MAEVE BRENNAN

Style, Wit and Tragedy: An Irish Writer in New York

ANGELA BOURKE

PIMLICO

Published by Pimlico 2005

2 4 6 8 10 9 7 5 3 1

First published in Great Britain in 2004 by Jonathan Cape.

Pimlico edition 2005

Pimlico
Random House, 20 Vauxhall Bridge Road,
London SW1V 2SA

Random House Australia (Pty) Limited
20 Alfred Street, Milsons Point, Sydney,
New South Wales 2061, Australia

Random House New Zealand Limited
18 Poland Road, Glenfield,
Auckland 10, New Zealand

Random House South Africa (Pty) Limited
Endulini, 5A Jubilee Road, Parktown 2193, South Africa

Random House UK Limited Reg. No. 954009

A CIP catalogue record for this book
is available from the British Library

ISBN 0-7126-9755-1

Papers used by Random House UK Limited are natural,
recyclable products made from wood grown in sustainable forests.
The manufacturing processes conform to the environmental
regulations of the country of origin

Printed and bound in Great Britain by Bookmarque Ltd, Croyden, Surrey

For Isabel

CONTENTS

Or you could say that an exile was a person who knew of a country that made all other countries seem strange.
– Maeve Brennan, 'Stories of Africa'

'I have a few jokes, but they all begin after we are all dead, if you know what I mean.'
– Maeve Brennan to William Maxwell, 1964

'I have been screaming for years that . . . writing is writing, and it is for the reader. For the reader *always comes first.'*
– Maeve Brennan to Gardner Botsford

'She wasn't one of us – she was one of her.'
– Roger Angell

Author's Note and Acknowledgements

On 14 December 1997, in the book-review section of the *New York Times*, Tom Kreilkamp of Cambridge, Massachusetts, read Jay Parini's glowing account of *The Springs of Affection: Stories of Dublin*, a new collection by a recently dead Irish writer whom Tom only dimly remembered. 'Here's one for Angela', he told Vera, his wife, after purchasing a copy of the book, which they later brought to me in Dublin. I had never heard of Maeve Brennan, but the review, comparing her to James Joyce, noted that most of her stories were set in Ranelagh, about two miles south of the centre of Dublin city, a neighbourhood where Tom and Vera had often stayed with me. Houses there were steadily being converted back to single-family use, following years of decay when their lack of central heating and their closeness to the city had made it more profitable for owners to carve them into bedsits for a transient population of students and young workers than to live in them themselves. Vera Kreilkamp, fluent teacher and critic of Irish literature in English, remembered Maeve Brennan's Long-Winded Lady pieces from *The New Yorker* magazine of the 1960s, and recalled reading some of her stories when they first appeared there. Now she recognised the turn of a staircase, the placement of windows, the distribution of space. Maeve Brennan's stories impressed her as much for their evocation of an intimately known place as for their literary authenticity and precision, and she wanted me to read them.

It took me months to begin reading *The Springs of Affection*. Meanwhile Fintan O'Toole, living in New York that year, published an essay in the *Irish Times* about the book and its author, noting that 'she was two things that it would have been hard to sustain in the Ireland for which so many people seem suddenly nostalgic, an intellectual woman and a writer.'¹ Ita Daly, herself a distinguished novelist and short-story writer, told me that Cherryfield Avenue, the street I knew better than any other in Ranelagh, was where Maeve Brennan had lived as a child. When I avidly read the stories, and began to talk about them to everyone I met, Colm Tóibín told me that Roddy Doyle's mother Ita was Maeve Brennan's first cousin. Within a week, my mother Rosaleen learned by chance that Ireland's best-known living writer was the nephew of her own neighbour and former Civil Service colleague, Máire Peoples. And so I discovered that Maeve Brennan's cousins, born Máire and Ita Bolger, were from Brighton Gardens, in Terenure, a few doors from where I lived as a baby, and a stone's throw from the house I grew up in. Although as a child I had seen a plaque unveiled in nearby Brighton Square, at one of the many childhood homes of James Joyce, it seemed astonishing to find literary connections in such modest, unheard-of, rows of houses as Brighton Gardens and Cherryfield Avenue. It was Nuala O'Faoláin, producing from her bag a proof copy of the newly discovered novella *The Visitor* in response to my asking if she had yet read Maeve Brennan, who first asked me 'Are you going to write about her?'

Writing about Maeve Brennan seemed at first unlikely, as most of my work draws on Irish-language sources. Soon, however, it became clear that Maeve Brennan's life did involve sources in Irish as well as English, and that it offered a window on one of the most passionate and problematic periods of Irish cultural history, the Gaelic Revival and the foundation of the Free State. More than that, however, hers was the story of an Irish woman intellectual as she negotiated an identity in mid-twentieth-century Manhattan, and through her writing became part of the consciousness of America. Meeting writers Katherine Powers and Ellen Wilbur in Cambridge, Massachusetts, both of them enthusiastic promoters of Maeve Brennan's work, and later, when I spoke to Christopher Carduff, the editor who has almost single-handedly brought her writing back into circulation, to Irish journalist Anna Mundow, and to storyteller, scholar and wise woman Jo Radner and feminist critic Susan Lanser, I heard the question again, 'Are you going to write about her?'

I could not have begun to write about Maeve Brennan without the discernment and encouragement of the individuals named above, or without the generous co-operation of many people who knew her, or her work, on both sides of the Atlantic. I could not have continued without the help of the many librarians and other experts who responded promptly to queries, facilitated access to material, and supplied photocopies. The support of family, friends and colleagues, who spotted references, offered contacts, information and insights, answered questions and did so much to nourish my body and mind, straighten my spine and uncross my eyes during the writing of this book, was invaluable. Most of those who supplied information or verified facts are named individually in the Notes, but I must record my most sincere thanks here to the Brennan and Bolger families and their relatives: to Johnny and Eileen Bolger, Matt and Jim Bolger, Emer Brennan and her sons Bob and Pete Brennan, Ita, Rory, Roddy and Shane Doyle, Joan Doyle, Clíona and Garrett Hickey, Yvonne Jerrold, Joseph Maher, Máire Peoples, Steven Vore, Pat Walsh and Stephanie Whiston for their enlightened kindness in facilitating my work, and for giving me such generous access to documents, photographs, memories and places. In County Wexford, Lizzie Doyle, Nicholas Furlong, Mairéad Parker and Jim and Monica Sinnott shared memories that greatly enriched my understanding of the Brennans' background. In Dublin, I am especially grateful to the late Aodhagán Brioscú, who lived next door to them throughout their time in Cherryfield Avenue and recalled for me a wealth of detail about those years. My sister Stephanie Bourke, my brother Cormac Bourke and my mother Rosaleen Bourke, Gerry Clarke, Kathleen Clune, Mike Cronin, Monica Cullinan, Ita Daly, Ronan Fanning, Maeve Gallagher, Fiana Griffin, John Harrington, Niamh Hayes, Patricia Kelly, Eithne Kiberd, Brian Lynch, Elizabeth McCrum, Margaret MacCurtain, Dolores MacKenna, Pascale McGarry, Deirdre McMahon, David Marcus, Gerald Mulroney, Eilís Ní Dhuibhne, Honor Ó Brolcháin, Nuala O'Connor, Margaret Ó hÓgartaigh, Séamas Ó Maitiú, Sean Ó Mórdha, Diarmaid Ó Muirithe, Tim O'Neill, Niamh O'Sullivan, Anthony Roche, Medb Ruane, Frank Smith, Nadia Smith and Ged Walsh helped with expertise and resources in many areas, in more ways than perhaps some of them realise, while in County Offaly, Stephen J. McNeill graciously searched out and supplied details about the background of Tim Costello, doyen of the long-disappeared Costello's Bar on Third Avenue, New York.

Travelling to New York, the warm hospitality of Lorna and Ed Goodman made my research a pleasure in every sense. Roger Angell, Kathy Biddick, Gardner Botsford, Clare Carroll, Williams Cole, Elizabeth Cullinan, the late Philip and Anna Hamburger, Madeline Gibson, Frances Kiernan, Mary D. Kierstead, Sabra Loomis, Francis W. Lovett, Lucy McDiarmid, Faith McNulty, Timothy Meagher, Heather Morgan, Maureen Murphy, Brian Ó Conchubhair, Philip O'Leary, Alastair Reid, Richard Rupp, Iris Snyder, John Updike and Wendy Wolf all either shared their own memories of Maeve Brennan, directed me to others who could, or facilitated my access to archive and library material. Karl Bissinger went further, in allowing me to use two of his magnificent portraits of Maeve Brennan, taken in 1948. For her courtesy in arranging this I also thank Catherine S. Johnson. I thank staff who helped me at the National Library of Ireland, National Archives of Ireland, University College Dublin Library, the British Library, London, the New York Public Library, the University of Delaware Library, Special Collections,

Newark, Del., and the University of Illinois Library, Special Collections, at Urbana-Champaign. Michael Steinman, on behalf of the Estate of William Maxwell, was most helpful in arranging access to the letters written by Maeve Brennan to Maxwell.[2]

I owe a particular debt to University College Dublin, the National University of Ireland, Dublin, whose award of a President's Research Fellowship for 2002/03 gave me the time and financial support to complete my research and produce a first draft. I thank the staff and my fellow residents at the wonderful Tyrone Guthrie Centre at Annaghmakerrig, where a week's residency primed the pump. A generous bursary from the Ireland Fund of Monaco allowed me to spend a month at the Princess Grace Irish Library, Monaco, in 2002, an Aladdin's Cave of mid-twentieth-century Irish and Irish-American writing, where Judith Gantley and Géraldine Lance could not have been more helpful; my sincere thanks are due also to Mr A.W. B. Vincent and Kieran McLoughlin of the Ireland Fund. In the spring of 2003, I was privileged to be the first Irish holder of a Bogliasco Fellowship in the Humanities, at the Centro Studi Ligure, in Bogliasco, Italy, a perfect environment for the writing of several chapters. Anna Maria Quaiat, Alan Rowlin and Ivana Folle work there with Gianni and Rita Migone and a support team to provide a setting that was at once magnificently stimulating and incomparably peaceful, and where my 'fellow fellows', especially Claudia Karolyi, were the best sounding boards a writer could desire.

Jonathan Williams, literary agent, placed his faith in this project from the beginning, and facilitated it right to the end, with imagination, energy and great kindness. It was my good fortune too to work for the second time with Will Sulkin, Jörg Hensgen and Lily Richards, and for the first time with Dan Franklin, Rosalind Porter and Chloe Johnson-Hill, all at Random House in London. Their scrupulous care for this project and its author, together with the commitment, generosity and grace displayed at every stage by Christopher Carduff of Counterpoint, have reassured me that humane values continue to inform publishing on both sides of the Atlantic.

Christopher Carduff has been godfather to this book from the beginning, as Vera Kreilkamp has been its godmother: separately and quietly, they smoothed the path of my research in the United States; they discussed the work with me at every stage, and read drafts as I produced them. Their comments, and those of Fiana Griffin, Elizabeth McCrum, Margaret MacCurtain, Jim McCloskey, Philip O'Leary, Will Sulkin and Jonathan Williams, have made this a much better book than it might otherwise have been, although the shortcomings that remain are of course no fault of theirs and I alone am responsible for the opinions expressed in it, and for the conclusions drawn. I thank them sincerely, along with anyone whose name

AUTHOR'S NOTES AND ACKNOWLEDGEMENTS

I have inadvertently omitted from the list above, as I thank Michael Hayes, who has been almost as patient with Maeve Brennan as he has with me, and whose love has sustained me throughout. Mo bhuíochas ó chroí!

Angela Bourke
Dublin, 8 April 2004, Holy Thursday

MAEVE BRENNAN

Homesick at *The New Yorker*

Introduction

Maeve Brennan was an Irishwoman and a New Yorker; an intellectual and a beauty; a daughter, sister, aunt, lover, friend and wife, but never a mother. She dazzled everyone who met her, and wrote some of the finest and most widely read English prose of the twentieth century, yet in her lifetime, when Irish writers were celebrated as never before, she was practically unknown in her own country. In the 1970s, her life was devastated by mental illness. She disappeared from view, and was all but forgotten. Recently rediscovered, however, her work has a special relevance now. Twentieth-century Irish society guarded its secrets closely, but Maeve Brennan's fiction offers unequalled portraits of people's circumstances and experience. Hindsight gives all her writing a new poignancy and edge, for readers now know that despite the best efforts of those who loved her, the laughing, generous, carefree woman who wrote with such unsparing clarity on the theme of home herself became tragically homeless for a time.

Maeve Brennan published fiction and essays whose truthfulness is at once shocking and consoling. As a child, she had lived through some of the most turbulent years of Irish history, and questions about being Irish, and female, were central to her writing, as to her life. Although she spent most of her adult years alone in Manhattan, she returned again and again in fiction to the Dublin and Wexford of her childhood. The issues she lived with and wrote about – identity, migration and memory – would become preoccupations of the late twentieth century. Patiently, almost without mercy, the stories she wrote about Ireland probe the discomforts of quiet, careful, middle-class people, offering an unparalleled, feminine, view of a society and a place; by contrast, her fictions set in America throw the life of privileged New Yorkers and their Irish servants into grotesque relief. All Maeve Brennan's stories transcend place, however, to reveal human nature in the way only great writers can. Republished since 1997, her various writings remain in the mind like previously unknown species of animal or plant, with an authority and inevitability that have made me want to investigate what I might call their ecology.

I grew up in Dublin, between the River Dodder and the Grand Canal, as Maeve Brennan did. I lived in a house of the same shape, played in a back garden like hers, and walked to the same kind of school, along the same kind of streets. I even pushed a little brother in a pram, as she had a generation earlier. As a child, I was sent with my younger sister in the summer holidays to spend idyllic weeks with farming relatives, as she had been. In my thirties, I lived for several extended periods in the United States, and tried to make sense of the interior dislocations I experienced there, although academic affiliations and the knowledge that I had a job and a house to return to insulated me from most of what my contemporaries experienced through emigration.

The house I came back to in Dublin was on Cherryfield Avenue, in Ranelagh; it is a stone's throw from the one Maeve Brennan lived in, which her fiction so insistently describes. The rooms were the same size; the light fell in the same ways. Reading her stories for the first time in 1998, I found myself back among the furniture and wallpapers of the neighbours who were elderly when I went to live in Ranelagh in the late 1970s. They were Maeve Brennan's parents' generation: the young men and women who moved into those houses in the 1920s, most of them recently married, many with young children. She captures the texture of their lives with uncanny precision: the house I moved into even had a carpet with big pink roses on it.

Sitting at tables in the windows of modest New York restaurants, or at her desk at *The New Yorker*, Maeve Brennan looked back at Ireland with a trained, observant eye from the 1940s until the 1970s, examining the physical and social structures among which she had grown up. Buildings and kin-groups of kinds that anthropologists, folklorists, sociologists and geographers have studied remained in her memory, their stories and conversations preserved in the amber of a troubled nostalgia. Her writing tells us not only what sorts of houses people lived in, and what rules governed their relationships, but also how it felt to dwell in those buildings and inhabit those relationships. She has left us an intimate history of Ireland in the twentieth century.

Maeve Brennan's fiction bores deep into her own memory, and her family's. It returns repeatedly to the same houses, and the same stages of a family's life. So many details of what she writes correspond to the facts of her own history that a reader might be forgiven for imagining that all she wrote was literally true. But it isn't, of course. The beam of light she shone into the past was unwavering, but narrow. The most memorable characters she created occupy the shadows at its edges, and their most intense encounters take place there. Recent studies of memory (including repressed memory and false memory) emphasise the importance of an audience or interlocutor in the process of remembering, and the extent to which memories are moulded by the act of translating them from private to public through telling. It seems that it is impossible not to recreate the past in telling about it, especially if we tell it often. As cultural psychologist Ciaran Benson puts it, 'My "life" will always be an edited version.'[1]

When the 'I' who remembers has lived turbulently and has a taste for drama, the episodes she selects for presentation will dwarf all others; when she is a writer of fiction, and lives far away from where those events took place, even they may well end up changed utterly. I had not been long engaged in researching Maeve Brennan's history when it became clear that memory and invention lie one upon the other in her writing, as in a pastry that has been many times rolled thin and folded back upon itself. To pick apart the delicate layers will destroy its structure, and yet to give a truthful account of her life and times, it will be necessary in places to mark a boundary. I have endeavoured to be true to the immediacy and flavour of her recall, but I have also felt it important to point out the differences between real events and people, and her depiction of them.

This book aims to place Maeve Brennan's own story in the context of the historical events that impinged on her life, and also to situate it among the changing currents of how people live and think: to take account of fashion and furniture as well as politics; of family history and landscape as well as literature. Maeve Brennan's life permits and even demands this approach, partly because the disarray of her later years meant that what might have remained for her literary executors was scattered and dissipated, all but impossible to reassemble into a single-stranded narrative. More importantly, her effect on the people who met her, her eye for human behaviour, clothing and interiors, her unsparing reading of literature, her memory of home and her courageous life as a woman alone in metropolitan America make her an icon of the twentieth century, even if she is not as well known as Marilyn Monroe, Billie Holiday or Colette.

Historical biography is 'the presentation and explanation of an individual life in history', according to the great French historian Jacques Le Goff, who defends the enterprise on the grounds that 'the time of a single life is a significant period for history'.[2] Because Maeve Brennan lived from 1917 to 1993, the light cast by her biography should easily reach into both the beginning and the end of the twentieth century. Ireland, where she was born and grew up, achieved political independence in her early childhood, largely through the activism of people like her parents. The new Irish Free State and its successor, the Republic of Ireland, proceeded to struggle with questions of identity and meaning throughout her lifetime. Maeve Brennan's own identity was insistently Irish, yet in Ireland she was a 'Yank': an exotic relative known through airmail letters and parcels, and periodic visits home. New York, where she spent her adult life, was a crucible of intellectual change, especially in the years after the Second World War, while *The New Yorker*, which employed, published and sheltered her for more than forty years, was perhaps the most influential magazine in the world. She wrote in its pages about her family and her childhood, and placed many of her fictional characters in the house where she had lived in Dublin. Her fiction editor and close friend was the legendary William Maxwell, much of whose own best writing does the same with the matter of his boyhood in Illinois.

Because she deals in memory preserved through generations, and because the rediscovery of her work has coincided with a period of extraordinary social change and reassessment in Ireland, Maeve Brennan's story extends in fact all the way from the nineteenth century into the twenty-first. Her parents, Bob Brennan and Una Bolger, came from two households in County Wexford that were only a few miles apart, yet different from each other in ways that lifetimes could not bridge. The roots of those differences, between the country and the town, tell us much about Maeve Brennan's preoccupations, and about Irish society. Like Dublin, where she grew up, both the childhood homes of her parents were distant from Manhattan by a week or more on board ship until mid-century. Throughout her fiction and letter-writing, her parents persist, fading but intrepid, walking alongside her life and inhabiting her memories, and so this study begins with them, and the places they came from. Una, especially, merits attention, for she starts out as a rebel and a feminist, but then in motherhood and middle age becomes reduced to silences and domesticities, her individuality occluded by her relationships and roles. She was one of the women active in the 1916 Rising, and in the Anglo-Irish War and Civil War that followed, but history has just begun to become acquainted with them, for it is only in this new century, with all the protagonists dead, that we can safely venture among the painful stories of that time.

Maeve Brennan will not become central to her own story until the fourth chapter of this book. Its opening narrative is intended instead to lay down the topsoil of culture and history out of which she and her memories grew, for Irish social history at the end of the nineteenth century and the beginning of the twentieth has a fascinating complexity that is often hidden from us behind the Great War and the Irish fight for independence.[3] Characterised by immense optimism, rapid social and intellectual change, and tragic compromises, it helps to account for the urgency with which Maeve Brennan wrote about the years that followed.

One of the most attractive characters in her fiction is Lily Bagot. Aged between six and nine in the stories written about her, Lily is clearly based on Maeve Brennan herself. In 'The Carpet with the Big Pink Roses on It', published in *The New Yorker* in 1964, she is seven, and lies on her stomach on the bare floorboards of the sitting-room. Her mother has taken up the carpet, to beat it clean in the back garden, and Lily is trying to retrieve a penny that she has dropped between the boards. She had wanted to sit on the carpet outdoors, and fly away somewhere, but Mrs Bagot had said no. 'The Carpet with the Big Pink Roses on It' is an innocent story, but one that brings the child's relentless questioning alive, as she badgers her mother about the nature of loss, and about what it means to have a stable home: 'If the house blew up, then would we get the money?' she asks. Mrs Bagot is tired. Privately she thinks it might be restful to do as Lily suggests and simply float away, instead of having to walk down the public street each time she leaves her house. In the end, she falls asleep indoors, and Lily sits alone on the carpet and travels far away, then home again, to the house that never blew up. Why Maeve Brennan ever imagined that such a house might blow up; how she came to live there; where her travels took her, and why the magic carpet always brought her back, are the subjects of this book.

List of Abbreviations

LWL Maeve Brennan, *The Long-Winded Lady: Notes from*
    The New Yorker (New York: Mariner, 1998)

MB   Maeve Brennan

NAI   National Archives of Ireland

NLI MSS National Library of Ireland Manuscript Collection

RB   Robert Brennan (Maeve's father)

RG   Maeve Brennan, *The Rose Garden: Short Stories*
    (Washington, DC: Counterpoint, 2000)

SA   Maeve Brennan, *The Springs of Affection: Stories of*
    Dublin (Boston and New York: Houghton Mifflin, 1997)

V   Maeve Brennan, *The Visitor* (Washington, DC:
    Counterpoint, 2000)

ONE

The Bolgers of Coolnaboy

At Enniscorthy, the ninety-mile road from Dublin to Wexford steps east across the River Slaney on a stone bridge that has been there since 1680. It still has fourteen miles to go. Swans feed below the walls of the town, and its streets and houses climb together on the opposite bank, up to the thirteenth-century castle and the cathedral. Enniscorthy is an old town, and an interesting one, given dignity and pleasure by stone and water: houses, quays and granaries, and the smoothly flowing river. The Slaney has almost no traffic now, but it is not so very long since boats carrying cargo, and even passengers, plied up and down from its mouth at Wexford and tied up at these quays. The railway has been coming through since 1872. A tunnel takes it under the town, and railway, river and road continue southward side by side.

Outside Enniscorthy, on the left, square redbrick towers show suddenly above the trees, like pieces from another landscape – in Italy, perhaps. St Senan's Hospital was built in 1865 as a lunatic asylum, but the high walls that surrounded it then have been taken down and a line of poplars grows along the roadside instead. Six miles farther on, halfway between Enniscorthy and Wexford, is Oylegate. The road moves inland here from a series of low bluffs along the river; it narrows between two brief rows of buildings, and traffic slows down.

Oylegate is a small village, with houses, shops and pubs, a Garda station, a primary school, a post office. The Catholic church is at the far end, on the right, separated from the road by gates and a long paved yard. Behind Oylegate's two rows of buildings lie generous fields and farmland. Their names, not written on any signpost, designate the townlands into which the land is divided: subdivisions of civil parishes, the smallest administrative divisions in rural Ireland. Coolnaboy, *Cúil an Átha Buí* – the Place by the Yellow Ford – is a typical townland name for this area.[1] It lies on the left as you enter Oylegate. Opposite Mernagh's shop, a pair of gateposts opens on to an unpaved private road – a lane, as it is called – that runs between the fields. It leads to the farm where Maeve Brennan's mother Una Bolger grew up, and where she herself spent long stretches of her childhood.

Living in New York City, writing for *The New Yorker* for thirty years, Maeve Brennan kept returning to this gateway, this farm and this lane, in memory and in fiction. Her stories lay bare the foundations of an emotional life assembled over generations. Often discomfiting, it is insistently rooted in place. She describes Coolnaboy with ethnographic precision, as a reservoir of certainty and human connection.

In 'Stories of Africa', an old bishop has come home to Ireland after many years as a missionary. Frail and humble, resigned to his coming death, he visits Delia Bagot and her children at their home in Dublin, and remembers the house where Delia was born, where her grandmother presided and her father was his childhood friend. He and Delia have never met, and Delia's father has been dead since she was two, but together they remember the farm they call Poulbwee, the bishop speaking first:

> 'I think of the days when I used to walk down the lane from the village of Oylegate to Poulbwee. It is a mile walk. You know it as well as I do. You must have walked that lane thousands of times . . . Your father and I used to walk along that lane from school every day, and then I would cut off across the fields to our place, Cooldearg . . .'
>
> 'It seems a very long time from those days to now,' Mrs Bagot said, 'and yet the lane is exactly the same. It's a full mile from the village of Oylegate to Poulbwee, and yet it never seemed like a mile. The lane is so nice, the way it turns around to suit the fields and then goes straight between the hedges when it gets a chance. And I used to like opening and shutting the gates as I went along.' [*SA* 291–2]

'There was murder if you didn't close those gates,' Maeve Brennan's cousins remember, at the beginning of the twenty-first century, and although the gates themselves are long gone, they can rhyme off their names in the order in which they used to open and shut them on the way from the house to Oylegate: the Big Gate, the Little Lane Gate, Bill's Gate (at the bottom of the field called the Racecourse), the High Field Gate, and the Top Field Gate. Maeve's writing recalls the house that stands behind the Big Gate:

> Poulbwee is a very long two-story farmhouse with a deep thatched roof. The house is whitewashed and the front door is painted green. The front door stands open on a square hall that is only large enough to step into. To the right is the door leading into the parlor. That door

is always kept closed. To the left is the kitchen with the door always open. The inside wall facing you has a very small window in it so that anybody sitting at the kitchen hearth can peer out and see who is coming along the lane. [SA 293]

Though it has changed with time, Coolnaboy still answers this description.[2] The lane winds between green fields for exactly a mile, and ash trees stand along the banks on either side; in spring, primroses bloom milky yellow in the grass at their feet. Farm buildings embrace the paved yard in front of the house, so that as the visitor emerges from the lane, it stands perfectly framed before her, thatched and whitewashed, with tall trees behind and a rosebush on either side of the front door.

It looked much the same in 1840, the year the Ordnance Survey came to County Wexford, surveying and measuring, and listing place-names for the new six-inch maps that would organise the taxation base once and for all. The six-inch map published in 1842 shows the fields as Delia Bagot describes them in 'Stories of Africa', with a lane that is not yet separately marked and fenced but that passes through field after field, gate after gate. The Survey's coming also prompted the making by private citizens of hand-drawn, coloured maps of individual farms. The house at Coolnaboy is pictured on one of them, with its windows, thatch and whitewash, and stands with its fields spread in front of it, each one separately coloured and named. This beautiful map is still kept at Coolnaboy, where Maeve Brennan must have seen it as a child. The Bolgers' house, perfectly symmetrical, with two windows on each side of the door and four more tucked under the thatch above, modestly echoes the façades of eighteenth-century Georgian mansions. It is a house in a storybook.

Houses like this in the south-east of Ireland are called by historians of vernacular architecture 'hearth-lobby' houses. Most are built of hard-packed earth on a stone foundation, and deeply thatched with reeds, and their small square entrance lobby marks a transition from the outside world to the private space within. The chimney is in the middle, so that the packed-earth gables do not need to be built high, and the thatch comes down low over them in a hipped roof. A small partition – a jamb wall – protects the hearth from draughts that blow through the open door. In old houses like this, from Kildare to Wexford, a tiny window in the jamb wall allows a person sitting at the fire to observe the door and whoever approaches it.[3]

'Your grandmother used to watch for me,' the Bishop said, 'and the minute I came around the last turn she would appear out at the door and stand there waiting for me. I could feel her smiling as I came

along down the lane. God bless her kind heart, she was never ashamed
to show you you were welcome, never ashamed, never afraid . . .'
[*SA* 293]

The Bolgers and their house are deeply rooted in their place, so that it
comes as a surprise to learn that the family has been in Coolnaboy for little
over a hundred years. The hand-coloured map of 1840 was made by William
Prandy, the then proprietor. By 1885, when George Bassett's *Wexford
County: Guide and Directory* appeared, the only farmers listed for Coolnaboy
were Nicholas Nolan and Patrick Ryan. A John Bolger, however, is listed in
the Oyle, the next townland to the south, which appears unpronounceably
on modern maps, as 'Theoil'.[4]

John Bolger, Maeve Brennan's grandfather, was born in 1842. He came
from the Oyle, and family tradition says that, because he did not own a
farm, the prosperous Whittys of nearby Pouldearg ('Pouldarrig' in some
documents) were not impressed when he wanted to marry their youngest
daughter Johanna. He spent ten years in Australia, however, working as a
miner, or perhaps as a sheep shearer, and returned with enough money to
buy his first farm.

Pouldearg, where her mother's family had farmed since 1666,[5] and where
her grandmother Johanna Whitty grew up, is another of the haunting, sunlit
places in Maeve Brennan's fiction. Only a couple of miles from Coolnaboy,
but on the opposite side of the Enniscorthy–Wexford road, it lies in another
parish (Ballinaslaney), and another barony (Shelmalier East), just south of
Oylegate on the bank of the Slaney, at the first place for some distance
where the land has easy access to the river. At one time, when the old coach
road still passed nearby, the Whittys of Pouldearg made ale and kept an
alehouse by the bank of the river. Their house was at a busy junction then,
where road and river met.

Pouldearg was a beautiful farm. The river flowed just below the house,
with swans gleaming white on the dark, slow-moving water. The green fields
of the opposite bank were far enough away to be mysterious, close enough
for comforting familiarity. Like Coolnaboy, the farmhouse was built of
packed earth, and thatched, but Pouldearg, a longer house, with fewer rooms,
was probably older. The land was excellent, and included a magnificent
orchard that was productive and profitable too. Pouldearg is *An Poll Dearg*,
'the red pool', or 'the red hole' (Maeve's invented 'Poulbwee' would be *An
Poll Buí*, 'the yellow pool'), and a gravel pit on the Whittys' farm brought
in extra income. When Maeve came here as a child in the 1920s, her grandmother's surviving siblings were old and unmarried. Eighty years later,
although its unspoilt view of water remains, their house has long since fallen,

and the orchard is swept away. Only one gable still stands, smothered in ivy, beside the track that leads to the water.

The elderly Whitty relatives Maeve met as a child had grown up with security in Pouldearg while less prosperous parts of Ireland were in the grip of famine. Her great-aunt Margaret was born there in 1841, followed by William in 1843 and then by Mary Kate (1846); Eliza (1848); Anastasia, known as 'Anty' (1849) and, in 1854, Johanna, who became Maeve's grandmother.

John and Johanna Bolger's first child, born on 11 September 1888, was christened Anastasia. Her family called her 'Anty', like her aunt in Pouldearg, but she would change her name to the more Irish-sounding Una in the early years of the twentieth century. Next came James, known to the family as Jim; then John; Elizabeth, whom they called Bessie; Ellen, known as Nellie, and finally Walter, who became Wat.

The couple prospered. John Bolger was secretary of the local Land League branch, which campaigned for tenants' ownership of the land they farmed, and when celebrations were planned to commemorate the centenary of the 1798 Rebellion in County Wexford, he helped to organise them.[6] In 1897 he paid £400 for the ninety-seven-acre farm at Coolnaboy and set about modernising it for his family. The house had originally been two cottages. Windows were to be enlarged, perhaps a new thatch put on, but as the family prepared to move in, John Bolger fell from his horse and died, aged fifty-six.[7] It was 8 September 1898, three days before Anastasia's tenth birthday. As though that were not enough, Nellie, the second-youngest child, died before she was six. Not surprisingly, Johanna Bolger is remembered as a strict and unsmiling woman. With her children, she moved into the large farmhouse among the fields, where the census returning officer found them at the end of March 1901.

The census documents for that year show the Bolgers' house at Coolnaboy as having ten rooms and eight out-offices: stable, coach house, cow house, calf house, dairy, piggery, fowl house and barn. It is a 'first-class' house, the best in the townland.[8] Six people slept there on the night of Sunday, 31 March 1901. They do not include Anastasia, who would become Una: she was aged twelve and a half, and already a boarder at the Loreto Convent in Enniscorthy. 'Every farm family was expected to contribute a son and a daughter to the Church', and so the eldest girl and boy were selected to be educated.[9] Jim in his turn would go to St Peter's College on Summerhill in Wexford, a boarding-school that was also a seminary, educating boys for the priesthood after their secondary education. For now though, still only eleven and attending primary school, Jim was at home. The sixth member of the household was the children's aunt, Mary Kate Whitty, Johanna's older sister, whose age is given as fifty-three.

Johanna Bolger was the head of family in 1901. Forty-seven, and widowed, the form gives her occupation as 'farmer'. She is a Catholic, and able to read and write, as is her sister (this was the only question the census form asked about education). All four children enumerated are listed as 'scholars', so even four-year-old Wat is walking through the fields to Oylegate every day, although unlike his older brothers and sisters, he cannot yet read. Mary Kate's occupation is not listed. She is clearly at Coolnaboy to help her sister with the care of the children, as unmarried aunts so often were in those labour-intensive households.

The 1901 census return for Pouldearg shows William Whitty, Mary Kate's and Johanna's only brother, as the head of family in their old home by the Slaney. He is fifty-eight, a farmer, and unmarried, and shares his six-roomed house with two more of his unmarried sisters, Margaret, who is sixty, and Anty, aged fifty-two. Three male farm labourers were also in the house on census night.

Detailed records are available for only one more census: that of 1911. By then, three of Johanna Bolger's children remain at home in Coolnaboy. John is twenty, Elizabeth eighteen, and Walter fourteen. Mary Kate Whitty is still here, but mysteriously has aged twelve years in ten: her age is given now as sixty-five. In Pouldearg, yet another of Johanna's sisters has moved back home. Eliza Harper, widow, aged sixty-one, now shares the farmhouse with her sixty-eight-year-old brother William and their two sisters. There is only one farm labourer.

In her story 'The Springs of Affection', Maeve Brennan wrote about these people and this place:

> Delia's mother's family, her old brother and her three old sisters, lived by the Slaney in a very big farmhouse, whitewashed, with a towering thatched roof. The size of the house and the prosperous appearance of the place impressed Min. Delia's aunts and her uncle were all unmarried, and they had all been born here. Min heard the house was very old, and that the family had been in this lovely spot beside the Slaney for centuries. [*SA* 337]

The statistics on marriage in Ireland in the late nineteenth century come to mind. Households like the Whittys', where several siblings aged together in shared celibacy, were not unusual.[10] Women's tenure in farm households was uncertain in the late nineteenth and early twentieth centuries. They might marry, as Johanna and Eliza Whitty did, if an appropriate 'match' could be made, but land belonged to men, and was passed to the next generation in the male line; their wives usually came from other farms, bringing dowry supplied by their fathers or brothers in the form of cows or cash or furniture, and this guaranteed their right to be housed. A widow might farm alone, as Johanna did, but sometimes a childless widow like Eliza, or one whose son was old enough to marry, returned to her parents' home years after they had died, to live with her own elderly siblings.[11]

The greatest security for a woman was in the house where she had been born: from there she could not be dislodged, although her life would not necessarily be pleasant. Unmarried daughters of any age were subject to their parents, or to a presiding sister-in-law if a brother had inherited, and they had no guaranteed income from the farm that could absorb all their labour. But it was not easy for a man to marry if his sisters were still about the place. Work was apportioned by gender, and a fully functioning household needed at least one woman to cook, bake, wash, tend the fire and the dairy, and care for poultry. Even where there were servants, the women of the house worked alongside them, and as long as sisters still performed their tasks in the way the household had learned to expect, there was no economic reason to bring in another woman.[12]

In a society that subjected all personal fulfilment to economic pragmatism and exalted the celibacy of its priests and nuns, marriage was necessary for procreation, but might safely be delayed until a man was in his forties, when his parents were retired from active work or dead. Even then, there could be friction between personalities, especially between a man's widowed mother or unmarried older sister and his much younger bride, while bedridden old people might not tolerate a stranger dealing with their intimate care. Marriage among these large families therefore required an elaborate choreography that would allow a sister to exit as a bride entered – often using the same dowry. Increasingly, especially where valuable farms were at stake, the dance became too complicated, with unacceptable age differences between men deemed marriageable and the women they wished to marry. Most of these difficulties could be overcome if siblings simply stayed together; if nephews were growing up elsewhere, even inheritance might not be a problem.

There were other outlets for emotion, in any case: the land itself elicited strong feelings in those who worked so hard on and for it. The title of Maeve's story comes from a phrase spoken by Delia's Aunt Mag – based perhaps on the real-life Margaret Whitty, seventy at the time of the 1911 census. She leans over the shoulder of Delia's new husband, Martin Bagot, as he stands in the garden of the unnamed Pouldearg on the afternoon of his wedding day, watching the river flow. She is taller than he is (the Whitty women were all tall), and stands behind him with her arms around his shoulders:

'I have a great fondness for the water,' she said. 'I couldn't be content any place but here where I was born and brought up. I've never spent a night away from this house in my life, do you know that? It's a blessing the day turned out so grand . . . The Slaney is in full flood, and the springs of affection are rising around us.' [*SA* 349]

One commentator at least has seen the Irish family of cohabiting adult siblings as not merely dysfunctional, but pathological, but others point out that children who grew up to live as the Whittys did had beaten the system, while an important study suggests that for Irish immigrants in America, siblings were what constituted family and belonging. Where marriage was largely a matter of economics, the relationship most often romanticised, spoken and sung about with nostalgia, was that of brothers and sisters, and the best-loved place was one's childhood home.[13]

Of course spinsterhood was not the future Catholic parents envisaged for their daughters; Anastasia Bolger, growing into her teens at the Loreto Convent, Enniscorthy, was destined to become a nun. Between 1851 and 1911, the number of nuns in Ireland increased from 1,000 to 9,000.[14] In Pouldearg, in the generation before Johanna and Mary Kate's, a second family of Whittys, distantly related, boasted two prominent Sisters of Mercy, as well as a Jesuit priest.[15] It was Anastasia Bolger's well-to-do Whitty relatives who paid for her education at the Loreto Convent.

Going to boarding-school, Anastasia left behind her widowed mother, her aunt, and four younger siblings at Coolnaboy. It may be that the deaths of her father and little sister, and her mother's reaction to those losses, made her glad to get away. Certainly, sending a girl to the Loreto Convent was an important status symbol: a signal that Johanna was managing very well despite her widowhood. Anastasia loved school, where her favourite subject was chemistry; she consistently came top of her class.[16]

From their foundation in Rathfarnham in the hills south of Dublin in 1821, the Irish Loreto nuns had been educators of middle-class girls, whose families could afford to pay for their education. Schools like theirs emphasised etiquette, deportment and 'refinement', alongside academic education and accomplishments like music and fine needlework. Photographs taken in the Loreto Convent, Enniscorthy, about 1920 show young girls in the school orchestra with their instruments, and also in the cookery kitchen, built in 1900 while Anastasia Bolger was a pupil.[17] Convent boarding-schools produced confident young women – ladies – whose expectations in many cases were of a life different from their mothers', and a role more autonomous than that available to daughters on farms. A significant number of their pupils entered the religious life when they finished school, finding there a congenial and orderly environment and a path to personal and spiritual fulfilment.[18]

Anastasia Bolger did not become a nun, but although she lived at Coolnaboy after leaving school, she did not like the farm. Her mother Johanna and Aunt Mary Kate were a formidable pair, who may not always have seen eye to eye, and the fastidiousness of a Loreto girl may have been difficult to accommodate in a working farmhouse without electricity or running water.[19] Anastasia listened to and read about the debates of the day. Wexford's lively social, cultural and political life was only seven miles away, and although she must have had chores and responsibilities at home, she soon began to join societies and attend meetings.

At eighteen, in 1906, Anastasia Bolger was smaller and slighter than her severe, black-clad mother, while her younger sister Bessie had easily outgrown her. Never talkative – one nephew described her in later life as 'a very gentle-going little person' – she was pretty, with a shy smile, cloudy green eyes and long, thick, brown hair. She loved flowers, and excelled at needlework. Most probably by this time she had a bicycle: it was the fashionable thing for young women in the early years of the twentieth century, and would have allowed her to travel easily and independently, if bumpily, from Coolnaboy to Enniscorthy or Wexford. (Pneumatic tyres had been invented, but were not yet generally available.)[20] Young women could also travel by pony and trap, of course, and the railway station at Macmine junction was only a couple of miles away, on the other side of the river. With a new century, and new legislation that allowed Irish farmers to own the land they farmed, change was everywhere. Anastasia joined the Pioneer Total Abstinence Association in May 1907, registering her name and address in Irish, as Úna Ní B[h]olguidhir, Geata na hAille.[21] Founded in 1898, 'the Pioneers' was just one of a range of new organisations that were harnessing young people's mobility, education and purchasing power to ideals of social reform and national liberation.

In 1892, in a famous lecture to the National Literary Society in Dublin, 'On the Necessity for De-Anglicising Ireland', Douglas Hyde, son of a Protestant clergyman from County Roscommon, had spelled out the implications of colonisation for Irish society, stressing the need for autonomous thinking in all areas of Irish life.[22] The following year he founded the Gaelic League, with the object of reviving the Irish language, and became its first president. In 1898, a young London-based Irish journalist and pugnacious phrasemaker called David Patrick Moran began publishing a series of much-talked-about articles in the *New Ireland Review*, developing Hyde's ideas, but with a decidedly sectarian twist. Two years later, aged thirty-one, he returned to Dublin and started a new weekly paper, the *Leader*.[23] By the time Anastasia Bolger left school, Moran's thoughts about a Gaelic, Catholic, industrially developed 'Irish Ireland' were available at newsagents' shops every week, alongside advertisements for Irish-made goods.

Known as 'the rebel county' since the United Irishmen's insurrection of May and June 1798, Wexford was steeped in a rhetoric of freedom originally drawn from the French and American revolutions. In 1898, spectacular centenary celebrations focused memory and language on the nationalist cause, this time with a Catholic emphasis.[24] The same year saw the start of a new weekly newspaper in Dublin. The *United Irishman*'s editor was twenty-seven-year-old Arthur Griffith, recently returned from South Africa, who propounded a new kind of politics, on the Hungarian model, urging Irish representatives not to take their seats at Westminster, but to set up their own assembly in Dublin. His pamphlet, *The Resurrection of Hungary: A Parallel for Ireland*, appeared in 1904, and in November of the following year he and Bulmer Hobson founded Sinn Féin, the first of many organisations to bear this name, which simply means 'Ourselves'.

A branch of the Gaelic League was formed in Wexford in 1899, a branch of Sinn Féin a few years later, and both did well, with many activities and growing membership lists. In Enniscorthy, the weekly *Echo* newspaper began publication in May 1902, its editor, William Sears, energetically promoting Irish Ireland. Week after week, in the top left-hand corner of its front page, immediately below the Births, Marriages and Deaths, the *Echo* carried a small advertisement in Gaelic script, with shaky grammar, but impeccable Irish-Ireland sentiment:

A Gaedhilgeóirí Má Theas tuighean uaibh éadach Gaedhealach tar
go dtí an Tig Gaedhealach, 6 Sráid na Slaighne, Inis Córthaidh
[Irish-speakers, If you want Irish clothes, come to the Irish House,
6, Slaney Street, Enniscorthy]

Another small ad, however, published in three issues of the *Echo* in January 1908, reminds us of the sort of life that was available to young women whose families did not have the means to send them to convent boarding-schools or keep them at home:

Wanted: Steady middle-aged girl as General Servant for farmer's place; must be recommended by her Parish Priest and last mistress; must know how to milk and wash and do general work; early riser; wages £7 per year to suitable person. Apply 73s, Echo Office, Enniscorthy.[25]

'Middle-aged girl' reads like an oxymoron, but 'girl' in the older Ireland meant an unmarried female, as 'boy' meant an unmarried male. A young woman whose family could not provide a dowry had no realistic prospect of entering the sort of marriage that could offer economic security. Thousands of such women emigrated to the United States every year, most of them to work as domestic servants and to be known as 'Bridget', whatever their given names. They saved their wages to pay the passage of their sisters, neighbours and nieces; they contributed to the building of St Patrick's Cathedral on New York's Fifth Avenue and to Catholic charities in Boston and other cities; they sent home the money that enabled their families in Ireland to install indoor plumbing, build an extension, re-roof the house, or pay off debt. Some saved nest-eggs that allowed them to come home and marry with dignity, or to start small businesses, but others returned with broken health to die, and many never came back.[26] In Maeve's story, 'The Bride', published in 1953, Margaret Casey, a maid in Scarsdale for ten years, is one of these women; Bridie, Agnes and the rest of the maids in her 'Herbert's Retreat' stories are others.

Women's issues were part of the new rhetoric of freedom at the beginning of the twentieth century. In the early 1880s, the Ladies' Land League had brought women together for political ends, and many of its members continued to be active. Campaigns were afoot for women's right to vote, and for their full access to higher education.[27] The Gaelic League enrolled women and men as equals in classes and other activities.[28] During Queen Victoria's visit in 1900, the unionist business houses of Dublin, many of them supporters of the Boer War, donated tons of biscuits, sweets and jam and thousands of buns for a 'treat' for 50,000 girls and boys in the Phoenix Park. Nationalists indignantly refused to allow their children to take part, however, and a Patriotic Children's Treat Committee emerged in response, with Maud Gonne, muse and nemesis of William Butler Yeats, as president.[29] She had been horrified to see ragged barefoot children hungrily eat the bread her own son offered them to feed the ducks in Dublin's St Stephen's Green and proposed an alternative outing the following year to Theobald Wolfe Tone's grave at Bodenstown, County Kildare. Despite its lugubrious venue, the treat was a success, and led to the setting up of a hugely influential women's organisation.

Maud Gonne founded Inghinidhe [pronounced Inini] na h-Éireann, the Daughters of Ireland, as a non-sectarian organisation in 1901.[30] It was at once a theatre company, a debating society, a nationalist pressure group and an educational forum. Members were actively feminist, and many were flamboyant, happily defying the rules of propriety and deference in which the Catholics among them had been schooled. They opposed the Catholic Church on issues like school meals for children, but ran into arguments with suffragists by refusing to campaign for a women's franchise if that meant recognising the right of the British government to rule Ireland. Some even maintained that the egalitarianism of their movement meant that Irish-Ireland women already were enfranchised![31] They opposed recruitment to the British army (and Irish women's fraternising with soldiers and police), and urged the buying of Irish goods and the wearing of Irish-made fabrics, sharing the ideals of Sinn Féin and Irish Ireland. Anastasia Bolger became a member of the Inghinidhe, and secretary of a new branch formed in Wexford in July 1908. She was nineteen.

A new column appeared in the *Echo* of Saturday, 4 July 1908. Entitled 'Women's Ways', it was written by 'Una'.

'I think every important paper should have a column devoted to the special interests of women,' it began. 'I said that some time ago to the editor of "The Echo", but being a mere man he did not seem to agree with me.' The tone is light and bantering, but the content is serious. 'Una' announces that the editor has called her bluff and invited her to contribute the column she has demanded, though he wagers that very few women will bother to read it. She continues:

> We women have to do half the brain work in everyday life and in many cases half the servile work too, and more than half. But when it comes to making laws for the two sexes, Man says 'I can do this by myself, thank you. You go home and mind the house.' And sometimes it happens that the man who sneers at the woman has not brains enough to keep the cat from the milk.
>
> Take the case of the Enniscorthy [Poor Law] Guardians and you have an instance of man's conceit. There are sixty or seventy of them in it. Someone suggested that ladies should be co-opted. Phew! they wouldn't hear of it. There were no ladies fit to sit on the same board with them. So plentiful was male ability in the [Poor Law] union [an administrative division] that as many as sixty clever men could be found, and not even three women, or two, or one! There's presumption for you!

The column made feminist politics local. It must have given rise to some heated discussions in the farmhouses and shops of County Wexford, as convent-educated girls began to discuss the functioning of public institutions. Further on, 'Una' told her readers, 'I am ready to assist in matters of dress, prices, diet, poultry, flowers, etc.'

Appearing monthly, the 'Una' column included recipes, ways of removing ink stains from linen, and other useful advice, but it also propounded the views of the Inghinidhe, as on 13 March 1909, when a piece headed 'Irish Girls' began:

> Ireland has need of the loving service of all her children. Irishwomen do not sufficiently realise the power they have to help or hinder Ireland's cause. If they did, we should not see the sad sight of Irish girls walking through the streets with men wearing the uniform of Ireland's oppressor . . .

Some six inches of the same column were devoted to 'The Irishwoman's Examination of Conscience'. A list of fifteen questions, it owes much to the examination of conscience that featured among the spiritual exercises of convent schools.

From November 1908 until 1911, the Inghinidhe had their own paper, edited in Dublin by Helena Molony.[32] Published on the first Saturday of each month, *Bean na h-Éireann* (The Woman of Ireland) included a gardening column written (though not signed) by Maud Gonne; a children's page, 'An Grianán', by 'Dectora' (Madeleine ffrench-Mullen);[33] recipes, fashion and travel notes; advertisements for Irish-made clothing, furniture and bicycles; fiction, poetry, and of course politics, which featured in articles, in correspondence and in Helena Molony's editorials. The magazine's writing, design and layout were professional and attractive; its content was varied, and highly relevant to the lives of young women in Ireland.

The Wexford branch of the Inghinidhe ('Daughters of Erin' in the pages of the *Echo*), met monthly in the Sinn Féin Rooms, Monck Street, Wexford, on the same day as *Bean na h-Éireann* appeared. On the following Saturday, 'Una' would report on the meeting in her *Echo* column and announce the date of the next one, informing readers that 'Rules, circulars, etc.' were 'to be had from the hon. sec., Miss Bolger, Oylegate'.

It is not possible to state with certainty that 'Una' was Anastasia Bolger, but it seems overwhelmingly likely. Anastasia was at the heart of nationalist feminism in Wexford, and she had certainly begun to be known as Una in Irish-Ireland circles. In 1908, a list published in the *Echo* of 'the generally recognised duties of a Gaelic Leaguer and Irish Irelander' included the obligation to 'use only the Irish form of your name and address in all correspondence, documents, licences, private, official or legal'.[34] In many, if not most, cases, this meant the restoration of native originals, repudiating forms imposed by British administrations over centuries; but some people adopted, or even coined, new Gaelic equivalents. Una had been one of the most popular names for girls in medieval Ireland; often anglicised as Winnie, or Winifred, it now became a nationalist substitute for Agnes and Anastasia as well.

In August 1909, Helena Molony referred to 'Una Bolger' in a *Bean na h-Éireann* editorial as having 'had a big share in the starting of Bean na h-Eireann'. The occasion for mentioning her name was to congratulate her and her husband on their recent marriage: on 6 July, Una Bolger had married Robert Brennan of Wexford, a fellow 'Irish Irelander'. Interestingly, the 'Una' column in the *Echo* had stopped in May, with no notice of a June meeting. As a woman of twenty, about to be married, Una Bolger would have been busy.

On 10 July 1909, a piece entitled 'Wedding Bells' appeared in the *Echo*:

On Tuesday morning, the pretty parish church of Oylegate was the scene of a marriage ceremony of more than usual interest to Wexford Gaels. The happy pair were Mr Robaird O'Brendainn, Wexford, and Miss Una Ni Bolguidir, Coolnaboy, Oylegate, and the ceremony was performed by Rev. James Murphy P.P., Oylegate. The bride was given away by her uncle, Mr William Whitty, Pouldarrig, and the brides-maids were Miss Elizabeth Bolger and Miss Annie Brennan. Eamonn O'Fodluda and Feargus O'Coiglaig, Lac gCarmain,[35] were 'best men,' and a number of prominent Irish-Irelanders from Wexford and Enniscorthy were to be seen in the church. After the ceremony the wedding party were entertained to breakfast at the bride's home, Coolnaboy, and then the pair got a hearty and enthusiastic send-off to Enniscorthy, where they took train for Dublin. Robaird has for many years occupied a prominent place amongst the workers for the Irish revival in Wexford County, as a member of the Committee of the Wexford Branch of the Gaelic League, and of the County Committee of Sinn Fein, while his bride has also been a patriotic and zealous Irish-Ireland worker, being county secretary of Inginidhe na hEirinn. They have been the recipients of many valuable and beautiful pres-ents from their host of friends, and from the national organisations for which they have done much valuable work; and they begin their wedded life with the heartiest good wishes for happiness of all who know them. We congratulate Robaird and his bride with all our hearts.

> Saol fada sonasac do an mbeirt acu
> Agus beannacht Do go a tir ar a bhosha.

As usual in this period of the Gaelic revival, the Irish text contains several typesetting mistakes, but the message is clear: 'A long happy life to both, and the blessing of God on their marriage.'

TWO

Bob and Una

Many years after she had run through the streets of Wexford as a child, Maeve Brennan's *New Yorker* story, 'The Springs of Affection', described them:

> The streets in Wexford are very narrow, and crooked rather than winding. At some points the Main Street is only wide enough to allow one car to pass, and the side path for pedestrians shrinks to the width of a plank. There are always children bobbing along with one foot in the street and one on the path, and children dodging and running, making intricacies among the slowly moving bicycles and cars. It is a small, worn, angular town with plain unmatched houses that are dried into color by the sun and washed into color by the rain. There is nothing dark about Wexford. The sun comes up very close to the town and sometimes seems to be rising from among the houses. The wind scatters seeds against the walls and along the edges of the roofs, so that you can look up and see marigolds blooming between you and the sky. [*SA* 320]

Maeve's father Bob Brennan[1] was a child in Wexford in the 1880s, when horses and ponies drew carts and traps through the narrow streets, and two-masted schooners – as many as thirty at a time – moored along the quays, loading and unloading in the heart of the town.[2] The little cargo boats called Slaney gabbards were here too, beginning their journeys up the river to Enniscorthy several times a day.[3] Trains had been coming to Wexford since 1872, but did not yet go as far as Rosslare, so Wexford was still the important port it had been since medieval times.

The Vikings built Wexford town, and named it, more than a thousand years ago, and for centuries it kept the same shape: a long, narrow network of streets along the side of a hill, pressing against a coast that runs north-east to south-west. Built just outside the Slaney's narrow mouth at Ferrycarrig, the town commands the broad harbour that opens to the east. Main Street runs roughly north and south, through the middle of the town, and until the end of the eighteenth century each narrow side street on its eastern side ended in a wharf. By the 1820s, however, broad quays had been built outside the wharves, on land reclaimed from the harbour, and by the time Bob was six, the trains of the Dublin, Wicklow and Wexford Railway travelled on an extended track along the water's edge. Later, the line would continue for a further six miles to the long sandy beach at Rosslare, where a sleepy seaside resort quickly developed into the fashionable Rosslare Strand, with two packed excursion trains running from Wexford every Sunday in summer by 1904.[4]

Bob's father, also called Robert, was forty when his son was born, on 22 July 1881. He and his wife Bridget already had a daughter, Tess, who was almost three.[5] Another daughter, Annie, later known as Nan, was born in 1884, and a fourth child, Christine, four years later.[6] Robert was for a time a dealer in cattle and pigs, and his son's earliest memories were of a house in John's Gate Street, behind which was a large yard divided into stalls that were almost always filled with cattle, sheep and pigs. Bassett's *Directory* of 1885 lists Robert Brennan as a cattle dealer in John's Gate Street, and a local ballad mentions him among a list of butchers and others who lost animals when a ship called the *Montague* ran aground on the Dogger Bank.[7] His business must already have been in decline in 1885, however. His son's memoir and Maeve's fiction both depict him as gullible and slow-thinking, marginal to the animated repartee of his family's life.

For most of Bob Brennan's childhood, his mother Bridget was the main breadwinner and the dominant personality in the family. Born Bridget Kearney, she was at least fifteen years younger than her husband, who may have married her as much for her quick wit and ability with money as for her beauty. To Bridget and her parents, Robert Brennan, cattle dealer, might have represented security; certainly there is nothing to suggest that it was a love-match. Bridget was a small, plump woman who always wore black; intelligent, energetic, optimistic and generous, she was light-hearted, at least in her son's eyes: 'My mother was never despondent . . . Every evening she used to recount the happenings of the day with a wealth of comic detail, mostly imaginary, and all the funnier because my father believed every word.'

Like the 'vivacious, quick-tempered' Bridget Bagot, in her granddaughter Maeve's short story 'The Springs of Affection', 'who read Dickens and Scott and Maria Edgeworth with her children', Bridget Brennan bought a sewing machine by instalments and worked as a dressmaker to support her family. While she sewed, she sang: Bob remembered her singing Thomas Moore's 'Irish Melodies', traditional ballads, solos from light opera and Stephen

Foster's 'Negro' songs. 'I learned them all,' he added. Of his father he wrote, 'I have never known a more credulous man, or one who could be more easily imposed on'. Eventually, when Bob was in his teens, and a star pupil at the Christian Brothers' school, the family rented a four-bedroomed house on the corner of George Street and Abbey Street, just yards from the ruins of Selskar Abbey and diagonally across from the barracks of the Royal Irish Constabulary. The house had doors opening on to both streets, and when Bob won an Exhibition worth £20 in the Intermediate examination, his mother used the money to open a shop on the Abbey Street side, in what had been a small parlour. The shop sold 'sweets, candles, matches, cigarettes, vegetables etc.'. In the evenings she made toffee in the kitchen, and sold that too.[8] Sixty years later, Bob Brennan's verdict on his childhood was, 'We were very poor, and we were very happy.' His daughter's short stories offer a more complex memory, however, which carries a flavour of authenticity despite its distance in time and its passage through the convoluted filters of a displaced personal history.

That square-shaped corner house where her grandmother Brennan lived until her death in 1938 – originally two houses, with two front doors and a dark, awkwardly shaped kitchen at the back – appears several times in Maeve Brennan's fiction. In 'The Rose Garden', published in *The New Yorker* in March 1959, and in some of her stories about Rose and Hubert Derdon, Rose's mother, Mary Lambert, lives there:

> The house was really two corner houses that had been knocked into one. The houses had been thrown together, and the staircase twisted determinedly from one house up into the other, although it was impossible to to tell whether it had been built from the first floor up or from the second floor down, the construction of it was so ungainly and uneasy. The stairs thrust its way, crooked and hard, up through the house, and some of its steps were so narrow it was difficult to find a foothold on them, and some started wide and narrowed to nothing at the other side, so that they could not be depended on going down as they could going up. It was a treacherous stairs, but no one had ever been known to slip on it, because it forced respect and attention, and people guarded themselves on it. [*RG* 185–6]

A small shop takes up 'what had once been the parlor of one of the houses'. There Mary Lambert sells 'bread, sugar, milk, tea, cigarettes, apples, penny sweets, and flour': 'The milk stood in a big tin can on the counter, with a dipper hanging from the side of it, to measure out the customers' pints. The same farmer who brought the milk brought eggs and butter.

There was a sack of potatoes slumped open against the wall in one corner' [*RG* 186].

In 'The Springs of Affection' this same house (without the shop) is the home of the Bagots: the resourceful, proud and cunning Bridget, her shambling, elderly husband, their three daughters, and their son Martin. That story tells of the impacted incomprehensions that could divide town-dwellers from their rural neighbours in the early twentieth century. It traces the cultural differences that grew like a thick hedge between families like the Brennans in Wexford and the Bolgers of Coolnaboy, seven miles away in a very different house. 'The Springs of Affection' renders these differences in painful, intimate detail, distilling a lifetime's observation of human discontent into a single character. Min Bagot remembers her brother's wedding as a gladiatorial battle, with her own family grotesque in defeat, and as she looks back on a life lived in the shadow of Martin and Delia's marriage, the unhappiness of exclusion is faithfully transmuted into spiteful cruelty. In this story, as elsewhere in her fiction, Maeve has planted personalities of her own creation in settings and circumstances that are recognisably those of her family. The liberties she took with the details of other people's lives provide her stories with unassailable emotional authority, but it is not surprising that they caused heartache and misunderstandings, and complicated her relationships as time went on.

When Martin married Delia, Min felt betrayed. Country people's accents were not the same as those in town – 'She didn't like the voices of the people out here in the country' – and neither were the things they talked about. 'They didn't talk, as Min understood talk. Here in the country they wove webs with names and dates and places.' Like the real-life Brennans, the Bagots lived in rented houses and flats in Wexford, and shared the familiar streets with strangers. The walls of a house defined the limits of the family who lived there, and kept it intact; those walls guaranteed recognition, but things were different in the country:

You had to own your place – not merely the house but some of the land. And the houses were miles apart from one another, and the families lived according to laws of succession that were known only to them, and people had to depend for recognition on a loose web of relationships, a complicated genealogy that they kept in their heads and reinforced by repetition on days like today when they were all gathered together. Min thought it would be pleasant to walk around the orchard once in a while when the weather was fine, but for a nice interesting walk she would take the streets of Wexford any time. [*SA* 339]

Wexford was never a big town, but its character was always urban: its identity, prosperity and pride came from its own ships, factories and foundries and not from its agricultural hinterland. For Min Bagot, as for Maeve in Wexford or New York, 'The town was always the same . . . always on the go, with people around every corner, and no matter who they were, you knew you had as much right there as they had'. [*SA* 338–9]

By his late teens, Bob Brennan resembled the fictional Martin Bagot in several ways. He had curly black hair and blue eyes, a devoted mother and three sisters, a lively interest in books, people and amateur theatre, and a comfortable clerical job in the County Surveyor's office (he worked from ten in the morning to four in the afternoon, and was paid six shillings a week).[9] The story of his gradual immersion in cultural and political national- ism is a paradigm of early-twentieth-century life in Ireland. As mass media and mobility brought Victorian and Edwardian consumerism sharply up against the idealism of a generation newly educated about its Gaelic past, and international events and movements reverberated through the streets of Wexford, Bob made choices that would shape his subsequent career, his marriage, and the way his daughter Maeve observed the world.

The 'gay' nineties were a light-hearted time, as Ireland followed the lead of London, where the middle-aged Edward, Prince of Wales, led a fashion- able set in assiduous and much-reported pursuit of fun. In Ireland, as in England, trains brought audiences to music hall and light opera, and carried crowds to the seaside, while the spread of newspapers and magazines put jokes and humorous writing into brisk circulation. Gilbert and Sullivan were in full flow, and Sir Arthur Conan Doyle's stories of Sherlock Holmes were appearing in weekly episodes in the *Strand* magazine. Bob could not afford to pay six- pence for the magazine, but the Mechanics' Institute provided a library and reading room on North Main Street:

> I used to hang around the reading room of the Mechanics' Institute in Wexford, waiting for the magazine to be placed on the table, so that I would be the first to grab it and breathlessly follow the latest adven- tures of Holmes in his life and death struggle with the arch criminal Moriarty while the bumbling Dr Watson looked helplessly on.[10]

Maeve inherited from her father a lifelong interest in detective stories and a finely tuned sense of the ridiculous. One of Bob's all-time favourite books was Robert Louis Stevenson's *The Wrong Box*, published in 1887.[11] A major departure from the Scottish Gothic and South Sea adventures of Stevenson's other work, it was written with his stepson, Lloyd Osbourne, mostly in

Samoa, and has since become a film, starring John Mills and Ralph Richardson. It reads like a cross between the Sherlock Holmes stories and Oscar Wilde's *The Importance of Being Earnest*, with a touch of Gilbert and Sullivan thrown in. Full of trains, uncles, general knowledge, misunderstandings and disguises, the book's non-sequiturs include this remarkable exchange as two brothers prepare to dispose of a body:

'If I could only see how you meant to set about it!' sighed John. 'But you know, Morris, you always were such a bungler.'

'I'd like to know what I ever bungled,' cried Morris; 'I have the best collection of signet rings in London.'[12]

A world away from the quiet seriousness of Coolnaboy, Bob's humour was honed on books like this one, as well as on his mother's hilarious improvisations. Amateur drama and musicals were a central part of Wexford's cultural life, and he was actively involved there too – once even taking part in a group that sang the 'Marseillaise' in blackface, wearing green sashes. And when the local *Free Press* offered a prize of three guineas for the best short story, Bob wrote 'A Three Hand Reel! or A Tale of Shelmalier', and won.[13] Devoted to self-improvement, he also attended evening classes, and often travelled by train to Dublin to hear a lecture or a concert, see a play or read in the National Library. At least once – when he took the Matriculation examination of the Royal University – he cycled there and back.[14]

Bob was seventeen when the celebrations marking the centenary of the 1798 Rebellion swept through Wexford. At eighteen, he was among the group that welcomed Douglas Hyde to Wexford, and became one of the first members of the Gaelic League branch that was founded there soon after.

On that first visit to Wexford, Hyde's attire at first dismayed and even embarrassed his hosts. 'Instead of the carefully-groomed, bespectacled professor we had expected, we saw a big, wide-shouldered man, carelessly dressed in homespuns and wearing a tweed cap,' Bob recalled.[15] This was his first encounter with the Irish-Ireland campaign for the use of Irish-made cloth. Tweeds were worn by gentlemen in the country, but not in town, where gradations of 'respectability' were scrupulously noted. At the Chicago World's Fair in 1893, however, weavers from County Donegal had been a central feature of the Irish Village organised by Ishbel, Lady Aberdeen, wife of the former Viceroy. The promotion of Irish cottage industry was an objective that nationalists shared with Viceregal society in Dublin.[16] Everything he wore was Irish, Dr Hyde announced proudly, as he and Bob walked through Wexford's narrow streets, and Bob marvelled that he gave no indication of noticing 'the ridicule which attended his course'.

Even the speech Hyde gave that evening had a tweedy flavour, as 'He drew a contrast between the heroic Gaelic Ireland of the past and the shoddy English-speaking Ireland of the present'. The English textile mills, whose low-cost fabrics endangered the Irish woollen industry, had given the propagandists a word that would run and run. 'Shoddy' was recycled fibre, woven together with new wool in English mills to produce a cheaper textile. 'Shoddy imported goods' became a catchphrase of the Irish-Ireland movement, turning colonialist rhetoric against the coloniser, and managing to suggest low standards in all spheres of English, and English-dominated, life, from mass production to sexual morality.

Tweed, still made in cottages in the west of Ireland by hundreds of local weavers, was the clothing fabric favoured by the gentry in their forays into romantic, craggy landscapes. It appealed to the aspirations of the socially mobile, therefore, while the sturdy self-reliance of its artisan weavers offered a satisfying link with the English Arts and Crafts movement.[17] With its peaty smell and rough feel, homespun tweed could even bring to mind walking holidays spent in Irish-speaking areas, in the idyllic western landscapes recently opened up by the railways and soon to be celebrated in Paul Henry's paintings of towering skies, peat bogs and huddled cottages.[18] In the nineteenth century also, Irish entrepreneurs had invested in the latest machinery from England; the number of commercial woollen mills rose from 11 in 1850 to 100 in 1904.[19]

A few years after Hyde's first visit to Wexford, tweeds had become the costume of the Irish Irelander. In 1908, the Enniscorthy *Echo* announced: 'To look a man, an Irishman, you must be dressed in native tweed. If you wear Carley's Bridge tweed you will realise the warmth of Home Grown wool, and the value of home spun tweed.'[20] 'All pure wool,' the advertisement noted; 'no inferior shoddy used'.

On the basis of what he had learned at the Christian Brothers' school, and what he could teach himself from books like Father O'Growney's *Simple Lessons in Irish* and Norma Borthwick's *Ceachta Beaga Gaeilge* (Little Lessons in Irish), Bob Brennan became the Wexford Gaelic League's first teacher of Irish. The classes paid him five shillings a week (almost as much as his job in the Surveyor's office), and entailed cycling to outlying villages to recruit new members for the League, as well as teaching in town.

In March 1901, it was nineteen-year-old Bob, not his father, who filled in and signed the census form in his distinctive handwriting. He gives his own occupation as 'clerk', his father's as 'victualler', his mother's as 'dressmaker'. His sister Teresa, twenty-two, is a milliner; his sister Annie [Nan], sixteen, a dressmaker; Christine, the youngest, is twelve, and a 'scholar'.

According to the form, all members of the family can speak both Irish and English (in their census return for 1911, however, when Bob was no longer living with them, his parents made no claim to speak Irish, although his three sisters did).[21]

The Gaelic League represented a new kind of nationalism. John Redmond's Irish Parliamentary Party had influenced hearts and minds in 1898, but the party's complacency was provoking increasing cynicism among Irish Irelanders. The Agricultural Co-operative Movement, started by Sir Horace Plunkett in 1894, was gaining ground, offering the prospect of economic independence to individuals who pooled resources, but Redmond's second-in-command, John Dillon, whose family owned a large shop in Ballaghadereen, County Mayo, became one of its most vocal opponents.[22] Increasingly associated with attitudes like his, the parliamentary nationalists became the *bêtes noires* of the Gaelic revival as it grew more articulately populist and anti-colonial. 'Gaels' in their twenties poured scorn on the fifty-year-old parliamentarians, calling them tools of the British Liberal Party and lambasting them as West Britons and Shoneens.

The term 'West Briton', still heard a hundred years later as 'West Brit', was coined by D. P. Moran of the *Leader*, as was *Seoinín* (or Shoneen), a 'little John' – a craven imitator of the coloniser's ways.[23] Like Griffith's *United Irishman*, the *Leader* urged opposition to parliamentary politics, but Moran gloried in the simplistic polarisations of Boer War jingoism. He developed a rhetoric of ridicule against the social climbers Dubliners called 'Castle Catholics', and his nicknames and shibboleths became part of the culture of Irish Ireland, reinforcing a sense of 'them and us'.

By the spring of 1902, some 28,000 Irishmen, including hundreds from Wexford, were in the Transvaal. Members of part-time militias, they had rashly signed up years earlier as 'available for overseas service' in return for an extra five shillings annually. Now they had been called upon to fight the Boers, and resistance to the war was growing among those at home. Arthur Griffith, James Connolly, W. B. Yeats and Maud Gonne were among the radical activists who formed the 'Irish Transvaal Committee', and as they compared Britain's policies in South Africa and in Ireland, it began to seem both heroic and feasible for a small aspiring republic, composed largely of farmers, and united by language and religion, to take on the mighty British Empire.

Bob saw a play in Dublin that spring, when he was twenty-one, that would remain with him all his life. *Cathleen ni Houlihan*, billed as the work of W. B. Yeats, but written in close collaboration with – if not entirely by – the fifty-year-old Lady Gregory, was first performed at St Teresa's Hall, Clarendon Street, on 2 April 1902.[24] It ran for three nights as part of a double bill staged by the Inghinidhe, along with *Deirdre*, by Æ, otherwise known as the nationalist writer George Russell. It was the first Inghinidhe production, and their blue banner with its golden sunburst hung near the stage. Lady Gregory herself was present on the first night, and over 300 people packed into the hall for each of the performances, with many turned away. Several of those present would write about the intense excitement they felt, and many years later, in one of his last poems, 'The Man and the Echo', Yeats would fret that the play had perhaps sent men to their deaths in 1916.[25]

Students in generations since have smiled at such a possibility (and Yeats's entitlement to ownership of the play is strongly disputed), but Bob was in no doubt that the play had done precisely as Yeats imagined, or feared. His generation, weaned on the 'green' rhetoric of the 1798 centenary, was now disenchanted with parliamentary politics. It found its own idealism expressed for the first time in one place that week. And despite the play's dingy surroundings and inadequate rehearsal time, it had glamour. Inghinidhe founder Maud Gonne, thirty-six years old, over six feet tall, and already legendary, played the elderly Cathleen in bare feet. Arriving late on the first night, she made her way in costume through the audience to the stage. Bob (who measured five feet six and a half inches), attempted to speak to her backstage, but gave up in the crush. He wrote: 'I had heard she was the most beautiful woman in Ireland – I thought she must be the most beautiful woman in the world.'[26]

Art and politics made a heady combination. Scholars had been editing and translating medieval Irish manuscripts and collecting oral traditions, and their publications offered a wealth of fresh themes and images to work with. One of the first productions of the Irish Literary Theatre, forerunner of Dublin's Abbey Theatre, had been a two-act play called *Maeve*, by Edward Martyn, performed at the Gaiety Theatre on 19 February 1900, in which the warrior queen of medieval saga rescues a modern Irish woman. In October the following year, also at the Gaiety, Douglas Hyde acted in his own new play in Irish, *Casadh an tSúgáin* ('The Twisting of the Hay Rope'), a comedy based on a traditional song from his *Abhráin Grádh Chúige Connacht*, or *Love Songs of Connacht* (1893). At Christmas 1902, Hyde published a new nativity play in Irish, *Dráma Breithe Chríost*, with an English translation by Lady Gregory. Thirty years later, as a schoolgirl, Bob's daughter Maeve would star in it.[27]

Lolly and Lily (Elizabeth and Susan) Yeats, sisters of the poet, with Evelyn Gleeson (who provided the capital), set up craft workshops for girls in Dundrum in 1902. Now a suburb in the foothills of the Dublin mountains, this was the last village on the Harcourt Street railway line before trains from Wexford reached the outskirts of Dublin. The women named their house Dun Emer (Emer's Compound), after Emer, steadfast, clever wife of the hero Cú Chulainn (in medieval saga, when he first saw her, she was training her companions in fine needlework).[28] Already a talented watercolour painter, Lily Yeats had worked at embroidery with William Morris's daughter in England; Dun Emer's first commissions included twenty-four sumptuously embroidered banners for the new Loughrea Cathedral in County Galway, designed by Lily's artist brother Jack B. Yeats and his wife Mary Cottenham Yeats in 'Celtic' medieval style. By 1904, when the Arts and Crafts Society of Ireland held its third exhibition in Dublin, Dun Emer was also producing fine printed books and handwoven rugs and carpets, and the Catholic Church had become firmly established as a patron of Irish arts and crafts. Various attempts were made to establish a national costume, with kilts for men and lavishly embroidered, loose-fitting gowns as evening wear for women. Most Irish Irelanders, however, were content to insist on Irish-made fabrics.

A few years later, an advertisement on the front page of *Bean na h-Éireann*, for Dripsey Woollen Mills in County Cork, used just thirty-two words to invoke not only the memory of the Yeats/Gregory play, but also the fashion sense, thrift, and economic power of 'sensible' nationalist women:

Dripsey!
The 'Kathleen Ni Houlihan' are Lovelier than ever!
The Prices Lower than ever!
By wearing Dripsey Dress Cloths the sensible Women of Ireland
have doubled the
Dripsey Mills in Two Years.[29]

Fifty years after this appeared, when Maeve Brennan in New York wrote about tweed as a fashion fabric, she was knowledgeably invoking something that had been part of her parents' lives before she was born.

As late as 1973, Maeve was avidly reading a magazine that also dated from this period, and one with which her father had a long association. Social reformers on both sides of the Irish Sea deplored mass production's ability to pander to people's basest instincts. In Wexford in 1902, John M. Walsh of the *People* printing works asserted cultural independence when he began publication of *Ireland's Own* as 'A Journal of Fiction, Literature and General Information'. A popular weekly of twenty-four pages, then priced at one penny, it is still in production more than a hundred years later:

'Ireland's Own' is intended to counteract the influence and displace a great portion of the vicious and undesirable literature that reaches this country weekly. It will not be by any means run on narrow lines, but will be broad and instructive – a journal that may be taken and perused with advantage by all persons in Ireland . . . its aim being to instruct, elevate and afford recreation to the people . . ., nothing that is not absolutely healthy will find a place in its columns. Our fiction, whether Irish or otherwise, will be pure, and ennobling in the lessons it conveys . . .[30]

Ireland's Own was an immediate success. By July 1904 hundreds entered a competition asking readers to identify twenty-four railway stations from photographs. First prize was a lady's or gent's Pierce free-wheel bicycle, made in Wexford, or a gold watch. When the winner was announced on 24 August, two pages of the magazine were packed with the closely printed names and addresses of competitors who had had twenty-two or twenty-three correct answers. Within ten years its circulation reached 30,000, and it continued to rise. The fiction it published told of adventure, villainy and bravery, all with an Irish flavour, and Bob soon began to submit his own stories.

Irish Ireland stood for a whole new way of life as the twentieth century began and Bob Brennan and Anastasia Bolger came to adulthood. The Gaelic League gave its young members co-educational language classes, dances, songs and music.[31] The first generation of ordinary people to own bicycles, they roamed the countryside to attend local festivals and meetings. Their programme of cultural renewal was part of an international movement towards physical and social mobility, for women as well as men, and marked a significant departure from the colonised acquiescence of the older generation. Although Hyde's vision for the League had been strictly cultural, many of its members joined Sinn Féin, of which Bob soon became County Secretary.

By the time Anastasia Bolger began to sample the cultural and political life of Wexford, changed her name to Una and first encountered Bob Brennan, D. P. Moran's rabble-rousing version of Irish Ireland was in its heyday. Bob tells in his autobiography *Allegiance* of a visit to Dublin, and an incident that later made him blush: 'One night a crowd of us went to the Gaiety Theatre to protest against a play called *Sappho*. We knew nothing about the play except that Moran in *The Leader* had said it was immoral'. He tells of the icy contempt with which their hilarious discussion of the episode was greeted next day at the National Library by a 'fairish, thin-faced fellow' who quickly left the company. The 'fellow' turned out to be James Joyce, whose *Chamber Music* (1907) had recently appeared.[32] Molly Ivors in Joyce's 1906 story 'The Dead' is a typical Irish Irelander, but it was in his excoriating portrait of the Citizen, in the Cyclops episode of *Ulysses*, that Joyce gave vent to his distaste for Irish Ireland's xenophobic excesses.

The nationalist movement accommodated many strands of ideology in the early twentieth century, however, and humour played an important rôle in winning it new recruits. D. P. Moran's gleeful pursuit of his adversaries with verbal caricature brought faithful weekly readers to the *Leader*. Always a fundamentalist, Moran dubbed the bearded mystic George Russell (Æ), who was neither Catholic nor Irish-speaking, 'the hairy fairy',[33] while Bob Brennan described the novelist George Moore, whom he used to see around the National Library, as looking 'like a very large pink cigar'.[34] The feminists in *Bean na h-Éireann* made extensive use of wit and humour too, and Russell's own writing style was full of jokes and mockery. '[W]hen man was created, and intellect given him,' he wrote, 'this very delicate gyroscope humour was given man to steady him. All the great tragedies of the intellect came from the absence of humour.'[35]

Russell edited the *Irish Homestead* for the Agricultural Co-operative Movement. Actor Máire Nic Shiubhlaigh remembered him 'muffled in his great tweed coat, peering pleasantly through a tangle of spectacles and beard . . . always ready to talk with us, listen to our theories'.[36] He was a poet and a Sunday painter, who Yeats said was in the habit of 'wandering alone among the hills, talking to half-mad and visionary peasants'. Mysticism notwithstanding, Russell was an energetic and practical facilitator of social reform and cultural revival, and his influence on young people was considerable. Married, with two small sons, he allowed the Inghinidhe to use his house on Rathgar Avenue in Dublin for rehearsals. He travelled the country on behalf of the Irish Agricultural Organisation Society, and made its newspaper a bible for creative, industrious Irish Irelanders like Bob Brennan and Una Bolger.

Published weekly, price one penny, the *Homestead*, with its philosophy of radical humanism and small-scale economic self-reliance, was a serious journal of social reform. Russell's philosophy is often identified as the source of a nationalist pastoral tradition, which found its most extreme expression in Éamon de Valera's St Patrick's Day broadcast in 1943. To some, he seemed nostalgic for lost landlordism, but many of the young people who read the *Homestead* were living on small farms and putting its teaching into action daily. Since about 1850, a growing urban demand for beef, combined with the new rail network and the availability of land after the Famine, had allowed a wealthy grazier class to develop in Ireland. When increasing conflict between the capitalist values of graziers and the interest of smallholders led to the so-called 'ranch war' of 1906–1909, the *Homestead* came out firmly on the side of the small farmer.[37]

Week by week, as Bob and Una were preparing to marry, the *Irish Homestead* exhorted, encouraged and informed, offering examples of farming and marketing practices in Denmark and elsewhere, as well as in Ireland. In the wake of the Wyndham Land Act of 1903, which provided for the smooth transfer of holdings from landlord to tenant, it advocated labour-intensive mixed farming and derided 'ranching'. The work of the grazier it characterised as 'opening and shutting gates'. Its notes on poultry- and bee-keeping were addressed to the beginner as well as to the experienced. Once, it offered a prize for the best essay on 'The Duties of Committee-Men of Co-Operative Societies'.

Every week, the *Homestead* offered a suggestion for 'seasonal decoration'. On 29 May 1909, this was 'sprays of yellow broom and the brown shoots of sycamore'; on 5 June, 'copper beech and double pink peonies'; on 19 June, 'white, mauve and purple violas, picked with long stems and arranged very loosely in low glasses'. Beauty was of as much concern in its pages as profit. Its articles assured idealistic young couples, determined to live in new ways in a self-sufficient Ireland, that the two could be combined.[38] Its issue of 29 May devoted pages to an ambitious initiative in daffodil-growing at Lissadell, County Sligo, by Sir Josslyn Gore-Booth, brother of W. B. Yeats's friends Constance (Countess Markievicz) and Eva (he was a landlord, but also a well-known advocate of co-operation). Innovatively for 1909, the article was accompanied by splendid photographs taken at Lissadell: a single specimen of *Narcissus* Madame de Graaf, and a whole field of *Narcissus grandis*. 'This flower-gardening is a more thrilling and exciting rural occupation than opening and shutting gates,' the article continued. 'A single bulb may be more valuable than a cow.'

Una Bolger's love of flowers was thus part and parcel of the new nationalism. The domestic arts at which she excelled did not conflict with her feminism. Rather, her generation of emancipated women cultivated gardening and needlework as powerful weapons against one of the great social problems of the day: the mass emigration of young women from rural Ireland. If country women's lives could be made more attractive, they reasoned, and their drudgery lessened, declining communities could flourish once again.

On social questions, the *Homestead* deplored 'the loveless marriage' – code for the practice, common among farmers, of marrying for dowry. On 28 August 1909, it asserted that 'every civilisation which has beauty in it has its roots in some way in a humanity which rates kinship of soul higher than cows or pounds, shillings, and pence'. The previous 12 June it had published a poem by James Stephens, entitled 'Woman to Man':

> You want a thing to cook,
> To wash and scrub and smile,
> To black your boots and brush your hat
> And kiss you goodbye on the mat,
> Then darn your socks a while.

'Household Hints' were equally irreverent. On 28 August 1909: 'The serpent tempted Eve with an apple; he knew very well he would have no chance with a potato. Eve would have felt no tempation to eat anything new if she had to cook it first . . .'

New organisations, expressing nuances of nationalism and liberation, were forming all the time. In 1908, Hanna Sheehy-Skeffington and Margaret Cousins founded the Irishwomen's Franchise League, and in the same year Seán Mac Diarmada moved to Dublin and began actively to revive the secret, oath-bound Irish Republican Brotherhood, known as the Fenians. Tom Clarke, who had served fifteen years in prison for Fenian activities in the 1880s and 1890s, had returned to Dublin from the United States and now became a mentor to the younger men. Along with other Gaelic League and Sinn Féin members, Bob Brennan joined the IRB, and was sworn in by Seán T. O'Kelly (later Ireland's second President), who had travelled to Wexford from Dublin for the purpose. Although an unwritten rule barred women from membership, Bob came to the conclusion that he could not keep his membership from 'the lady who was to be my life partner'. He insisted that Una Bolger be admitted, so as to share his secret, and she was duly sworn in – believed to be one of only two women IRB members ever.[39]

Bob retained his taste for adventure stories, and his sense of humour. Erskine Childers' spy novel, *The Riddle of the Sands*, published in 1903, impressed him, and he wrote occasional pieces for *Ireland's Own* and for the *Echo*. A short item in the *Echo* of 14 February 1908 could well have come from his pen. Under the title 'The Nu Spelin Leag of Amurrika', the writer commented 'It wud giv us a sik feelin about the diafram to eat an eg spelt with wun "g".'

After her wedding on 6 July 1909, Una Bolger became known as Una Brennan (and briefly as O'Brennan), though her own family continued to address her and refer to her as 'Anty'. The newly-weds travelled by train to Dublin the same day. Their wedding photograph, reproduced in *Allegiance*, shows Una with piled-up hair, wearing the long-sleeved white blouse and high-waisted skirt of her wedding 'costume'. The setting, and the couple's pose, are identical to those in a photograph of Éamon de Valera and his wife Sinéad, taken when they married the following year.[40] The two couples did not yet know each other, but it seems that both patronised the same photographer in Dublin, probably a member of the Gaelic League. In Maeve's story 'A Young Girl Can Spoil her Chances', Hubert Derdon remembers his wife Rose walking in Dublin's St Stephen's Green, 'in a navy blue skirt and a long-sleeved white blouse and no coat. It must have been a very warm day. The navy-blue skirt had a matching coat that went with it. She called this outfit her costume, and it had been her wedding dress' [*SA* 89]. Maeve would have seen these clothes in her parents' wedding photograph throughout her childhood.

The *Oireachtas* – the Gaelic League's annual cultural festival – was held in Dublin a few weeks after Bob and Una married. *Bean na h-Éireann* approved:

> Picturesque figures in the National costume appear in the streets, homespun-clad men with an intense enthusiasm in their faces, women joyous and beautiful, mixing with the men in free comradeship, and the music of the Gaelic everywhere.[41]

But the Brennans were already back in Wexford. On 31 July 1909, three weeks after their wedding, the *Echo* published a short item:

Wexford Notes
A RESIGNATION

> The Secretary of the Wexford County Council has received from Mr Robert Brennan, Wexford, intimation of his intention to resign the position of Assistant County Surveyor at an early date.

Bob's job had involved cycling around the county, inspecting some 400 miles of roads. His political activities had long been an embarrassment to the parliamentarian majority on the Council, and an accident on a bridge had now given them an excuse to censure him. Bob insisted that the bridge in question was not his responsibility, but 'Una and I decided at once that I should resign,' he writes, 'and I did so'. William Sears, editor of the Enniscorthy *Echo*, immediately offered him work, and he became the newspaper's Wexford correspondent, at a salary of £1 per week.[42]

After their marriage, the Brennans lived in rooms above a shop at 24 North Main Street, Wexford, and Una continued as secretary of the

Inghinidhe, her name and address now given in Irish in the monthly *Echo* report as 'Bean Ni Bhreandain [Mrs Brennan], 24 Sraid Mhor Thuaidhe, Loc Garman'. The young couple may have spent their first Christmas with the Bolgers at Coolnaboy, for the *Echo*'s Wexford Notes on 1 January 1910 included the following report of a loss suffered by Una's uncle, making a local incident the basis for a swipe at the police:

> On Christmas night the tails were cut off two horses belonging to Mr William Whitty, Pouldarrig. The idea of the thieves is to steal the hair for selling purposes. It seems to be a profitable and safe method of robbery. The thieves can't be caught – at least they don't be caught. The police are too busy greasing their hair and looking dignified to interfere with the marauders. Last year there was a surfeit of this sort of outrage in the district. The tails were cut off horses belonging to Mr John Murphy, Ballinaslaney; Mr W. Ronan, Turkyle; Mr Laurence Cummins, Ballylucas, and several others. In one instance two good horses were completely spoiled for the fair. It is believed that the work was carried out by tramps. Of course if we had a proper police force in the country such things could not happen in such a wholesale fashion.

Later items detailed the preparations being made for the grand reopening of St David's holy well, Ballinaslaney, on the small road that led to Pouldearg, in March 1910. The well's popularity had been growing among pilgrims and Sunday cyclists, following a series of apparently miraculous cures attributed to its water. A number of holy wells were restored and opened to the public in this period, in ceremonies cannily designed to combine the energies of Catholicism and nationalism with young people's mobility. Until the early nineteenth century, large crowds of pilgrims had come by river and road to St David's well (especially on the 'pattern' or patron day, 1 March, still observed in the twenty-first century).[43] One hundred years later, its reopening marked a new pride in Irish traditions. Without any overtly political connotation, reopened holy wells could become centres of assembly for the young men and women most likely to espouse the nationalist cause.

Bob and Una soon began to put the utopian ideals of Irish Ireland into practice. With money given to Una by her Whitty relatives, they bought a large house with ten acres on Summerhill, on the outskirts of Wexford town. The house, called Summerville, was big enough for them to take in another couple as lodgers. They planned to make money from poultry, gardening and bee-keeping, and borrowed £300 – a considerable sum – to stock the land. On 28 May 1910, the *Echo* carried a small prepaid advertisement in the column 'Births, Marriages and Deaths' on its front page:

bIRTH [*sic*]

O'Brennan – On Saturday, May 21st, at Summerville, Wexford, the wife of Robert O'Brennan, of a daughter.

Bob and Una called their daughter Emer. She was a lovely baby, but almost nothing else in their plan went right. They made cold frames of glass, and tried to sell them to vegetable growers, but couldn't; they raised plants for sale, but had to dump most of them; they grew tomatoes and calculated that if they had a full crop for forty-two years, they might be able to pay the cost of the greenhouse. Eventually, even their bees died.[44] Una became pregnant again, and gave birth to a boy whom they named Manus.[45] That baby lived for less than a year. Maeve's fiction makes many references to Delia and Martin Bagot's infant son who died, and to the long-lasting effects of that bereavement on Delia and on their marriage.[46] The loss of her own elder brother before she was born must have coloured – or perhaps drained the colour from – her parents' lives and her own childhood.

By 1912 Bob was County Secretary of both Sinn Féin and the IRB, but these too were in decline. Only the Gaelic League still drew new members. His career in journalism was progressing, however, and Una's younger brother, Jim Bolger, joined the staff of the *Echo* too. William Sears was a supportive employer, and his paper was committed to the same ideals as the Brennans were, celebrating all that could be celebrated locally, heaping scorn on the British administration in Ireland, the police and the Irish Paliamentary Party, and raising readers' consciousness about nationalism and women's issues.[47]

As well as reporting on local news, the work of the courts and the deliberations of the County and District Councils (and attempting to farm), Bob was writing weekly detective stories for *Ireland's Own*, sitting up until four on a Friday morning to finish them, and carrying them to the post office in time for the early morning collection. He had invented a bucolic, one-eyed detective called Crubeen Patch, and from 1912 to 1914 produced over a hundred stories about him, each of some 7,000 words. They were signed 'R. Selskar Kearney' (Kearney for his mother's maiden name; Selskar for the abbey beside her house), and reportedly helped raise the magazine's circulation to 80,000. The outbreak of war in 1914 put paid to a plan to publish them in book form, however.

The years leading up to the Great War were marked by increasing militancy. The *Echo* was initially proud and supportive of Pierce's foundry in Wexford, which made farm implements for world-wide export, as well as the Pierce free-wheel bicycle, but in February 1912 it reported on a lockout at the foundry, describing the scab labour that had been brought in from Britain and paraded through the streets of Wexford under a police escort as 'the scum of the British Isles'. Then in August 1913, when a group of Dublin employers sought to ban the Irish Transport and General Workers' Union, the great Dublin strike and lockout followed. Within a month, 20,000 were out of work. The union set up soup kitchens in its headquarters, Liberty Hall, and James Connolly founded the Irish Citizen Army to protect the workers. The Brennans sheltered two fugitives at Summerville, hiding their presence for weeks from the family with whom they shared the house.

In the north, the Ulster Volunteer Army formed to oppose Home Rule. Nationalists responded by founding the Irish Volunteers in November 1913 and proceeding to drill, with marching and rifle practice. 'We all joined up,' Bob wrote. Six months later membership had climbed to 27,000.[48] A women's auxiliary, Cumann na mBan, came into being the following April, and along with her fellow members of the almost-defunct Inghinidhe, Una became a member. Gaelic League classes in various parts of Ireland were now regularly followed by military drills. Despite its founder's determination to keep the League apart from politics, its membership was heavily involved in the IRB.

In April 1914, with the Home Rule Bill on its way through Westminster, the Ulster Volunteers illegally imported quantities of rifles from Germany at Larne, Bangor and Donaghadee, but the police did nothing to stop them. Then on 26 July, Erskine Childers' fifty-foot yacht, *Asgard*, landed 1,500 rifles and ammunition at Howth, near Dublin. Volunteers marched from the city to receive them, but were intercepted by police and army on their way back. Some of the rifles were captured, and three people were killed in the disturbances that followed. The immediate result of the Howth gun-running, as it came to be called, was a huge increase in recruits to the Volunteers.

War broke out in Europe a week later. John Redmond called on Irishmen to join the British army, and a majority of the recently recruited Volunteers enlisted, but the IRB stepped up its preparations for armed revolt. Bob began to carry an automatic pistol. Jim Bolger was arrested and taken to Arbour Hill Barracks in Dublin, charged with treason and sedition. Una and Bob managed to visit him before his trial, where it was feared he would be sentenced to death; but he and his fellow defendant were acquitted.

By 1916, the Brennans had abandoned their attempt at farming and moved back into Wexford with their five-year-old daughter, to rooms at 28

North Main Street. On 1 March that year, a concert to commemorate the 1803 execution of Robert Emmet was held in Enniscorthy's Athenæum, beside the Castle at the top of the town. The printed programme advertised 'Orator P.H. Pearse, recitations Máire Nic Shiubhlaigh, etc.'. Delivering his lecture, Patrick Pearse, Commandant of the Volunteers, was flanked by a guard in full uniform with rifles and fixed bayonets. His performance left no doubt that an armed uprising was imminent. A few days later, orders came from him naming Bob as brigade quartermaster in Wexford, with the rank of captain.[49]

Easter Sunday, 23 April, was the day planned for the Rising. Bob would have an important role, but Una, as a member of Cumann na mBan, was scheduled to take part as well. They brought Emer to Coolnaboy, to stay with her grandmother. Her Aunt Bessie was twenty-three, her Uncle John two years older; Wat, the youngest uncle, was nineteen, and he became especially fond of the little girl. Emer was the first of several grandchildren to be petted and kept safe in that house, where nationalist politics were strong, but the sound of gunfire far away.

A great deal has been written about the events of Easter weekend 1916: the orders given and countermanded, the rising that finally occurred in a few centres on Easter Monday, the Proclamation of the Irish Republic, read by Pearse at Dublin's General Post Office, the uncompromising British reaction, and the surrender of the Dublin insurgents on 29 April. Enniscorthy was one of the very few places outside Dublin where the Rising actually took place. Peter Paul Gallagher cycled there from Dublin with an order to block the railway line, to prevent reinforcements reaching Dublin. Some 300 men turned up to occupy the town, and the Constabulary retired to barracks. The Volunteers set up their headquarters at the Athenæum, where they put up a notice proclaiming the Republic. Cumann na mBan organised food kitchens and first-aid posts, and Una and two other women raised the green, white and orange tricolour above the building. Men and women held out there for the rest of the week, until written orders to surrender were brought from Pearse in Arbour Hill Barracks.

At 2 p.m. on Monday, 1 May, Bob and five other officers surrendered to the British in Enniscorthy. Una took a train back to Wexford. The men were brought first to the RIC barracks in George Street, Wexford, where Bob could look out the window and see his mother's house and shop across the heads of the crowd gathered in the street. Later, they were transferred to prison in Waterford, where their height, weight, age, hair and eye colour and other details were entered in the prison register. The charge recorded against Bob was that he did 'Feloniously levy and aid and assist in levying war against our Sovereign Lord the King'.[50]

Within days the prisoners were transferred to Dublin. They knew already that Patrick Pearse, Thomas MacDonagh and Tom Clarke had been executed by shooting on 3 May, with further executions carried out daily. The six Wexford prisoners were court-martialled and condemned to death also, but the number of executions was starting to turn public opinion in Ireland, Britain and the United States in favour of the insurgents. The men's sentences were commuted almost immediately to five years' penal servitude, and before the end of the month they were transferred to Dartmoor in south-west England, a place Bob had read much about in the stories of Sherlock Holmes. He would not return to Ireland for more than a year, until a general amnesty was declared in June 1917. Una managed to visit him once in Mountjoy Prison before he was moved to England.[51] She may not yet have known it when she saw him, but she was pregnant again.

THREE

Belgrave Road

Una Brennan was not the only woman left to cope alone after the 1916 Rising. While the Great War raged on in Europe, some 130 Irish prisoners, most of them young men, and many of them married, were sent to various British prisons, with no indication that they would be free in less than five years. Several others had of course been executed. Twenty-nine-year-old Joseph Mary Plunkett, already dying of tuberculosis, had married his sweetheart, the talented cartoonist Grace Gifford, in Kilmainham Jail just before he was shot. Thomas MacDonagh, husband of her sister Muriel, had been one of the first executed, along with Pearse, on 3 May, and Muriel was left with their four-year-old son Donagh. Like Una Brennan, Éamon de Valera's wife Sinéad, formerly known as Jennie Flanagan, was pregnant when her husband was arrested. She had been de Valera's Irish teacher before their marriage in January 1910; they already had four children, and he was in Dartmoor with Bob Brennan when their fifth child, Ruairí, was born in November 1916.[1]

Through Cumann na mBan, Dublin offered a network of support for women. Trains from Wexford terminated at the top of Harcourt Street, from where it was a short walk to the Cumann office in Sinn Féin headquarters at number 6, near the corner of St Stephen's Green. Since a spectacular accident in 1900, when an engine overran the end of the platform and crashed through the wall to hang above the street, all trains were required to make a preliminary stop at Ranelagh, a mile south. An active nationalist community had grown up there, with many feminists and republicans living in the area.[2]

Ranelagh station on Dunville Avenue served the township of Rathmines, a thriving suburb first incorporated in 1847. Red pillar-boxes on the stately, tree-lined Palmerston Road were embossed with Queen Victoria's discreet 'VR', while new ones in smaller, neighbouring streets bore the florid monogram of King Edward VII. Separated from the increasingly nationalist Dublin city by the Grand Canal, Rathmines had always been Protestant and unionist. The spire of Holy Trinity Church rose above its house roofs, and the Union Jack flew from the 128-foot clock tower of its red sandstone town hall. The builder of several of the residential streets, however, was a Catholic, Patrick Plunkett, grandfather of Joseph, who had been executed in May although terminally ill. Aged one hundred in 1917, Patrick Plunkett still lived at 14 Palmerston Road, while his grandson's in-laws, the Giffords, were at 8 Temple Villas, at the top of the same road. Their other son-in-law, Thomas MacDonagh, had been a university lecturer and poet, a friend and colleague of Pearse. He had liked to recount how the lace curtains at the windows of their unionist neighbours would twitch with outrage as he walked by, wearing the tweed kilt that proclaimed him to be an Irish Irelander.[3]

Rows of redbrick houses were still being built in Ranelagh and Rathmines for a growing middle class, and more and more of the new householders were Catholic.[4] There was even a new Catholic church on Beechwood Avenue, its belfry incorporating what looked like an Irish round tower.[5] As the train from Wexford crossed the high viaduct over the River Dodder at Milltown and ran past allotments before reaching Ranelagh station, the Church of the Holy Name appeared on the right, above the rows of grey slate roofs and redbrick chimney-pots.

Joseph Plunkett's sister Geraldine lived with her husband Dr Tommy Dillon in one of the older houses, around the corner from her grandfather, at number 13 Belgrave Road. Tommy Dillon, a university lecturer in chemistry, had not been involved in the Rising (he and Geraldine had married on the morning of Easter Monday, 1916), but he had supplied expertise with explosives.[6] Other prominent nationalists rented houses from the Plunketts: Dr Kathleen Lynn, aged forty-two, a rector's daughter from County Mayo, was a devout Protestant and resolute nationalist, who had attended the wounded around City Hall and Dublin Castle on Easter Monday. She shared number 9 Belgrave Road with her friend Madeleine ffrench-Mullen ('Dectora' in *Bean na h-Éireann*). Like the Dillons, Lynn was a friend of the Brennans, a familiar figure in suit, collar and tie, as she cycled all over the neighbourhood, her stethoscope about her neck.[7] According to one account, even when on the run, she 'managed to continue her work without hindrance from the authorities. She evaded capture by dressing as she put it "like a lady, in my Sunday clothes and feather boa, and walking instead of cycling".'[8]

Cullenswood House, on Oakley Road, was a stone's throw from the Ranelagh-Rathmines station and from Belgrave Road. It had been the home of Patrick Pearse, and the first site of his school, St Enda's. His mother still held the lease, and Cullenswood House became a home from home for many: Dublin lore says that several rebel women had their babies there.[9] Una, however, had already lost one child in infancy. She may have stayed with Geraldine and Tommy Dillon during her pregnancy, leaving Emer with her mother and Bessie at Coolnaboy, but she did not give birth at Cullenswood House.

Maeve Brennan was born at Denmark House, 21 Great Denmark Street, Dublin, on Saturday, 6 January 1917.[10] A large Georgian townhouse, across the street from the Jesuit Belvedere College, it was a nursing home run by forty-year-old Miss Estrea (or perhaps Astrea) Cutler. Miss Cutler was a member of the Church of Ireland, originally from County Kildare, who had described herself in the 1911 census as a 'hospital nurse/matron [of] nursing home'. Denmark House was close to both Eccles Street, where James Joyce placed Leopold and Molly Bloom's home in *Ulysses*, and Sackville (now O'Connell) Street, where the main action of the Rising had taken place the previous Easter. It had eleven rooms, with thirteen windows overlooking the street, and was evidently a highly respectable establishment. In 1911, in addition to several boarders, it had housed two hospital nurses besides Miss Cutler, and two patients (both Protestant), with their newborn infants; by 1916 it even had a telephone.[11]

Denmark House may have been part of a feminist network, perhaps recommended to Una by Kathleen Lynn (its next tenants, from 1919 to 1922, were the Irish Women Workers' Union). One advantage of giving birth there was that it obviated the embarrassment of registering the father as a resident in one of His Majesty's prisons. The new baby's parents were named as Robert Brennan, journalist, whose dwelling place was given as 'Denmark House, Great Denmark Street', and Una Brennan, formerly Bolgar (*sic*), of the same address. The details were supplied by the midwife, Elizabeth McFarland.

The baby was registered as 'Meave Brigid Clarke Brennan', and while 'Meave' may have been a simple error, like 'Bolgar' for 'Bolger', it also reflects the unfamiliarity of the name. Brigid, or Bridget, was Bob's mother's name, and also that of the saint most often invoked during the Revival as a model for women; Clarke was probably for the executed Tom Clarke, but Maeve, like Emer, was a name from medieval saga. Stories about Cú Chulainn's wife focused on her discretion and skill at needlework, but Maeve, or in Old Irish, *Medb*, was the demanding, fiery warrior queen against whose forces the young hero was pitted. In a long, apparently unpublished, essay on Irish history and pseudo-history, which Maeve Brennan wrote in the US some time after the end of the Second World War, she refers to 'Queen Maeve of Connacht, who was red-haired and bad-tempered and loved war'.[12] Not many people in 1917 would have known that her name was cognate with the English word 'mead', and meant roughly 'she who makes people

43

drunk'. For the new baby and her parents, it was enough that it stood for defiant and confident nationalism.

When their second daughter was born, Una had not seen Bob for seven months. He was in Lewes Prison in Sussex, to which all the Irish prisoners had been transferred in early December, brought by train in chains and convict clothing from other jails.[13] The Irish prisoners organised themselves effectively for recreation and education. Most were devoutly religious, and morale was high. Experts in various areas shared their knowledge: Éamon de Valera gave lectures in mathematics; Bob delivered a series of talks on bee-keeping; prisoners kept up their study of Irish and other languages. Bob's autobiography records witty exchanges between prisoners and prison staff, and details some of the stratagems the men used to communicate and to support each other. Ordered to make jute doormats, Tom Doyle from Enniscorthy contrived to weave into them harps, shamrocks and round towers, visible only at certain angles, using a slightly darker shade of fibre for the design. Bob himself wrote two full-length mystery novels during the time he spent in Lewes.[14]

The first four years of Maeve's life were at once a time of displacement and danger, and one of the most densely inscribed periods of Irish history. Writing about them in the 1950s, her father's colleague and friend Frank Gallagher would call his book *The Four Glorious Years*, for it seemed to him that idealism and self-sacrifice had been at their highest then, and utopia within reach.[15] On 18 June 1917, under a general amnesty, the Irish nationalist prisoners were released from English prisons and returned triumphantly home, where huge crowds turned out to greet them, and Bob met five-month-old Maeve for the first time.

Bob resumed his job as a reporter for the *Echo*, and took over command of the Volunteers' Wexford Battalion. For the rest of the summer, as they drilled, he delighted in reporting the decisions of one public body after another to rescind their earlier resolutions condemning the Rising. Throughout Ireland, with the exception of the north-eastern area around Belfast, disillusion about the war in Europe, fear of conscription, and disgust at the treatment of those arrested in 1916 was turning public opinion more and more in favour of the nationalists. In a by-election in East Clare in July, Éamon de Valera resoundingly defeated the Irish Parliamentary Party candidate.

De Valera had emerged as the Irish prisoners' leader in Dartmoor, and Bob, who met him there for the first time, had come to revere him. Born in New York in October 1882, but brought up by his maternal grandmother and unmarried uncle in a spartan labourer's cottage by the side of the road outside the village of Bruree, County Limerick, de Valera had been known in primary school as Edward Coll. He had single-mindedly reinvented himself, however, using his father's Spanish surname, after winning a scholarship at the age of sixteen to Blackrock College, a high-class boys' boarding-school south of Dublin. De Valera became a lecturer in mathematics, learned Irish at Gaelic League classes, and later ran Irish summer courses in Tawin, County Galway, changing his first name to Éamon. Cerebral, principled and ambitious, he was a clever strategist, totally committed to the nationalist cause. More militant members of the movement saw him less as a leader than as a conveniently moderate spokesperson and figurehead, but Bob Brennan wholeheartedly embraced the vision he offered.

As released prisoners travelled about the country in the summer of 1917, speaking to enthusiastic crowds, Dublin Castle reacted to its loss of control by banning unauthorised uniforms. Many arrests were made. In September, eighty-four republican prisoners in Mountjoy Jail went on hunger strike to demand political status. A young Kerryman called Thomas Ashe was serving a sentence with hard labour for making an allegedly seditious speech. Force-feeding in the prison caused him internal injuries, and he died on 25 September, with Dr Kathleen Lynn in attendance. Ashe had been a teacher and a traditional musician, and his enormous funeral on 30 September marked a watershed in public opinion: led by armed Volunteers in uniform, 20,000 people followed the coffin to Glasnevin cemetery, where Michael Collins spoke, and thousands more lined streets along the route.[16]

Bob was soon arrested again, when he paraded his men to honour Count George Noble Plunkett, father of Geraldine Dillon and the executed Joseph. He and two others were hauled off to Cork Prison, where they joined about sixty prisoners from Cork and Kerry. It was not a long stay. Fearing more hunger-strike deaths, the authorities suddenly released all republican prisoners at the end of November. Una may have gone to stay with the Dillons in Belgrave Road, for their neighbour Kathleen Lynn recorded in her diary on 20 November 1917, 'B. Brennan released from Cork jail after hunger strike'.[17]

Back in Wexford with Emer and Maeve, the Brennans were able to employ a maid, and go out walking in the evening.[18] Bob was thirty-six, Una twenty-eight. Then in January 1918, at a Sinn Féin meeting in Dublin, de Valera told Bob of a plan to set up a new Press Bureau, and offered him the job of running it. This new office would co-ordinate publicity and put Sinn Féin on a secure footing for the next election. By April the Department of Propaganda was established in 6 Harcourt Street, and Bob and Una had moved with the children to Dublin.[19] They rented one of the Plunkett houses, at 10 Belgrave Road, next door to Kathleen Lynn and just a few houses from Tommy and Geraldine Dillon. Sighle Coghlan, who had been a teacher with Pearse at St Enda's School, lived two doors away with her husband Seumas and their small children.

Maeve's novella *The Visitor* (2000), which she wrote in the 1940s, is set in a house like 10 Belgrave Road, of which there are many around Rathmines. A flight of granite steps led to the heavy front door with its brass door-knocker, letterbox and knob. A metal plate halfway up the steps could be lifted to allow coal to be poured down in sackfuls several times each winter. Tall, twelve-paned sash windows lit the main rooms. Below the front steps, another, smaller, door gave access to the broad, low-ceilinged kitchen with its iron stove, the scullery, and the coal-hole. These tall houses, their ceilings decorated with elaborate plaster mouldings, heated by fires for which maidservants carried coal-buckets up many stairs, were the homes of the confident middle class, both Catholic and Protestant. Behind them ran a network of lanes, where red valerian still grows on top of high granite garden walls, with back entrances from which the dustbins were regularly collected and their cargo of ashes and cinders emptied.

Bob's salary was £3 per week. From the front garden gate of number 10, he could turn right to catch the train to Harcourt Street at Dunville Avenue, or left, past Holy Trinity Church, to where the number 14 tram passed along Upper Rathmines Road. Always a keen walker, he could get to his office in less than half an hour by following Mount Pleasant Avenue as far as the Grand Canal.

Allegiance recalls a visit that Una paid him at 6 Harcourt Street, and her first encounter with the austere de Valera:

> One day Una, who with the children had joined me in Dublin, came into the office to see me. She sat on the table at which I was working. Dev came in suddenly. He frowned severely on seeing, what he thought, was one of the girls from the Cumann na mBan office, which was on the same floor. Una, in spite of all her troubles, still looked about nineteen. Dev came right to the point. 'Look here,' he said, 'you shouldn't be coming in here.'
>
> 'Why not?'
>
> 'Do you know Mr Brennan is a married man?'
>
> 'Well,' she said, 'I ought to,' and she explained the situation. He laughed heartily and ever afterwards, whenever he met her, he recalled the incident with glee.[20]

It was the sort of story that de Valera's followers used to tell in tones of wonderment.

From her new home, Una could walk with Emer and baby Maeve up

Palmerston Road to Palmerston Park, a half-moon of Victorian public garden with a duck pond, lawns and brightly coloured flowerbeds laid out behind iron railings. With its high trees all around, it may be the model for Noon Square, where Mrs King lives in *The Visitor*. After all Una had been through, life in Rathmines was comfortable. Summary arrests and draconian censorship continued throughout Ireland, as the British authorities attempted to keep control, but she was soon pregnant again.

In May 1918, in reaction to a supposed 'German plot', Éamon de Valera, Arthur Griffith, Countess Markievicz, Maud Gonne and several others were again arrested and jailed. On 18 May, the night following these arrests, Bob was nominated National Director of Elections and Director of Publicity for Sinn Féin.[21] For the next six months he worked sixteen to eighteen hours a day, including Sundays, setting up election machinery, and writing and editing 'vast numbers' of handbills and pamphlets for distribution around the country.

By the autumn, no election date had been set but candidates had been selected for each constituency, and Frank Gallagher, a frail-looking, dark-haired young man of twenty, had joined Bob in Harcourt Street. Gallagher had begun his career as a journalist with the *Cork Free Press*. Irrepressibly cheerful and a tireless worker, he lilted scraps from Gilbert and Sullivan operas and traditional songs as he prepared and corrected copy, and 'smoked and smoked and smoked'.[22] He was to become one of the most influential journalists of his generation.

Sinn Féin had just published its election manifesto, and Bob was still working flat out, when his third daughter was born, on 16 October 1918, in the Coombe Women's Hospital, Dublin. Maeve was not yet two; Emer was eight and a half. The baby was christened Ita Deirdre: Ita for a holy woman of medieval Munster, Deirdre after another heroine of the Ulster cycle of sagas; the family called her Derry.

Maeve's fiction, like much of that published in *The New Yorker* in the mid-twentieth century, is often indistinguishable from memoir. The seven stories in the first part of *The Springs of Affection* (1997), all appeared in *The New Yorker* between February 1953 and January 1955. They are written in the first person, and the characters are Maeve's family, even to their appearance, names and ages.

In 'The Clever One', Maeve recalls, 'The first word I ever remember hearing about Derry was that she had been underweight when she was born and that her health was precarious' [*SA* 57]. Derry was born at the height of the virulent Spanish-influenza epidemic, when healthy young adults and children died in their tens of thousands all over Europe and North America. Pregnant women were especially vulnerable. As Frank Gallagher travelled the country to make election speeches for Sinn Féin, he saw funerals from train windows everywhere.[23] Twenty thousand people died in Ireland, and the effects in Dublin, particularly in poorer areas, were devastating.

On Sunday, 27 October 1918, Kathleen Lynn wrote in her diary, 'Brennan came in evg. Very hopeful all round.'[24] It seemed that Una and the baby would survive. Lynn herself was arrested the following Thursday, 31 October, but was released after an intervention by the Lord Mayor of Dublin, and on 2 November she and Alice Barry set up an influenza hospital at 37 Charlemont Street, just across the Grand Canal from Ranelagh. Later, she and Madeleine ffrench-Mullen would found St Ultan's Infant Hospital there.[25]

Derry was less than four weeks old when the Great War ended on 11 November. Parliament was dissolved the next day, clearing the way for an election, but on 20 November, Bob was arrested once again. Kathleen Lynn wrote in her diary, '6 Harcourt St raided & B. Brennan taken, his house searched, he is in Arbour Hill'.[26]

Una managed to visit her husband just once at Arbour Hill Barracks before he was transferred to England:

> Una came in, looking very thin and pale. Her fourth baby was only a few weeks old. My young lieutenant very kindly walked to the other end of the cell and turned his back. She told me she had found out where I was after endless enquiries all day and all night and that Countess Plunkett, finding her almost exhausted from the search, had insisted on driving her around in a cab which was waiting outside . . . She brought me some clean underwear and a suitcase, fearing I might be deported.[27]

Within days, Bob was 'carried off untried to Gloucester Jail'.[28] In *Allegiance* he gives a comic nine-page account of the journey. It recalls the Charlie Chaplin films of the time – except that Bob supplies a soundtrack. He won round his military escort – a weary but good-hearted sergeant and two privates – by procuring a bottle of whiskey from sympathetic crew members on the rough sea crossing. They travelled to Birmingham, where the sergeant, in Brennan's account, told some acquaintances about what was going on in Ireland while they waited for their next train:

> 'Why, look at this man,' he cried, pointing dramatically at me, ''E's a white man, ain't 'e? Don't tell me, I know it. Me and my mates know it. Well 'ere 'e is going to some bleeding prison in England and 'e don't know where, but I can tell him now, it's Gloucester. Well 'ere 'e

is, dragged out of 'is bed, away from 'is wife and kiddies, and all for wot? Nobody knows, because see there's no trial, no warrant, no sentence, no judge; just like Russia and the Czar. Well if that's plying the gyme I'm a mug, we're all mugs.'[29]

The four men got to Gloucester at 5 a.m., and lost their way in the unlit streets until eventually the three soldiers fell asleep on a canal bank. While they slept, Bob asked a passer-by for directions to the jail and then guided his companions the rest of the way. Because it was Sunday, however, the jail did not open until seven o'clock, and they were refused admittance; Bob led the soldiers to the police station around the corner, where they promptly went to sleep, and he was able to engage an Irish sergeant in conversation. His account, for all its slapstick quality, is a transformation of several tropes of popular colonialist writing, neatly reversed to show the Irishman as honourable, intelligent, resourceful and chivalrous, while the inept and clearly inferior representatives of empire express their instinctive homespun philosophy in dialect.

Bob spent much of his time in that prison with Arthur Griffith, and formed a regard for him that was strong enough to survive the bitter political split that came later. Tommy Dillon was also a prisoner in Gloucester, and back in Belgrave Road, with several small children between them, Una Brennan and Geraldine Dillon did their best to cheer each other up. They had 'a dismal Christmas, food-wise', at number 10.[30] Afterwards, Una took the children to her mother's house again. In fact most of Derry's first three years were spent at Coolnaboy, being looked after by her Aunt Bessie.[31] In 'The Clever One':

'The first time I remember seeing you,' [Maeve tells Derry] 'was before we went to live in Ranelagh. It was when we were living in the house on Belgrave Road. You must have been about eighteen months old, I suppose. Someone was holding you in their arms and you snatched Emer's cap off her head and threw it in the fire, and she cried. It was a new woolen cap she had.' [SA 56]

In the story, Derry has no memory of Belgrave Road. Neither had the real Derry, although the family lived there until the end of 1920.

Ranelagh railway station was less than a ten-minute walk from the Brennans' house. Going back to Wexford, Una would have had to manhandle her babies and their bags up the wooden steps to the platform above the road, but Emer, whom Maeve describes in one story as 'my elder sister and my mother's chief prop' [SA 37], was old enough to help, and in later years Una would stay at home while she accompanied her younger sisters to Wexford. Once on the train, they could relax until they came to Macmine Junction.

Belgrave Road was becoming known as 'Rebel Road'. On 26 November 1918, suffragist and pacifist Hanna Sheehy-Skeffington moved into number 7 with her nine-year-old son Owen.[32] Widowed by the summary execution of her husband, Francis, who had attempted to prevent looting following the Rising, she was a passionately articulate proponent of women's rights. In December, when the general election was held at last, giving the vote for the first time to women over thirty and to working men, Bob was still in jail, but Una was eligible by three months to vote. Sinn Féin swept to victory with seventy-three of its candidates elected. Sheehy-Skeffington led a victory procession in Dublin.[33]

The elected Sinn Féin representatives had never intended to take their seats in the House of Commons. Instead, Dáil Éireann, the Parliament of Ireland, met in Dublin. On 21 January 1919 it endorsed the declaration of the Irish Republic, first proclaimed by Pearse at the General Post Office on Sackville Street in 1916. That same day, to the dismay of moderates in the movement, the Irish Republican Army (as the Volunteers had come to be called), killed two armed RIC officers in an ambush at Soloheadbeg, County Tipperary. The Anglo-Irish War had begun in earnest. Those arrested at the time of the 'German plot' and later were still in English prisons, but on 6 February de Valera made a daring escape from Lincoln Jail and was smuggled back to Ireland. On 5 March, after five months in prison, Bob was released from Gloucester on a week's parole to visit his seventy-eight-year-old father, who was seriously ill in Wexford. He never went back, for his fellow prisoners were all released within days.

That spring, the IRA carried out regular attacks on RIC barracks. In early June de Valera travelled to the United States to lobby support and raise money for the Republic. At his first American press conference, in Fenway Park, Boston, on 23 June, a reported 50,000 people came to hear him speak.[34] He would be away from Ireland for a year and a half, allowing the more hawkish Michael Collins to increase his influence in the republican movement. In September, the British government proscribed Dáil Éireann as a dangerous association, sending its members into hiding. Bob too went underground, to continue his work in secret, for like his colleagues, he no longer felt safe in his own home.

The Propaganda Department's most urgent task was to make sympathisers in other countries aware of what was going on in Ireland. All reports in the British press were heavily censored, and it was vital that other states recognise the new government. London-born Desmond FitzGerald had been appointed Director of Publicity for the Dáil. An internationally respected poet, who spoke French fluently, he now travelled to London to make contacts among international journalists, while in Dublin, Bob sent a message to Kathleen McKenna to say that she was needed. The teenage daughter of an old friend of Arthur Griffith, she had that summer volunteered her services as a typist.

McKenna presented herself without delay at 6 Harcourt Street. Her job was to type and mimeograph each issue of a brand-new publication, the *Irish Bulletin*, which would appear daily. Its purpose was to counteract British propaganda and make the underground elected government's positions known, at home and abroad. Produced by seasoned journalists Brennan and Gallagher, the *Bulletin* would describe in meticulous detail, but without sensationalism, the outrages committed by British forces in Ireland, and the indignities to which IRA prisoners were being subjected.[35] The first issue appeared on 11 November 1919, the first anniversary of Armistice Day, and was posted to about thirty newspapers and individuals. Circulation increased steadily in the months that followed, as Brennan, with Desmond FitzGerald, Anna Fitzsimons (always known as 'Fitz'), Frank Gallagher and later Erskine Childers gathered and verified information and wrote it up. Within a year its circulation had risen to 600.

Robert Brennan senior died in Wexford on 20 November. In 'The Springs of Affection', which draws on many details of Bob's life before his marriage, Martin Bagot's father has been dead for nine years by the time he and Delia marry, allowing Min to remember a charmed period during which the young Bagots lived with their mother in peace and laughter. But Maeve cannot have known her grandfather, and perhaps his place in his family's history was so slight that she simply did not know the date of his death.

Sleeping in safe houses, using false names, and producing the *Bulletin* in secret, while Dublin Castle scoured the city to discover who was producing it, and where, was a heart-stopping business, a real-life version of the cloak-and-dagger stories Bob loved. Crown forces carried out lighting raids on buildings, and searched civilians in the street. With dozens of mimeographed copies hidden in deep pockets sewn to her underskirt, Kathleen McKenna cycled across Dublin among foot patrols and the Crossley tenders that had become a familiar sight in the city streets, posting bundles of *Bulletins* in red pillar-boxes here and there so as not to arouse suspicion. *Bulletin* staff took sworn statements from victims and witnesses of atrocities, and deciphered military orders and other secret Dublin Castle documents intercepted in armed raids. Anna Fitzsimons became particularly skilled at code-breaking.

Within a month, Harcourt Street had been raided so often that the *Bulletin* had to move. It was mid-December, and Kathleen McKenna's memoir in the 1970 *Capuchin Annual* (p. 509) tells how Una made the Brennans' house available for the work on condition that men were not seen coming and going. With Bob on the run, that would have made their home even more vulnerable than it already was:

> Mrs Robert Brennan kindly agreed that I, personally, might turn out the *Bulletin* in the basement of their home in Belgrave Square [*sic*], Rathmines, until a suitable 'dug-out' could be found. After all a type-writer and duplicator were not incriminating, there was always a good fire in the kitchen where in the event of a surprise raid by day documents could be destroyed while nothing 'seditious' would be left in the house by night. Keeping in contact with No. 6 (which though raided continued to be used as Sinn Féin headquarters), I typed and duplicated the *Bulletin* in Brennans for about ten days. As this house had but recently been subjected to an excruciating nocturnal raid by British troops who had caused Mrs Brennan and her three young children untold sufferings, every effort was being made to obtain another site and so liberate Brennans from the additional peril the presence of the *Bulletin* caused.

It was a considerable relief when the *Bulletin* found a new home, just before Christmas 1919.

Maeve was about to turn three. Local elections were being held in Rathmines, and her father was a candidate. Other Sinn Féin nominees included the family's next-door neighbours, Kathleen Lynn and Madeleine ffrench-Mullen. Together the Sinn Féin candidates issued an illustrated newsletter, the *Cuala News*, whose lively rhetoric suggests that Bob wrote it: a copy was among his papers when he died:

> The existing Freemason and Orange Council accuses us of introducing politics into Municipal affairs. The Rathmines Urban District Council *is* and always has been the most politically bigoted Council in all Ireland. It is *essentially* and *distinctively* a political body. The Union Jack is at least as much a political emblem as the Green Flag or the Republican Tricolour, and the Union Jack, emblem of our subjection, floats from Rathmines Town Hall on the slightest provocation.
>
> Rathmines has been, and is at the moment, the convalescent home and the asylum of Freemasonry and Orangeism. I write of these things from other than a religious standpoint. I speak of them as political or economic institutions which have brought sorrow, tragedy and heart-break on the world.[36]

Bob was not elected.

Kathleen McKenna may have been confused about the timing of the 'excruciating nocturnal raid' on the Brennans' home: raids were common, but other records describe a truly terrifying one that took place after the election, in late February 1920. London had begun to recruit an *ad hoc* force of former soldiers to serve in Ireland. Kitted out in a motley of police and army uniforms, they soon became known as the Black and Tans. By November their number would reach 9,500 and their behaviour would provide most of the *Bulletin*'s copy. In February, a curfew was imposed from midnight to 5 a.m., and within weeks had been extended to begin at 10 p.m.

Bob Brennan's *Allegiance* describes what happened on the night of Friday, 27 February:

> Like everyone else engaged in the struggle, I changed my sleeping quarters frequently. I stayed in my own home at rare intervals. On one such occasion, Una and I were talking over the fire when suddenly at five minutes before the curfew hour, which, at that time, was ten o'clock, I got the impression I should not stay . . .

He went out the back door and across two garden walls to the home of Sighle and Seumas Coghlan, who allowed him to stay the night:

> I awoke from a sound sleep to find the room flooded with light. There was an enormous cat purring somewhere. I rolled out of bed and crept to the window. The light came from the headlights of a lorry and the purring noise from the powerful Rolls Royce engine of an armoured car. The road from end to end was lined with armed men. There was a second lorry in front of my house. This was the dreaded raid. Men in uniform moved to and fro in the headlights . . .[37]

He heard voices from the direction of the Dillons' house at number 13 say that they had arrested two men. Tommy Dillon was probably not one of them: he had recently been appointed Professor of Chemistry at University College Galway, and his daughter Eilis (who would become a distinguished novelist and children's writer), was born in Galway a week later.

Bob was worried about his own family, but did not dare go home until daybreak:

> When I got over the wall I saw Una standing at the window, pale and silent. I had never seen her so near a break. She had been crying. They had kept her downstairs all night away from the children and they had

grilled her and our eldest child, Emer, aged nine, for hours, on my activities and whereabouts. Una had very narrowly missed having a bayonet run through her at the foot of the basement stairs in the dark. The rooms looked as if a herd of wild cattle had been through them. The two younger children, Maeve, aged three, and Deirdre, one and a half, were hysterical, which was not to be wondered at. It was of this raid that Erskine Childers wrote: 'This is not civilised war'.

Bob's autobiography describes his first meeting, in June 1919, with Erskine Childers, who would become one of the most important publicists for the republican cause. Bob was working in his office in 6 Harcourt Street when: 'I looked up from my desk to see a spare, worn, prematurely aged man with clear, kindly eyes, youthful and alert. He was rather nervous and apologetic.'[38] Bob, of course, already knew of Childers as the author of *The Riddle of the Sands* and the daring yachtsman who had landed guns at Howth in 1914. Childers had resigned his position as Clerk of the House of Commons in 1910 to work for Irish Home Rule. On the outbreak of war, however, he had joined the Royal Navy, and had later been awarded the Distinguished Service Cross. Described by Frank Gallagher as small and slight, with a quiet, musical voice and a brilliant smile, Childers was an attractive character. He immediately put his talents to work on behalf of Dáil Éireann.

With his American wife, Mollie Osgood, their children and her mother, Childers moved into a large modern house at 12 Bushy Park Road, Rathgar, about a mile from Rathmines, on a bluff above the River Dodder. Their long back garden adjoined a 'pocket farm' called Danum (now the High School, it was the home of Ernest Bewley, founder of Bewley's Cafés), and the combination of open fields and riverbank made their home an ideal hideout for men on the run. Bob stayed in the Childers home several times in the spring of 1920. Childers was hard at work in his study upstairs on a series of eight articles for the English *Daily News* entitled 'Military Rule in Ireland', but the two men had time to discover a shared passion for Robert Louis Stevenson's *The Wrong Box*.[39] A passage from *The Riddle of the Sands* may explain something of what this kind of humour still meant to the two men in 1920, as they worked to stay one step ahead of the Crown forces:

[A] sense of the ludicrous came to my assistance . . . Humour . . . Romance . . . the ancient inspiration which, under many guises, quickens thousands of better brains than mine, but whose essence is always the same; the gay pursuit of a perilous quest.[40]

The first of Childers' *Daily News* articles, called 'Military Rule in Ireland: Its Purpose and Methods', appeared on 29 March 1920. As an established author and decorated war hero, Childers appealed to the decency of the British public to repudiate the things being done in Ireland in their name. His second article, published on 7 April, was entitled 'What It Means to Women'. With names, addresses, times and dates, it detailed the traumatic effects of raids by police and soldiers on private homes in the small hours. Its final example, under the heading 'Another Young Mother's Ordeal', described the raid on the Brennans' home a month earlier:

> The next case is that of Mrs Robert Brennan, of 10, Belgrave Road, Rathmines, whose husband is hiding from arrest, a marked man for no reason save that he is a responsible literary worker for the Republican cause, to whose integrity, broad-mindedness, and charm all who know him will bear witness.
>
> His young wife, alone in the house with three little children, is roused by knocking on the night of February 27 last, runs down in her nightdress, asks permission to dress, and gets for an answer, 'Damn you, open, or we'll smash it in.' In they rush, sweeping her aside, bayonets at the charge. An agonising time follows. One soldier is drunk, and uses foul language. In spite of passionate supplications to be allowed to go to her children, *she is kept apart under guard while their rooms are searched*, and the search throughout is conducted with a roughness and insolence worthy of veritable Huns. Nothing found. No apology.
>
> This is not civilised war.[41]

No wonder the children were hysterical. The title story in Maeve's 1969 collection *In and Out of Never-Never Land* places her own *alter ego*, Mary Ann Whitty, in East Hampton, New York, on the Fourth of July. The neighbouring house catches fire, but Mary Ann knows nothing until she hears the rumbling of the fire engines outside: '. . . she thought, What a big oil truck. But then came more rumbling and grinding, and she thought, Armored cars' [RG 297]. To a modern reader, armoured cars may suggest the vans used to transport money to and from banks, but to Maeve, who lived in cities, surrounded by traffic noise, for almost all her American life, armoured cars, 'rumbling and grinding', can only have meant the terrifying vehicles that drew up in front of her house with searchlights blazing, when she was a small child.

Skilled propagandist that he was, Childers drew further use from that night of raids in Belgrave Road. His next article was entitled 'Looting'. He had not fully understood the procedure adopted in raids, he wrote, 'until I was able to observe for myself the behaviour of two officers who, at the head of a large force, including a tank, raided my house at 1 a.m. and made themselves as insolently at home there as in a section of a captured enemy trench.' He added details of nine cases, most of them affecting women. The first, headed 'No Apology: No Redress', was that of Kathleen Lynn, whose home had been raided on the same night as the Brennans', but at 1.30 a.m., so that he could give it the following day's date:

Dr Kathleen Lynn lives (and practises) at 9, Belgrave Road, with her friend Miss ffrench Mullen, and a maid: three women in all. She herself was out attending a case of sickness when at 1.30 a.m. on February 28 last the soldiers charged in, refusing her friend time to dress. Miss ffrench Mullen, in spite of strong protests, and the maid were both kept isolated under guard while the house was searched. Dr Lynn returned to find a scene of disgraceful disorder, and the following articles missing: a 4lb box of chocolates emptied, cigarettes taken, and a hypodermic record syringe, a small hot-water bottle in a velvet case, and an embroidered lace collar stolen. This may be called a mild case of hungry soldiers pilfering and curio-hunting. A claim was lodged in vain; no redress. Nothing incriminating found; no apology. Four officers were present.

During his time on the run, when army lorries roared through the streets after curfew, arresting anyone they found abroad, Bob found shelter one night with a Latvian man called Yohan Climanis and his Irish wife Maria at their home above a butcher's shop on Terenure Road, Rathgar.[42] Thom's *Directory* shows that in 1920 the fourth shop from the top of Rathgar Avenue on what is now Terenure Road East was that of James A. Doyle, victualler and poulterer. In its gable wall, the door through which Bob was pulled to safety can still be seen. Almost eighty years later, Jim Bolger's grandson Roddy Doyle borrowed the Climanis episode and developed it with operatic flourish in his novel of the Anglo-Irish War, *A Star Called Henry*. He had grown up seeing Bob's autobiography *Allegiance* on the bookshelf behind his father's chair, and his wife was Erskine Childers' granddaughter.[43]

Incident followed incident in 1920. Frank Gallagher was arrested in March, spent ten days on hunger strike, and was released.[44] County Council elections in June renewed Sinn Féin's mandate, with its candidates winning majorities in twenty-seven of the thirty-three councils. Republican courts heard cases, and plaintiffs ignored the official assizes, resorting to them instead.[45] From Monday to Friday every week, the *Bulletin* appeared. Its staff flitted with their equipment from one hideout to another. Then in October, with the assistance of solicitor Michael Noyk, Una Brennan rented a flat that could be used as an office, at 11 Molesworth Street in the heart of unionist Dublin. Masquerading as international oil importers, the *Bulletin* staff came and went without detection.

Sunday, 21 November has gone down in history as the first of Ireland's Bloody Sundays. A young medical student, Kevin Barry, had been hanged at Mountjoy Jail three weeks earlier, as anxious crowds waited outside, singing and praying, hoping for a reprieve. In Galway, a week before, the Black and Tans had killed Father Michael Griffin, a Catholic priest. Michael Collins planned a major attack on Dublin Castle's spies. Armed IRA members were able to mingle with large crowds on their way to nine o'clock Mass, for attendance was universal among Catholics, and those wishing to receive communion had to fast from midnight, so went early. Like characters in spy novels, they wore trenchcoats, whose deep pockets allowed them to conceal their weapons. Walking into bedrooms all over Dublin, they shot dead thirteen men, and wounded six others. Reprisals were speedy and furious. The Black and Tans and Auxiliary Police rampaged through Dublin, ending up at Croke Park, where 8,000 spectators were attending a Gaelic football match. They opened fire on the crowd, killing twelve men and women, and injuring sixty more.

Bob and Una had intended taking their children to Croke Park that day. Bob was rarely at home, and outings meant the family could be together, but on their way to the tram they met Kathleen Lynn, who told them the city was in an uproar:

From the tram we saw ample evidence of the military activities. Armoured cars and soldiers in lorries were patrolling the streets, holding up and searching pedestrians and cyclists. When we got to Nelson Pillar, however, we saw that there were huge crowds going to the football match and we decided that the crowds might be too much for the children, so we went out to Dollymount [north of the city, by the sea] instead. There was a cold wind blowing on the Bull [W]all and we set out to return rather earlier than usual.

We were on the top of an open tram running in from Fairview when we saw vast numbers of people running from the direction of Croke Park, some of them bleeding from head and face. They were crowding the trams. An old friend, Paddy Devlin, a Gaelic sports writer, whose pen-name was Celt, came up on top of the tram. I asked him what had happened and he said that the Tans had driven into the Park and opened fire on the football crowd. Some of the players were killed, he said, and a lot of spectators.

At the Pillar Una left to take the children home and I went to the *Freeman's Journal* office to find out what had happened . . .[46]

Maeve was almost four. She must have been terrified by what she saw from the top of that open tram. After Bloody Sunday, the Brennans decided that Belgrave Road was no longer safe. Una again took the children to Coolnaboy, and left them with Bessie and her mother. She and Bob rented rooms from a unionist landlady in Rathgar Avenue, near George Russell's home, telling her that they were Mr and Mrs William Kearney, and that Bob was an official at the Department of Agriculture; Tommy and Geraldine Dillon even joined them there for a while, when Galway became too dangerous for them.[47]

De Valera arrived back from the United States at Christmas 1920, and immediately asked Bob to set up a Foreign Office and become the Dáil's Under-Secretary for Foreign Affairs. Pretending to represent an insurance agency, Una rented premises for the new office, this time using the name Lewis (perhaps a joke, after Lewes Prison). Bob's colleagues included the writer Máirín Cregan (married to Dr Jim Ryan from County Wexford and later the mother of a political dynasty), Una's brother Jim Bolger, and Frank Kelly, husband of the *Bulletin*'s Anna 'Fitz', and as skilled at codes and ciphers as she was. Una bought an old wardrobe; Bob and Frank Kelly made a secret compartment in the top of it, and every night they hid away their files. As an extra precaution, they rented a second office, on Kildare Street, across from the Shelbourne Hotel, where they pretended to market an Irish-made disinfectant called Iresol. When their landlady enquired why they had no customers, Máirín Cregan fobbed her off with some bottles of the (real) disinfectant.[48]

For all the camaraderie of his daily life, Bob was feeling strain. His nominal boss was Count Plunkett, Minister for Foreign Affairs (who was also his landlord and Geraldine Dillon's father), but correspondence between Bob and de Valera suggests that the lines of command were anything but clear.[49] In February Bob had 'what was tantamount to a breakdown', and was forced to lay off work for some weeks. The *Irish Bulletin* continued to appear without him, and in April he was out of the office again.[50] Negotiations between Dáil Éireann and the British government came to a head while he was ill; truce terms were agreed on 9 July 1921, and came into effect two days later. Republicans no longer needed to live in hiding, but as Bob wrote in *Allegiance*, 'Instead of getting better, I got worse'. Perhaps he was simply exhausted, or it may be that he did not know how to face turning forty. Although he was clever and personable, de Valera trusted him, and others liked him, it is not clear that they had much faith in his judgement.[51] For Una too, it must have been another difficult time.

Their children were still in Coolnaboy. Emer, who had just turned eleven, was attending the national school in Oylegate, just inside the gates of the church where her parents had been married. Derry must have spent her days under Bessie's eye, but Maeve was four and a half that summer, and she too started school. Maeve was upset on that first day at school, and Lizzie Doyle from Coolamain, a girl from Emer's class, stayed with her, 'to pacify her'. Eighty years later, Lizzie Doyle still remembered Maeve's tears.[52]

The Brennans had hardly ever lived together as a family, and had not owned their own home since leaving Summerville in Wexford years before. Now, Bob and Una looked for a house to buy. In October, however, 'as much in the interest of [his] health as of the service', Arthur Griffith suggested that Bob take advantage of the Anglo-Irish conference that was to be hosted by Prime Minister David Lloyd George in London in a few days' time, to obtain a passport, and that he should make a tour of European cities, visiting the various envoys of Dáil Éireann in his capacity as Under-Secretary for Foreign Affairs.[53] When the five plenipotentiary negotiators went to London on Sunday, 9 October, Bob accompanied them. He continued to Paris, where Sean T. O'Kelly was the Irish envoy. While Griffith, Collins and the other plenipotentiaries began talks with the British, Bob spent time with O'Kelly and with the consul Leopold Kerney and his French wife Raymonde. The depression that had been with him for months suddenly lifted as he fell in love with Paris.

From Paris he travelled to Madrid, Salamanca and Barcelona, then to Geneva, where he met Ireland's representative Michael MacWhite, and Berlin, where the envoy was Nancy Wyse Power. He was dining with her and three others on 6 December when they heard the newsboys call a special edition. That was how Bob learned that a treaty had been signed in London, committing Irish elected representatives to take an oath of allegiance to King George V, and retaining six counties of Ireland for Britain. He started for Dublin at once.

FOUR

Cherryfield Avenue

'The Morning after the Big Fire' was the second of Maeve Brennan's stories to appear in *The New Yorker*. First published on 7 February 1953, it begins, 'From the time I was almost five until I was almost eighteen, we lived in a small house in a part of Dublin called Ranelagh.'

Ten days after Bob left for London in October 1921, Una completed the purchase of a house on Cherryfield Avenue, less than a mile from Belgrave Road. When Maeve collected twenty-two of her short stories in 1969 as *In and Out of Never-Never Land*, three of the book's four sections consisted of stories set here; the second of them, with its seven auto-biographical pieces, was called simply '48 Cherryfield Avenue'. The house is the linking motif in the posthumous 1997 collection, *The Springs of Affection*, subtitled *Stories of Dublin*. William Maxwell, Maeve's editor and friend, called it 'her imagination's home'.[1] As the editor who had worked on all her *New Yorker* fiction, he could describe it as though he had walked through it:

> It has a bow window and there is a tiny grass plot in front, a walled garden in back with flowers and a yellow laburnum. The front door leads into a narrow hall. Past the stairs, down three steps, is the kitchen. The front and back sitting-rooms are separated by folding doors. One room is heated by a coal-burning fireplace, the other by a gas fire. Upstairs there is linoleum on the floor of the back bedroom, none in the front one. [*SA* 6–7]

Like Balzac, whom she called 'the Master' (*LWL* 19), Maeve noticed, remembered and wrote about the tiniest details of this house and garden, which sheltered her childhood from the continuing political turbulence outside, and against whose walls she measured her own growth. Those walls house and contain her best fiction, supplying the three-dimensional frame that her writing so intricately fills in with thoughts and emotions that had lain in her mind for decades.

Number 48 Cherryfield Avenue had been built for barely ten years when the Brennans moved in. The land had been part of an estate owned by the Bewley family, importers of tea and coffee, just outside the boundary of Rathmines township, on Sandford Road, Ranelagh. In 1905 a building contractor called William George Bailey bought a large field from the Bewleys, near the end of the number 11 tram route (older people knew it as Baron George's Fields, and remembered picking blackberries there). Bailey was a Methodist, the son of a successful manufacturer of marquees, flags and rope – commodities much in demand in Dublin during years of royal visits and nationalist rallies. He built a pair of large redbrick houses at the upper end of his new site, and named them Cherryfield and Hollybank. Cherryfield was for his own family (aged thirty-four, he was married, with three children); Hollybank became the home of his sister Mary Jane and brother-in-law Adam Henry Gibson. Gibson was also the business partner of William Bailey Senior, who lived with him and his family.[2]

The two new houses faced away from Sandford Road and towards the two imposing houses where members of the Bewley family still lived. They were attached, and it may be that Bailey intended them to form the nucleus of a new street or square as Dublin expanded along its tram routes; no further houses joined them, however. Instead, Bailey laid out a street of sixty smaller houses running up from Sandford Road to the back of his brother-in-law's house, along the northern edge of the field. With slate roofs, stained glass in their front doors, bay windows that let in plenty of daylight, and sills made of granite, the two rows of redbrick houses were desirable starter homes for young middle-class couples. They also attracted a number of single women.[3]

When Hollybank Avenue was completed, Bailey built another row of houses parallel to it. Numbers 1–27 Cherryfield Avenue shared their back garden walls with one side of Hollybank Avenue. The materials used were less expensive than before, but the design was almost identical: instead of red brick, these houses were built with breeze blocks made of cinder from the Gas Company, and finished with stucco.[4] Inside, they measured just under 1,000 square feet. A scaled-down version of Dublin's older terraced houses, they were shaped like piano keys, with a lower, narrower 'return' projecting from the back of each pair, so that the kitchen and bathroom windows of adjacent houses faced each other across tiny paved yards and garden walls. Each had a garden beyond the yard, seventeen feet wide, the same as the house.

Modest though they were, these houses reflected the aspirations of those who lived in them. Considerably wider (at forty-two feet) than most side roads in Ranelagh, Hollybank Avenue and Cherryfield Avenue allowed cars to pass easily up and down, and park on either side. They also let sunlight reach into the houses. A path of red quarry tiles led to each front door, which was set back in a square porch and raised by a single step. Bay windows gave extra light to the front rooms, upstairs and down; patterned glass in the front door lit the hall without compromising privacy; mouldings decorated the ceilings downstairs, and electric light fittings hung from plaster centrepieces. On Cherryfield Avenue the tall windows at the backs of the houses had sliding sashes, as in Hollybank Avenue, which could be opened at the top or bottom, but those in front were stylishly modern. Hinged at the sides, the large window in the middle of each bay was divided down the middle and could be thrown fully open, while the largest of the three bedrooms had an extra, similar, window over the front door. Maeve's fiction refers several times, as the houses' occupants must have done, with some pretension, to 'French windows'. Beside the fireplaces of polished slate in the front sitting-rooms, a brass electric bell-push could summon the maid from the kitchen. Instead of being in a basement, this was three or four steps down from the hall; its floor was made of the same red tiles as the front path, and a small black range burned coal for cooking and heating. A door beside the sink led to the back garden. Above the kitchen in the return, a tiny third bedroom behind the bathroom could accommodate a resident maidservant at a discreet distance from the rest of the household.

James Hill and Son, Expert House Furnishers, had a showroom at 10, 11 and 12 Bachelor's Walk, Dublin, with displays of furniture, room by room, for various types of 'Model Home'. Large numbers of young people were setting up house at a distance from where they had grown up, drawn to the city by their own literacy, numeracy and ambition, and by a proliferation of jobs in administration and business. The new houses they moved into would be too small to accommodate either interfering in-laws or the heavy furniture of earlier times, so the layout of their homes could express their relations with each other, and their sense of their place in the world.[5]

On 2 March 1910, an advertisement by Hill and Son on the front page of the *Irish Times* offered a complete inventory of furnishings for 'The Bungalow' — a house of about the same size as those on Hollybank and Cherryfield Avenues (dining-room, drawing-room, best bedroom, spare bedroom, hall and kitchen) — for a total price of £59 10sh. Clearly, their service was not only practical; it had to do also with educating customers in the niceties of domestic life and guarding them against social gaffes. Here is what they recommended for a 'best bedroom':

Satin walnut bedroom suite comprising wardrobe with bevelled plate-glass door, panelled front, and with deep drawer at bottom. One 3 ft 6 in. dressing chest with three drawers and bevelled swing glass. One 3 ft 2 in. washstand with marble top, tiled back and pedestal cupboard, fitted with towel rails. One cane-seated chair, set of toilet ware [i.e. a large jug and basin, with chamber-pot]. One 4 ft 6 in. satin walnut bedstead to match. Woven wire spring mattress. Hair mattress. Feather bolster and two pillows. Felt pad. Fender and [fire-]irons. Roller blind, white pole and lace curtains. Art carpet.

In 'The Springs of Affection', Min Bagot recalls how Martin rejected the wedding gift his mother had wanted to give him and Delia:

A big round mahogany table and four matching chairs that must have had pride of place in some great house at one time. She kept that furniture up to the nines, polished and waxed till you could see to do your hair in it. But Martin turned up his nose at it. No secondhand stuff for him and Delia, and the mahogany was too big and heavy anyway. He didn't want it. He and Delia went and ordered furniture made just for them; new furniture, all walnut – a bed, a chest of drawers, a wardrobe, a washstand, and two sitting-room chairs so that Delia could hold court in style when they had visitors. [SA 353–4]

Mahogany represented the stultifying past; walnut or fumed oak the young twentieth century. Delia Bagot, in Maeve's story 'The Twelfth Wedding Anniversary', 'liked things that matched' [SA 231]. Matched sets of new furniture made in solid wood could offer a reassuring metaphor of what came to be known as the nuclear family, gathered around its hearth, resisting difference and intrusion for the foreseeable future.[6]

By 2 April 1911, census day, Bailey had built thirty-eight houses on Cherryfield Avenue. All but one were occupied, and number 39 was 'building'. A breakdown of the census return shows a demographic distribution more like that of Belfast than modern Dublin, with five different Protestant denominations represented and several of the adults born in England. Seven of the heads of household were Catholic, but there were four 'mixed' marriages. Among individuals, only nine men were Catholic, as against twenty-seven women, but most of that discrepancy is accounted for by a total of twelve maidservants, eleven of whom were Catholics.[7]

Two unmarried women with income from investments, both members of the Church of Ireland, were among the heads of household, but most householders were couples in their twenties and thirties. Eighteen houses had children under seven, and many of those were infants. The men included a veterinary surgeon, an optician, a wine manager, a mechanical engineer, a professor of music, a teacher of chemistry, and several clerks and commercial travellers.[8] Servants were aged between sixteen and twenty, and all of them were female. Cherryfield Avenue was a place where Charles Pooter would have felt quite at home.[9]

When the Brennans moved in, their neighbours on one side were Catholic nationalists; on the other, Protestant unionists.[10] Henry and Mary Briscoe had bought number 47 in 1919. Henry was a civil servant, based in Dublin Castle. Brought up in Glasnevin in north Dublin, where his father Hubert had been the landlord of the Tolka House pub, he and his brothers had been educated by the Christian Brothers at O'Connell Schools. Mary, his wife, was cheerful, pragmatic and intrepid (she once climbed out of one upstairs window and in another, to rescue her four-year-old daughter who had locked herself in the bathroom). Originally from County Meath, and more outgoing than the shy and quiet Una Brennan, Mary had grown up in Ringsend, Dublin, where her father, Daniel Halton, kept a grocery called the Limerick House on Bridge Street. The Briscoes had three small sons, Kevin and Brendan, aged five and three, called after early Irish saints, and their baby brother Hubert, born in 1920, who was named after his grandfather and uncle. Their youngest child, Ita, was born in 1924. Maeve would borrow the Briscoes' names and some details of their lives for the fiction she wrote in New York.

When Una stood in the kitchen of her new home and opened the back door, she faced a high wall about six feet away across the paved yard. Beyond it, across another six feet of concrete paving, was Mary Briscoe's back door. Farther down the garden, in the wider part, where the concrete ended and the grass began, the wall was lower, with trellis on top, but a gap in the trellis allowed the two women to talk across the wall. Maeve described this arrangement in 'The Twelfth Wedding Anniversary':

> Where the cement joined the grass, the garden wall that separated Mrs Bagot from her neighbor dipped suddenly to a height of only five feet, and along this low part Mrs Bagot had put up a green wooden trellis. She had extended the trellis to about a foot above the wall, and there she trained ivy and something she called 'the vine,' but for politeness' sake she left an open space where the red-haired lady next door, Mrs Finn, could peer through and make remarks. [*SA* 216]

This trellis appears behind a smiling, snaggle-toothed Maeve, photographed with her mother when she was about twelve.

On the Brennans' other side, in number 49, lived the Pearsons, a Protestant couple with one son. Every year on 5 November, the boy and his friends lit a bonfire in the back garden to celebrate Guy Fawkes Night, commemorating the foiling of a Catholic plot to blow up London's House of Commons in 1605, when Guy Fawkes was burned to death. Innocuous though Guy Fawkes celebrations might seem in Britain, in Ireland they represented polarisation and sectarian ill-feeling: Catholics celebrated Hallowe'en on 31 October instead.

As 1921 ended, with Bob's return to Ireland and the move to their new house, the Brennans had been married for twelve and a half years. The movement to which they had dedicated their adult lives was on the point of splitting over the Treaty, and they had been apart from each other, and from their children, for a considerable time. Christmas was a chilly time to move house. Apart from the range in the kitchen, the only sources of heat were coal or gas fires, rarely lit until evening. 'The Clever One' has Maeve remembering this time as she talks to Derry years later:

> 'The next time I have a clear memory of you,' I continued, 'you must have been about three. We were living in Ranelagh. I went into the front bedroom and found you wandering around in your skin, crying for someone to dress you, and I dressed you.' [SA 57]

Una was too conscientious to have left three-year-old Derry alone upstairs, distressed and naked, unless she herself was seriously distracted. As the political crisis developed, Maeve would have been almost five: old enough to find clothes and help a younger child to put them on, but young enough to remember that as an achievement.

The debate on the Anglo-Irish Treaty began in Dáil Éireann on 14 December. On 7 January 1922, the day after Maeve's fifth birthday, the Dáil approved the Treaty by sixty-four votes to fifty-seven, allowing a border to be drawn that would divide the Irish Free State from the new entity of Northern Ireland. Frank Gallagher describes how de Valera buried his face in his arms and sobbed aloud after the votes were counted, after which 'Deputy after Deputy broke down in that strained room, not on one side, but on both, and the passing of the Treaty was accompanied by the sound of brothers' weeping who till now had stood together in death's face.'[1]

Suddenly de Valera and his supporters were out in the cold, rejecting the newly established Irish Free State and excluded from its administration, while Michael Collins became chairman of the Provisional Government. It was the beginning of the split that has divided Irish politics ever since: between those who accepted the Treaty with its compromises, including partition of Ireland, north from south, and those who did not. Bob resigned as Under-Secretary for Foreign Affairs. Much of his effort in that position had gone into organising an Irish Race Congress, *Aonach na nGaedheal*, to be held in Paris during the week of 21–28 January, with the objective of fostering international cultural and economic links. The congress went ahead, and he attended, as did de Valera, Countess Markievicz, Eoin MacNeill, Douglas Hyde, and delegates representing Irish emigrants settled all over the world. The agenda was frustrated, however, by conflict about the Treaty among the delegates from Ireland.[12]

There followed a period of confusion and bitter disillusion for Bob and all those who remained committed to a republic whose only boundaries would be the seas around Ireland. Bob's former boss Desmond FitzGerald had taken the pro-Treaty side and continued as Director of Publicity for the Provisional Government, becoming Minister for External Affairs the following September. Bob, however, maintained an anti-Treaty diplomatic and propaganda service, urgently re-establishing contact with sympathetic Irish envoys abroad – including Harry Boland in the United States and Seán T. O'Kelly and Leopold Kerney in Paris. From an office in Sackville Street, Dublin, continuing to operate as though the Treaty had not been signed, he worked with them to undermine the international credibility of the Free State.[13]

More militarist opponents of the Treaty refused to await changes in world opinion, and violence became inevitable. On 26 March, the IRA split formally into pro- and anti-Treaty forces. Armed units of anti-Treaty IRA became known as 'Irregulars'. They stole arms and ammunition and raided houses, shops and post offices for money and supplies, launching attacks on Dublin and on Free State institutions throughout the country. On 14 April, a group of Irregulars led by the uncompromising Rory O'Connor captured the Four Courts in central Dublin, on the north bank of the Liffey, and held out there for over two months. In June, when a general election showed strong support for the Treaty and Britain pressed for its implementation, O'Connor began to threaten an invasion of Northern Ireland. With British artillery, Michael Collins gave the order to attack the Four Courts. Three miles away in Cherryfield Avenue, the Brennans heard the attack:

On the morning of the 28th June a little after four o'clock, Una and I were awakened by the noise of heavy explosions. We both said: 'They have attacked the Four Courts.' I cycled into town. The streets were quiet till I reached the quays, where I found groups of people looking on at the bombardment . . .

I went to my office in O'Connell Street and tried to put things in some sort of shape so that it could be carried on in my absence. Then I went home and told Una I was going to join up.[14]

That day, Bob Brennan and Éamon de Valera, aged forty-one and almost forty respectively, rejoined the Volunteers and were sworn in. Once again they were on the run, this time from their own countrymen. The Civil War would be a nightmare of blood and betrayal, quite unlike the Anglo-Irish War. Among their opponents were people they had known for years, alongside whom they had worked and trained, and with whom they had shared prison cells, while many of their fellows were much younger men who had taken no part in the Troubles until now. Some of the time, Una travelled too, since women aroused less suspicion than men, while men accompanied by women were less at risk of apprehension and arrest. Once more, Maeve and her sisters were removed to Coolnaboy. Bob travelled to Cork to edit the *Cork Examiner* on behalf of Sinn Féin and prepare daily dispatches which Erskine Childers would transmit by cable from Valencia Island in County Kerry. He stayed at the home of Mary MacSwiney, whose brother Terence had died on hunger strike in October 1920, and among his helpers were the young writers Frank O'Connor – then known by his real name, Michael O'Donovan – and Seán O'Faoláin. In September 1922, however, Bob became ill once again and was forced to return to Dublin. Mary MacSwiney became Director of Publicity in his place. When she was jailed in November 1923, O'Faoláin, who had been Assistant Director since May, took over as Director.[15]

Alone with the children in Cherryfield Avenue, Una had been working to re-establish a normal life. Maeve began to attend primary school at Muckross Park, the Dominican convent on nearby Marlborough Road. Bob slept in safe houses, sneaking home from time to time to see his family, and once at least, Una brought Maeve to see him at someone else's house. She was five, she tells us, contentedly stringing beads in the front sitting-room, the first time Free State agents searching for her father invaded the house on Cherryfield Avenue. Her story 'The Day We Got Our Own Back' begins (with one telling childish adjective): 'One afternoon some unfriendly men dressed in civilian clothes and carrying revolvers came to our house searching for my father, or for information about him' [*SA* 37]. The men could not easily be denied admittance, for they came on behalf of the government of the day, but they acted with all the insolence Erskine Childers had observed among the occupying British forces a couple of years earlier. 'They camped around the room,' Maeve writes, 'talking idly among themselves and waiting.' Had her father returned home while they were there, he would have been arrested and court-martialled. Judging by the fate suffered by so many of his comrades, he might easily have been shot.

Even while on the run, and in spite of having been ill again, Bob found time for joking and play-acting. One of the best-known safe houses for republicans was the home of Seamus Moore and his two sisters, Bride and Mary, at 51 Lower Beechwood Avenue. Another visitor, 'Todd' Andrews, who described Bob as 'the leading Republican propagandist', recalled meeting him at Moore's during the Civil War when he and his IRA commanding officer John Dowling called there one evening. Seán Lemass, Sinn Féin's young Director of Communications, was there too, when the conversation turned to the Abbey Theatre, and the writings of George Moore:

> Dowling and Brennan held the floor in a witty and fascinating exchange of repartee. Brennan, being more knowledgeable on the subject than Dowling, provoked him into wild assertions about the merits of Moore and Yeats, as genuine Irishmen rather than as artists. Seán Lemass was so obviously bored by the talk that he finally left the group, standing up ostentatiously to gaze gloomily out of the window. It was the first indication I had of Lemass's contempt for what he regarded as intellectuals.[16]

Lemass would go on to lead the Irish state out of economic stagnation in the 1950s: unlike the older generation, he would place his faith in economists, not poets or humorists.

The Civil War left a legacy of bitterness that lasted for generations. Without Britain and the Black and Tans as their common enemy, nationalists discovered and acted upon animosities against each other, but Brennan's own account focuses on moments of comic relief. Anna 'Fitz' and her husband Frank Kelly printed the weekly *Republican News* on a platen press, hiding out in stables and garages:

> On one occasion when the place she and Frank were staying at was raided in the middle of the night, they both escaped by the back. Fitz crossed a field and coming on a mansion, she climbed through a window, only to discover it was a maternity hospital. To the astonished matron she said: 'It's not twins. It's politics'.[17]

Bob's capacity for finding humour in all situations did not fit him for leadership, but it may well have been the key to his effectiveness as a diplomat in later years.

At least once during the Civil War, Una Brennan entrusted documents to Mary Briscoe next door for safe keeping.[18] A year or so after the first raid on 48 Cherryfield Avenue, Free State agents arrived again: 'They pulled all the beds apart, looking for papers and letters,' Maeve writes [*SA* 40], 'and they took all my father's books out of the shelves and shook them, and they looked in all the drawers and in the wardrobe and in the kitchen stove'. In her story, the children's mother had been doing housework, shining the brass rods that held the red stair carpet in place, and polishing the linoleum in the dining-room. Una Brennan's earlier life had been full of mobility and political conviction, so the story's emphasis on these domestic chores is noteworthy. (Maeve as an adult almost never cooked or ironed, although she did sometimes scrub floors.) In Belgrave Road, where the danger to her and the children had been immediate, Una had allowed only Kathleen McKenna to work on the *Bulletin* in their home. In 'The Day We Got Our Own Back', the men's invasion is less a physical threat than a sacrilege against domestic ritual, a pollution of the sacred space of home. Their boots scar the newly polished linoleum in the dining-room; in the kitchen, they leave tea, sugar, flour and salt spilled all over the red-tiled floor, but they get their comeuppance before leaving, when one man thrusts his arms up the sooty chimney in the front sitting-room, and comes out black all over. It is the only time the narrator can remember her mother laughing heartily.

This second raid that Maeve recalled may have been the occasion of which Bob wrote:

> [A]fter the outbreak of the Civil War, my house was being raided by a party of Free State soldiers and they came upon [a note from Arthur Griffith, repaying a loan of a few pounds and apologising for his delay in returning the money]. Seeing it, they decided they had come to the wrong house and they promptly left.[19]

The soldiers may have been young, and unaware of how recently all had fought together; evidence of friendship between their leader and the man whose house they were searching was enough to convince them that they had made a mistake. Erskine Childers was not so lucky. Long suspected by the Free Staters of spying for the British, and intensely disliked by many members of Dáil Éireann, he was arrested on 10 November 1922, and found to be in possession of a handgun. That Free State leader Michael Collins himself had given it to him counted for nothing when he was tried at Portobello Barracks on 18 November and sentenced to death by firing squad. Collins himself was already dead: ambushed and killed at Bealnablagh, near Macroom, County Cork. And Griffith too had died, aged fifty-one, in August, worn out and disillusioned by the violence. The conflict had descended to new levels of bitterness. After Childers' sentence was carried out on 24 November, the Irregulars decided to shoot members of Dáil

Éireann. When they assassinated Sean Hales on 7 December, the government retaliated with the reprisal execution of Rory O'Connor, Liam Mellowes, Dick Barrett and Joe McKelvey at Mountjoy. Little remained on either side of the 'gay pursuit of a perilous quest' of which Childers had written in *The Riddle of the Sands*.

The Civil War continued for several more months, with ambushes, booby traps and appalling atrocities on both sides. Sunday, 8 April 1923 saw the formal launch of a new political party, Cumann na nGaedheal, led by William T. Cosgrave, President of the Free State government. On 30 April, the IRA Chief of Staff, Frank Aiken, called a unilateral ceasefire and on 24 May de Valera ordered all republicans to dump arms. By June, when the war finally ended, 927 people had been killed, including 77 executed by the government.

How should a family live after events like these? While those who had embraced the Treaty enjoyed increasing prosperity, republicans experienced serious difficulty in earning a living and supporting a family. Employment in the public sector was conditional on an oath of allegiance to the Free State, and hundreds – including de Valera – were arrested for activities perceived as subversive, and sent to prisons and internment camps.[20] Bob supported his family by a variety of jobs, including some commercial travelling: Una had taken over his calls when he was on the run, in order not to lose his income. Emer was now thirteen. Quiet and unassuming, devoted to her little sisters, she was a major support to Una. But she had finished primary school, and a decision had to be made about the next step in her education. From Paris, Leopold and Raymonde Kerney sent word that she would be welcome to live with them and their two young children, and to attend school there.[21] The Brennans gratefully accepted. On at least one occasion, Bob accompanied Emer to France and then disappeared, living there for some time under a false name. Emer did not come home for Christmas 1923. On Christmas Eve she wrote on the back of a small picture card, 'To my dearest little sister Meave [*sic*] from Emer'. The front of the card was printed 'Meilleurs Vœux pour la Nouvelle Année'.[22]

Maeve and Derry went to St Mary's National School on Belmont Avenue, a short walk from Cherryfield Avenue. In Maeve's story 'The Shadow of Kindness', this is where 'the school building, gray and high, with a few large, oblong, institutional windows, fitted and matched the yard exactly, as though a child had drawn and colored it'. Delia Bagot walks there every day at midday to bring lunch to Lily and Margaret, but also so that she can watch the youngest children 'stumbling like moths from one side of the yard to the other and beating at the air with their hands, and looking up at their teacher as though they imagined she produced the light by which they played' [*SA* 250–1].

The centre of Dublin lay in ruins, but most of the fighting had been in rural areas, and ordinary life went on. A new children's library opened in 1922 in the Carnegie Library opposite Rathmines Town Hall. It was followed in 1923 by the Stella Picture Theatre, farther up the street. Across from the Stella, on the corner of Castlewood Avenue, was the imposing Lee's drapery, built in 1910, whose newspaper advertisements for household linens, sewing fabrics and children's clothing continued to appear. Una's brother Jim Bolger was living in a flat at 1 Castlewood Avenue with his wife Ellen and baby daughter, Máire. He applied to the Civil Service, and was accepted, despite his politics. In 1923, just before their second child Joe was born, the Bolgers moved a little farther from the city centre, to a redbrick house very like those on Hollybank Avenue, at 25 Brighton Gardens, Rathgar.[23] It was near where Bob Brennan had sheltered from the Black and Tans with Yohan and Maria Climanis above the butcher's shop in 1920.

In Cherryfield Avenue, Una spent most of her time at home. Dinner for families was in the middle of the day, with meat, potatoes and vegetables, or fish on Fridays; tea in the early evening was a much lighter meal, without potatoes. Milk and bread were delivered daily in horse-drawn wagons, and a 'pig man' collected food scraps. Fresh meat and vegetables were available in Ranelagh, a ten-minute walk away. Fires had to be lit, and grates cleaned out; coal deliveries and chimney-cleaning had to be arranged. The Brennans' house had no back entrance, and no flight of front steps with coal-hole beneath. Two or three times a year, black-faced coalmen would run through the house at a trot, without speaking, each with a heavy sack on his shoulder, and stoop in the door of the wooden shed behind the kitchen to pour coal with a throaty roaring sound into the mysterious glittering darkness. Children watched solemnly, standing well back, as the empty sacks were counted and the money handed over.

A laundry van called, but most clothes had to be washed at home, dried on a line in the back garden – or in the kitchen, if the weather was wet – and ironed. In Maeve's story 'The Beginning of a Long Story', when it rained for days on end, 'The mother finished the washing early and pegged it across a line she had put up under the kitchen ceiling. The arms of the father's shirts hung down like streamers, stiff and dry, and brushed the mother's light-brown hair as she moved about the kitchen' [RG 212]. The Brennans had no maid, but by the mid-1920s, although huge numbers of young girls still went into domestic service, that was not unusual.[24]

On Mondays – the traditional washday – the *Irish Times* published a regular column called 'Woman and her Home'. Advertisements ran alongside it in 1925 for floor and furniture polish, and for the new electric Hoover – 'It Beats as it Sweeps as it Cleans'. Another, headed 'Spring-Cleaning Time is Frazerton Time!', showed overalls cut like contemporary clothes:

loose and straight, with a dropped waist and a hemline below the knee: 'Attractive aprons and overalls . . . They have all the stern qualities you expect of an Overall or Apron. Yet in them you are becomingly clad – ready for any unexpected visitor.'

Apart from deliverymen of various kinds, and occasional relatives or friends who dropped by unannounced, the most common callers at these houses where women were at home all day were pedlars and people who asked for scrap metal or cast-offs, or begged for money. These are the people who feature again and again in Maeve's stories. Mary Briscoe used to welcome a man called Hairy Joe, who was tall and bearded and carried a basket full of plants in pots. She referred to him humorously as 'His Hairiness', but used to buy plants from him, and give him food – dinner or tea, according to the time of day – which he would sit on the step of the porch to eat. If he arrived between meals, he got a cup of tea with bread and jam.[25] At Coolnaboy, when Una was growing up, visits from poor men and women had been a part of life, and in Maeve's stories the children's mother accepts their claims on her in Dublin in ways that give her satisfaction, but sometimes embarrass her, or lead people to accuse her of allowing herself to be exploited.[26]

Una knitted and sewed for herself and the children, but her recreation and pleasure was her garden. At home in Coolnaboy she had loved flowers; in Ranelagh she made a flowerbed in the tiny front garden, under the bay window, with crocuses in spring, peonies and poppies in summer. She grew more flowers at the back, in beds around the edges of the grass. In 'The Poor Men and Women', Maeve gives a list, mixing the seasons together: lupin, London pride, wallflowers, freesia, snowdrops, lilies of the valley, forget-me-nots, pansies, nasturtiums, marigolds and roses. Nasturtiums covered the trellis on the Briscoes' wall. In one corner, following the fashion of the time, Una had made a careful rock garden [*SA* 134, 219]. She grew geraniums in a large pot. A laburnum tree had been in the back garden when they moved in, pressed against the wall on the Briscoes' side, visible from the back sitting-room window downstairs. Every year in May and June its heavy drooping heads of small deep yellow flowers lit up the garden. Maeve was never a gardener, but that laburnum glows through many of her stories, even finding itself in the garden behind Mrs King's house in her novella *The Visitor*, where it appears three times.[27] Writing this description of Rose Derdon, Maeve must have been remembering not just the look and smell of the flowers, but their feel between her fingers:

> She smiled hardly to see it, the generous little tree, a furious yellow,
> a million blossoms, lifting itself as near to glory as color could bring

it. That spindly trunk, thin as a leg, was glorious for them every summer, boiling in the sun with smell and color. She had to smile, knowing the look of the shapely little blossoms, each one as yellow as the next, the petals of them unusually smooth, to see and to rub. Her fingertips tingled, and she caressed the complicated lace of her best cloth, spread on the table for John. (*SA* 139)

Indoors, Una had ferns: a collection of them in pots on a table in the bay window downstairs, the tall ones twined around bamboo canes. They are another fixed point in her daughter's stories.

Children played on the streets in Dublin in the 1920s, but the Brennans and the Briscoes kept mostly to themselves when their children were small. The women spoke from garden to garden, but did not visit each other's houses. As Kevin and Brendan Briscoe grew older, kicking footballs around their small back garden and muddying the house with their shoes, their mother Mary had the grass replaced with concrete paving, just as Mrs Finn did in Maeve's story, 'The Twelfth Wedding Anniversary', 'making a hard gray surface where grass and flowers might have grown' [*SA* 217]. (Mary Briscoe was a gardener, however, like Una. She retained her flowerbeds around the walls, and a large lilac in one corner.) Maeve and Derry played in their own back garden. Girls' games had more rhymes and singsong formulas than boys' did: 'In and out go the darky bluebells' was one, 'I sent a letter to my love, and on the way I dropped it', another. Growing up next door, younger than Maeve or Derry, Hubert Briscoe felt a certain envy when he heard them skipping with a rope on the cement paving outside their back door, chanting together 'A tisket, a tasket, / A brown and yellow basket.'[28]

Una always dressed her two young daughters alike, as Maeve records in 'The Clever One'. She tied their hair with ribbons, and she made almost all their clothes. In Coolnaboy, her mother's young neighbour never saw her sitting down without a piece of needlework in her hands, and used to watch in fascination as she bit the thread off between her teeth. Years later, in diplomatic circles in Washington, DC, Una was renowned for her fine hand-work.[29] She used a sewing machine too – another recurring feature of Maeve's remembered house – and Derry had a toy one, as little Ita Briscoe did next door, when she was old enough.

Maeve writes that 'Derry's delicate health . . . loomed as importantly in my childhood as the Catholic Church and the fight for Irish freedom' [*SA* 57], and in story after story of hers, a little sister is upstairs in bed with a cold. Sometimes it is Margaret Bagot, who is subject to crying fits and is 'always missing days at school, always having colds and coughs' [*SA* 277]. In 'The Beginning of a Long Story', eight-year-old Ellen's younger sister is in bed

73

with a cold, and this is not unusual: 'Johanna was capricious at the best of times, but when she was in bed sick she was very hard to deal with' [*RG* 211]. 'The Clever One' suggests that Derry showed symptoms of St Vitus's dance when she was six or seven, and refers to her 'keeping the house in an uproar over her health for years on end'. Derry did not go to school much as a child, because of recurrent ill health. The two sisters got on well together, but it is clear that, at least in Maeve's memory, the roles they were assigned within the family were very different. Both were intelligent, and pretty; nevertheless, '"Derry has the beauty," [people] used to say, "but Maeve has all the brains."'

Brains and beauty were a binary pair, never found together in the same child, according to a common opposition that carried a strong message about what the future held for girls. Reserving femininity to those who stayed silent or were not considered brainy, it expressed some of the ambivalence people felt about women's intelligence and ambition, and their demands to be heard. Women's education was proceeding in Ireland, of course. Early in the twentieth century, *Bean na h-Éireann* had been active in twin campaigns to make Irish an essential subject for Matriculation, and to have women admitted to degrees on the same basis as men at the new National University of Ireland, and both aims had been achieved by 1910. Dedicated unmarried nationalists like Dorothy Macardle at Alexandra College and Louise Gavan Duffy at her own Irish-speaking Scoil Bhríghde, were transforming their activism into opportunity for the daughters of their generation, preparing girls for Matriculation. After the Civil War, however, women who had been articulate and active in the nationalist and feminist movements for years, working and facing danger as equals with men, found themselves relegated to the home in much the same way as American and British women would after the Second World War. In the rhetoric of *Bean na h-Éireann* and the *Irish Homestead*, housework had been an integral part of nationalist activism, associated with husbandry in the building of community, but nobody was expected to take it very seriously; the *Echo*'s 'Una' column had presented its tips on stain removal side by side with feminist polemic. Now, however, housework was elaborated as an end in itself, and the subtext was that those who did it were not fit for the demanding world of paid work. The obverse was true too: brainy, talkative girls would not grow into mothers and homemakers. Although as Anastasia Bolger, Una Brennan had been top of her class in the Loreto Convent, and had loved chemistry, her daughter's stories give her no intellectual role. As in the years after the Second World War, peace brought a renewed need for domestic stability. As business and manufacture recovered, they needed markets, and so women must make homes and go shopping, and men must have jobs.

In Maeve's autobiographical story 'The Old Man of the Sea', she knows about Sindbad the Sailor because she has read the *Arabian Nights*. Brains suggest masculinity, and even brawn. The real Maeve was small-boned and elfin, but in these stories she is 'the large, hardy twin' who talks all the time, while Derry, 'the thin, pale one', is always silent. Derry is 'tiny' in 'The Clever One', and 'only weighs about half a pound' in 'The Lie'. In 'The Beginning of a Long Story', Ellen, modelled on Maeve, is 'as warm as a little bull', 'strong as a little horse . . . growing too fast, growing out of her clothes, getting bigger every time you looked at her' [*RG* 222]. In 'The Lie', Maeve's declaration that she had no interest in sewing seems not so much a statement of liberation (although it may be that) as acquiescence in the role assigned to her [*SA* 44]. In 'The Clever One', the conversation between her and Derry as adult sisters takes place in Derry's home in Washington, DC, as Derry hems a pink cotton dress for her older daughter. Maeve, one imagines, simply sat and smoked, behaving like a visitor – or a man.

Maeve is Mary to Derry's Martha, and in many ways she has chosen the better part, for she often manages to feel important. There is a cost, however, and it pains her deeply. When she looks back in 'The Clever One' at all the dishes she washed because Derry pretended to be too sick and frail to help her, she realises, 'I hadn't really minded doing the washing-up alone, since I always received high praise from my mother for doing it' [*SA* 58]. Her fury in 'The Lie' is born of hurt. At nine years old she impulsively flings herself into her mother's lap and is pushed away: she is too big; too heavy. Una is tiny, like Derry, but Maeve is different from them, and so, except when she washes dishes, she is excluded from the feminine magic that holds the home together. One critic identifies what happens next as Maeve's loss of innocence and the moment of her expulsion from Paradise: in her rage, she breaks her sister's toy sewing machine, then lies about her crime. It is when she inadvertently reveals her lie that she feels the end of the special bond she has enjoyed with her mother until now: 'I saw the little joke die, and I knew that I had killed it'.[30] Maeve's later writing will insist on the importance of truth, and jokes will often be where it shows most clearly.

Most views in these stories are from inside the house. The Brennans' and the Briscoes' side of Cherryfield Avenue was built along the curving eastern boundary of the field William George Bailey had bought in 1905. Beyond it were more fields: the grounds of Milltown Park, a Jesuit house of studies, with tall trees all along its avenue, and beyond that, fronting on to Milltown Road, a large field that the Jesuits had recently leased to a new soccer club called Shamrock Rovers. 'Association' football had been played in Dublin since 1890, when the Irish League was formed, but with partition came a split, and in 1923 the Football Association of the Irish Free State was recognised for international competition. Glenmalure Park, Milltown, came to represent an urban, English-speaking Irish masculinity, with little access to political power, quite unlike the Gaelic Athletic Association, based in Croke Park, which forbade its members to play, or even to attend, 'foreign games'.

Between Milltown Park and Cherryfield Avenue lay the Norwood Tennis Club and McCabe's garage, which Maeve calls McRory's. Not many people had cars in Dublin in the 1920s, but a lot of those who did played tennis: it was a genteel sport whose popularity was growing enormously as the middle class expanded. Switzer's and Hely's stores in Dublin regularly advertised tennis rackets for sale. Some clubs were exclusively Protestant; others, set up in reaction, were for Catholics. All were social centres where the marriageable young could meet, but it was generally agreed that the Protestant clubs served better afternoon teas.[31] Norwood Tennis Club was largely Protestant, and most of its members came from larger houses than those on Cherryfield Avenue. Its entrance was just around the corner from the Brennans' house. Beside the little grocery shop that William McCabe's two sisters ran on Sandford Road, a lane led past the garage to the club's grass courts and deckchairs, and the wooden Victorian pavilion.

The tennis club features in story after story by Maeve Brennan. In summer, she and Derry could watch from the back bedroom window as men and women in whites ran about the courts. They heard the pocking sound the balls made against the rackets and the 'intent and formal cries' of voices calling scores. Every Saturday night in summer as they lay in bed, the sound of dance music came from the pavilion. At tournament time they witnessed the pristine colonial drama of the prize-giving ceremony, conducted against fresh paint on a special platform by 'a lady in a wide hat and a flowered chiffon dress' [*SA* 19].

McCabe's garage caught fire one summer night in the mid-1920s. In number 47, the three small Briscoe boys stood at their bedroom window and watched a display that was far more exciting than any Hallowe'en or Guy Fawkes Night: flames shot high as the wooden building collapsed and petrol tanks exploded. Maeve was already familiar with gunfire and explosions, but years later she wrote: 'It was a really satisfactory fire, with leaping flames, thick, pouring smoke, and a steady roar of destruction, broken by crashes as parts of the roof collapsed' [*SA* 16]. As so often in her writing, a single adjective, 'satisfactory', makes clear the child's restricted point of view.

In Maeve's description of the change the fire made in her familiar landscape, we can read a metaphor of her father's political position in the 1920s. His adult life had been sustained by the romantic-nationalist conviction, fed on translations of medieval sagas about sacral kingship, that Ireland's beautiful green countryside, its language and history, were connected, mystically and inevitably, with the Sinn Féin politics he espoused; now, however, new structures were in place:

> It was not long before the McRorys put up another garage, made of silvery corrugated-metal stuff that looked garish and glaring against our garden wall; it cut off more of our view than the old building had. The new garage looked very hard and lasting, as unlikely to burn as a pot or a kettle. The beautiful green courts that had always seemed from our window to roll comfortably in the direction of the old wooden building now seemed to have turned and to be rolling away into the distance, as though they did not like the unsightly new structure and would have nothing to do with it. [SA 19]

The tennis club was undamaged by the fire, and the tournament went ahead, even as men with Dublin accents shouted hoarsely in the 'dark shambles' that the fire had left. Nearly eighty years later, McCabe's is called the Sandford Service Garage. Frank and Fred Smith, whose father first went to work there as an apprentice mechanic in 1925 and took over the business in 1946, own and run it.[32] The corrugated-iron building that Maeve disliked so much still stands: Frank Smith remembers peeping through a gap in its wall at the tennis players when he was a child. Houses replaced the tennis club in the 1950s, but charred timbers are still visible behind the lock-up garages along the lane.

FIVE

Remembering Shadows

Maeve's seven stories about her own family say very little about her father, although 'The Day We Got Our Own Back' is constructed around his absence. In 'The Morning after the Big Fire', Maeve hears his voice outside her bedroom door, and later he takes part in conversations about the garage that has caught fire. In 'The Lie', when she comes home after telling her sin in confession, he asks a simple question that leads her to betray herself, as her mother immediately understands. The story ends with his reaction:

'What's going on around here *now*?' my father asked, bewildered.
He got no answer.

Unsatisfactory marriages loom large in Maeve's writing. By contrast with the autobiographical stories of mother and children, in the fiction she wrote about the Bagots and the Derdons the central characters are a husband and wife. The same is true of 'The Beginning of a Long Story' [*RG* 204–22], about an unnamed family who live in the same small house with dark red carpet on the stairs, french windows in the front and a tennis club beyond the back garden. Bewilderment still rules, however. Children in the stories, and readers outside them, observe a couple's incompatible aspirations, their apprehension about each other's reactions, and their inability to speak about what is important to them.

And yet these stories are about love. One of the last short stories Maeve published was 'Christmas Eve', which appeared in *The New Yorker* on 23 December 1972. Martin Bagot stands on the linoleum in the hall of his house, looking at the umbrella stand and the chair (both mentioned, along with the linoleum, in the advertising of Hill and Son, Expert House Furnishers, in 1910), and tries to reassure himself that his family has everything it needs. This is one of Maeve's poetic meditations, inserted seamlessly into the fabric of a prose that is in every other way remarkable for its unassuming clarity and even practicality:

> Nobody ever sat on the chair and nobody ever stood long in the hall. It was a passageway – not to fame and not to fortune but only to the common practices of family life, those practices, habits, and ordinary customs that are the only true realities most of us ever know, and that in some of us form a memory strong enough to give us something to hold on to at the end of our days. It is a matter of love, and whether the love finds daily, hourly expression in warm embraces and in the instinctive kind of attentiveness animals give to their young or whether it is largely unexpressed, as it was among the Bagots, does not really matter very much in the long run. It is the solid existence of love that gives life and strength to memory, and if, in some cases, childhood memories lack the soft and tender colors given by demonstrativeness, the child grown old and in the dark knows that what is under his hand is a rock that will never give way. [SA 307]

In these stories, most of which she wrote when she herself had been married and divorced and shared her life with a dog and several cats, Maeve attributes a kind of higher wisdom to animals. In the 1920s the Brennans had a dog called Bennie. The fictional Bagots have a rough-haired white terrier of the same name, and two cats, Minnie, thin, black and agile, and Rupert, a big, soft, lazy orange cat.[1] All are former strays. Their personalities are minutely observed, and in a household of anxious people, they are a source of calm kindliness and humour. Delia Bagot first saw Bennie on the street, on her way home from Mass; he was being tormented by boys, and she rescued him. In 'The Shadow of Kindness', he has been in the house for five years and she does not know how old he is: 'Sometimes he seemed like a puppy and sometimes he was a very thoughtful, grown-up dog. He was very faithful' [SA 243–4]. He sleeps on Delia's bed, and follows her attentively around the house and garden, while the children talk uninhibitedly to him in ways they cannot do when their father is there. In 'The Sofa', Bennie is closer to Delia than Martin is: 'He must brush against her every chance he got . . . he must at all times know that she was still herself. Verification, ascertainment, recognition, and silence – Bennie lived in the blazing humility of perfect love' [SA 259].

Martin Bagot does not like the animals: sometimes he remembers to ask the children 'How is Minnie?' or 'How is Rupert?', but in fact he hates the dog and the cats, and in the past he has demanded that Delia get rid of them. It is the only thing she has refused to do. These details wind themselves with such consistency through so many of the Bagot stories that it is hard to believe Maeve has invented them.

Delia and Martin do not share a bed. Four of the eight stories about the Bagots make this point quite firmly, while in the final one, 'The Springs of Affection', Min Bagot notices that the double bed they bought when they married has vanished from their house [*SA* 354]. Martin works in an office and comes home very late – at one or two in the morning – so he does not want to be woken early. He has taken to sleeping in the little boxroom above the kitchen, behind the bathroom, so as not to wake Delia and the children when he comes in, and so that they will not disturb him in the mornings. His books are in that room too. 'The Twelfth Wedding Anniversary' probes the texture of the silences that have allowed this arrangement to become fixed, and Delia finds herself wondering if the shape of her life and Martin's could perhaps have been dictated by the house's layout: '[I]f the little room had never existed, he would never have had the idea of shutting himself away from her. What an alarming truth it was that if they had had a smaller house they might have been happier. And yet, the house was quite small' [*SA* 220].

Martin is not unhappy that they sleep apart – only suffocated by the possibility of closeness, and filled with irritation at Delia's panicky humility and guilt about his own unkindness to her. He loves his family, but they must deal with him on his terms.

Several of the stories suggest that the distress in the Bagots' marriage dates from the birth and death within three days of their first child, Jimmy. He was born in that house, three years before Lily, and Delia and Martin have never been able to meet across the grief that remains. When the elderly retired missionary bishop visits Delia in 'Stories of Africa', full of nostalgia and interest in her life, she tells him about Jimmy, and is consoled by his ability to embrace the dead along with the living. As she gives the bishop a verbal tour of her house, Delia mentions that the room they call the boxroom has a nice window overlooking the garden. That is all she says, however, for 'Mrs Bagot's husband slept alone in the boxroom, but she wasn't going to tell that to the Bishop or to anybody else.'

In houses built so close together, people did not need to be told things to know them. For years, Bob had been kept away from his family repeatedly by his commitment to an Irish Republic and his loyalty to de Valera. Now armed violence had ended, and his home was safe, but from 1924 he worked on a campaign to set up a newspaper that would articulate the point of view of those who still opposed the Anglo-Irish Treaty, the so-called 'third Sinn Féin party'.[2] He still wrote fiction and continued working as a journalist, now on a short-lived paper called *Sunburst*. The Briscoe children next door were aware that Mr Brennan worked unusual hours, and that he needed sleep. To them he seemed cross. Their bedroom and their parents' room shared walls with the two main upstairs rooms of the Brennans' house, and the boys knew that Una had asked Mary Briscoe to keep them quiet in the mornings. They were greatly relieved when he moved into the small boxroom, which shared a wall with the Pearsons' house instead. From their kitchen, after their own father had gone to work, they could hear him singing 'The Boys of Wexford' as he shaved in the bathroom, whose window faced theirs.[3]

Otherwise, Bob was not at home much, except on Sundays. He joined the Royal Dublin Society, which had moved to new premises in Ballsbridge in 1925 after yielding Leinster House to the Free State for its houses of parliament. Long a cultural mainstay of Anglo-Ireland, the RDS had more than trebled its membership between 1919 and 1926. Bob went every Saturday to its library, a short bicycle ride from Cherryfield Avenue, along the River Dodder. He also liked to take long walks: in the other direction, the path by the Dodder led right up into the foothills of the Dublin mountains.[4]

Before any of the Bagot stories, 'The Beginning of a Long Story' was published in *The New Yorker* in February 1961. The father is called John:

> Sometimes after tea he went to see a play in town, but the mother never went with him, because she had the children to mind. He said that when Ellen was bigger she could go with him. He liked to go for long walks in the Dublin hills on Saturdays and Sundays in the good weather, and in the summertime he often went to Wicklow and had a few days by himself. He said that when Ellen's legs were longer she could go on the walks with him, too. [*RG* 220–1]

The mother in this story is simply 'the mother'; she has the same very long hair that Una Brennan and Delia Bagot have. There are three little girls. Ellen is eight, Johanna, six, and the youngest is Bridget, who must be one of the most vividly drawn four-year-olds in English: she walks around with shiny transparent coloured paper stuck to her face, announcing that she is a bathroom window. Johanna is in bed with a cold; she does not say much, but when she speaks, it is crisp and final. Ellen is a reader, with an urgent imagination. When everybody else falls asleep in the daytime, she stays awake, as Lily Bagot will do in 'The Carpet with the Big Pink Roses on It', and the story is told through her eyes.

The long story that is beginning here is one that will continue in Maeve's fiction about the Bagots; it is about the mother and father sleeping apart.

At first, the mother is gentle, affectionate and generous, although she wears 'a frightened, afflicted smile'; the father is exciting and funny. The children run delightedly to meet him when he arrives home from work, and he constructs elaborate comic routines for their amusement. On the second page, we learn in passing that the parents share a big brass bed in the front bedroom; much later, that the back bedroom has 'two narrow beds for Ellen and Johanna and a high-sided iron cot, painted white, that Bridget still [sleeps] in'. There is a third bedroom: the little boxroom above the kitchen, beside the bathroom. In it, the father has 'a gramophone and a set of French Linguaphone records, and a set of the *Encyclopaedia Britannica* that he was buying in installments'. Also in the room is 'a lumpy little bed . . . a spare bed'. By the end of the story, it is clear that the small bed is where the father is sleeping, on this particular night at least.

Maeve uses the same dramatic irony in this story as in her one novella. When *The Visitor*'s central character, Anastasia King, was small, her mother crept into her bed one night, saying 'I'm cold, pet, and you're warm as toast always.' Anastasia did not know for years what that meant, but her cheery revelation at breakfast the next day allowed her icily overbearing grandmother access to the fragile privacy of her parents' marriage. 'The Beginning of a Long Story' leaves the reader to put two and two together when the mother fits herself into bed beside Ellen: '"Oh Ellen, don't wake up," the mother said. "I'm perishing with the cold and you're as warm as a little bull always. I'll just get warm. I'll just lie here a minute"' [*RG* 221].

That Maeve observed and was troubled by what she interpreted as a fracture in her parents' relationship cannot be doubted. That Bob sometimes slept alone in the tiny boxroom is registered also in 'The Morning after the Big Fire', where 'he had been awakened by the red glare of the flames against his window'. By then the little girls were sleeping in the big front bedroom, and Una had the back room, from the window of which she allowed them to watch the fire.

Bob had suffered some sort of breakdown over a period of months in 1921, and had been ill again in September 1922. In August 1924, when the Civil War had been over for more than a year, the *Dublin Magazine* published a very short story by 'R. S. Kearney', the pen-name he had used for his 'Crubeen Patch' stories in *Ireland's Own* and for a mystery novel written in prison and published in 1921.[5] The new story was called 'Solo?' It was prefaced by the note: 'My only excuse for this story is that I dreamt it all word for word exactly as it is set down here.'

'Solo?' is a surreal transformation of a clichéd theme but, unlike some of Bob's other writings, it is not funny, merely preposterous and strange. As it opens, the narrator, Black, has a pistol in his hand, and a huddled form lies on the floor. Black has just shot Tommy Smith, but Smith turns out to be identical quintuplets called Theocritus, Telemachus, Themistocles, Thucydides and Theophrastus – all known as Tommy, and all married to Elsie, whom Black has been trying to protect. Brown, Smith and Robinson have already murdered three Tommys, and when the case comes to court, the judge himself shoots the fifth, whereupon '. . . Elsie flew to him and flung herself sobbing into his arms'.

Throughout Bob's writing life, he embraced the conventions of English popular fiction. The stories he wrote were always literate and well crafted, but none of them attempted to explore motivation or emotion, and none revealed the man behind them. For all his allegiance to the idea of a de-anglicised Ireland, he gave many of his characters quintessentially English names, and placed them in neutral settings that were English by default. In the 1920s, living in Cherryfield Avenue, he invented a jaded American millionaire-turned-detective called Oscar van Duyven, who operates in France (although at least two stories about him are set in Ireland, and Irish characters have walk-on parts in others).[6] Van Duyven is thirty-five and unmarried, a manufacturer of electric fans that are found 'in every hotel from Tokio [sic] to Lisbon . . . from Peru to Yokohama'. As he is about to leave Paris to return to New York, van Duyven's interest is aroused by a clever seventeen-year-old hotel messenger who shows him a telegram in cipher – 'not a letter code but a word code' – and they embark on the first of many adventures. Bob had travelled in France in 1921, and had been in Paris again for the Irish Race Convention in January 1922, and at some stage with Emer, but the van Duyven stories rely heavily on what he must have gleaned from maps and guidebooks. Much depends on the names of streets in Paris, and characters have surnames like Curie and Perrier. Van Duyven's young sidekick is called Pierre Lemasse. Seán Lemass, by now a leading member of Sinn Féin, was the young man who had stared gloomily out a window in Beechwood Avenue during the Civil War, while Bob debated literature tongue-in-cheek with John Dowling, and Todd Andrews looked on admiringly. While still a schoolboy, he had fought in the GPO during the 1916 Rising. He was elected to Dáil Éireann for South Dublin in a dramatic by-election in 1924 and would succeed de Valera as Taoiseach in 1959.

Fictional detectives are not normally married with young children. The van Duyven stories are pure escapism – for their author, clearly, as well as for potential readers – and even carry a homoerotic charge, which may be entirely due to the conventions of the genre. As one story opens, van Duyven and Pierre are wrestling together; in another, set in Dublin in Horse Show Week (early August, when accommodation was always scarce), men have to share hotel bedrooms. A 'splendidly built, foreign-looking' young man, who turns out to be 'Liban, the Marathon Runner', offers his room-mates a drugged pipe, but Pierre foils his attempt at robbery.[7]

In 1926, the London publishers John Hamilton issued Bob's Oscar van Duyven novel, *The Toledo Dagger*, this time under his own name. The blurb promised:

A thrilling detective story, the scene of which is laid near Monte Carlo. Leon Darracq is found stabbed in a locked room at the villa of M. Rodin, a wealthy retired jeweller. Suspicion falls on all the guests, but the police are baffled. An American, Van Duyven, and Pierre his valet succeed in discovering a good many mysteries connected with the case but the murderer is eventually revealed in an unexpected way.

Maeve was nine when *The Toledo Dagger* appeared, and she must certainly have read it. In her own fiction, Martin Bagot's library included 'books by Sidney and Beatrice Webb, Darwin, Shakespeare, Turgenev, Edgar Wallace, Wolfe Tone, W. B. Yeats, James Joyce, Chekhov, Ibsen, Molière, Edgar Allan Poe, and others', and it seems reasonable to infer that Bob Brennan had these books too. Maeve read the *Arabian Nights*, as we have seen, and devoured the fairytales of Hans Christian Andersen: along with magic carpets, his figure of the Little Mermaid is a recurring theme in her later writing. Although many nationalist Catholics saw English newspapers, and comics especially, as a symptom of the polluting godlessness that lay across the Irish Sea, she and Derry loved comics, and were allowed to buy them at the local newsagent's, the Elm in Ranelagh.[8]

While Bob continued to work with de Valera for a Republic, the Free State government was setting about repairing the physical damage of the Civil War and creating an infrastructure in line with modern needs. The Minister for Finance, Ernest Blythe, ensured his place in history in 1924 when he reduced the old-age pension by a shilling a week. The government agreed on the need for an Irish broadcasting service and renamed Sackville Street, Dublin's central thoroughfare, after the 'Liberator' Daniel O'Connell. The street had been laid waste in the fighting, but by the spring of 1925 its restoration was well advanced. Work had begun too on rebuilding the Custom House, destroyed by fire in 1921. Reports and letters in the newspapers discussed proposals to develop a hydroelectric scheme on the River Shannon, and to abolish income tax.

In Ranelagh, William George Bailey built a new row of twenty houses alongside his brother-in-law's and another beside his own house, extending

Hollybank and Cherryfield Avenues. In March and April 1925, a small ad appeared in the *Irish Times*, under Houses and Lands for Sale:

> Bailey & Sons, Builders, have new houses at Upper Cherryfield Avenue, Sandford Road, Dublin, containing 2 reception, 3 bedrooms, bathroom, kitchen, electric light and gas. Prices semidetached with motor garage £800; without: £725. Inspection invited.

The new houses were the same size as the Brennans', but new design influences had crept in, and horizontal lines replaced many of the verticals of those down the street. Instead of slates, these houses had red tile roofs, while garages attached to some of them reflected the fact that ordinary people were buying cars: a five-seat touring car cost £375; a Peugeot Baby Quad could be had for £175. Cloche hats were fashionable for women: pulled down over the ears, they would not blow away in an open car. Most buyers of the earlier houses had been young couples, but many of these new ones were occupied by single women.[9] As in Britain, the Great War had left many young women who might have married to face life alone. Maeve's stories make no mention of the new houses; perhaps, since hardly any children lived in them, she did not notice them.

Business people, who had a powerful incentive to re-establish normal life, were strongly represented among those who had accepted the Treaty. The unionist *Irish Times* expressed approval of 'our government of young men' as it applauded the economic progress that had been made, and noted a resurgence of social life. W. B. Yeats had won the Nobel Prize for Literature in 1924, and on 29 April the following year the newspaper published a photograph of him with Dr Oliver St John Gogarty (James Joyce's Buck Mulligan), at a race meeting at Punchestown, commenting, 'There can be no question . . . that the Free State is emerging from the darkness into the sunshine. Gatherings like Punchestown prove the growth of a healthy reaction against the gloom and horrors of recent years.'

If 'The Beginning of a Long Story' is full of rain, sunshine streams into the childhood Maeve describes in the stories about the Bagots. There are eight of them, and they began to appear in *The New Yorker* in May 1964. Lily Bagot is seven in 'The Carpet with the Big Pink Roses on It', and Margaret is five. Lily is a form of Elizabeth, so that these girls have the names of the British princesses who were children in the 1930s. Not giving them the names of Irish warrior queens or saints may have been a way of achieving fictional distance, but Lily and Margaret Bagot are clearly modelled on Maeve and Derry Brennan.

Lily and Margaret sleep together in a big brass bed in the back bedroom, where the wallpaper is patterned with faded garlands of blue flowers and a fire is sometimes lit in the small iron fireplace. Margaret spends a lot of time there alone, sick in bed, drawing with crayons or dozing, with the cats curled in beside her, but Lily is always awake. Margaret is 'very defenceless and unsure of herself', yet like Derry in 'The Clever One' and Johanna in 'The Beginning of a Long Story', she has the power to stop her older sister in her tracks with a single deadpan sentence. Lily is always reading; she writes letters, asks questions, experiments with a penny to see if it will fit between the floorboards, and uses sheet after sheet of paper to work out codes: 'Lily was always hoping to discover a code that would be easy to write and impossible for anyone but herself to understand' [SA 243]; 'she was very clever and always got good marks' [SA 245, 300]. In all this she takes after her father, and he always asks about her schoolwork and takes an interest in her, but in more than one story, she is 'a bit too sure of herself, perhaps'. Being sure of yourself can make you vulnerable, the adult Maeve writing about Lily suggests. People may look at a child who is too sure of herself 'with the ugly eyes of suspicion', or the child may say too much, and give herself away. In a culture that still has as its ironic mantra 'Whatever you say, say nothing', and at a time when false names, safe houses and coded messages had so recently been facts of life, Lily was 'very soft, very nice to people who maybe wouldn't understand that it was her nature and that she wasn't the fool she seemed to be'.

In 'The Shadow of Kindness', the children are away and Delia Bagot is alone in the house. Just a day earlier she has put them on the train and sent them to visit her sister and brother in the country. She imagines Lily now, watching through the rain for the postman to arrive on his bicycle down the mile-long lane, and it is clear that the farm she is thinking about is Coolnaboy.

From Cherryfield Avenue to Ranelagh railway station was a walk of perhaps fifteen or twenty minutes. The Harcourt Street line closed down in 1958 and would not reopen for almost half a century, but Gerald Mulroney, born three years after Maeve, in 1920, shared his memories of trips to the seaside from Ranelagh station:

> Mr Carey was the stationmaster, a kindly man who knew his passengers by name, and who was not offended if some overburdened mother asked for help with her luggage up the long flights of wooden stairs which led to the platforms. His office was a snug one, with an iron stove glowing in the winter, and beside the hatch carefully arranged rows of cardboard tickets for stations from Harcourt Street to remote and romantic places like Woodenbridge and Wexford. Below these was a machine which printed the date on the ticket with an impressive bang as Mr Carey stamped on the foot pedal.[10]

Passengers reached the down platform through a tunnel lined with white porcelain bricks, some of which bore the legend 'Ham Baker & Co., Westminster, London'. Gerald Mulroney often wondered, as Maeve may well have, 'if Westminster was not an unusual address for a firm making porcelain bricks'. He recalled the race to secure a corner seat so as to be able to lean out of the window, although anyone who did so risked a smut in the eye from the steam engine.

Every summer, Maeve and Derry spent a month away from home, the first half at Coolnaboy, the second with their father's mother in Wexford town. 'Grandma's' long black skirts had deep pockets that always seemed to be filled with sweets. She would reach in and pull out a handful of sweets, or even a half-crown for each of them: a huge sum then. Maeve loved the time in town: streets and shops and the many different things there were to read. It was a foretaste of the life she would have in Manhattan, a place where she could be herself. In her fiction, Wexford town is the scene of complex, difficult, adult emotions, not childhood pleasure; only Coolnaboy features in the stories of childhood, and then always with nostalgia.

Una's youngest brother Wat, who had been so kind to Emer at the time of the 1916 Rising, when she was six, now farmed Coolnaboy, while their sister Bessie ran the house and dairy and looked after the poultry. Johanna Bolger died in December 1925 (de Valera travelled to Oylegate for the funeral), but Mary Kate Whitty lived on. Seventy-nine years old when her sister died, she had been in bed upstairs in her tiny room under the eaves for more than ten years, and Bessie still tended to her every need. Nobody knew what was wrong with her, and everybody, except apparently Bessie, thought that perhaps nothing was. It was said that she had retired to bed in a huff when someone had criticised her gravy, and had not got up since. She was a big, handsome woman with snow-white hair, who spent her time praying and reading religious books, collecting stamps for the missions, and twisting long pieces of newspaper into 'paper matches' or 'spills'. From her window under the thatch at the end of the house, however, she could see all that went on. Mary Kate's sister Anty in Pouldearg, famous in County Wexford as a lacemaker, had been dead since 1919; Margaret had died at eighty-two in 1923, and their brother William had died nine months before Johanna, aged eighty-three. The Whittys' nephew, Una's brother John, had inherited the farm at Pouldearg. Mary Kate became a legend in the family, to the extent that staying in bed all day or retreating from life was known as 'doing a Mary Kate'.

When the children played in the orchard, they knew that Mary Kate might be spying on them. Maeve and Derry used to tease her, by creeping to her door and knocking on it. 'If I could get out of this bed!' she would expostulate, threatening them. 'Oh but you can't!' they would cry, and run away. Near the orchard was the haggard, where hayricks were built to feed animals through the winter, then came the Barn Meadow, and after that a field called the Slang, part of the Parkers' farm in Martingale. The Parkers' house was several miles away by road, but the children could easily run across two fields from one farmyard to the other. Mairéad Parker was four in 1925. In the years that followed, she played with the Brennans every summer and remembers Maeve as forever doing crosswords. Maeve walked with 'a little short step'; she had lovely dark hair, which she wore in two long plaits, and to the younger child she always seemed happy. Both Brennan girls were 'devils after cats', and at least once Derry climbed a high wall to reach a nest of kittens. Derry loved all animals, and was never seen with a book. Maeve read all the time; she was curious about everything, and friendly with everyone. Nan Cullen helped Bessie in the house at Coolnaboy. She had had little formal schooling, but her mother was a traditional herbalist who made ointments, and she knew a great deal about her natural environment. When Nan Cullen took the three little girls out for a walk, Maeve was the one who pestered her to name the wild plants and tell them about their uses.

Lizzie Doyle, older than the other children, lived in another beautiful thatched house, in Coolamain, near Martingale. She was the girl from Emer's class at Oylegate national school who had consoled Maeve on her first day there in 1921. She and Mairéad Parker still remember Maeve's charm and Bob's wit and energy. Once when Wat Bolger and others ran out of material for a fund-raising concert they had organised, Bob quickly wrote a play. Bob and his sister Nan visited Coolnaboy on another occasion, when Bessie had just sent a chicken to a Jesuit priest for his table. Bob looked at the rooster that was running in the yard with the hens and remarked, 'He's a very proud cock: there's one of his people in the Jesuits!' Una, on the other hand, never made jokes. She was quiet, and much smaller than Bessie, who was strong enough to lift the heavy Mary Kate in bed. Her hair was luxuriant, but always in a bun, and her eyes were beautiful. The young girls thought of her as a good historian, skilled at conversation, who always seemed to be doing needlework.

Most of the time, Maeve and Derry were in Coolnaboy without their parents. 'They would be falling in love with their aunt and with their uncles. They would come back at the end of the month pining for the farm and the animals and all the freedom they had down there' [*SA* 243]. By contrast with the narrow, L-shaped house in Ranelagh, whose every corner emphasised the need to fit in, Coolnaboy was comfortably symmetrical, with a broad and kindly face. The big thatched house was the calm, uncontested master of the acreage in which it stood. The farm was a good one, but the Irish economy was struggling, and Wat and Bessie were not rich. In the 1930s, when Jim Bolger's children spent summers at Coolnaboy after their own young mother's death, their dinner most days consisted of boiled potatoes eaten with home-churned butter. The household almost never ate butcher's meat. Occasionally they had bacon, but the meat most often eaten on special days was chicken. On Fridays they ate two fried eggs for dinner; the sea was less than ten miles away, but Coolnaboy was too far from any harbour to get fresh fish. Bessie used to walk with her butter and eggs to Oylegate, where the local shopkeeper exchanged them for tea and sugar. The house had no electricity, and no running water. Bessie did most of the cooking over the open fire, and lit oil lamps and candles in the evenings; water came from a well behind the house. The huge clay and wattle chimney, supported on its jamb wall, projected four feet into the kitchen, where children could stand under it and look up at the stars.

For little girls whose own home was filled with strain, days spent among the gentle rhythms of a farm run by people who had lived on it since childhood were a healing liberation. All three adults in the house were unmarried, although Wat was in love with Lizzie Doyle's older sister, Katie, from Coolamain, and Bessie was courted by a famous Wexford hurler. He was Mike Parker, little Mairéad's uncle, and he managed the neighbouring farm at Martingale after his brother died. Bessie was thirty-two in 1925, but while Mary Kate Whitty still lived upstairs, needing care of the most intimate kind, she had to stay in Coolnaboy. She could not bring a husband to live there either, for the farm could support only one family, and since Wat had inherited it, custom ruled that his wife must live there when he married. It would be ten more years before Bessie could marry and move to Kilmuckridge, and until she did, Wat could not marry. Mike Parker, in any case, was responsible for his own two elderly aunts, and could not move while they lived. Whatever she may have felt about her own situation, Bessie was selfless and cheerful, welcoming and generous to the Dublin children, and they loved her. Despite her limited resources, 'she was very fond of giving away money', especially when poor people came to the farm looking for help.

The Bagot stories make only passing mention of the children's aunt in the country, but in 'Stories of Africa', the bishop remembers the gentle generosity of Mrs Kelly, Delia's grandmother, who used to watch for him to come along the lane for his breakfast after he had said Mass: 'I could feel her smiling as I came along down the lane. God bless her kind heart. She was never ashamed to show you that you were welcome, never ashamed, never afraid. She was very gentle' [SA 293]. Many details and sequences in

Maeve's fiction correspond with disturbing, if sometimes misleading, precision to facts selected from her childhood and her family's history. In fact Una Brennan's grandmother never lived in Coolnaboy.[11]

The bishop in 'Stories of Africa' has been an exile for all his adult life, as Maeve was:

> But the kind of exile he felt, living inside his own body and dragging along while the priest within him strode proudly, that was an entirely different kind of exile — somebody inconsolable and stubborn who was not intelligent enough to understand the earthly sameness between his own and other countries and who therefore in bewilderment tormented himself about the *difference*. Or you could say that an exile was a person who knew of a country that made all other countries seem strange.

The place that has stayed with the bishop throughout his exile is Poulbwee — Maeve's Coolnaboy — and the woman whose kindness has stayed with him all his life is almost certainly modelled on Maeve's memory of Bessie.

Delia Bagot misses her children while they are away, and prepares an elaborate welcome for them, with a special cake, and all the flowers from the garden cut and placed around the house. But when weeks remain until their return, she feels so unmoored that she cannot eat. Putting on the light in their empty room, she suddenly sees her shadow on the wall and realises that although she and her mother had not looked alike, their shadows do, and that her mother's shadow is there on the wall, appearing and disappearing at the touch of a light switch. She goes downstairs, consoled profoundly by what she has seen, and prepares a meal for herself: 'She felt very hopeful all of a sudden. It was wonderful how seeing that shadow had raised her spirits. It was wonderful knowing that the shadow was upstairs and that it would never go away. It was almost like having someone in the house' [SA 254].

Maeve felt accepted and free in the sunlit spaciousness of Coolnaboy; she ran happily through the streets of Wexford, 'making intricacies among the slowly moving bicycles and cars', but whatever its compromises and disjunctions, only the small angular house in Ranelagh, where she lived with her parents, sisters and animals, was home. The last piece of writing she ever published appeared in *The New Yorker* on 5 January 1981, the day before her sixty-fourth birthday. It was written in New York, when her mind was deeply troubled, but in it she returns once more to Cherryfield Avenue, to a time when she was about eight:

> Yesterday afternoon, as I walked along Forty-second Street directly across from Bryant Park, I saw a three-cornered shadow on the pavement in

of the emotional climate in her childhood home – makes details stand out with violent clarity. Her descriptions of the houses she lived in and visited, and the accounts she gives of certain events, are vivid and full of authority, and many are independently attested as true to fact. This should not, however, reduce the historical figures who were her relatives to the roles she has written for them. The Derdons and the Bagots of Maeve's fiction remain frozen in their twisted postures of mutual incomprehension, but her parents, Bob and Una, living in Cherryfield Avenue, moved on. Their son Robert was born when Maeve was eleven. Much of her fiction, however, deals with little girls aged eight and nine, as she returns again and again to a seam of memory that runs through the middle of the 1920s in Ireland.

By 1925, the poachers-turned-gamekeepers who were the Free State government, along with the diehard republicans who opposed them, were middle-aged. For members of Sinn Féin, excluded from public administration by their own policies, and watching the membership and revenues of their organisation steadily dwindling after an initial burst of energy in 1923, the sense of unreality must have been considerable as the Cumann na nGaedheal government got on with the business of governing.[4] In July 1925, the Shannon Electricity Act gave the go-ahead for the hydroelectric development agreed in February 1924 with the Siemens Schuckert Company of Berlin, to make feasible the delivery of electric power to rural areas. On the first day of 1926, the new Dublin Broadcasting Station, 2RN (later Radio Éireann), began transmission.

The Christmas and New Year period was always special for Maeve, perhaps because her own birthday fell on 6 January, the Feast of the Three Kings (also called 'Little Christmas' or 'Women's Christmas' in Ireland). In the frugal 1920s, when streets were dark, houses were cold and food plain, and almost everyone was a churchgoing Christian, the twelve days of Christmas were marked out dramatically by song, firelight, candlelight, prayer and an abundance of sweet, spiced food. In the last piece she published, written when the past had become much more vivid to her than the present, Maeve focused on a New Year's Eve when she was a little girl and 'something marvelous happened' on Cherryfield Avenue:

> [I]n the late afternoon word went around from house to house that a minute or so before midnight we would all step out into our front gardens, or even into the street, leaving the front doors open, so that the light streamed out after us, and there we would wait to hear the bells ringing in the New Year. I nearly went mad with excitement and happiness. I know I jumped for joy. That New Year's Eve was one of the great occasions of our lives. [*LWL* 268]

Maeve's birthday was the last day of the holidays. In 1926, she was nine. The 'birthdays of all of us were celebrated with presents in the morning and a very special birthday-cake high tea in the evening', she wrote [*LWL* 267–8]. The cake would have been home-made: only on the most intimidating occasions, like the visit of a bishop, would the married women of that time have bought a cake [*SA* 280]. Very likely, Una baked a pair of sponge cakes in shallow round tins, and sandwiched them together with whipped cream and home-made jam; the top might have been iced for a birthday, or simply dusted with icing sugar. A special birthday 'tea' would have been the family's evening meal, eaten at 5.30 or 6 p.m. in the back sitting-room, around a table set with a starched white cloth and fine china. The butter would be shaped into 'curly balls' between two wooden butter-pats for the occasion, and presented in glass dishes. Father and mother might start with a small savoury course, perhaps a slice of ham with a tomato, or a boiled egg – the sort of food Rose Derdon prepares for Hubert's tea – but children would work up from plain, home-made bread-and-butter to bread with butter and jam – perhaps the raspberry, damson or gooseberry jam Rose Derdon makes – then scones or buns, or a fruit bread with butter, with the birthday cake coming at the end.

After tea on the evening of Maeve's ninth birthday, the Ranelagh branch of Sinn Féin held a special meeting in Rathmines Town Hall, where the speakers included Seán Lemass, Constance Markievicz, Seán MacEntee and Éamon de Valera. Always a master of abstraction as a way of diverting the attention of an audience, de Valera began his long speech with an exhortation to nationalists to save the Irish language before it was too late; he then moved on to the need for sobriety among the young men of Ireland, and bewailed the state of the nation and the economy, advancing statistics to show that the government's talk of prosperity was mere propaganda. Laying all the blame on those who had signed the Treaty, he advocated magnanimity towards them, and then indicated that he would be prepared to enter the Dáil if the oath of allegiance to the Crown were removed.[5] This last was nothing less than a total reversal of Sinn Féin's policy since the Civil War. It caused shock and consternation, but for those republicans who wished to hold more than merely ideological positions, it must have seemed like the only move that could break the stalemate.

From 9 to 11 March 1926, at the Rotunda, Dublin, Sinn Féin held an extraordinary *ard-fheis*, or party congress, with more than five hundred delegates, to discuss the new development. At the end of the meeting, de Valera resigned as president and was replaced in the chair by Mary MacSwiney, leader of those who would not hear of compromise. Afterwards, 'a great hush descended on the party' as it attempted to come to terms with the schism between those of its members who would bend and those who would not.[6] Bob, of course, sided with de Valera. On 16 May, de Valera launched his new party, Fianna Fáil (the Soldiers of Destiny), at a meeting in the La Scala Theatre, in Prince's Street, Dublin. Over the months that followed, increasing numbers left Sinn Féin to join Fianna Fáil, and efforts were revived to start a newspaper. Once again, Bob Brennan was given a central role, and a full-time job.

In an undated typescript memoir headed 'The Start of the *Irish Press*', Bob describes the newspaper project, of which he was appointed organiser.[7] With two secretaries, he established an office in Dame Street. It was decided that a company should be set up with a capital of £200,000, half to be raised in the United States, and the rest in Ireland in £1 shares, subscribed in five instalments. Quotas were established for each parliamentary constituency; local committees were set up, and thousands of people, even in the poorest parts of Ireland, scraped together the money to buy a single share. They paid two shillings on application; five shillings on allotment; five shillings two months later; four shillings two months after that, and a final four shillings after a further nine months. (None of these investors ever received a dividend.) Among the leading businessmen who made up the board of directors was the Wexford industrialist Philip Pierce, and over the next few years, Bob travelled all over the country with him in his Rolls-Royce, 'at that time a novelty in Ireland', as he notes, with considerable understatement. Perhaps this was the inspiration for the car in which Mrs Sheffield Smith takes Lily and Margaret Bagot for a drive while the bishop visits their mother in 'Stories of Africa'.

In the general election of June 1927, the 'conditionally abstentionist' Fianna Fáil party won forty-four seats, against Cumann na nGaedheal's forty-seven; the depleted Sinn Féin party won only five. That August, de Valera led his party into Dáil Éireann. Shortly afterwards, when a by-election was called in County Dublin, Bob became a candidate. A flyer dated 15 August 1927 is headed, 'Brennan stands for Peace Unity Progress', and pledges that Fianna Fáil will remove 'the ever-present menace of Civil War and disturbance'. At a second general election, in September, smaller parties were routed as Cumann na nGaedheal held on to a majority, but Fianna Fáil won a further thirteen seats. The new party settled down to learn about parliamentary democracy, preparing itself to govern.

Meanwhile de Valera had begun his fund-raising drive in the United States. He and Frank Gallagher were in the US from March to May 1927, and again for six weeks from December. Gallagher's diaries and letters describe the crowds that gathered and the wads of cash that were subscribed at meetings from coast to coast, as de Valera reactivated his 1919 networks among Irish-Americans. Ernie O'Malley was already in the US, travelling and speaking about his IRA experiences, collecting money for the new newspaper while writing *On Another Man's Wound*, his memoir of the Anglo-Irish War. De Valera's first trip raised funds for Fianna Fáil, but the second was explicitly in aid of the newspaper project, and channelled substantial funds into his personal control.[8]

Bob was not elected to the Dáil. Una was pregnant and on 24 April 1928, when she was almost forty and Bob was forty-seven, Robert Patrick was born. In 'The Barrel of Rumors' [*SA* 30–6], Maeve's baby brother is Robert, but while they still lived in Ireland the Brennans called their son 'Pat', or 'Padens', possibly a version of the Irish 'Páidín' ('little Pat'), the name he was called in his Irish-speaking primary school. Later, in the United States, he too would be known as Bob.

Una may have found it difficult to care for an infant along with her other children, as well as running the house, especially as Bob was so frequently away. Maeve and Derry could spend a month of the summer in County Wexford, but the new school year would bring a demanding timetable, along with coughs and colds, puddles and raincoats, and the need to set fires and clean out firegrates. Una was a gentle and loving mother, but boarding-schools were widely regarded as offering the 'best' education, and she herself had attended one. At the end of the summer of 1929, when Robert Patrick was sixteen months old, Maeve, aged twelve, and Derry, almost eleven, started at boarding-school in Kilcullen, County Kildare, twenty-seven miles from Dublin.

The bus from Dublin to Kilcullen took about an hour, travelling through Naas towards the flat horse-racing country of the Curragh, until it crossed the Liffey on one of the river's many loops through County Kildare. From the bridge, the road climbed between two rows of small shops to a cross-roads at the edge of the village, and there, on the right-hand corner, behind an iron gate, stood the long, grey flat-fronted buildings of the chapel, convent and school with their separate entrances, and nineteen windows in a long row on the second floor. Una handed over her daughters to the care of Sister Mary Agnes and Sister Mary Stephanie, then caught the bus back to Dublin, where seventeen-year-old Emer had been left in charge of the baby.

Maeve kept the letters Una wrote to her at boarding-school.[9] They all begin, 'My dearest little Maeve and Der'. Una hopes the girls are happy, and sends them parcels from time to time with treats. Maeve is clearly the one who is expected to read the letters, and convey their messages to her sister. Her mother writes, '. . . also Maeve get Der a badge for her gym dress, I know she wants it.' In her short story, 'The Devil in Us' [*SA* 47–55], and again in a piece called 'Lessons and Lessons and Then More Lessons'

[*LWL* 220–4], Maeve recalls the Cross and Passion College. A proof copy of 'The Devil in Us', dated 9 April 1953, even gives Sister Agnes and Sister Stephanie their real names, although by the time the story appeared in print on 3 July 1954, they had been changed to Veronica and Hildegarde.[10] The school had about sixty students, all girls, aged from seven to eighteen. They wore navy-blue uniform dresses, with long black stockings and black shoes. Women from later generations who attended the school remember the locked, glass-fronted bookcase that housed the school library, just as Maeve describes it, and the long walks in crocodile away from the village and among the fields through the 'flat and spiritless countryside' of County Kildare's stud farms.[11] Secondary schooling was a privilege available to only a small proportion of girls in Ireland, and many of those at Cross and Passion would have been the daughters of well-to-do farmers, as Una Brennan had been in her Loreto days, when she was Anastasia Bolger. Maeve's friend Gardner Botsford mentions that on her twelfth birthday she was given a riding crop, 'because she loved horses so much, even though her family could never . . . have afforded to keep one'.[12] Perhaps she had asked for it in anticipation of going to boarding-school. In their first year, the girls slept in a brand-new extension with central heating, and each had a cubicle with her own basin and cupboard.

All seems to have gone reasonably well for Maeve at first. The school laid great emphasis on religion and on sin, but so did the rest of Irish society at that time. For all the optimism the *Irish Times* expressed in 1925 about the Free State's 'emerging from the darkness into the sunshine', the 1920s had been a grim time. Lacking the modern factories that might have driven new prosperity, the cities south of the border were notorious for their slums. Poverty was widespread in rural areas too, and they suffered a constant haemorrhage of emigration, especially of young unmarried women and men. Economic caution and social conservatism among the better-off Catholic farmers and their relatives, now the leaders of society, fostered a culture of denial and silence after the unforgettable horrors of the Civil War. The same factors discouraged early marriage, and, by extension, sex, and even romance. The Irish Free State was not alone in seeking to 'turn back the tide of filth', which many in Europe saw advancing in the aftermath of the Great War, but its moves to regulate morality and the media had a decidedly sectarian slant. Private divorce bills (the only kind of divorce available) became illegal in 1925, much to the disgust of W. B. Yeats, who spoke eloquently in the Senate against the move. Catholic bishops and clergy fulminated against the evils of jazz, the dangers of immodest dress, and condemned even the most innocent of sexual relationships outside marriage – what they called company-keeping. The number of Protestants in the population continued to fall; red pillar-boxes were painted green, and Catholic Ireland gloried in its insularity.[13]

Nineteen twenty-nine marked the fiftieth anniversary of an apparition of the Virgin Mary at Knock, County Mayo, with a large increase in pilgrimages to the shrine. In June, the Free State issued its first commemorative postage stamps, celebrating the centenary of Catholic Emancipation. The fifteen-hundredth anniversary of Saint Patrick's first arrival in Ireland with the Christian message was also approaching, in 1932. An application had been made to Rome some two years earlier to hold a commemorative Eucharistic Congress, and permission was now granted. Throughout almost two centuries of agitation for Irish independence, Saint Patrick had been a figure around whom both Protestants and Catholics could assemble, but now he was to be defined once and for all as Catholic.[14] On 16 July 1929, again despite strong opposition from W. B. Yeats and others in the Senate and elsewhere, the Censorship of Publications Act became law. One of the first books to be banned was Margaret Mead's *Coming of Age in Samoa*, published the previous year: despite its name, the Free State would be neither an island of sun-warmed idleness and sexual experimentation, nor a place where the contemplation of alternative ways of living would be encouraged.

Maeve's story 'The Barrel of Rumors', published in February 1954, seems to refer to the late summer of 1929. She was 'about twelve'; the baby is described as 'about two', but he was not yet old enough to have much hair or talk intelligibly (Robert Patrick would have been sixteen months old in August 1929). The Poor Clares' monastery is on Simmonscourt Road, near the RDS in Ballsbridge: a convent of enclosed nuns who conduct a life of prayer and silence, speaking only during their daily recreation.[15] At the end of the 1920s, when Catholicism dominated Irish life and thousands of young women entered convents, enclosed orders captured the imagination in a special way, and rumours about them abounded. It was typical of devout women like Una to take parcels of food to the monastery for the nuns' support, or to send their daughters instead when they were old enough (one of Una's letters to Maeve and Derry in Kilcullen mentions that 'Emer and the baby went to the poor Clares today').[16] It was equally typical for the sisters to offer prayers in return, along with medals and holy pictures, and to talk to young girls about the possibility that they too might 'have a vocation'.

In the story, Maeve places her baby brother in the 'turn', as the nuns call the rotating barrel that allows them to receive gifts of food, and sends him to visit them on the other side of the wall that separates them from the world. Who could invent the detail of placing the parcel of food on the 'warmed-up spot' where the baby had sat, 'matter-of-fact and friendly', for his trip into the unknown? 'The Barrel of Rumors' is a simple enough story, yet layers of troubled understanding show through it (and its title), in a way that suggests they were already present in 1929. A vocation for the religious life was something every young Catholic girl was expected to consider seriously. The mystery that veiled the apparently ordered, quiet life of the cloister was never far away. For girls approaching puberty among the middle class, its mystery could seem more accessible and welcoming, and to offer greater prospects of achievement and autonomy, than those of sex and procreation. Mysteries hold terrors, however, and a girl who became a nun risked vanishing for ever into a 'crevasse in Irish family life', as the Derdons' son John did in 'An Attack of Hunger' when he became a priest [*SA* 148]. Pink and cheerful baby Robert may enter the nuns' world until he is three, and still return, but he arrives among them fully clothed, bathed and brushed, and he cannot bring any message back from the other side. Maeve's first, alarmed reaction to the idea of putting her baby brother in the barrel reflects her fear that he is simply to be given to the nuns, like a packet of salt, or a cake, never to be seen again. Babies are what those women most significantly lack, but that fact is never mentioned.

Living in New York, and working at *The New Yorker*, Maeve used to make hilarious capital of the fact that her boarding-school had been called Cross and Passion. During her childhood in Ireland, of course, passion meant only the sufferings of Christ on Calvary. Images of blood and suffering were everywhere: convent schools were decorated with portraits of teenage virgin martyrs, and all Catholic churches displayed the fourteen pictures or carvings of the Stations of the Cross. In the kitchen or hall of most houses, a small red light burned day and night before a picture of the Sacred Heart: the adult Jesus pulling back his garments to show the wounded heart in his bloody chest. (In Maeve's story 'A Free Choice', one of these lamps in the wealthy Ramsays' house suddenly goes out, frightening Rose.) As in other Catholic countries, such images were entirely domesticated, and went unremarked, except in the observations of Protestants and in children's nightmares; they feature strongly in the writings of James Joyce, however.[17]

It has been suggested that the nineteenth-century Irish Gothic fiction that culminated in Bram Stoker's *Dracula* owes its origins to Protestant unease in an overwhelmingly Catholic society. Transylvanian and British settings obscure the Irish origin of much important Gothic fiction. The connection went unnoticed in the early years of Irish independence, but began to provoke serious discussion at the end of the twentieth century, when critics pointed out the relevance of Gothic fiction to nineteenth-century Ireland.[18] Tod Browning's film, *Dracula*, with Bela Lugosi in the title role, was released in 1931, as was *Frankenstein*, with Boris Karloff. By contrast with its attitude to sex in film and literature, the Free State regarded the Gothic as an aspect of modern international culture that could be welcomed and embraced, its erotic aspects sufficiently concealed.[19] On 23 April 1932, the *Irish Press* carried a small headline at the bottom of its front page: 'Uncensored Film: Why Free State Board Passed Frankenstein'. The article referred to the Karloff film, banned in Belfast, but passed by the Free State Board of Appeal after it had been rejected by the censor. It quoted Senator J. T. O'Farrell, chairman of the Free State Censorship Appeal Board as saying, 'We failed to discover anything of a very terrible nature in the film, and were unanimous in passing it for exhibition.'

Speculations about nuns sleeping in their coffins in Maeve's 'The Barrel of Rumors' echo the discussion of the Cistercian Abbey at Mount Melleray in Joyce's short story 'The Dead'. In that story, the Protestant Mr Browne is 'astonished to hear that the monks never spoke, got up at two in the morning and slept in their coffins'.[20] But Joyce had read Bram Stoker, and Maeve had undoubtedly seen the *Dracula* film, though she knew Joyce's work well by the time she wrote her own story. Images in 'The Barrel of Rumors', of cells and dormitories, and coffin lids left leaning against the wall, 'like hockey-sticks and bicycles', must be drawn from her experience of boarding-school. The irony of that vision was not unique to her, of course: it was implicit in the culture all around her, and explicit in the jokes her father made. On the one hand, the immense authority of the Catholic Church could, as this story relates, calmly forbid a woman ever to see or speak to her daughter again, although she might live nearby, so that for fourteen years she would strain to hear the girl's voice among the choir of nuns; on the other, the delight in language and repartee, the sense of the ridiculous, which offered a child surreal images of nuns walking about carrying coffins under their arms, was capable of subverting all and every authority.

So thoroughly was sex expunged from any discourse that might touch a convent schoolgirl that Cross and Passion students 'grew up on murder'.[21] Like horror films, murder stories reiterated received ideas about good and evil, and were judged appropriate reading for young people. Maeve's father wrote fiction and drama that dealt with murder, along with stolen jewels, missing works of art, long-lost relatives and the other paraphernalia of 1920s detective stories, and some of his writings dipped into the surreal. Although they steered firmly away from sex, and indeed from love, they were always light-hearted and usually funny. The vision the boarding-school offered of the world its girls might inhabit, however, was neither joyful nor kindly, and Maeve hated her memories of Cross and Passion. 'The Devil in Us' describes the school's penitential food and the deadly narrowness of the constant search for sin, with its consequence of guilt and apprehension.

'Lessons and Lessons and Then More Lessons' was published in 1962, but tells of an incident from the early 1950s, in the University Restaurant on Eighth Street, in Greenwich Village, where the author sat with a pile of books and a martini at three in the afternoon. The piece ends with her realisation, when two nuns walked into the restaurant, that '. . . my right hand, with the empty martini glass in it, had somehow gone under the table and was hiding there behind the tablecloth. It was the moment of no comment. It was the moment of no comment' [*LWL* 224]. The repetition marks a thud of recognition.

Maeve may have been culturally deprived at boarding-school, but she seems to have taken part in at least one school play: Shakespeare's *A Midsummer-Night's Dream*.[22] Meanwhile her father and many of the family's friends were writers and keen theatregoers, and in Dublin she read books, saw films, and went to the theatre. In her story 'The Clever One', she sat in the back garden with her sister, both of them still very young: '"When I grow up," I said to Derry, "I'm going to be a famous actress. I'll act in the Abbey Theatre, and I'll be in the pictures, and I'll go around to all the schools and teach all the teachers how to recite"' [*SA* 60]. Derry's succinct response, '"Don't go getting any notions into your head"', is typical of the younger sister in several of Maeve's stories; its language, unfortunately, was that of many Irish adults at the time and for years after.

Notwithstanding the prevailing dourness, 1928 had marked the first production by Dublin's new Gate Theatre Studio – *Peer Gynt* at the Peacock Theatre – as well as the beginning of Taibhdhearc na Gaillimhe, an Irish-language theatre in Galway. Both were overseen by a twenty-nine-year-old Englishman-turned-Irishman called Micheál Mac Liammóir, actor, painter and writer. With his partner Hilton Edwards, Mac Liammóir brought a cosmopolitan refinement to the Irish stage and injected a new gorgeousness into the myths of nationalism on which Maeve had been reared.[23] 'Brilliant but dangerous' was supposed to have been John Charles McQuaid's description of Edwards and Mac Liammóir. Shortly to become president of Blackrock College, McQuaid would wield enormous influence in public life, even before becoming Archbishop of Dublin in 1940. The story of Dublin's culture for the next seventy years could be told as an epic conflict between the forces he and the two actors represented: McQuaid, the aseptic, asexual authoritarian appeared to hold all the cards, yet by the end of the twentieth century the legacy left by the two playful gay Englishmen was the more cherished and less problematical.

In Maeve's 'The Beginning of a Long Story', eight-year-old Ellen is reading a book about 'the adventures of a fifteen-year-old Spanish princess in a strict girls' school in England'. In their second year at Cross and Passion, instead of having private cubicles, Maeve and Derry slept upstairs in older, less comfortable, dormitories with communal bathrooms. Boarding-schools were staple settings for English adventure fiction, and Maeve seems to have tried strenuously to adapt her own school to a fictional ideal. Government policy had begun to encourage the teaching of Irish, and the nuns embraced the new policy, promoting its use throughout the school. The Irish language had been a linchpin of the movement that had brought Maeve's parents together. It had transformed ordinary lives into stories that were as good as any found in books, but it was also what made those adventures with secret codes and daring escapes unique to Ireland, and bound them into a powerful myth of national identity and destiny. Maeve was in her element, as her niece relates:

> [S]he started a secret society and organised a group of girls to be 'Gaelic Leaguers'. The girls bought Irish books with their own money to teach themselves Irish, and had secret signs. Because the society was secret and the girls would not divulge the purpose of it, they got in big trouble. The day girls were expelled. Maeve was not expelled. She was a boarder. The irony is that the nuns would have strongly approved of the purpose of the society had they known what it was.[24]

Maeve has left no account of this episode, but it tallies with a note by an interviewer for *Time* magazine in 1974: 'She began secretly writing a journal and poems as a girl in convent school. "But", she later remarked, "the nuns found them."' 'The Devil in Us', about the nuns' childish but vicious persecution of four girls, conveys the growing unhappiness of Maeve's second year at boarding-school. A letter she wrote to William Maxwell from London in 1957 suggests that it was substantially true, for Maeve recalled that she had never felt so holy as she did after the nuns in Kilcullen explained to her in public that she was 'damned, damned, damned'.[25]

Although she escaped expulsion, Maeve's (and Derry's) time at Cross and Passion came to an abrupt end before the close of their second year. Things were going well for their father. Bob had taken a walking tour alone through Cork and Kerry in summer 1929, and returned refreshed to his fund-raising campaign. The Wall Street crash in October had of course affected the newspaper project, but arriving in New York only weeks later, de Valera had been able to raise £60,000 in six months. By spring 1930, the campaign had exceeded its target, and a limited company had been set up; the board of directors had acquired the old Tivoli Theatre on Burgh Quay to use as a premises, and had begun converting it for newspaper production.

Bob and Una had at last made the final payment on the loan of £300, which they had taken out to stock Summerville twenty years earlier in Wexford, and Bob had written a play.[26]

On 19 May 1930, *Bystander* opened at the Abbey Theatre. Set in 'Blackmoor Prison', it drew on Bob's considerable experience of British jails, and offered Dublin theatregoers a refreshing novelty: a new play by an Irish writer, but with a non-Irish theme. Cries of 'Man away, Sir!', 'Alright, Sir!' punctuate the script – words that the many former prisoners who saw the play must have recalled from the time when gates were opened and shut on them throughout the day.[27] The production was by Paul Farrell, who also starred as Ebenezer Jones, a clerk who dreams of freedom after twenty-three years trapped in the routine of the prison service. Mary Manning played Lady Sterne, wife of the prison governor, while Brefni O'Rorke, called in at short notice, played Bystander, a laconic, urbane newcomer who sets all the prison's certainties in uproar. On the opening night, Rosamond Jacob, feminist nationalist and friend of Hanna Sheehy-Skeffington, drew Bob on to the stage to receive the applause of a delighted audience. She wrote to him the following day: 'Dear Bob, Hearty congratulations! I hope you were pleased, but why be so coy? It was hard manual work to get you out; my arms nearly broke off with it . . .'[28]

Critics praised the play lavishly, singling out Paul Farrell for commendation. Sheehy-Skeffington, writing in the republican newspaper *An Phoblacht* on 22 May, called his part 'one of the greatest roles played in the Abbey'. On a tiny postcard addressed to Bob in Cherryfield Avenue (but without a house number), she wrote: 'I enjoyed Bystander immensely. It's really wonderful & a glorious contribution to prison literature. Paul surpassed himself & Brefni suited wonderfully. It ought to have several runs. Am urging all I know to go & see it. HSS'.[29] Sheehy-Skeffington had herself spent time in Holloway Prison in 1918. In Wexford, the *Free Press* published a photograph of Bob, describing *Bystander* as 'probably the most successful production of the Abbey Players for a long time past'.

Maeve and Derry were to have time off from school to see the play, which would run for only a week, and the nuns in Kilcullen had been asked to put them on the bus to Dublin: Maeve was thirteen, and Derry eleven. Maeve was sick, however, and Una was dismayed to discover that Derry had been sent on the bus alone, and without appropriate clothing. Derry did not return to school. Instead Emer, now twenty, was dispatched to pack up both girls' belongings and bring Maeve home. Maeve turned out to have blood poisoning, caused by a whitlow on her finger, which was then treated in Dublin.[30]

Maeve and Derry were next enrolled in a pioneering Irish-speaking day school, with no nuns. Louise Gavan Duffy, born in Nice in 1884, was the youngest daughter of Irish rebel turned colonial statesman Sir Charles Gavan Duffy and his third wife, Louise Hall. At the time of her birth, her father was sixty-eight and had retired from public life in Australia to live in France. Louise was brought up bilingual in French and English, and first heard Irish spoken when she came to Dublin for her father's funeral in 1903. On returning to Ireland in 1907 to attend university, she set about learning the language, with considerable success. With Mary Maguire, who later married the poet Pádraic Colum and emigrated to New York with him in 1914, she taught in Patrick Pearse's short-lived school for girls, Scoil Íte (St Ita's). Gavan Duffy spent Easter Week 1916 in the GPO, providing food for the insurrectionists – although she told Pearse frankly that she disagreed with their action, as it was bound to fail. Then in 1917 she opened a new school, Scoil Bhríghde (St Brigid's, now spelt Scoil Bhríde), at her home on St Stephen's Green, to offer secondary education to girls through the medium of Irish, teaching Irish history and fostering 'a proper spirit of nationalism'.[31] Within a year she had more than a hundred pupils. Her philosophy of education echoed Pearse's own, growing out of the same cosmopolitan humanism that had informed the language revival in the early years of the century, and emphasising the development of the whole person. Former colleagues and pupils have left many testimonials to Louise Gavan Duffy's vision and influence as an educator. Teaching by example and persuasion, and instilling a love of learning without resorting to punishment or fear, she laid great emphasis on voluntary work for charity as well as for the Catholic missions, to which she was devoted. Scoil Bhríghde was almost unique among Irish Catholic secondary schools in being run entirely by laywomen, and was one of the first outside the Gaeltacht to teach all subjects through Irish. It also encouraged the use of the language outside the classroom: Maeve's class-mates later wrote to her in Irish.

Bob had known Louise Gavan Duffy since the early 1920s, when her house was one of the safe places where the staff of the *Irish Bulletin* could meet: Erskine Childers described its raiding and looting by British forces on 3 April 1920.[32] (In *The Toledo Dagger*, Bob's fictional detective, van Duyven, stays in the Villa Marguerite, on the French Riviera – the name of the Gavan Duffys' house in Nice.) In 1926, faced with severe financial problems, Scoil Bhríghde sought recognition by the Department of Education, and became a national school so that the Department of Education undertook to pay its teachers' salaries. The kindergarten admitted boys as well as girls, while the senior classes prepared girls for Matriculation. In 1931, through an imagin-ative co-operation between the Department of Education and University College Dublin, the school moved from 55 Pembroke Road to 19 Earlsfort

Terrace, a stone's throw from the university, where the number of pupils eventually reached 300.[33] This former townhouse, its classrooms heated by open fires, was where Maeve and Derry would go to school for the remainder of their time in Ireland, and Robert Patrick would join them there when he was four. It was an easy trip on the number 11 tram or on the train from Ranelagh to Harcourt Street, and a short walk from there to Earlsfort Terrace.

Maeve was happy at Scoil Bhríghde, where Louise Gavan Duffy herself taught English, French and Religious Knowledge. Among Maeve's papers at the University of Delaware – carried to America and kept through many moves – are school reports for herself, Derry and Robert Patrick, and photographs taken at the school. Maeve's reports cover the years 1930–1934; Derry's are for the first two years, and one report for Robert Patrick, or 'Páidín', shows that he attended Scoil Bhríghde in 1932/33.[34] Another box of Maeve's papers contains numerous mementoes of a religious retreat with her classmates in 1933, along with a single sheet of letterhead paper, dated during the school holidays, 30 December 1931, a week before her fifteenth birthday. On it is written: 'Dear Miss Brennan, I have written my name three times with pleasure. Jack B. Yeats'.[35] Almost thirty years later, in the *Irish Press*, Bob wrote a short memoir of the painter, whom he had known well. Using Maeve's meeting with him to illustrate Yeats's generosity, he gave a vivid picture of his daughter as a teenager:

> [L]ong before I had met him socially, I used to see him nearly every Saturday when I went to the RDS Library. At the time, I lived in Cherryfield Avenue, Ranelagh, and, a few hundred yards away, in Marlborough Road, he lived. One day my daughter, Maeve, raced in in a great state of excitement.
>
> 'Do you know, Daddy,' she cried, 'I was talking to Mr Yeats and look what he gave me.'
>
> She had followed him into his house to ask for his autograph and he gave her, not merely his autograph, but a hastily drawn sketch which she still keeps by her.[36]

Maeve spent four years at Scoil Bhríghde. Her marks – except in mathematics – were good from the beginning, and in English they were excellent: Louise Gavan Duffy commented glowingly on Maeve's interest and aptitude in her annual reports. Gavan Duffy's teaching must have laid the groundwork too for Maeve's lifelong engagement with French language and literature. Her marks faltered a little here at first (down from 72 per cent in her first year to 49 per cent in her second), but Gavan Duffy's former pupils agree that she had only to raise an eyebrow or express some disappointment to make them behave and strive to do better. In eighth class, the highest grade, where Maeve would spend two years, she worked at her French and made steady progress.[37] She had a very sweet voice, her teachers noted, and was good at singing.

Eithne Keegan (now Kiberd), was Maeve's classmate, and remembers her as 'very nice, quite jolly' – an easygoing girl who did not play games. Eithne herself excelled at camogie – a girls' version of the men's fast, skilful game of hurling, played with smaller sticks than the men's. It was a nationalist alternative to the hockey played at schools like Cross and Passion. In 'The Devil in Us', Maeve writes, 'I detested hockey and basketball and all the other sports we were expected to practise', but among her papers is a photograph of twelve smiling Scoil Bhríghde girls in gymslips and white blouses, with their camogie sticks. Maeve is not included, of course, but she has written the players' names on the back. Two of them wear the *fáinne*, a flat, ring-shaped, gold pin in the lapel that denotes proficiency in speaking Irish; it was the highest level of a graduated system of incentives to use Irish in the school. A later photograph shows Maeve herself wearing it proudly.

In summer, although the Department of Education made no provision for educational travel, teachers at Scoil Bhríghde took the girls on expeditions outside the city. Eithne Kiberd remembers climbing the Sugarloaf in County Wicklow; others recall trips with Miss Gavan Duffy to the archaeological monuments of the Boyne Valley and to Carton House in County Kildare. In the autumn and spring there were outings to the National Gallery, the National Museum, and to the cathedrals and other important buildings of the capital, as well as visits to the theatre.

Between 1930 and 1933, under Micheál Mac Liammóir's direction, An Comhar Drámuidheacta (the Gaelic Players, founded in 1923), presented twenty-seven plays in Irish at the Gate Theatre. They included works by Molière, Chekhov, Sheridan, Shaw and Eugene O'Neill, translated by Mac Liammóir and others, as well as several new plays by young writers.[38] Students from Scoil Bhríghde were regular attenders, and some even acted in the plays. The Gate's programme in English was flourishing too, with new plays and classics, splendid costumes designed by Mac Liammóir, and a growing reputation among actors. In 1931, its winter season featured a sixteen-year-old American called Orson Welles in several plays.

Every summer, the girls went back to Coolnaboy and Wexford. Their young cousins Máire, Joe and Ita Bolger were now regular summer visitors to Coolnaboy as well: their mother Ellen, Jim's wife, had caught pneumonia in 1929, and died within a week. Ita's son, the novelist Roddy Doyle, presents his mother's stories of early childhood and those visits in his memoir, *Rory and Ita*.[39] Mary Kate Whitty still lay upstairs in bed, praying and eating peppermints, and Bessie still ministered to her and to everyone else. Sometimes there would be visits to Pouldearg, but Una's brother John had remained unmarried and the house there had begun to look neglected. In Maeve's 'Stories of Africa', the old bishop recalls going back to his own old home, which the story calls Cooldearg:

> My mother was dead and there was only my brother at home. He never married, and I suppose the loneliness got in on his mind. He lost heart. All the time I was there he kept talking about how he was going to sell up the place and go to America. He had already sold off all the stock and all the furniture out of the parlor, furniture that had belonged to our great-grandmother, and before that. [*SA* 293]

Each year, when their visit to Coolnaboy ended, Bessie would drive the Brennan girls into Wexford town in the pony and trap and drop them off at their grandmother's house. Bridget Brennan still lived at the corner of Abbey Street and George Street and kept her shop downstairs, selling sweets, candles, vegetables and other staples. Two of the children's aunts, Tess, the eldest, and Nan, still lived with her. Like Clare and Polly Bagot in 'The Springs of Affection', Tess and her youngest sister, Chrissie, had both married Protestants. John Griffin was a farmer when Tess first met him in her mother's shop, but his family had cut him off when he became a Catholic in order to marry her. He lived with her in the Brennan home and did odd jobs (at one time he was a coal merchant; he also worked as an auxiliary postman). They had no children. In 1930 Tess was fifty-one, and had begun to have the violent headaches that would lead to her spending the rest of her life in hospital. Nan, still unmarried at forty-five, lived there too, although by now she had her own business, and she took care of the household when Tess was unable to. Chrissie and her husband John Williamson had their own home. He was a draper from Northern Ireland, who had inherited the shop where he worked after his employer died; their children were younger than Maeve or Derry.

In the 1901 census, when she was sixteen, Nan Brennan had been described as a dressmaker. Her first training came from her mother, but in 1907, a young woman of her own age, an English-trained dressmaker called Bridget Larkin, married James Sinnott, the head waiter at White's Hotel in Wexford, and they took a lease on a house owned by the hotel at 95 North Main Street.[40] The ground-floor shop was rented to a butcher, but above it was a large room, lit by three tall windows, one of which squinted down Charlotte Street to the harbour. Bridget Sinnott soon opened a dressmaking business there, while she and James and their children lived on the floors above. Nan Brennan served her time as an apprentice to Bridget Sinnott, and the two became firm friends. The business expanded to employ as many as fifteen young women, all of them cutting and tacking (i.e. basting) cloth and working at sewing machines in the same long room.

James Sinnott was as enterprising as his wife. After his marriage, he gave up waiting on tables to run his own chauffeur business – his were the only cars for hire in Wexford at the time. In 1920, the solicitor M. J. O'Connor persuaded him to join him in building a hotel at Rosslare Strand, using timber and glavanised iron recycled from Kinnock's munitions factory in Arklow, County Wicklow. Within ten years he bought out his partner, and became sole proprietor of the Golf Hotel. In 1930, the Sinnotts moved to Rosslare Strand; Bridget gave up her dressmaking business, and Nan Brennan took over the lease of 95 North Main Street.

This was the flat that Maeve described in 'The Springs of Affection', with the workroom 'running the full width of the narrow old house' [*SA* 318], which later becomes Min Bagot's living-room. The life Maeve gives to Min in that story is very like what Nan's was, especially when she lived there full-time after her mother's death, but there were cruel omissions. Nan's sewing and reading are there, and her daily trips to buy a newspaper and food, but Maeve's story leaves out her lifelong involvement in Wexford's cultural and political life, and the affection in which so many people held her. She and Bridget Sinnott went to every show at Wexford's Theatre Royal; Bridget's children called her 'Bren', and regarded her as part of their family (it would have been unthinkable to use her first name, but equally unsatisfactory to call her, as everyone else did, 'Miss Brennan'). Every week, James Sinnott sent a car for her, and Nan spent the weekend by the sea with her friend. In winter, she helped to manage the hotel linens, the two women stitching and mending as they talked. Bridget looked forward to Nan's visits, for life in the hotel could seem monotonous after her lively sewing room in town.

Nan Brennan was resolutely single, showing no interest in men, except as friends (of whom she had many), but she loved clothes, and dressed well.[41] For teenage girls who came to Wexford from the Cross and Passion convent with its relentless self-denial, or indeed from the high-minded bluestocking atmosphere of Scoil Bhríghde, Nan's flat must have been a fascinating place, as Maeve's photographic recall attests. Cherryfield Avenue, two miles from the centre of Dublin, was essentially suburban, but 95 North Main Street, Wexford, with the bustle of the town below its windows, and all the goods and services one might need close at hand, was urban. Fabrics, fashion magazines and patterns lay all around on the long table in the big front room; tucked into the bookcases were programmes from Wexford's many concerts and plays.

And Nan was independent. For her there was no worry about laundering shirts on wet days, or boiling potatoes in time to have a hot dinner on the table at one o'clock. Instead, she prepared ladylike little meals when she was hungry, or had a guest – scrambled eggs on toast, with tea and cake, or sandwiches cut small – and her offerings were always beautifully arranged with fine china and a white tablecloth starched 'like iron'.[42] Her dressmaking work was excellent, but rather than maintain and develop the business Bridget Sinnott had built up, 'dressmaking for the whole county', as Bridget's son remembered it, or employing and training relays of young seamstresses, Nan suited herself, and worked just as much as she wished, often cutting and sewing into the night, but sleeping late the next morning. Those who knew her realised that she was sensitive, and easily hurt: she could speak sharply. They knew that she had wanted to be a teacher, but had not been encouraged: her mother had kept her at home on the day of the examination that would have admitted her to training. Well read and well informed, she used to read the *Financial Times*. Whether or not either of them realised it, Nan Brennan must have been a role model for Maeve years later, when she went to live alone in New York.

Nan was devoted to her brother Bob, and intensely proud of him, as was Maeve. *Bystander* was revived at the Abbey in December 1930, but already there was talk of a new play, this time a comedy, set in Ireland. On 5 November 1930, 'Irish Theatre Notes' in the *Daily Express* quoted the actor Jimmy O'Dea: 'I don't know when I enjoyed reading anything as much as Mr Brennan's new play . . . It is very daring, but great comedy, without a dull second, and it is written with such a rare understanding of the theatre that it acts itself.' On 23 March 1931, Bob's three-act play, *Good Night, Mr O'Donnell*, opened at the Olympia Theatre for a week's run.

The Olympia, a Victorian music hall, was much larger than the Abbey, and *Good Night, Mr O'Donnell* ran twice nightly. Described as a 'Comedy Mystery Drama', and resembling a French farce, it starred Jimmy O'Dea and Harry O'Donovan, with Noel Purcell – a team much beloved of Dublin audiences for decades afterwards. O'Dea was thirty-two. He played Kerryman Jimmie O'Donnell, 'bright and naïve and undoubtedly good-looking', newly arrived in Dublin during Horse Show Week and reduced to sleeping on a shake-down in the drawing-room of Mrs Fennessy's Private Hotel. The script explains that this was formerly the home, first of an English judge called Billington, who unjustly condemned an innocent man to hang and whose guilty ghost haunts the house, and later of Colonel Savage Blunt, who was 'on duty' in Dublin Castle when the Crown Jewels were stolen (in 1907), and who turns out to have been the thief. This fictional hotel was also a safe house for the IRA during the time of the Black and Tans, and still contains a secret room. The action all takes place in the drawing-room, with rival villains prowling through as Jimmie O'Donnell tries to sleep. There are exits and entrances through door and window; the secret room and the jewels are discovered, and a marvellously melodramatic housemaid whose long-lost love, last seen 'riding a wild mustang on the plains of Santa Fé', turns up as the investigating policeman – through the window, of course.

By 28 April, Geraldine Dillon, the Brennans' friend and neighbour from their days in Belgrave Road, was writing to Bob from Taibhdhearc na Gaillimhe, the Irish-language theatre in Galway:[43]

> Dear Bob,
> I believe we will be able to do 'Goodnight Mr O'Donnell' all right. Sorry for not writing before but we were in the throes of producing Sierra's 'Two Shepherds' – a good production tho I says it as shouldn't – we will get someone to translate Mr O'Donnell & if it were good enough it would be taken by the Gúm – what business arrangements do you suggest?
> Please let me know
> Yours sincerely,
> Gerry

'The Gúm' is An Gúm, the Irish-language publisher set up by the Department of Education in the mid-1920s to ensure the supply of text-books and reading material for learners and others. Liam Ó Briain, Professor of Romance Languages at University College Galway (UCG) and a leader of the movement to create a theatre in Irish, had persuaded Mac Liammóir to join An Taibhdhearc, and provided plays translated from several European languages. His translation of *Good Night, Mr O'Donnell* opened at the theatre in Middle Street on St Patrick's Day 1932 as *Oidhche Mhaith agat, a Mhic Uí Dhomhnaill.* Writing to Bob, Geraldine Dillon hoped that he would attend, and bring Una, 'if you can persuade her to come'. Una apparently could not be persuaded, but references in Maeve's later correspondence make it clear that she accompanied her father. It was her first time in Galway, and the trip was exciting. Bob was an important figure now, and she was at least as well able as he was to speak and understand Irish. At fifteen, fully in tune with the combination of romantic nationalism and practical creativity that An Taibhdhearc represented, she was old enough to take an intelligent part in adult conversations, but young enough to be impressed. An Taibhdhearc was closely linked to UCG through Liam Ó Briain and Professor of Chemistry Tommy Dillon, Geraldine's husband. Owen McKenna, Professor of Mathematics, was another language activist at the university, and brought his children to An Taibhdhearc's Christmas pantomime each year. His daughter Siobhán was not quite nine in 1932, but she would begin her acting career at An Taibhdhearc as a teenager, and go on to make an international career.[44]

On 9 May, Liam Ó Briain wrote to Bob that he had completed a clean copy of his translation of the play, and sent it to An Gúm. The letter ends:

> 'Twas a marvellous play of its type. The swiftness of it, the direct action of it – even going over a badly-typed copy, correcting in-numerable mistakes, I was enjoying every minute of it. I hope we will be able to revive it this summer, although the man we had playing Jimmie has had a falling-out with someone & left us & one or two others have gone away. But there are always others. I believe when it is available in print & Gaelic dramatic work begins to spread through the country, that it is certain to be performed often & you firstly, & I, very much secondly, can feel we have made Jimmie O'Donnell give the revival a push along. And when it appears, if you have still any influence left with the 'Irish Press', see that it gets a good puff in it, won't you.[45]

Ó Briain was right: *Oidhche Mhaith agat, a Mhic Uí Dhomhnaill* was published by An Gúm (Bob received a princely £5 as an advance on royal-ties), and played in professional and amateur theatre all over Ireland for many years.[46] It was well constructed, funny, totally 'clean', and easily performed in schools and halls, with several roles for young people. It also had the advantage of not being set in a country kitchen. As Jimmy O'Dea had remarked, 'it acts itself'.

A few months later, Maeve herself was on stage. Each year before the Christmas holidays, Scoil Bhríghde performed Douglas Hyde's nativity play *Dráma Breithe Chríost*, an occasion for pupils to donate parcels of their toys and clothing for distribution to Dublin's many poor children, bringing them as gifts to the manger. Maeve played An Dara Bean (The Second Woman), in 1932, just before her sixteenth birthday. Created by Máire O'Neill at the Abbey in 1911, this was one of the play's two leading roles.[47] A photograph among Maeve's papers shows her in the final tableau with her hair loose over her shoulders and covered with a veil.[48]

The first issue of the *Irish Press* had appeared on Saturday, 5 September 1931. Frank Gallagher was its editor, and Bob Brennan the general manager. A front-page photograph showed Mrs Margaret Pearse, mother of the executed Patrick and Willie, setting the presses rolling, as de Valera, Gallagher and Brennan looked on. Also in the picture were Dr Jim Ryan, Fianna Fáil TD (Dáil deputy) for County Wexford (husband of the

Brennans' old friend Máirín Cregan), and Father Gregory, a Franciscan priest. Next door to the Brennans on Cherryfield Avenue, eleven-year-old Hubert Briscoe took a keen interest in the 'dummy' newspapers that preceded the first issue and in the excitement of that day. The paper was a success from the start. As historian Joseph Lee puts it, 'Its ebullient free-wheeling polemical style outraged genteel spirits, but for a stridently popular paper, it descended to the gutter level remarkably rarely'.[49]

The *Irish Press* soon sold twice as many copies daily as the 'quality' *Irish Times*, and easily exceeded its targets. Gallagher, a democrat and republican to his fingertips, was an experienced journalist with a highly developed sense of 'spin'. He trained his staff to disentangle news from propaganda in what they were told, and to pitch the stories they wrote in ways calculated to grab attention and mould minds. He and Bob both revered de Valera, and threw their energies into making *his* newspaper as lively and as trusted as the *Irish Bulletin* had been ten years earlier. Their success translated into results for Fianna Fáil: in February, the party won seventy-two seats in the general election, against Cumann na nGaedheal's fifty-seven, and de Valera became president of the the the Free State's Executive Council.

Perhaps the biggest story the *Irish Press* covered in its first year was the Eucharistic Congress of 1932 – the thirty-first such congress of the Catholic Church – held in Dublin from 22 to 26 June. Originally planned and programmed by the Cosgrave government, it gave de Valera a huge propaganda opportunity – at once a chance to wipe out the stigma of excommunication that still hung over former members of Sinn Féin by showing them acting in close concert with the Church, and an occasion to bring people together from all corners of Ireland in a spectacular rally of national identity. Twenty thousand priests took part, many of them from overseas,[50] but the major attendance came from within Ireland. People who had never left home before made the journey to the congress. Charles McGlinchey, a weaver, tailor and storyteller from near Clonmany, in Inishowen, County Donegal, recalled it twenty years later as one of only two expeditions he had made away from home in his life: 'I raked the fire myself one Saturday morning in 1932 and went to the Eucharistic Congress in Dublin and didn't get back till Monday evening. The fire was living in the rakings all the time.'[51]

Dublin was not a tourist city. The bay was filled with cruise liners, chartered as temporary hotels, but most people could not afford hotels of any kind. Many knew Boston or Glasgow, but not the capital of their own country. Dubliners opened their homes to country relatives and tidied their children out of sight to make room for visitors. In the ancient tradition of pilgrimage, people willingly put up with discomfort, sharing beds and sleeping on floors or in bathtubs. Following the opening ceremonies on

Wednesday there was a men's Mass on Thursday, a women's Mass on Friday, and a children's Mass on Saturday. Charles McGlinchey would have been in time for the final Pontifical High Mass in the Phoenix Park, celebrated by Ireland's Cardinal McRory with cardinals from Europe and America, where the Irish tenor John McCormack, a papal count since 1928, sang César Franck's 'Panis Angelicus' to a crowd estimated at over a million.

Maeve was the only one of the Brennans who attended. School groups were marshalled by colours, and with other senior girls from Scoil Bhríghde, she wore a green hat. She might have preferred to stay at home: Derry and the other junior pupils got a day off school. Hubert Briscoe was a student at Synge Street Christian Brothers' school, where nationalism was as much part of the curriculum as it was in Scoil Bhríghde. Three years younger than Maeve, he was chosen for the choir that sang hymns in Irish before and after the Mass on Saturday. Eighty thousand children attended.[52] Poet Máire Mhac an tSaoi, whose father Seán MacEntee was Minister for Finance, was twelve also. She wore a red-and-white striped cotton dress and a wide-brimmed straw hat, and speaking on radio seventy years later recalled the 'big element of secular triumphalism' that went along with all the devotion, and the 'splendid thread of worldly satisfaction' that ran through the proceedings. Middle-class houses flew yellow-and-white papal flags, but she looked enviously at the glittering altars decked with lights, which adorned tenements in the poorest parts of the city. 'Exultation, happiness, hope' were the emotions she remembered.[53] Maeve gave Cardinal McRory's surname to the garage owner in her story, 'The Morning after the Big Fire'.

Her own first published writing appeared a few months later. Maeve was barely sixteen when the *Irish Press* printed her essay about a 200-year-old collection of pamphlets on Irish economics that she had discovered in Coolnaboy. Burgh Quay was not a happy place, however. As one veteran journalist put it, 'The early years [were] characterised by an odd mixture of passion, devotion, intrigue and penury.'[54]

Hours at the newspaper were long and wages low. Frank Gallagher insisted on the highest standards. Added to his own experience as a working journalist, he had made a fact-finding tour of England after his appointment, interviewing newspaper editors about what would now be called 'best practice', but the directors of the *Irish Press* expected everything to be done on a shoestring. Then early in 1933, sensitive to the opinion of his American investors, de Valera introduced a young 'efficiency expert' called John J. Harrington, who proceeded to alienate many of the newspaper's most valuable workers. Gallagher defended his staff, but found his position increasingly difficult. A folder of his papers in the National Library of Ireland still smells of the cigarettes he smoked as he drafted document after document about the situation.[55]

On 8 July, Gallagher sent a furious memo to Bob Brennan as general manager, for submission to the board. The directors had refused to sanction a payment he had recommended, of £5 expenses to a correspondent who was moving to London. Having felt for some months that he lacked the board's confidence, Gallagher was outraged now at the attitude displayed by Bob, whose job it was to convey the board's decisions to him. He begins, 'The Board's refusal to grant the £5 recommended by me to Mr McLoughlin, together with some of your remarks at our conference today, makes it necessary that the Board be acquainted with the following facts . . .'[56] Gallagher and Brennan had been friends, and when Gallagher died in 1962, Bob would write a warm obituary; here, however, their relationship was clearly breaking down. Although de Valera was the Controlling Director, with supreme authority at the newspaper, it apparently did not occur to Gallagher to doubt his good faith; Bob, however, seems to have accorded the whole board the same unquestioning loyalty.[57]

On 3 September 1933, Frank Gallagher tendered his formal resignation to the board, which ignored it, apparently on the grounds that his had been a political appointment by de Valera, and so could not be terminated except by him. Gallagher struggled on until the end of June 1935, but in December 1933, de Valera, who controlled both newspaper and government, leant down and plucked Bob out of his job as general manager.[58]

Bob's photograph appeared, two columns wide, in the middle of the *Irish Press* front page on 12 December, above the fold. A banner headline, 'The New Spain Survives Widespread Revolt' ran along the top, but that story was fitted down the left of the page, reassuring readers that the Madrid government was in control, but noting rumours that a detachment of the Spanish Foreign Legion was to be brought from Morocco that night.[59] 'Mr R. Brennan's New Post' was the heading on the smaller story in the centre of the page: 'Diplomatic Appointment Abroad'. Summarising Bob's involvement with the republican movement and with the *Irish Press*, the article said only that he had been 'appointed to an important diplomatic post abroad'. Messages of congratulation rolled in, by letter and telegram, from friends, colleagues and neighbours. Bob kept a bundle of them, all with the same date: 12 December 1933. Aged fifty-two, he was to be Secretary of the Irish Legation in Washington, DC.

SEVEN

Mr Brennan Goes to Washington

None of Maeve's fiction deals with her move to America: all the characters she wrote about are either younger or older than she was in those years. It was by far the biggest upheaval in her life, however, and somewhere within it must lie the hinge between the self she was as a child in Ireland and the woman she became, who remembered that life with such bitter, compassionate clarity.

A photograph from the Brennans' last months in Cherryfield Avenue seems to have been taken in the back garden in summer. Emer on the left holds an unidentified baby on her lap; Una, with hair drawn back in a bun and eyes downcast, smiles slightly as she sits sideways on a deckchair, while Robert Patrick, on the footrest in front of her, is a sturdy child in tweed jacket, short pants and knee-high socks, who looks as though he has just been running. Sitting calmly on the grass beside him, wearing a short-sleeved summer dress, is Derry, with short hair. Maeve is behind her, perhaps seated on a kitchen chair, her long dark hair parted at the side and tightly plaited. She wears a coat over her dress and glowers at the camera with narrowed eyes. In her final year at Scoil Bhríghde, she was still getting excellent marks, but teachers noted that she could be headstrong or wilful (*beagáinín ceanndána uaireanta*). Under *Órdú* (Neatness), one of them has written, 'Go dona, ach bíonn a cuid leabhar go slachtmhar' ('Poor, but her books are well kept).' She was seventeen, and against all expectations, preparing to move to America.

Irish teenage girls did go to America of course, in huge numbers. They went to the spinning mills of Massachusetts and Connecticut, and to factories and domestic service in New York, Boston, Philadelphia and Chicago. Unlike other Europeans, however, who migrated in family groups or allowed women to travel only after men had established themselves in the New World, most young Irish women left home in groups of two or three. They maintained extensive networks that allowed nieces to join aunts, and sisters to live near each other, and conducted an informal collective bargaining that raised their living standards gradually.[2] But these were not girls like Maeve: they did not study French or go to the theatre; their fathers did not travel around Ireland in Rolls-Royce cars; their homes did not have electricity, or telephones, or, in many cases, indoor plumbing. Maeve would meet some of them in the years that followed, when she was an honoured guest, and they were working as maids. Most of the Irish girls who went to America in the 1930s came from country districts and small towns in the west. An agricultural labourer's cash income in 1934 was only £12 and 6 sh. per half-year, and small farmers were not much better off. They could not afford to keep grown daughters at home, or provide them with the dowry necessary to marry. For many families too, the money the girls sent home from America was badly needed, especially around Christmas.[3]

Had Éamon de Valera not sent her father to America, Maeve might have spent time in France after finishing at Miss Gavan Duffy's school, but it is more likely that she would have stayed in Dublin. We have seen her at eight years old, in her story 'The Clever One', declaring that she would be an actress, and act in the Abbey Theatre. That may still have been her ambition at seventeen, or she could have joined the civil service, or even the *Irish Press*, but she would probably have gone to university. Maeve's class at Scoil Bhríghde was preparing for the summer 1934 Matriculation examination of the National University of Ireland, and her own exam timetable and admission card were among the documents she kept for most of her life.[4] Éamon de Valera was Chancellor of NUI, whose largest constituent college, University College Dublin, was just across the street from Scoil Bhríghde. Trinity College was less than a mile away, beyond St Stephen's Green. It would be ten years before John Charles McQuaid, as Archbishop of Dublin, formally prohibited Catholics from going there, but for a Catholic girl, especially one whose parents and older sister had not been to university, UCD would have been the obvious choice. By 1934, about a third of its 2,000 or so students were women (the proportion would fall again from the mid-1930s), and most of those were in Arts, where Irish and English had the highest enrolment of first-year students. Many of the 600 women students were young nuns, destined to be teachers. As a lay student, therefore, Maeve would once again have been among a privileged few.[5]

De Valera had selected Bob as his, and Fianna Fáil's, man in Washington. The Free State's Dominion status did not entitle it to independent diplomatic representation, but the Cosgrave government had managed in 1924 to have an Irish 'Minister Plenipotentiary' accepted in Washington — effectively the first Dominion ambassador. Michael MacWhite, whom Bob had met in Geneva in 1921, was now the Minister, and Bob would join him in the Tracy Place office.[6]

All through the Anglo-Irish War, the Civil War, the years out in the cold, and the years of parliamentary opposition, de Valera had looked to the United States. It was the land of his birth, where his mother still lived (in Rochester, New York), and his speaking tours had helped him to build extensive networks of personal loyalty across the nation. A man with many enemies, those who believed in him were disciples, rather than friends, and Bob was one of them. He had not been shrewd or resolute enough for the convoluted politics of the *Irish Press*, but his personal devotion to de Valera made him completely trustworthy, while his nimble wit and ability to get on with people meant that the Chief could rely on him to present the new government's often jesuitical positions in palatable form. Seán Lemass was now Minister for Industry and Commerce, so Bob's mystical-literary idea of Irish destiny, and his tendency to make jokes, may have made him a safer bet in Washington than at home. Although a faithful servant to Fianna Fáil, he might not have found a role among the hard-headed realities of government.

On Burgh Quay, the *Press* was fast becoming a place 'of desolation, doom, suspicion and intrigue', but Christmas and New Year saw the Brennans preparing for Bob's departure.[7] Maeve's seventeenth birthday was the last she would celebrate in Cherryfield Avenue. Within a couple of weeks her father would leave for America, and the rest of the family would follow later.

Bob's ship had probably not yet docked in New York when Maeve wrote to him from Cherryfield Avenue on 3 February.[8] It was a Saturday afternoon and she filled both sides of a thick sheet of ochre-coloured linen-weave paper before scribbling '(More later)' in the bottom right-hand corner and abandoning it, perhaps because it was time for tea.

Maeve's first letter to her father is chatty and vivid, but it leaps from topic to topic as though she were gesticulating at his ship as it disappeared from view. The expensive paper, the great distance the letter will cover, her own reputation as 'the clever one' – the child who takes after her father in his love of words and stories – all seem to make her giddily self-conscious. The letter has no paragraph breaks, and while it demonstrates that Maeve at barely seventeen could write, its opening tells us how circumscribed her life had been until then. A visit to the dentist seems to be a rare event, and may have been made in preparation for the move to the US. (Irish dental care was notoriously poor for much of the twentieth century, and Maeve never had good teeth.) The pious 'T.G.', for 'Thank God', recalls the convent education that maintained a vestigial fear of ill luck or the evil eye, so that every good fortune must be acknowledged as God's gift, especially when writing. The reference to the Christopher medal, which shows the patron saint of travellers carrying the Christ child on his shoulder across a river, does the same. These medals were a traditional gift for those who emigrated: a talisman to keep them safe and a charm against falling away from the Catholic faith. Jimmy O'Dea, of course, was the young actor who had played Jimmie O'Donnell in Bob's play; the Brennans used to meet him at Sunday Mass, probably in Donnybrook:

My Dear Daddy,
I hope you're grand. We all are (T.G.) Emer brought Der and me to the Dentist on Friday. He waffled our heads around a lot and worked us up and down in his chair. It must be great fun for him. I don't like to feel at his mercy that way. I nearly asked for a large twopenny stamp in the Elm yesterday. I just wasn't thinking at all. Bob learned this 'pome' from a kid at school 'Click, Clack, Click, the monkey on the stick'. Derry and I were listening to him saying it last night and it's now 'Feedle Foodle Feedle, the monkey on the needle'. How did you like your Christopher ~~Meadle Meddel~~ (Mummy said meddle, Der said medle, Emer said medal) medal? Der and I got it [in] the Dublin Art Shop. Jimmy O'Dea was very intrigued (pronounce intreeged) about it. (Can you be intreeged about) . . .

Maeve is flexing her writing muscle, building vocabulary, playing happily with words on the page, scrupulous about apostrophes and inverted commas. She and Derry have been to two of the bookshops on the quays along the Liffey in the afternoon, walking past their father's former office on Burgh Quay. Maeve has spent one shilling and sixpence on a second-hand copy of the poems of Robert Herrick, while Derry, almost two years younger and with none of her sister's intellectual pretension, has bought a book called *Everybody's Strange Facts*. Five-and-a-half-year-old Robert Patrick (who still called himself Pat) is 'Bob' in this letter.

The Mr Ridgeway Maeve refers to in the next passage must have been a civil servant detailed to see Bob off at Cobh, County Cork, where he had boarded his ship. Maeve indulges in the kind of joke her father loved, calling the tender that carried him to the anchored ship the 'delicate and sore':

Have you got large sloping ears. If so you are a great philosopher and statesman. Der is reading 'Everybody Strange Facts' [*sic*] and of course if you have large and sloping ears it is a strange fact. Ha ha what a joke!! Mr Ridgeway rang Mummy up. Isn't it disgraceful. When you're away too. Adding insult to absence (more mirth). He said you didn't move off in the delicate and sore till 6.o. Der and I went into [town] to the Dublin Bookshop this afternoon. We felt quite sad passing the 'Press ("cause they couldn't come in and scrounge cash off me.' said he, gritting his teeth). We spent an hour there and I got a copy of Herrick's poems for 1/6. Der got 'Everybody's Strange Facts' (see above). We went over to the other side then to Webb's [on Aston Quay] and didn't like that place so much. We got a Dundrum 'bus home then. You left your new nailbrush behind I hope you got another. I'm going to the Gate on Monday, the Comhar Drámuidheachta are producing 'Céad Blian ag Fás'. I'm going on Saturday as well 'Storm Song'. D[orothy] M[acardle] said it wasn't very good except for one scene. Mrs Briscoe got knives and things in the dustbin (her own) today and she had a row with Mary. (More later)

The Briscoes next door had a maid called Mary Power, who must have scraped their dinner plates with some abandon. Mary Briscoe would have opened her kitchen door to search the dustbin when 'knives and things' went missing, and Maeve, through her bedroom window just above, would have heard every word of the row that followed. These were the kinds of stories she used to save up as a child, to tell her father when he came home from work. She has a life outside the house now, though, where there is more to do than overhear raised voices from next door and worry about nailbrushes. Twice in the coming week she will be at the theatre: on Monday (with a school group, perhaps), to see a Comhar Drámuidheachta production at the Gate, and again on Saturday, for the Gate's own production of Denis Johnston's new play, *Storm Song*.[9]

In her letter, Maeve calls the Irish-language play *Céad Blia[i]n ag Fás*: 'A Hundred Years Growing', though in fact it was *Céad Bliain d'Aois*, 'A Hundred Years Old', a translation of *El Centenario*, by S. and J. Alvarez. Produced by Micheál Mac Liammóir, it received only one performance at the Gate, on 5 February 1934.[10] This slip-up shows Maeve's immersion in the Irish-language culture of the time: Muiris Ó Súilleabháin's autobiography of Blasket Island life, *Fiche Bliain ag Fás*, subsequently translated into English as *Twenty Years A-Growing*, had been published by the Talbot Press the previous year.

Maeve did not continue her letter until the following Saturday, 10 February. By then she had seen *Céad Bliain d'Aois*, and heard about An Comhar Drámuidheachta's progress with a revival of *Oidhche Mhaith agat, a Mhic Ui Dhomhnaill*, the translation of Bob's *Good Night, Mr O'Donnell*, due to run from 12 to 17 March. She had heard a radio talk on Tuesday by Dorothy Macardle, the *Irish Press* drama critic and a family friend who took a particular interest in her, and had even listened to coverage of an international rugby match played at nearby Lansdowne Road:

Imagine, it's just a week since I started this! We're going to have black pudding for tea. England beat Ireland! We listened to the report over the wireless but Der and I went to the library before the end! We're going to 'Storm Song' at the Gate tonight. Emer and Der and me. Hilton Edwards is sick so Denis Johnston is taking his part. It's the first Denis Johnston play I've ever seen! Miss Gavan Duffy wanted to know were you lonely going away – imagine her unbending that much. They've started on the rehersals [*sic*] of your play and they've chosen an absolutely lovely girl to play Molly. She's the girl who danced on the drawing pin [probably a reference to a remark passed by Bob at an earlier performance] – Niamh Nic Gearailt. I was at the Comhar on Monday and she had a teeny part. She's a dote. It'll run for a week, because they're doing it at the Peacock. They're playing at the P[eacock] from now on. I'm wondering who they'll get in the Comhar to play Jimmy though. I hope Séamus Ó hÉilidhe plays Lizzie [the housemaid, presumably played in drag] – his brother it was that played Jimmy in Galway. Dorothy Macardle gave a grand lecture on the wireless last Tuesday. She said in writing to me that she'd enjoy my appreciative(?) ear next time. That was 2 weeks ago and my ear still blooms in its old place. I'm in the back sitting room and the lady from Athlone is reading the news – isn't the Irish team the limit! If me & you were there we could duck like you did that time. Or we could foul during the scrums. I'll shut up now but I'll write next Saturday.

Best Love, Maeve

Denis Johnston, thirty-two, was a member of the Gate's board. His first play, *The Old Lady Says 'No!'*, staged in 1929, had been successful enough to secure the new company's future. His fourth, *Storm Song*, about a film director on the Aran Islands, was based on his own experience: he had worked on Robert Flaherty's *Man of Aran* and had also written the screenplay for the 1933 silent film version of Frank O'Connor's story 'Guests of the Nation'.

Maeve's knowing that Johnston would act in his own play that night shows how important the theatre had become in her life. Niamh Nic Gearailt, the 'absolutely lovely girl' she mentions as the romantic female lead for her father's play, was twenty-five, and a promising actor. Her mother Máire Ní Chinnéide had been involved in the language and cultural revival since the beginning of the century, and it was she who had persuaded the seventy-year-old storyteller, Peig Sayers of the Blasket Islands, to dictate her autobiography in Irish for publication.[11] Tomás Ó Criomhthain's *An tOileánach* (later translated as *The Islandman*) had appeared in 1929, and Ó

Súilleabháin's *Fiche Bliain ag Fás* had been out since April. *Peig*, the first woman's autobiography in this genre of nation-making books, would be published in 1936. Under the Fianna Fáil government, the Irish-speaking islands off the west coast, celebrated as repositories of authentic Irishness throughout the Revival, were being mined with a new urgency for images and ideas, and cinema audiences were waiting impatiently for *Man of Aran*. After two years of filming, and various delays, the *Irish Times* had announced on 11 December that it was finally on its way to completion.

That a girl so determinedly unsporty as Maeve should get excited about a rugby match seems strange at first, but in 1930s Ireland, rugby football – brought to Trinity College Dublin by former pupils of Rugby school in the 1850s – was just beginning to be taken up by the Catholic middle class, and its heroes were well-fed, well-built young men.[12] That Saturday, despite a strong start by Ireland, England scored a decisive victory. The live 'running commentary' from Lansdowne Road by former Irish international player W. P. Collopy was a major technical achievement in 1934, and more importantly, the Brennans had a radio in the back sitting-room.[13] A new transmitter in Athlone, County Westmeath, had extended radio coverage to the whole country a year earlier (it had even been rushed into service ahead of schedule to cover the Eucharistic Congress in 1932).[14] Radios were expensive: in 1933 the *Irish Times* advertised a Philco Five Star Baby Grand, 'a perpetual season ticket to the whole world of radio entertainment', for twenty guineas – about one hundred times the price of a ticket to an international celebrity concert at the Theatre Royal. The Brennans owned one of perhaps 100,000 radios in the Free State, while the number of households with telephones was considerably lower. The cost of telephone installation was high, and Maeve's teasing implication that there was something improper in her mother's receiving a phone call from a man suggests that they had not had theirs for long.[15] The 'lady from Athlone' was still reading the news when Maeve signed off. She added a postscript: 'P.S. news still on. Is it really as cold as that over there?'

The news was broadcast between 6.45 and 7 p.m., so it seems that Maeve worked on her letter both before and after tea, starting when she and Derry came home from Rathmines library. It would have been dark outside as she sat at the drop-leaf table in the small back sitting-room with the linoleum on the floor, in the heat of the gas fire, while Una or Emer fried black pudding in the kitchen. Salty and savoury, quick to cook, black pudding was weekend food, served in small quantities, and Bob was probably one of the many Irish men who could never have enough of it: Todd Andrews recalled lovingly that he once ate a plateful intended for a whole household, while on the run in west Cork during the Civil War.[16]

Emer helped their little brother to write to his father that day too. Robert Patrick used the same ochre-coloured paper, printing in capitals, all but one of the 'S's written backwards:

DEAR DADDY,
HOW ARE YOU. I AM WELL. ARE YOU HAVING A NICE TIME.
WE GOT THE PHOTOS TODAY. WAS THE SHIP NICE. BEST
LOVE FROM PAT

A line of 'X's follows, and a line of noughts. Emer has annotated the noughts as 'hugs', and added a note in pencil: 'He wrote all this himself! Love, Emer'.

Bob had written two letters home by the time Maeve wrote to him again, on 21 February. The paper this time is thinner, pale grey, with the address, '48 Cherryfield Avenue, Sandford Road, Dublin', stamped on it in blue Gothic type. 'Isn't this swank?' Maeve writes in a PPS at the top of the first page, 'A man came travelling for it to the door & I got such a surprise because he didn't have an English accent I got Mum to buy some!!!' Door-to-door salesmen in Dublin tended to be from England: Maeve is being patriotic, as well as 'swank'.

Bob had landed in New York by now, and may already have been in Washington. At any rate he was living in a hotel, and seeing a lot of movies. Again, Maeve's tone is bantering, with knowing references to the clichés of popular culture. She starts off with the high-minded nationalist snobbery that sees America as a philistine place but then gets down to the films she has seen at the Sandford Cinema, just down the road:

My dear Daddy,
I was glad to read your two letters (I did) and to see that you are behaving. I think American Air must be having a bad effect on you – going to the pictures every night of the week indeed. Wouldn't mind if it was the Gate. Ha ha – you can't turn that place into a Gate Theatre!! I was at a gorgeous picture last Saturday, when I went up to the Sandford with Derry. It was a pioneer picture (not about temper-ance)[17] and I thought it was grand. Anne Harding and Richard Dix were in it. I never cried at the pictures – not even at Cavalcade[18] – but I positively howled at this one. It was terribly suspenseful and you needn't say I'm sloppy – it wasn't a widowed mother (or a wicked one, it's all the same) weeping over her dying suffering and forgiving child! I didn't like the sad bits much they were too harrowing – but as a whole it was grand. It's name, by the way, was 'the Conquerors'.[19]

One of the family's women friends had also taken Maeve in search of high culture:

> I was at the 'OP' with G. O'B.[20] on Friday night. 'Rigoletto'. She said that Gilda was a young and fair creature so naturally I was waiting for her to appear. The sad old father came on (clown at a palace – tear behind the smile – I could go on Mary Manning-wise about him forever) and sings at length and then the partition opens and <u>she</u> trips out – at first I imagined it was Noel Purcell dressed up – a girlish figure with an indescribable <u>red</u> wig hanging down her back (I mean the plait of it was) She wore a sluttish blue dress and her face – whenever she opened her mouth (I really don't mean to be vulgar) you could almost see her tonsils! G. O'B. gave me her OP glasses & I was almost afraid to look, for fear I would see them. Anyway I disgraced myself and giggled like——! It was terribly funny. All the same I pitied her. She's been singing for 30 years, so G. O'B. told me!

Dublin had no regular opera season until the Dublin Grand Opera Society was founded in 1941, so this production of *Rigoletto* by the O'Mara Opera Company was a rare treat for aficionados. Like Dorothy Macardle, who had managed to write to Maeve even when hard at work on her voluminous history of the nationalist movement, *The Irish Republic*, 'G. O'B.' has found the time to spend an evening at the opera with this clever teenager. Perhaps she was offended by Maeve's giggles, but it is more likely that she had to leave early to catch a bus. Maeve was clearly quite comfortable alone – even when she recognised a man in front of her as he gave a Fascist salute during the national anthem:

> G. O'B. left before the end and when they played the Soldier's Song I stood all alone and looked patriotic & all of a sudden I noticed a <u>small mangy</u> man about a seat away but in front of me, who had come in in the middle of the last act, standing with one arm extended. I didn't know what he was at for a while and then I saw it was an old enemy of mine who swore to teach me catechism and the pomps of the devil once & when he turned I was sure! Gearóid O'Sullivan!! Stupid little ass. As he turned he happened to glance at me and I glared at him but he didn't wither up just then. He looked silly.

The right-wing organisation known as the Blueshirts had been much in the news. The self-styled National Guard, banned since August 1933, shared many members with Cumann na nGaedheal. Eoin O'Duffy, whom de Valera had dismissed a year earlier as Commissioner of the the Free State police force, the Garda Síochána, was its leader, and an admirer of Benito Mussolini. Gearóid Ó Súilleabháin, formerly one of Michael Collins' closest confidants, seems to be the person mentioned here. He had been a member of the Free State army council until 1924, when mutiny forced his resignation, and ten years later was both a Dáil deputy and a barrister. An outspoken critic of de Valera, he is the first of many people in Maeve's life for whom she professes an uninhibited and cheerful dislike. Too late, she has thought of a way of making fun of him:

> I wish I'd thought of doing some of that drill I learned in Kilcullen – I didn't think of it till after. You know the 'Pyrammus [*sic*] & Thisbe' thing out of the Midsummer Night's Dream? I started to do Thisbe at obair baile [Irish for homework] the other night for the edification of Der & Bob. And here Bob [Robert Patrick] started (clutching me) 'Oh Maybelle, my sweet Maybelle – I cannot live without thee' & so on! I was flabbergasted! Isn't that a grand word!

Maeve's five-year-old brother is already being initiated into the family's theatrical games. 'Maybelle' seems to be her melodramatic *alter ego*: she will sign herself that way in later life when writing self-mockingly to friends. For now, though, she is full of high spirits, and adolescent zeal:

> I saw Jimmy O'Dea come in late to mass on Sunday & after I was talking to him. 'You were late at mass' sez I while my sooty bule (blue) eyes twinkled roguishly 'No' sez he 'But you're earlier at mass since your father went away'. But I got my own back (fuaireas mo dhruim féin) He thanked Mum for your book in Irish & sez I 'Can you read it?' 'No' sez he 'Ha ha' sez he 'Ha ho' sez I and so on! He had 2 English papers (the Sunday Times was one) under his furtive arm & she had the Dispatch. I'll stop now (did I hear a sigh of relief)
> Love, Maeve

She adds a postscript: 'P.S. I've written to Grandma'. Bridget Brennan was seventy-seven, and still in good health in her house in Wexford town.

Bob's 'book in Irish' must have been Liam Ó Briain's translation of his play, *Oidhche Mhaith agat, a Mhic Uí Dhomhnaill*, now published by An Gúm. Maeve's aside in Irish, 'fuaireas mo dhruim féin' is a bilingual pun that was part of a joke her father used to tell about learners of Irish: literally it means 'I got my own back' – but only if 'back' is a noun.[21] The title of her story 'The Day We Got Our Own Back', like Rose Derdon's pencilled petition in 'The Poor Men and Women' – I want my own back, I want my own back' [*SA* 140] – echoes the family joke.

Man of Aran opened in London at last in April 1934. Its depiction of heroic and elemental characters wresting a living from the edge of the Atlantic drew criticism from social realists, but the film found immediate and wholehearted acceptance among the people Maeve most admired, and she herself must have loved it. The Dublin première was on 6 May, with de Valera and W. B. Yeats among the dignitaries present. Dorothy Macardle wrote in the *Irish Press* the following morning,:

> These are our countrymen and their actual, constant achievements are no less than these . . . We have become almost resigned to being traduced . . . Not three generations of protesting could do as much to rehabilitate the Irish people in the imagination of the peoples of other countries as this faithful and beautiful motion picture will do.[22]

Ireland's place in the imagination of the peoples of other countries had been Bob's whole preoccupation since the time of the *Irish Bulletin*. It was once again his full-time job, and this time his family would be actively involved. It would be a few more months before they would pack up to join him in Washington, however. On 8 May, Mary Kate Whitty died at Coolnaboy, aged eighty-eight. She had never married, and had not been seen in public for more than twenty years, so her funeral passed off quietly, the *Echo* noting only that Oylegate Fianna Fáil Cumann had passed a vote of sympathy with the Bolger family of Coolnaboy on the death of their aunt: all the power of Mary Kate's personality had been exercised, and would be remembered, within the family. Bessie was forty-one, Wat thirty-seven, and at last they could begin to think of independent lives.

For Maeve, it would mean big changes in a place she loved, for Bessie would move to Killincooley, Kilmuckridge, when she married Mike Parker, and Wat would marry Katie Doyle and bring her to live in Coolnaboy. In Dublin, meanwhile, the school year was not yet over, and Maeve had to sit the Matriculation exam at the end of June. On 6 August, her Uncle Wat wrote to her from Coolnaboy, 'I suppose we may expect you down soon'.[23] Like all his letters, this one offers unstinting affection and welcome, and a sense that Una's children have unquestioned rights in her old home. We can assume that they did go to stay with him and Bessie one more time.

There was still the house to sell. Whenever the Brennans returned, it would not be to Cherryfield Avenue, for as Maeve writes in 'The Beginning of a Long Story', 'It was a very ordinary house, a regulation uniform for the lives of certain families, or for some families at a certain stage of their lives. It was better than a workingman's house but not good enough for a successful man and his family to live in' [*RG* 204–5]. By mid-September, Fianna Fáil's General Secretary, Paddy Morrissey, had arranged to buy it. The sale was not yet complete, but Una signed a document giving power of attorney to her solicitor, then with Emer, Maeve, Derry and Robert Patrick, she travelled south to board the *Manhattan*, which would call at Cobh on its way from Southampton to New York.[24] The family stayed overnight in Cork and went next day by tender to the ship.

When the Brennans had left, fourteen-year-old Hubert Briscoe climbed over the back garden wall to explore. In the tin-roofed coal-shed behind the kitchen he found old copies of the paper *Sunburst*, and two small books in Irish, which he kept.[25] Both had belonged to Bob when he lived in Wexford.

Forty years later, her life fallen apart, Maeve told a friend who visited her in hospital that she had felt 'desperate about being uprooted' when her family left Ireland.[26] As far as her younger sister could see at the time, however, she was excited, eager to know about where they were going, and reading avidly about America in the newspapers. Already, as they sailed out of Cobh, they were in a new world. The *Manhattan* was an American passenger liner, staffed like a luxury hotel, with cabin maids, valets and hairdressers: more crew than passengers. Every day, deckhands put out rows of reclining deckchairs, and waiters served 'elevenses', soup, and afternoon tea as the passengers lounged. The ship had a library, and a special area for pets. Movies were shown in the afternoons (*The Barretts of Wimpole Street* was one); they dressed for dinner and a dance-band played.[27]

From New York the Brennans went by train to Washington, DC, where they stayed at the Fairfax Hotel on Massachusetts Avenue, a short way from Union Station. Farther along were Dupont Circle and Kalorama, where most diplomatic missions, including the Irish Legation, were concentrated. Across the steep-sided Rock Creek lay Georgetown. Originally a tobacco port on the Potomac, with picturesque old houses and a famous Jesuit university, its buildings were not so different from those of Georgian Dublin. A formal photograph of the family found among Maeve's papers seems to have been taken soon after their arrival, for the girls wear American-style clothes.[28] Maeve looks young, and, for her, quite plump. Her most striking feature is the long, thick, glossy, dark plaits that hang, tied with bows of broad ribbon, over her shoulders.

Soon, the family moved into a five-bedroomed Spanish-style house, rented for them by the Legation, on Cathedral Avenue. Washington was Southern, and largely Protestant, and it was segregated. Eleanor Roosevelt would make history in 1939, when the Daughters of the American Revolution, who owned the city's Constitution Hall, refused to allow the

African-American singer Marian Anderson to perform there: the First Lady arranged for Anderson to give a concert on the steps of the Lincoln Memorial, with her audience out of doors on the Mall. Coming from a country as complacent about its racial homogeneity as Ireland was in the 1930s, the Brennans must have experienced a whirlwind introduction to multiracial society. Bob at least would certainly have felt an affinity with Frederick Douglass, the Washington slave who became a United States ambassador. Douglass had written an autobiography and had visited Ireland in 1845, during the Famine.[29] The children's formal education, however, was to remain resolutely Catholic and white. Robert Patrick started almost immediately at a parish primary school, while Maeve and Derry were enrolled, once again, in a school controlled by nuns. Emer, now twenty-four, found an office job and began to sample Washington's social life.

Immaculata Seminary was a high school and junior college for women only, run by the Sisters of Providence until it closed in the late 1970s. Located on Nebraska Avenue near Tenley Circle, it adjoined the campus of American University. Maeve lived with her family and followed Immaculata's two-year college course. On 6 January 1935 she wrote in her new diary: 'My birthday. Felt really and awfully older by far. Became 18. This is age!'[30] The Irish Legation hosted a reception for the Abbey Players that day, and Maeve attended their performance of Sean O'Casey's *The Plough and the Stars* the following evening. Diary entries over the following months show her making friends with other girls, attending an Irish class, and walking with her father. The ten-mile-long Rock Creek Park was nearby, but its wooded slopes were no substitute for the landscape they were used to, and on 23 February she was homesick: 'but where can you walk here?' she wrote in her diary, 'Oh for the Dublin mountains!' Other things she had taken for granted were equally unavailable: the Brennans' new home had central heating, so they had no need for fires, and Americans drank coffee, not tea.

Exposed to the sort of 'beauty' education she would not have encountered at Scoil Bhríghde, Maeve is bemused but attentive: on 28 February, 'Irish class girl offered me a facial'. On 3 March she writes, 'Wore my green dress to Mass under my coat and felt lovely'. On 19 March the entry is longer, as she describes her reaction to American beauty culture as presented at Immaculata College: 'A woman came in and gave us a "Beauty Talk"!! "How to Care [for] the Skin". It was interesting of course. These things always are. Anyway she gave everyone advice on their complexions but I asked for no advice. I didn't think I needed it.'

Maeve may have been experiencing culture shock, as she realised that in America, all women, and not just a minority, expected – or were expected – to be 'beautiful'. Her bluestocking mentors and wholesome friends in

Dublin would have been embarrassed to show so much concern about their appearance, and would have found wearing make-up 'common'. American women and girls used make-up enthusiastically, however, and one of the world's leading fashion magazines, *Harper's Bazaar*, based in New York and part of the Hearst empire, had recently begun to devote the whole of each August's issue to 'college fashions', with photographs taken on American campuses.[31] The same magazine published excellent new fiction – a hint that beauty and brains did not have to be mutually exclusive. Maeve began to watch her weight – her diary makes many references to dieting – and when Bessie sent shamrock for St Patrick's Day from Coolnaboy, Maeve's entry for 8 March reflected on the letter that accompanied it: 'Shamrock from Bessie & a letter today – Mike Parker is going to another part of the county to live & she is lonelier than ever. When I think of that wasted life I fume. But what's the use. She is now 42. Her youth has passed by. I'll hold onto mine. I want happiness. And I'll try to have it.' Bessie and Mike Parker would not marry for more than another year.

The only other record of Maeve's time at Immaculata Seminary is a photograph that shows her in yet another nativity play, this time as Mary, with a swaddled doll on her lap. Her hair is long and loose, below her shoulders, but full of kinks as though recently unplaited. She is thinner than in the family portrait.[32]

Graduating from Immaculata in 1936, Maeve moved to the adjacent American University for the last two years of her Bachelor's degree. She still kept up with friends in Dublin: a sixteen-page letter in Irish from a Scoil Bhríghde classmate refers to her correspondence with at least one other, while giving news of several more.[33] In a co-educational environment for the first time, however, she threw herself into student life, appearing often in yearbooks and directories.[34] In 1937, when she was twenty, *AUCOLA,* the yearbook of the American University College of Liberal Arts, listed Maeve Brennan as one of its eight sub-assistant editors (the editor and all the other members of the governing board were men), and as a copy reader for the student newspaper, the *Eagle*. An English major, she was a member of both the French Club and the German Club, and a member of the all-female Phi Mu 'fraternity'. Phi Mu's activities for 1937–1938 began with 'a formal tea, followed by a circus party, an Alice-in-Wonderland at-home, and a hay-ride to Rixey Mansion'. The French Club held monthly meetings that featured plays, talks, musical programmes, a bridge party and a tea dance. The German Club was more serious, and *AUCOLA* 1937 noted that 'Many of the programs of the German Club center interest in the cultural and political aspects of the present-day Germany'. At a special meeting in February, a Dr Gewehr spoke on 'Germany's Position as a World

Power'; Maeve was among the eighteen students photographed with him.

Maeve's yearbook photograph for 1937 shows her looking quietly amused, with her plaited hair up, twisted around her head, and a scarf knotted at the neck of her light-coloured ribbed sweater. By now the Brennans had moved to a larger, Victorian house at 3602 Newark Street, where for the first time they had household help. An African-American man called Tom was handyman-gardener, and also cooked and cleaned. Una suffered from severe arthritis; she was ill for long periods and Emer gave up her office job to take over the running of the house.

Letters from the Brennans told their friends in Ireland about their new life. One of them, Bob's former colleague Máirín Cregan, was writing books for children and teenagers.[35] Her 1941 novel *Rathina* uses letters from America in a way that underlines how exotic the Brennans' lives must have seemed to those at home:

> Mrs Donovan read them out to the family; and though Joan and Ben found it difficult to grasp the significance of 'Coast to Coast,' 'Middle West,' 'Arizona,' and 'Pullman,' they were thrilled by reference to skyscrapers, soda fountains, dimes, dollars, and black servants. In the trains real Negroes brought you tea and coffee and looked after you in sleeping cars. In one home which he visited the children actually had a black nurse, whom they simply adored![36]

Despite what their friends at home may have imagined, however, the Brennans had not come to a glamorous place. As one popular guidebook puts it, 'Between the wars, foreign diplomats looked on Washington as a hardship post, a somnolent backwater lacking any finesse of culture or cuisine.'[37] Franklin D. Roosevelt's New Deal, begun after his inauguration in 1933, was creating jobs in the administration, but the temporary office buildings that had housed the last war effort still cluttered the Mall, and the effects of the Depression, when hunger marchers had been driven out of Washington with tanks and tear-gas, could still be seen.

Back in Ireland, de Valera's repudiation of the terms of the 1921 Treaty had led to the so-called Economic War with Britain; and many of the Brennans' women friends were increasingly disillusioned by his policies.[38] Hanna Sheehy-Skeffington was one of the most vocal, but even the faithful Dorothy Macardle, whose monumental study *The Irish Republic* appeared in March 1937, objected to new strands of legislation discriminating against women. Since 1932, married women had not been allowed to work as teachers; the Criminal Law Amendment Act of 1935 had made artificial contraceptives illegal, and it had been followed by the Conditions of

Employment Act, whose Section 16 gave the Minister for Employment power to curtail the number of women working in any branch of industry. Sheehy-Skeffington wrote to the *Irish Press* before that bill passed into law that it 'out-Hitler[ed] Hitler'.[39]

Equality between women and men had been at the heart of the national emancipation movement to which Bob and Una's generation had dedicated so much of their youthful energy, but de Valera had never espoused it, and now his resistance to women's autonomy was about to be enshrined in Ireland's new Constitution. He published it in draft form on 1 May, to spirited opposition from women's groups, expressed in the pages of the *Irish Press* and elsewhere, but it came into effect on 29 December 1937 with only minor changes. Its wording relegated women to a passive, supporting, domestic role, spoke of their 'life within the home' rather than their work, and ignored those who were not mothers. To Una, as to many other members of Cumann na mBan, it brought political disillusion and enduring dismay, especially in view of the active and often dangerous role they had played in bringing the Free State into being.[40]

Emer accompanied Bob on a trip home to Ireland that summer, going with him to County Wexford, where they visited Bessie in her new home near the sea at Killincooley. Jim Bolger's daughters were visiting from Dublin, and eleven-year-old Ita stored up a memory of Emer that was still vivid sixty years later: 'She was a lovely person, very gracious, tall and slim. I still remember her magnificent coat. It was beautiful, tweed, completely lined in fur, real fur. It was absolutely beautiful, and she was so slim — it was gorgeous.'[41]

In Washington, life was at least comfortable. Emer often accompanied Bob to functions, but when Una was well enough to take part, she enjoyed the social round of diplomatic life too. Her dignity and gentleness, combined with her skills as a needlewoman and gardener, gained her respect and friendship, while the refinements of her convent education stood her in good stead. She took pride in keeping her house beautifully: her granddaughter still has the book on etiquette that she bought about that time.[42] Maeve and Derry were less enthusiastic. Derry found work at a riding stable, Maeve at the Intimate Bookshop, where she was paid $5 a week (later increased to $12). Bob took advantage of his writing background to make contacts among journalists as well as diplomats, and in September 1937 the Hedgerow Theatre presented his play *Bystander*, the programme noting that it was 'the one hundred twenty-fifth production'.[43] Meanwhile Maeve studied seriously, even taking courses during Washington's sweltering, sticky summer weather. A postcard written to her at Newark Street, signed 'Love, Marian', and postmarked 10 August, ends: 'I hear that you are very busily preparing for exams with the rest of the ambitious summer school goers. Anyway I know you will make out on top. You never do otherwise; but "good luck" in spite of the fact.'[44]

After three years in Washington (almost four for Bob), the Brennans assumed that they would soon be recalled to Ireland. Maeve had determined to specialise in library studies, a field in which she could expect to find employment at home, and wrote to Dorothy Macardle about her plans and recent adventures. Macardle wrote back on 10 December from her new home, Creevagh in Dundrum, just weeks before the new Constitution took effect, beginning her letter 'My dear Maeve', and signing it 'Yours with love'. She was thirty-eight, and the independent State for which she had worked and gone to prison offered little of what she had hoped for:

> I am glad to know you are making steadily for library work. But how I hope you won't encounter heartbreak and frustration when you come back here. The country is going through a phase when scarcely any body is interested in anything but money and factories. People who care about thinking and reading are getting desperate. If you find you can't do your best work here I think you'll just have to go where you <u>can</u> do it – but you'll want, I know, to stay in Ireland and hope you'll continue to.
>
> I wonder when you are coming home.[45]

Maeve was working hard, but she was no longer just 'the clever one'. An undated newspaper clipping among her father's papers shows an oval photograph headed 'Beauty', and captioned: 'Miss Maeve Brennan, daughter of the Secretary of the Irish Legation and Mrs Robert Brennan, is a real Irish beauty.'

Michael MacWhite, Irish Minister to the US, was transferred to Italy early in 1938. Bob became Chargé d'Affaires at the Irish Legation, and newspapers began to pay more attention to him and to his three attractive daughters, speculating that he might be promoted to replace MacWhite.[46] Maeve graduated in June from American University. Bessie wrote with a thousand congratulations, adding, 'I hope your Mammy was strong enough to be present.' Then, on 26 August, Bob's appointment as Irish Minister was confirmed. The *Washington Star* reported:

> The Minister was an important figure in the Irish revolutionary move- ment after the World War. He has three daughters named for the early queens of Ireland – Emer, Maeve and Deirdre – and a young son, Robert . . . Miss Maeve Brennan, the second daughter, was graduated

from the American University in June, and is at home with her parents now, as is her older sister, Miss Emer Brennan. Deidre [*sic*] Brennan, the youngest girl, attended an art school in Washington last year, and though her plans are not definite for the coming winter, may again take an art course. Robert, the Brennans' only son, attends grade school here.

Mr Brennan is not only a political figure in Ireland, having taken an important part in the Irish Revolution, but is known as a playwright, and Mrs Brennan is an artist at needlework.

On 1 September, the Brennans moved again, this time to a larger house at 2425 Kalorama Road, close to Rock Creek Park and the Irish Legation. They now had three maids – two young African-American women called Sylvia and Rose, and Ethel, who was very old, as well as a chauffeur called Peterson, who drove the Minister in a Chrysler. A Washington newspaper of the time printed a circular photograph of 'Miss Maeve Brennan, charming young daughter of the new Irish Minister and Mrs Robert Brennan'. Maeve looks grave and beautiful, with her hair combed straight back from her forehead and pinned up; her eyebrows are dark and carefully shaped.[47]

Four weeks after the house move, Bridget Brennan died in Wexford, aged eighty-one. The *Echo* described her as 'widow of the late Robert Brennan, and mother of Mr Robert Brennan, Irish Minister to the US', but her son did not return from Washington for her funeral: travel took almost a week each way by sea, and the Legation was busier than ever.

About two million US citizens were second-generation Irish. The new Constitution declared Ireland a 'sovereign, independent and democratic state', and claimed 'the whole island of Ireland, its islands and the territorial seas' as the national territory, so relations with the United States were crucial. Bob had been in Dublin six months earlier, when de Valera agreed plans for an Irish pavilion at the New York World's Fair, to be held in 1939. Amid fears of war with Germany, the Economic War with Britain had ended within days of that decision, and although the Border remained, and Ireland paid £10 million in final settlement of Britain's demands for land annuities, the three Free State ports reserved under the Anglo-Irish Treaty were handed over to Irish control. In June, Douglas Hyde, who had many American connections, was inaugurated as Ireland's first President. As Irish Minister in Washington, Bob concentrated his efforts on obtaining America's support for the ending of partition and for the maintenance of Irish neutrality in the event of war.

There were lighter moments. On 17 July, eleven years after Charles Lindbergh's solo flight from New York to Paris, a young airman called

Douglas Corrigan took off from New York, supposedly to fly to California. He had been refused a permit to fly the Atlantic in the single-engined plane he had bought for a song and rebuilt, but he did it anyway. Claiming that his compass had failed, he landed the next day in Baldonnel Aerodrome just north of Dublin. In Ireland, despite official misgivings, he became a celebrity: President Douglas Hyde went with his aides to meet him at Baldonnel and see the tiny aeroplane for himself, while Éamon de Valera allegedly thanked Corrigan for putting Ireland back on the map.

Within a week of his triumphant return to New York on the *Manhattan* (his plane was dismantled and crated for the voyage), 'Wrong Way' Corrigan was in Washington. His escapade could not be approved formally, but Bob kept a photograph that showed him sitting at a dinner table between Monsignor (later Bishop) Fulton Sheen and Corrigan, 'the man who flew to Ireland by mistake', while another showed Maeve and her two sisters among a group of young people at a 'green' dinner, held in his honour at the Mayflower Hotel, Washington, where even the potatoes and dessert were dyed green, and all the Corrigans in Washington were invited.[48] On 10 August, the *Evening Star*'s Social Calendar published a photograph of the whole Brennan family in evening dress, announcing: '. . . Mr and Mrs Brennan will receive the young flyer, Douglas Corrigan. The informal reception for the flyer will be held this afternoon in the Legation and only members of the Brennan family and the Legation staff will be present.' Maeve was expected to help her parents entertain. At seventeen, she had written sarcastically about the roguish twinkle in her own sooty blue eyes, but that was in Ireland, where the joke lay in the distance between media celebrations of femininity and the realities of a puritanical society in a rainy climate. In Washington, where 'beauty' was taken seriously, journalists were capable of portraying her and her sisters in stereotype, without any saving irony.

Maeve had always been more like Bob than Una in personality: where Emer and Derry were quiet, she was volatile. Popular, witty and wickedly clever, when her parents seemed set to remain in Washington, she had decided to continue in full-time education. Emer and Derry moved steadily forward into the kind of domesticity at which their mother had always excelled, but Maeve fell in love recklessly and had her heart broken more than once. A postcard sent to her at 2425 Kalorama Road, Washington, on 17 February 1939, by a friend whose signature is illegible, asks 'How is S?'. More than a year later, Derry, called away at short notice to accompany Bob on one of his trips, wrote to her: 'Hope you had a nice week and that Solly is well'. Solly Paul was Maeve's Jewish boyfriend. She was very much in love with him, so when he decided that he could not marry a gentile, and broke with her, she was distraught.[49] Allowing for the distortions and exaggerations of memory, however – especially in times of difficulty – another name seems to have been even more significant in Maeve's early personal history, for she would speak in later life of theatre critic Walter Kerr as her great lost love.

Asked to supply a short biography of his daughter thirteen years later, when the *Irish Digest* republished some of Maeve's *New Yorker* stories, Bob wrote, 'She took a degree in Arts at the American University, Washington and another in Library Science at the Catholic University of America'. The latter university has no record of Maeve as a graduate of its library school, or of its English Department, but she certainly studied there from 1938 to around 1940, and spoke to friends about it in later life.[50]

Walter Kerr also came to CUA in 1938. Born in 1913 to a Catholic family in Evanston, Illinois, he wrote film reviews for the local newspaper while still a young teenager, and later attended university in his home town. Northwestern University specialised in theatre studies, and theatre became his passion. As a playwright and director, he was able to integrate the intellectual excitement he found in twentieth-century literature with both his strong Catholic faith and his sense of fun. He graduated with a BA in 1937, followed by an MA in 1938, and moved almost immediately to Washington, to take up a teaching position in CUA's Department of Speech and Drama.

At twenty-five, Kerr was ambitious, good-looking, witty, and hugely energetic. Along with his classes for graduate students, he gave a lecture on 'Audience in the Theater' to the Blackfriars group early in his first semester, and followed it with another on 'Poetry in the Theater' to the Washington Poetry Society in January. During that first academic year, he published two plays, prepared another for publication, and directed both Shakespeare's *Coriolanus* and his own verse play *Hyacinth on Wheels* at the university. He also took part in two productions for radio station WMAL, and directed a show called 'Magic' for the Washington Blackfriars. The next years were equally active in the Department of Speech and Drama, whose flamboyant students and central place in university life gained it nicknames as 'screech and glamour' and 'smooch and dreamer'.[51]

It is not difficult to see what would have attracted Walter Kerr and Maeve to each other. Both were handsome, clever and amusing; both were celebrated publicly in Washington, but they also shared a more modest background, where idealism and public service came clothed in Catholic imagery. Kerr would have appreciated invitations to the Irish Legation, and the Brennans' association with the Gate and Abbey Theatres, while Bob, loath to part with any of his daughters, would have found a Catholic son-in-law who so strongly resembled him more acceptable than most. Still very much her father's daughter, Maeve may also have seen Kerr as a man Bob could take seriously.

By August 1939, talk of war was everywhere, but Maeve escaped to the beach at Margate, New Jersey with her mother, sisters and Robert Patrick. Bob joined them at weekends, until news of the trade agreement signed by Hitler and Stalin brought him hurrying back to Washington by train. The family returned a few days later. On 27 August, six recent graduates of the National University of Ireland were among a large number of young people who arrived in Washington, accompanied by priests as chaperones, for a one-week international conference on 'The Role of the University in Catholic Action'. In her column in the *Washington Times Herald*, Una's friend Betty Hynes described a tea party she and Bob held for them:

> Mrs Brennan, in crisp blue and white polka dot linen with sharp white accents at its high neckline, and the minister, cool in a white suit, wandered among their callers, helping now and then to pass sandwiches or fetch a glass of sherry for a guest.
>
> Miss Emer Brennan, her eyes as blue as the print of her frock, sat smiling behind the tall silver tea service, while the two other daughters of the house, Maeve in brown and white polka dots and Deirdre in white, helped entertain the visitors . . .[52]

All three of the Brennans' daughters were expected to help in entertaining visitors, but now it began to seem that Maeve, the least domesticated, would soon have to do most of the work, for Emer, thirty in May 1940, and Derry, twenty-one, were both engaged to be married. Emer wrote to Nan Brennan in Wexford on 20 April describing her Danish fiancé Svend Yort and the plans for their wedding on 17 June. In answer to her aunt's question about a wedding present, Emer sensibly and patriotically opted for Irish linen. Nan duly sent a gift of sheets, for which Emer thanked her promptly in a letter written on 6 July, adding a kindly and detailed description of the wedding and her honeymoon.[53] Meanwhile, working at the riding stable, Derry had met a young aeronautical engineer who had come to Washington to buy aircraft for the French airforce, and remained after the outbreak of war to work on behalf of Charles de Gaulle's Free French. Half English and half French, Gilbert Jerrold was the great-great-grandson of Douglas Jerrold, the nineteenth-century satirical journalist and prolific contributor to *Punch*. They too were married in Washington in 1940.

Emer had a baby daughter, called Una after her mother, and Derry's son Jan was two months old when another journalist wrote a long piece about the Irish Minister and his family in the summer of 1941.[54] The Brennans had moved house yet again. At sixty, Bob was still as energetic as ever, and he and Maeve were clearly close:

> Summer or winter he moves about the capital with a brisk energy that takes him in and out of many places in the course of a day. He goes, whenever time permits, on his own two feet. He would like to take long walks with his family, or go bicycling with his pretty daughter Maeve, who is a 24 year old feminine version of her father's quick wit and mind, and his son Pat, who at 13 is taller and heavier than his father.

According to the writer, Maeve was by now librarian at CUA's Catholic School of Social Service. On 16 June 1942, the *Irish Times* printed her photograph on its front page, with the same information. Wartime shortages had by then reduced the newspaper to four pages, and the few pictures it published were of cheerful, innocuous subjects; the rest of the front page was all war news. Maeve stands before a large painting of George Washington, holding a stack of five thick books and smiling broadly. Wearing a wool plaid jacket over a crisp white blouse, she has had her hair cut, and it reaches only to her shoulders. (In another photograph, apparently from the same time, she wears the *fáinne* that marks her as an Irish speaker.)[55] The information in the caption was out of date, however: by June 1942, Maeve had left Washington.

The absence of graduation records at CUA suggests that Maeve did not complete her degree in Library Science, while subsequent references in her letters and conversation point to some great unhappy upheaval in her life about this time. Certainly, her parents were not pleased about her decision to move to New York. Apart from missing Maeve's company, or worrying about her safety, Una, suffering with arthritis and long dependent on Emer, would now have no daughter to call on for help with her duties as a diplomatic wife, or in the running of the house. Thirty years later, however, in the midst of mental breakdown, Maeve spoke at length to a young woman friend about things she had only hinted at before. She had been in love with Walter Kerr at CUA, she said, and they were engaged to be married, then one day, walking into the cafeteria, she spotted him, deep in conversation with 'a big girl' on the other side of the room. Something in the way they behaved together made her continue through the room without speaking to him; later, he ended their engagement and, she said, her heart was broken.

This is one of the few moments in Maeve's story when the naked pain that is so strong in her fiction speaks through her own voice and body. That it tells the truth, at least about her memory, is clear from an exchange overheard between William Shawn and Edith Oliver, his assistant at *The New Yorker*, about 1960. Kerr was by then drama critic with the *New York Herald Tribune*. He had been married for seventeen years to the 'big girl', and *Please Don't Eat the Daisies*, his wife Jean's series of vignettes about life with her drama-critic husband and four sons, was a bestseller.

Mary Kierstead, who was Shawn's secretary, heard Oliver mention Kerr's name to the *New Yorker* editor.

'Walter Kerr will never work here,' Shawn said.

'Why?' asked Oliver.

'Because of Maeve,' was the answer. Most people who knew Maeve by that time found her enchanting, but inscrutable, and few of them dreamed that she possessed anything as old-fashioned as a broken heart, but Walter Kerr would have been a natural for *The New Yorker*, and Shawn's refusal to consider hiring him was firm enough to remain a puzzling memory.[56]

EIGHT

Away from Home

Maeve's 'Talk of the Town' pieces for *The New Yorker* are filled with references to her early life in Manhattan, when she lived in Greenwich Village and worked in midtown. A natural chronicler, she scrupulously counts years and provides dates alongside memories, much as she carefully noted her own age in each of her stories about childhood.[1] In July 1941, she writes, as a visitor to New York, she walked into the University Restaurant on West 8th Street for the first time, and ordered a dinner of lamb chops [*LWL* 197]. This does not read as though she had company; instead, we see her embarking on a long-time pattern of sitting alone, in this restaurant and others, observing all around her. The following winter, when the Japanese bombed Hawaii's Pearl Harbor and America entered the war, was her first in New York City.

Maeve's first job was at the New York Public Library, at 42nd Street. Soon, however, she found a position on New York's most exciting magazine for women, *Harper's Bazaar*. As the daughter of the Irish Minister in Washington, of course, she had connections. It would be impossible to trace them all, but *Harper's Bazaar* was part of William Randolph Hearst's publishing empire, and Bob's contacts in the newspaper world included leading Hearst journalist Joseph Kingsbury Smith, whose correspondence with Joseph Stalin was making international headlines that year.[2] More importantly, perhaps, Carmel Snow, the *Bazaar*'s indefatigable and visionary editor, was Irish.[3]

Born in 1887, in Dalkey, on the coast south of Dublin, Snow was the daughter of Peter White, Managing Director of the Irish Woollen Manufacturing and Export Company, who had worked with Lady Aberdeen in 1893 to prepare the famous Irish Village as a showcase for Irish tweed and handcrafts (complete with Blarney Stone), for the Chicago World's Fair. Travelling around the west of Ireland to recruit the forty 'colleens' required to staff the Village, however, Peter White contracted pneumonia. When he died a few weeks later, his wife Annie went to Chicago in his place, accompanied by her youngest sister Agnes Mayne, but leaving her six young children with relatives. Annie White managed the 'colleens' and more than sixty other employees, made the Village a huge success, then opened a shop for Irish imports on Wabash Avenue and sent for little Carmel and her sister Christine. Later, she ran a successful dress business in New York.[4]

Carmel White grew up in the American fashion world, wearing *haute couture* and travelling to Paris for the collections, but she also made regular visits to relatives in Ireland and revelled in her Irishness. When she married the wealthy Palen Snow in 1926, she took his surname, dropping her own to avoid confusion. She retained a trace of Irish accent, however; was pleased to be described as both 'fey' and 'fiery', and professed a devout Catholicism throughout her life. The austere new Archbishop of Dublin, John Charles McQuaid, was almost her first cousin, for her Aunt Agnes had married McQuaid's widowed father when John Charles was fourteen months old; astonishingly, he did not know until he was sixteen that Agnes was not his mother. Agnes was the sister sent to Chicago with Annie White in 1893. McQuaid, who met Carmel Snow during at least one of her visits to Agnes in Dublin, was Éamon de Valera's influential friend and confidant.[5]

Snow kept in touch with Irish literary life on both sides of the Atlantic. Pádraic and Mary Colum, old friends of the Brennans who had been living in New York since 1914, ate at her table regularly, while Frank O'Connor, Bob's colleague twenty years before on the *Cork Examiner*, was just one of the Irish writers who featured in *Harper's Bazaar*. The first place Snow remembered vividly from her childhood was the Maynes' large house, Cremorne, in Terenure, where she had lived after her father's death. It was close to where Jim Bolger lived and where Bob had found shelter with Yohan and Maria Climanis. Maeve's memories were of the same part of Dublin, as was her accent. She had resisted picking up Americanisms, and still sounded much as she had in Ireland, although her grooming and appearance by now were all American. Nineteenth-century stereotype had represented Ireland as a starving, rain-sodden land of beggars and inept servants. Well-off New Yorkers made comedy of the pronunciations and pronouncements of domestics like Bridget Keogh, the treasured 'little Irish maid' who worked for Snow, but they found the voices of educated Dubliners beguiling. Maeve's way of speaking, pitched between the rolling consonants of the Gate Theatre and the Celtic Twilight's Anglo-Irish drawl, could call up Irish Revival images of a land of homespun-clad poets, descended from kings. For Snow, who liked to recall that 'in Ireland your sheets are always of linen' (even if patched), and once noted that 'my aunt Agnes uses a magnum of champagne for a hot-water bottle', it would have been highly acceptable. Maeve became a fashion copywriter on her magazine.

Travelling to Paris with her mother and sister, Snow had learned to remember the top of a dress while Christine remembered the bottom, so that their mother could copy the pattern later.[6] This ability to remember and describe the precise details of fabric, cut and stitching was what Maeve now perfected. Before fashion began to be mass-produced in the 1960s, the careful descriptions and sketches of top fashion journalists percolated through lesser publications to the humblest rural dressmakers. Glossy magazines like *Harper's Bazaar* carried essential technical information for the women everywhere who sewed and altered their own clothes, or who instructed dressmakers on what they wanted. Maeve couldn't sew, but she had seen it done and heard it talked about all her life, and was well acquainted with her Aunt Nan's workroom in Wexford.

Back in Ireland, Maeve's new job was noted. When Máirín Cregan's novel *Rathina*, published in the US in 1942, won the Downey Medal for young people's fiction the following year, wartime travel restrictions prevented her going to New York to receive it, so Bob accepted the award on her behalf. Writing to thank him, early in 1944, she added: 'I enclose a cutting from [the Irish] Independent. Is this true about Maeve? If it is I wish her every success. I think it is one of the nicest jobs of literary work, to be on a magazine of that kind'.[7]

Already, by the end of the 1930s, *Harper's Bazaar* had become, as Snow put it, 'a kind of Mecca for lively young women who had too much vitality to expend it all on social life'.[8] Heiresses with famous last names took the bus to 572 Madison Avenue to work long hours for low wages. Art director Alexey Brodovitch was the most influential magazine designer of his time, pioneering new ways of making text and images flow together on the page. Snow knew all about what she called 'the architecture of clothes'; more importantly, perhaps, she understood fashion as a dynamic part of culture. She looked towards Paris – 'a city where millions of clever hands are at work [to produce] a new twist, a new cut, a new stitch' – but also coaxed her American models to stand or move naturally while being photographed, and identified the talent that could convey the excitement of these new ideas to American readers. Diana Vreeland, whom she hired in 1939 and who later became editor of *Vogue*, epitomised the combination of aggressive stylishness and witty, privileged insouciance that typified *Harper's Bazaar*.

By the time Maeve went to work at the magazine in 1943, the occupation of Paris meant there were no longer any couture collections to report, while wartime restrictions curbed its extravagance by limiting the amount of fabric that could be used in clothing. Even so, increased advertising meant more pages to fill, and talent continued to flow towards *Harper's Bazaar*, throughout its 1940s heyday. Soon after Louise Dahl Wolfe photographed an unknown young woman who had changed her name from Betty Jean Perske to Betty Bacall for a cover in March 1942, Hollywood adopted her as Lauren Bacall. (Maeve used to say that when Bacall departed for California, she announced that she would 'either become a movie star or marry one'.) Along with work by Dahl Wolfe and others, photographs by Edward Steichen and Martin Munkacsi appeared regularly in the magazine, alongside fiction by Colette, Virginia Woolf, and newcomers like Carson McCullers, Eudora Welty and Truman Capote. (In *Breakfast at Tiffany's*, Capote's 1958 novella, the fashion model who gatecrashes Holly Golightly's party has just finished a photo shoot for the *Bazaar*.)

Wartime shortages meant that the only way to be allocated more paper was to start a new magazine, so the Hearst organisation gave over the seventh floor of the Madison Avenue building to a new venture. With Eleanor Ryan ('Barry'), as editor and Lillian Bassman as art director, *Junior Bazaar* gave photographer Richard Avedon his first magazine work, and allowed several other talented young people to find their feet. Maeve Brennan, copywriter, was one of them.[9] Even after it began publication in 1945, however, *Junior Bazaar* remained under the benevolent eye of Snow and Brodovitch. As Snow put it, 'A confused world of novices in ballet slippers and wide hair ribbons, an atmosphere of slightly amateurish fervor, was just to my taste', and she made frequent visits to the seventh floor.

For Maeve, already at work on some of her most powerful fiction, this bustling world offered a way of forgetting what she had left behind. At the time she moved to New York, she had not lived apart from her family since the bleak, disastrous time at boarding-school ten years earlier. Her departure from Washington seems to have been sudden; that it was also a heart-sickening and terrifying separation is clear from a letter she wrote to William Maxwell in about 1970:

> The last week or so, 2 or 3 times, I woke up with the most painful awful feeling of irrevocable separation from something I could put my hand out and touch – I was in New York City & had come from Washington & they were in Washington & the sense of time drawing tight from nowhere to nowhere was, the 2 or 3 times or so, agonising, as though the feeling I woke up with was incurable & would last for every minute as long as I lived. It was as though I could see them & they were wondering about me & didn't know I was dead. And I <u>didn't want them to know</u>.[10]

This follows a detailed reference to her father, and it is clear that 'they' are Maeve's parents. While in Washington, she had attended Mass each

Sunday with Bob and Una at St Thomas's church and participated in the careful social life her father's position demanded. Now, with 'time drawing tight from nowhere to nowhere', she was alone: removed from her family emotionally and spiritually as well as physically. She felt she had abandoned them, and the manner of her leaving Washington seems to have been the source of what she would later call 'the disgusting guilt I feel about my family'.[11] Meanwhile one Washington admirer pursued her to New York with gifts, and pestered her in ways she found disturbing. She became really frightened when a box of flowers arrived from him with all their heads cut off.

In Washington, her father was embarking on the most delicate period of his diplomatic career. US troops landed in Derry, north of the hated Irish border, on 26 January 1942, and he was charged with conveying de Valera's protests to President Roosevelt.[12]

On first arriving in New York, Maeve lived at the Holley Hotel, on the corner of Washington Square West and Washington Place. (A small, old hotel between tall apartment buildings, it was torn down in the mid-1950s to make way for New York University's Hayden Hall.) Looking across at the 'worn-looking' studio buildings on the south side of the Square, Maeve thought them beautiful and romantic, and longed to find an apartment, or even a room, in one of them. Perhaps she still thought of returning to Ireland, but the war in the Atlantic made that impossible, at least for the moment. The area around Washington Square, with its handsome old townhouses and public park, is a part of New York that looks a little like Dublin, and in those early days Maeve tramped in and out of building after building, searching for a place to live [*LWL* 216]. She spent one summer in a tiny room at 224 Sullivan Street, another in a larger room on Hudson Street. By 1944 she had settled in 'one enormous room at the top of a beautiful house' at 5 East 10th Street, a few blocks north, just off Fifth Avenue [*LWL* 113, 195].

Every room she rented had a fireplace, as though she hoped to find again the feeling of home she had left behind in Dublin, where 48 Cherryfield Avenue, the house that 'never blew up', had been heated by coal fires. Guns and explosives had been part of her childhood, and some people's houses had indeed blown up. Bob, and even Una, had spent long periods on the run while their children were young, sleeping and eating where they could. Before the years in Cherryfield Avenue, houses where they lived had had their front doors kicked in or had had to be hastily packed up and abandoned. Even since coming to America, despite the considerable comfort of their lives, the Brennans had moved house often, at the behest of politics. Now, alone in New York, Maeve thought long and deeply about her parents, about marriage, and about the idea of home.

Details in one of her finest stories, published twenty years later, reveal that she began work on it about the time she arrived in New York. Its title, 'A Young Girl Can Spoil Her Chances', comes straight from the speech of County Wexford, and the voice that speaks it must be female. It is a middle-aged woman's dire warning to a younger one about the way she is conducting her relationships with men, or a man. In the story, as it appeared in *The New Yorker* of 8 September 1962, Rose Derdon's mother utters the words in a long, remembered, sequence about Hubert and Rose's courtship: 'They say a young girl can spoil her chances, but a young man can spoil his chances just as easy and just as much' [*SA* 81]. Mary Lambert (named in other stories, though not in this one) is a venomously self-defending woman – one of several in Maeve's fiction – and her dismissive cruelty has turned her daughter into the colourless woman whose timidity now so enrages her husband.

By the time 'A Young Girl Can Spoil Her Chances' was published, it had become a layered, complex narrative of some 13,000 words, the longest of Maeve's stories about the Derdons. Its evocation of place in the streets of central Dublin; its dwelling on the ashes of a marriage; the sickening ebb of feeling as the man at the centre of the story finds himself wanting, bear comparison to James Joyce's 'The Dead', and yet this story is wholly original, and entirely feminine. Its co-ordinates are domestic – the walls and stairs of the house; the preparation of ordinary meals; the fireside needle-work – and its expert construction suggests the skills of a seamstress and keeper of linen rather than any more workmanlike analogy. It begins at breakfast in Cherryfield Avenue and ends there on the same day at teatime; within it, however, lifetimes and histories are folded and pressed.

The day of the story's action is Tuesday, 9 September, the forty-third anniversary of Rose Derdon's father's death. Rose herself is almost fifty-three, for he died two days before her tenth birthday. In fact it was not even a full two days, and Rose has spent all her life since then searching for and puzzling about that uneven piece of time that broke off suddenly beneath their feet, when her father was lost and she was left behind.

Maeve's mother Una turned fifty-three on 11 September 1941, three (not two) days after the forty-third anniversary of her own father's death.[13] By the following July, she and Bob had been married for thirty-three years, as Hubert and Rose are in the story. Like Hubert Derdon, Bob had been twenty-eight at the time of his marriage. Maeve's fiction engages often in this sort of calculation, and she could simply have decided to locate the story in 1941–1942, but nothing within it dates it for the reader. Instead, external evidence suggests that she began to write it during those years, and used it to work out a private numerology.

Most tellingly, 9 September was a Tuesday in 1941 – a fact readily established with modern computers, but less easily discovered ten, fifteen or twenty years after the event. A proof copy of this story, dated 15 March 1961 and now in the University of Delaware, sets its action on the forty-fourth, instead of the forty-third, anniversary of Rose's father's death. There is little to choose between the two, unless the story is following the dates of Una's life.[14] In that proof copy too, Hubert and Rose live not in Ranelagh, on the south side of Dublin, but in Drumcondra, a northside suburb with similar houses. The rooms where they lived after their marriage are 'in a house off Hollis [i.e. Holles] Street', not, as in the published version, in the (invented) Somerville Street, off St Stephen's Green, which must derive its name from Summerville, the house Bob and Una bought just outside Wexford in 1910. When she first wrote this story, therefore, Maeve had not yet begun to plant her fictions in the house and street in Dublin that she remembered best. (By contrast, in the first Derdon story she published, 'The Poor Men and Women', in *Harper's Bazaar*, April 1952, Hubert and Rose live in the small house that is clearly identifiable as 48 Cherryfield Avenue. It is a twenty-minute bus ride south of O'Connell Bridge; a tennis club lies behind it, there is a laburnum tree in the back garden, and a table of ferns stands in the bow window at the front.)

Knowing something of Maeve's state of mind when she began to write 'A Young Girl Can Spoil Her Chances', we hear those words echo in her mind. Perhaps Una had spoken them to her, or another woman relative had written them in a letter when Emer and Derry were preparing to marry and have children, but Maeve was falling in and out of love instead, and choosing to continue her education. Before the outbreak of war in Europe, many states had moved to curb the freedom of their citizens and especially of women.[15] 'How I hope you won't encounter heartbreak and frustration when you come back here,' Dorothy Macardle had written, in the letter already quoted in Chapter 7. In an Ireland increasingly walled around with xenophobic suspicion, influential critics condemned modernism as un-Irish, and criticised the National Gallery for exhibiting paintings of nudes.[16] The 1937 Constitution had given expression to a growing conservatism that relegated women to the home, a change mirrored in the falling proportion of women among students at University College Dublin. With many more children than their counterparts elsewhere in Europe, Irish married women were especially constrained.[17] The title of Maeve's story echoes a backlash of Victorian righteousness that cautioned young women against competing with men, much less outshining them, and warned of the dangers of too much education. That attitude would find widespread support in America too, when the war was over.

As Maeve's first love returned to his Jewish community to find a wife, and Walter Kerr prepared to marry a woman ten years his junior, it is easy to imagine an Irish woman's voice suggesting complacently that Maeve had 'spoiled her chances'. Easy, too, to understand the fury this would have provoked in Maeve – for its irrelevance to the life she had chosen as much as for its lack of sympathy. All the raging bitterness of 'A Young Girl Can Spoil Her Chances' is directed at mothers. Mary Lambert is a monster, but one who is capable of kindness, as when she fills a basket with food for her daughter to take to Dublin after her marriage. Mostly, though, she thwarts and belittles her, bullying all the space around her, so that Rose grows up wary and weak, and hurries to efface herself at any hint of disapproval. The story's full-blown anger, felt by Hubert, is reserved for Rose herself, as his son's mother:

> But when he got to that point in his thoughts Hubert would have to stop himself, because he would begin to feel his anger against her getting out of hand. The anger was dreadful because there seemed to be no way of working it off. It was an anger that called for pushing over high walls, or kicking over great towering, valuable things that would go down with a shocking crash. The thing he really wanted to smash was out of his reach and he did not even know what it was, but when he thought of things that were out of his reach but that he could smash if he could reach them, he felt better. [*SA* 78–9]

By the time 'A Young Girl Can Spoil Her Chances' appeared in print, Maeve had been married, but was once more living alone. The story is clearly informed by experience of living in a couple, and yet the kind of anger it expresses reads vividly like that of a girl against her mother. A hundred irritations against Rose's humility, her 'cringing and running out of the room', her gentle distress that is never expressed in confrontation, but only passively, suggest the strategies a mother might employ to cope with her young adult daughter's furious, disruptive unhappiness. They also articulate the daughter's answering frustration. In families that had moved country, the ordinary tensions between mothers and daughters were amplified, as daughters embraced the culture of their new environment, while mothers continued to behave as they had in the old country. The aspects of Rose's behaviour that most infuriate Hubert in this story might have been expected of women in Ireland, but would have seemed odd indeed among forthright young Americans.

In later years, writing to William Maxwell, Maeve would reach towards understandings and explanations of what she saw as her mother's unhappiness, but writing this story, she seems merely furious and impatient towards Una as she pursues a life that will abandon all pretence of following in her footsteps as quiet homemaker or gardener. The world Maeve had come to in New York did not require her to cook, or sew, or even hand canapés around, and did not particularly expect her to marry. In Washington she had been noticed as beautiful; now in Manhattan she became intimidatingly stylish as well. She grew her hair long again, but instead of plaiting and winding it around her head, or wearing it loose around her shoulders, she tied it in a ponytail or piled it on top of her head. With a slash of dark lipstick drawn confidently across her mouth, she dressed more and more often in black. Part of the enduring fascination of her writing is the consciousness it reveals behind the laminations of that mid-twentieth-century image of femininity.

In pieces she wrote in 1962 and again in 1966, Maeve recalled the room she lived in on East 10th Street in the 1940s. It was on the sixth floor, under the roof – impossibly hot in summer and bitterly cold in winter (the fireplace didn't work) – but its wall of casement windows looked south at roof gardens and roof terraces, and a 'huge and always changing sweep of sky'. There was no elevator, and the stairs were dirty, and one stifling Saturday night in summer, when she had dressed with special care, she lost her footing on the last flight: 'I tripped and tumbled head over heels down to the bottom. My arms were dirty and my white gloves were ruined and my hair was down and I thought of myself living in that hot, dirty house, and I sat on the floor in the hall and cried with rage' [*LWL* 113–14].

At *Harper's Bazaar*, all the women editors wore white gloves (they wore hats in the office too), and there was no shortage of places to go to on Saturday, or any night. However, some of the many homosexual men at the magazine did not scruple to round out their own fashionable social life at the expense of the eager young women who worked there. The most senior women, like Snow, Vreeland and 'Barry', were happily married to wealthy men, but the status of single women was more ambiguous, especially if they lived in New Jersey or the Bronx, or even in Greenwich Village, rather than on the Upper East Side. The men needed female escorts, but their world floated on alcohol – three martinis before lunch was not unusual – and the young women could suffer emotional damage. Photographer Karl Bissinger, who joined *Harper's Bazaar* in the 1940s, recalled a private secretary called Ellen McCool. Brought up in New Jersey by Irish parents, she became mentally ill while working at the magazine and died later in hospital, 'totally, totally lost'.[18]

Bissinger photographed people surrounded by the detail of their lives, and his portraits of 'the luminaries of high Bohemia – writers, artists, musicians, painters, journalists' – are alive with his insights into personality.[19]

Maeve was McCool's friend, but Bissinger could see no vulnerability in her. To him she appeared watchful and disdainful, as well as beautiful and very elegant. He and she were sent on assignments together, and he might have got to know her better if he had not sensed an enormous anger in her and, as a young man recently arrived from Ohio, feared her amused New York contempt were he to say something that might reveal him as a hick. Years later, reading the fiction she had written during that time, he would be struck by the profound sensitivity it revealed, and by how well she had concealed it. Still, Maeve must have trusted and respected him, for she asked him to photograph the Irish playwright Denis Johnston when he came to New York in 1948, and when she wanted portraits of herself, it was Karl Bissinger who took them. One of them is on the cover of this book.

Although she maintained her connections with the Irish theatre, Maeve was by now resolutely unsentimental about the politics of her native land. New York in the early 1940s was full of military officers on furlough: young and dashing in their various dress uniforms, they were also lonely, and terrified of dying painfully and soon. A photograph Maeve kept in her album shows her on the street with three men in uniform, beside the awning that sheltered the entrance to Number 1 Fifth Avenue. In the same box, in a file marked 'Correspondence', she kept a V-mail signed by Lieutenant C. L. Shipley, and sent to her at 224 Sullivan Street from SS *Dashing Wave*, FPO San Francisco.[20] Another young officer, this time with literary leanings and Irish connections, met her briefly, and was immediately smitten.

Francis W. Lovett, of the Colorado-based Tenth Mountain Division, was in his mid-twenties, a fiction writer and an admirer of the acerbic *New Yorker* writer Dorothy Parker, when he and two companions walked into the Algonquin Hotel in March 1944, hoping to catch sight of the famous Round Table group. Lovett's college room-mate, John Armington Laidler, was in US Navy uniform, but Lovett and Carl Henry Maas both wore the dress uniform of their 'ski troop': jacket with green silk scarf, tailored ski pants, and square-toed boots with white gaiters. They sat drinking Jamaica rum daiquiris and conducting a deliberately preposterous conversation – 'a game we played for the benefit of unsuspecting onlookers' – until they attracted the attention of two young women who sat at the other end of the bar. Maeve's companion was a colleague called Rhona (or perhaps Roma) Ryan, and both young women, trained to examine and describe fabrics, cut and stitching, were fascinated by the Mountain Division uniform. Laidler left to catch a train, but the other two men remained. Lovett had an uncle in Northampton, Massachusetts, who liked to hold forth about the 'fight for Irish freedom': '[W]e turned the talk to Ireland . . . and Maeve irritated me when she said something about licking old wounds instead of getting on with things. There was a bit of vitriol in her tone, but she looked so pretty that I began to melt in earnest.'[21]

Lovett found Maeve challenging as well as beautiful. He worked hard to impress her, and was rewarded with a lively and memorable conversation about Somerset Maugham's *The Razor's Edge*. However, he too encountered the hard edge Karl Bissinger would observe, both in the 'vitriol' of her reference to Irish nationalists 'licking old wounds' and in her dismissive response at the end of the evening, when he asked if she would write to him. He and Carl Maas had boasted to her and her friend about their unit and about Colorado, describing the extreme conditions they were trained to endure, and how they had learned to build igloos and dig snow caves. Each recruit to the mountain troops had had to submit three letters of recommendation as skier or climber in order to enlist, and now Maeve asked him 'Why did you get your three letters and enlist in your troop?' He said something calculated to make her think about him – about loving climbing mountains, or getting higher than the horizon – but her reply was devastating: 'I will not write to any man who has a death wish,' she said. Lovett didn't dare to kiss her, although he wanted to. He never saw her again.

One of the first friends Maeve made in New York was Brendan Gill of *The New Yorker*, who was three years older than she was. Son of a wealthy Irish-American Catholic doctor from Hartford, Connecticut, he had married at twenty-two, the day after his graduation from Yale, and had joined *The New Yorker* in 1938. His wife Anne came from a Protestant family who knew Catholics only as servants, and the name of the Church of the Immaculate Conception, where their daughter's wedding was celebrated, seemed to them odd to the point of indecency. Within a few years, Gill had ceased to be a Catholic, and 'was often to be found attacking the Immaculate Conception in the nearest neighborhood bar', but he had made a name for himself 'as a writer of stories about priests, nuns, and sad young men about to be gobbled up by Mother Church'. That Maeve had gone to a school called Cross and Passion became a running joke between them in Costello's saloon on Third Avenue. He and Anne, their three children and a nursemaid, lived in an old redbrick townhouse on the Upper East Side, where they gave many parties.[22] Through him, Maeve met other leading *New Yorker* writers, among them Joseph Mitchell, already a master of interview technique when he joined the magazine in the same year as Gill, and Philip Hamburger, who had arrived in 1939 and initially shared an office with him. Charles Addams, whose Gothic cartoons for *The New Yorker* gave rise to a flourishing cult in various media, was another member of Gill's circle; he too became Maeve's friend, and, for a time, her lover.

Maeve may have met Brendan Gill as early as 1939, when the World's

Fair, 'World of Tomorrow', opened at Flushing, just outside New York. In the early summer of that year, along with other young holders of press passes, Gill 'all but lived on the fairgrounds'.[23] Alongside the General Motors Futurama, and other displays of how technology would make America's future both glorious and comfortable, more than sixty nations, Ireland among them, exhibited in the Fair's Government Zone at the north end of the fairground. US President Franklin Roosevelt had invited Éamon de Valera to open the Irish Pavilion in mid-May, but in late April concerns about the impending war caused him to cancel his trip, and Seán T. O'Kelly, Vice-President of the Executive Council, went in his place. As Irish Minister, Bob was closely involved in the arrangements and especially in the opening of Michael Scott's award-winning building of steel, concrete and glass, designed to show the shape of a shamrock when viewed from the air.[24] It is likely that Maeve accompanied her father to the Fair at least once. Gill certainly seems to have met him then, for he was granted an interview with de Valera in Dublin soon afterwards, probably by means of a letter of introduction.

Gill's autobiography describes how he left his job at *The New Yorker* that summer when his father announced that he and his younger son Charles were planning a trip to Ireland, and invited Brendan and Anne to accompany them. They landed at Cobh at a time when all the liners going in the other direction were full of Americans hurrying home. There they hired 'a big Buick' with a driver, and proceeded to tour the country. In Dublin in August, de Valera, who, as President of the League of Nations was 'widely assumed [to be] the best-informed man in Europe on the war question', assured Gill that there would be no war. Arriving back in New York, Gill repeated this to a reporter from his hometown newspaper, the Hartford *Courant*, who duly published it on 3 September, the same day as the paper announced Hitler's invasion of Poland.

By 1944, Maeve Brennan and Brendan Gill were good friends. She may have shown him some of her writing, for on 24 July he sent her a postcard at *Harper's Bazaar* marked with the superimposed crosses of a Catholic bishop's permission to publish and the words 'Imprimatur, Bishop Gill'.[25] By the time of Franklin Roosevelt's final election campaign that autumn, they were widely believed to be lovers. (Gill's autobiography discusses New York in some detail as 'the ideal place in which to commit adultery'.)[26] Philip Hamburger tells of standing near the corner of Fifth Avenue and 10th Street on a rainy day in lower Manhattan, waiting for Roosevelt's car to pass. The President was already in poor health, and ought not to have been out, but he was seeking a fourth term of office and was due to speak at Madison Square Garden that evening. As Hamburger stood among the crowd that had gathered, Gill emerged from Maeve's apartment building. Spotting

Hamburger, he asked him, 'What are you doing here?' Hamburger explained, and together the two men ran beside the President's car as it passed along Fifth Avenue.[27]

It was while living in that sixth-floor apartment at 5 East 10th Street and working at *Harper's Bazaar*, in 1944 or 1945, that Maeve completed the manuscript of her novella, *The Visitor*. It is a book that screams quietly, and with terrifying precision, echoing some of the themes in 'A Young Girl Can Spoil Her Chances' but presenting them in very different ways. Although Rose's mother in the short story and Mrs King in the novella are unlike each other in status and social setting, they share a vindictive coldness, and inflict similar injuries. The surface Maeve presented in those years (to men at least) was glamorous and brittle, but the writing she produced tells of wounds that were deep and exquisitely painful. *The Visitor* may be 'the acting out of a nightmare of harsh choices facing a young woman on the threshold of her future, who feels she must reject her past if she is to thrive, but dreads the consequences'.[28] It is possible too that her recurring dream years later, of 'the most painful awful feeling of irrevocable separation from something I could put my hand out and touch' (quoted above from a letter to William Maxwell), was not so much a recollection of that period of her life as a re-entering of her own fiction. By her late twenties, though, when she must have written *The Visitor*, Maeve's descriptions of pain and of tortured, public, craziness had the authority of lived experience.

Maeve's conversation with Francis Lovett at the Algonquin may have been fuelled by alcohol, but the cynicism she showed, about the 'fight for Irish freedom' that had been so much part of her parents' lives and about the eager military courage of her young American contemporaries, suggests extreme disillusion at twenty-seven and a bitter distance from her earlier patriotic idealism. She was in touch with her family, however. She grieved when Derry's second son died as an infant, and was overjoyed when her daughter Yvonne was born, in May 1944. Gilbert Jerrold's work for the Free French took him for long periods to Algeria, where he had founded the École Nationale Professionelle de l'Air in Cap-Matifou in 1943. With the children, therefore, Derry moved from their house in Maryland to New York City. One day when Yvonne was about two, Maeve arrived with a huge cardboard box from a department store, out of which she produced a magnificent yellow organdie dress. Yvonne's earliest memory of Maeve is of walking down the street between her mother and aunt that day, wearing her new dress, with each of them holding one of her hands.

The Visitor, discovered at the University of Notre Dame Library in 1997 among the papers of Maisie Ward, of the Catholic publishers Sheed and Ward, remained unpublished during Maeve's lifetime. At the time she completed it, she had published no fiction that we know of. She may have sent the manuscript to Ward for general literary advice, perhaps failing to keep – or even make – a carbon copy.[29] *The Visitor* is both like and unlike her other writing, and on the surface, given that it is the work of a New York fashion copywriter in her twenties, its subject matter is surprising. Although the book's central character is a young woman, there is no mention of New York or even of America, no reference to the war or to fashion, and what small social life it depicts is narrow, sour and elderly. It tells the story of an interior life lived against the chilly backdrop of an unwelcoming Dublin, and, in Christopher Carduff's words, sounds the three notes that will recur in Maeve Brennan's later work: a ravenous grudge, a ravenous nostalgia, and a ravenous need for love.[30] The wry and sometimes hilarious humour that will flash through some of her later writing is absent, however, and the only pet is a remembered cat.

The heroine of *The Visitor* has Maeve's mother's given name, Anastasia, but she looks a little like Maeve: 'Her hair was dark and brushed smoothly back from her forehead. Her mouth was stubborn and her eyes were puzzled under faint, flyaway brows.' Aged twenty-two, Anastasia King is an only child, and an orphan, and has just returned to Ireland following her mother's death in Paris, where they have lived for six years. It is November when she arrives, but nothing in the book suggests what year it is; instead, the gaunt houses of the Victorian suburb where her father's mother lives with Katharine, the kindly and powerless housekeeper, seem fixed in timeless decay:

> All the houses in the square were tall, with heavy stone steps going up to the front doors. They were occupied by old people, who had grown old in their houses and their accustomed ways. They disregarded the inconveniences of the square houses, their dark basements and drafty landings, and lived on, going tremulously from one wrinkled day to the next, with an occasional walk between the high stone walls of their gardens. [*V* 13]

Winter in Dublin is dark and rainy, but snow is rare, and there is nothing like the cold of New York. The flowerbeds in the gardens show only black soil, the wooden seat under the laburnum tree never dries enough to sit on, and night comes early. In the house, Katharine keeps the kitchen stove in the basement lit day and night, and toils upstairs with tea trays and with coal to feed the big fire in the living-room, where the windows look out over the park and the dark trees, and Mrs King sits, lonely and satisfied, irritated by any change, resolutely withholding all that her granddaughter craves.

With its tall houses and iron railings, and its tree-surrounded park where nursemaids come to sit in the green, 'not mysterious' middle space while children play, Noon Square resembles Palmerston Park in Rathmines. By the 1940s the area was home to many of the leaders of Irish society, in politics, the law and academic life. Mrs King's house is like the one where the Brennans lived on nearby Belgrave Road: its front door is reached by a tall flight of stone steps, in the side of which, at another door below, deliveries are received and poor men and women knock to ask for alms. Details are described precisely:

> Anastasia looked suddenly up at the mirror that hung over the mantel. It did not lie flat against the wall, but hung out slightly at the top. It reflected the fringed hearthrug where she had played when she was a little child, hearing the conversation go to and fro over her head. [*V* 13–14]

Maeve lived in Belgrave Road until she was four. The hearth she describes here seems to be the same one as in her story 'The Clever One', where she remembers her baby sister Derry at about eighteen months old, throwing Emer's woollen cap into the fire. Other details of the life of Mrs King's house come from Cherryfield Avenue, however: the laburnum tree in the back garden; the sun that lay across the cement outside the back door, where the cat waited for her breakfast on long-ago summer mornings; a young architect whose name is Briscoe.

Anger lies at the heart of *The Visitor*: an anger that explodes like the crashing of cymbals in the last pages, after the slow, sad, incomprehensions that have gone before. As so often in Maeve's writing, Christmas provides a high point. Coming at the middle of the book, it offers hope, with the possibility of action, and even approval. Day after day, Anastasia makes her way to the centre of Dublin, to the elegant shops on Grafton Street, where she finds pleasure in choosing presents: three each for her grandmother and Katharine, and one for Miss Norah Kilbride, Mrs King's elderly spinster friend, who will come to Christmas dinner. She wraps the gifts carefully, and hides them. One afternoon in a department store, which must be either Switzer's or Brown Thomas, opposite it, she believes she catches sight of her dead mother. Pursuing her through the crowds, she makes her way to a church – Clarendon Street church is just around the corner – where she lights a votive candle and kneels a while, feeling at last that she can leave her mother to rest in peace. Her own fragile peace is soon shattered, though, when her grandmother makes it clear that Christmas has been an end, not a beginning, and Anastasia understands that she has no home after all.

This has been the book's whole message, as it will be the central motif in all Maeve's best writing. Early in *The Visitor* it finds expression in one of the lyrical meditations she inserts so surely and seamlessly in her narratives. The words are enigmatic, yet they seem rational and true, with the private logic of remembered shadows:

> Home is a place in the mind. When it is empty, it frets. It is fretful with memory, faces and places and times gone by. Beloved images rise up in disobedience and make a mirror for emptiness. Then what resentful wonder, and what half-aimless seeking. It is a silly state of affairs. It is a silly creature that tries to get a smile from even the most familiar and loving shadow. Comical and hopeless, the long gaze back is always turned inward. [*V* 8]

In *The Visitor*, Norah Kilbride confides in Anastasia King about her love for a young architect called Frank Briscoe, years before, when she was twenty-eight, and how they defied Miss Kilbride's autocratic invalid mother by carrying on a sexual relationship downstairs while she lay in bed above. Frank Briscoe drowned on holiday in Killiney, however, and Norah Kilbride lived on as her mother's slave: a 'killed bride'. She dreams of 'a doubtful deathly union with her long-lost young hero, with whom she had once struggled in valiant, well-dressed immodesty on a small settee, for love's sake'. When she too dies, Anastasia so violently rejects the possibility of becoming like her – eternally a visitor and socially a virgin – that she breaks the promise she has made, to slip a wedding ring on to the dead woman's finger. Instead, she misses the funeral, further alienating her grandmother, and consigns the ring to the deep oblivion of an old quarry.

The Visitor's descriptions of Norah Kilbride's past – real or imagined – and of the state of Anastasia's parents' marriage when she was a child, could not have been written by a person without sexual experience. Some of the book's fury can be traced to the diary entry Maeve wrote at eighteen about her Aunt Bessie's 'wasted life'.[31] But the culture Maeve had been brought up in offered no possibility of sexuality outside marriage. Indeed, had *The Visitor* been published when it was written, it would almost certainly have been banned in Ireland, as were Kate O'Brien's *The Land of Spices* (1941), and Edna O'Brien's early novels, twenty years later. Like them, it laid bare the sexual needs so resolutely hidden behind social decorum and Catholic observance in Ireland, and more shockingly, perhaps, demonstrated a young unmarried woman writer's familiarity with them. We have no record of Maeve's making a journey back to Ireland between 1934 and the late 1940s, and travel would scarcely have been possible during the war, although her father did manage at least one visit on diplomatic business.[32] Had she gone back there in her twenties, she would have found a country that offered no place for her, as she must surely have recognised.

The Visitor ends with Anastasia standing in the street outside her grandmother's house, barefoot and recklessly singing, 'sudden and loud as one in a dream, who without warning finds a voice in some public place'. This is what she has seen poor men and women do on the worst winter days, in order to be let in by the basement door and given a meal in Katharine's warm kitchen. For Anastasia King, the nourishment of home is not to be found by the conventional adult way that leads up the steps and through the front door. Instead, she must take the route that children take, and beggars (a word that children must not say). The song she sings is a children's parody of a famous hymn. Aptly, it is about 'a happy land, far far away'.

One aspect of Maeve's Irishness fitted easily with her life in Manhattan, especially after the war ended. She knew writers and actors, and was much involved in entertaining members of the Abbey Theatre Company when they came on tour. Siobhán McKenna had joined the Abbey in 1944 and Karl Bissinger noticed that she 'caused quite a stir' when she first came to New York. In 1947, when Kathleen Hoagland published her monumental, *1000 Years of Irish Poetry: The Gaelic and Anglo-Saxon Poets from Pagan Times to the Present*, 'Miss Maeve Brennan of *Harper's Bazaar*' was among those she thanked for their help.

A favourite place for Irish writers, and later for writers of any nationality, was the saloon run by Tim and Joe Costello at 44th Street and Third Avenue, where the elevated railway kept rents down. It was only a few blocks from *The New Yorker*, many of whose writers and artists gathered there at the end of the day. A long mahogany bar ran down one side, and on the wall opposite, reflected in the mirrors behind the bar, James Thurber had drawn a series of large cartoons. Under them were six or eight booths, where corned beef and cabbage, and other unpretentious food, was served.[33]

Born in Ferbane, County Offaly in 1895, Tim Costello had fought on the republican side in the Civil War, and was one of the many who had emigrated to the US soon afterwards. He sold bootleg whiskey until Prohibition ended in 1933, when he and his brother opened a legitimate saloon.[34] Presiding over his Third Avenue bar as though it were a 'rambling house' in Ireland, where neighbours gathered to chat and tell stories, he became a reticent mentor to a whole generation. Faith Corrigan, who married the *New Yorker* writer John McNulty in 1945, was a year younger than Maeve. She first visited Costello's with McNulty in 1942, and noted how Tim Costello's own presence made it somehow a salon as well as a saloon:

He was a big upright man from Ireland with shrewd blue eyes and a mouth that tended to be slightly pursed. It was the expression of a man who sees everything, but withholds comment. When he was amused his smile went wide, his eyes sparkled under bushy eyebrows, and he would polish the glass he was drying even more vigorously. He was a man of dignity and pride who disliked anything phony, especially phony Irishmen. John told me how Tim had disposed of one such St Patrick's Day patriot who stood at the bar, flushed with drink and wearing kilts. Tim gave him a withering glance and said 'Pull up your socks, Hiawatha!'[35]

John McNulty, born in Lawrence, Massachusetts, of parents from Counties Clare and Mayo, had an unerring ear for the ways people really spoke and a brilliant ability to capture their stories on paper. For *The New Yorker*, he wrote a series of articles about Costello's, sixteen of which he collected as *Third Avenue, New York* in 1946. It followed Joseph Mitchell's 1943 collection, *McSorley's Wonderful Saloon*, and established Costello's as a unique and special place. Tim Costello was well acquainted with Bob Brennan through their shared political history, and he took a special interest in Maeve, who in 1969 would write of her own *alter ego* that 'she wishes Tim Costello hadn't died'.[36] Costello's was not one of the places Maeve wrote about – John McNulty was understood to have prior rights there – but she often ate or drank there. Faith McNulty remembers the first time she saw her. It was in the offices of *Harper's Bazaar*, and Maeve was sitting cross-legged on top of a table or desk. She was 'like a pixie', McNulty said: fascinating and unforgettable.[37]

At the beginning of 1947, Bob and Una were recalled to Ireland and began their preparations for departure. Emer and Derry were both married with children; Maeve was established in New York, and Robert Patrick was in Dublin, having graduated from his military academy and gone to study engineering at Trinity College. Following the lifting of war restrictions, de Valera's government planned to manage relations with the United States through two major new initiatives: transatlantic air travel and short-wave radio. An Irish–American agreement on air traffic, signed in Washington on 3 February 1945, had made Shannon a compulsory port of call for all transatlantic flights, and a customs-free airport was to be opened there.[38] Bob had played his part in that achievement, but now he was required to draw on his American contacts and experience to bring the new short-wave service into being. The government announced that he would be the new Director of Broadcasting. He was almost sixty-six.

De Valera had made broadcasts to the United States in 1935, for the

World's Fair in 1939 and again, famously, on St Patrick's Day, 1943, when he had articulated his pastoral dream of Ireland as 'a land bright with cosy homesteads'. His plan now was to re-establish and maintain contact with his huge American constituency, and he was confident that his followers would tune in to regular broadcasts of news and entertainment from Ireland. On 23 April, Patrick J. Little, the Minister for Posts and Telegraphs, introduced his budget estimate for wireless broadcasting. James Dillon of Fine Gael was the most articulate in the growing parliamentary opposition to Fianna Fáil. In a series of colourful contributions to the debate, he accused de Valera of gathering his old guard around him and asserted that 'the real explanation of the short-wave station is that the Taoiseach wants to go to America', and that 'Robert Brennan is being brought back from America to sound the Taoiseach's praises over the radio'.[39]

Newspapers in Washington and Dublin noted Bob's transfer too. In the *Irish Times*, Sarah McClendon wrote from Washington: 'Evelyn Peyton Gordon, one of the better known society columnists, who mixes political news with social reporting, speaks of Mr Brennan's accomplishments here and of his ability to make and keep friends during the ticklish war years.' In a long, quoted, passage, Peyton Gordon noted that the three Brennan daughters would remain in the US, as two of them were married, while 'Maeve, the dainty and exotic, is a member of staff at Harper's Bazaar and is doing a most successful job as such'.[40]

That spring, as Bob and Una Brennan prepared to leave, tributes and thanks poured into the Irish Legation in Tracy Place. Arriving in Dublin, they stayed in a hotel at first, and Bob resumed his old habit of taking long walks by the Dodder. Between Rathfarnham Bridge and Orwell Road, he noticed a house for sale: a bungalow with Tudor-style gables, and one small dormer window that peeped from its red-tiled roof. Across the street, the back gardens of houses on Bushy Park Road, where he had once lived on the run in the home of Erskine Childers, descended in wooded terraces to the water. In between, the river foamed over a weir; ducks and water hens swam, or flew low over the water, and men fished. Not waiting to consult Una, Bob contacted Michael Scott, by then the city's best-known architect, and asked him to inspect the house. By coincidence, the young architect from Scott's office who carried out the survey and wrote the report was the Brennans' old neighbour Hubert Briscoe, whose own commitment to things Irish had by now led him to change his name to Aodhagán Brioscú.

On 2 June 1947, Bob wrote to Maeve from 42 Dodder Road, 'our new address'. He and Una had been in residence for a month, and he found it idyllic: the house was spacious and well laid out; the good-sized garden at the back had the biggest bank of forget-me-nots he had ever seen, and beyond its wall Jersey cows grazed knee deep in lush grass and buttercups, in acres of fields that stretched away towards the Dublin mountains. They had been able to buy electrical appliances – said to be unobtainable in Dublin – and even had a telephone.[41]

Bob's career in radio did not last long. At a general election held on 4 February 1948 the Fianna Fáil party lost its overall majority, and two weeks later a new coalition government, led by John A. Costello, came to power. Determined to redress the conditions of poverty in which so many Irish citizens still lived, the new government set about making economies, and in May the new Minister for Finance announced a decision to abandon both the short-wave radio project and the transatlantic air service.[42] The five Constellation aircraft intended for the service that was to have been inaugurated on St Patrick's Day were sold, and Bob retired as Director of Broadcasting without regret. Always less impelled by personal career strategy than by a desire to do a good job for a cause he believed in, he had long wanted to do more writing. Now he disappeared into his study after breakfast every day, working on a political memoir and on the clever, escapist fiction he had been producing since his Crubeen Patch stories for *Ireland's Own*. Una began to create a new garden, in so far as her arthritis and trouble with her eyes allowed. For breaks, Bob walked contentedly along the river, taking many photographs, delighted whenever he spotted a kingfisher flashing blue-green under one of the bridges.

Oidhche Mhaith agat, a Mhic Uí Dhomhnaill, the Irish-language version of *Good Night, Mr O'Donnell*, had been revived at the Abbey shortly after the Brennans' return to Dublin. Now there was talk of making it into a film. Asked to provide further details about the theft of the Crown Jewels as background, Bob researched the matter in some detail and wrote it up. He also worked on his autobiography, provisionally entitling it *Personal Experience*, and finished a new detective novel. In October 1948 the *Irish Press* published a shortened version of his essay, 'Where Are the Crown Jewels? A Dublin Castle Mystery', and he began to make regular contributions to the paper. When he had to spend three days in bed with a cold, he wrote a play, which he read excitedly to Una and Robert Patrick, and sent to Dorothy Macardle for her opinion. On 21 June 1948 he wrote Maeve a long, affectionate letter that shows she had at last made a trip back to Ireland:

I take my usual walks by the river. It is really very beautiful. I took a lot of photos of it and sent them to Emer. Of course you were here and you saw it. I mean you didn't see it because you take no interest in scenery, you are so much interested in people. Of course I'm interested in people too but I've seen an awful lot of them. You do of course in

67 years and maybe that's why I'm beginning life all over again by taking notice of the thousand and one things on this riverbank that are not people . . .[43]

However modest Bob's political ambition, he still hoped for a major success as a writer, and he did not hesitate to enlist Maeve to help him. Much of this letter is about his new novel, *The Man Who Walked like a Dancer*. Set in Washington, it features a millionaire bachelor hero, not unlike Oscar van Duyven, a cast of Irish-American policemen and a beautiful, witty, independent young woman called More Shaughnessy. The hero, Peter Paul Rosegarland, explains that his name was given to him by the nuns who found him as an infant on the morning of the feast day of Saints Peter and Paul. He had been left in the revolving basket through which they received alms, wearing a silver necklace modelled like a garland of roses. This plot detail recalls the Monastery of the Poor Clares in Dublin, and Maeve's story, 'The Barrel of Rumors', but Rosegarland is also the name of a place near Wexford. Rosegarland and More share an appreciation of Stevenson's *The Wrong Box*, and the plot echoes that book in places, as when the dead body at the centre of the mystery is spirited away. Maeve, and her brother, had already read the book and she made suggestions when Bob wrote to her, but he wanted to make some changes to the typescript, which he seems to have left in her care. His letter ends with a suggestion that she contact the director John Ford for advice about its film possibilities. Ford had not yet begun work on *The Quiet Man*, but had visited Ireland as early as 1921 and had been planning that film for years: Maureen O'Hara had undertaken as early as 1944 to star in it.[44] Lest Maeve be reluctant to contact Ford, Bob reminds her, 'As you will remember, he was very friendly.' His letter finishes wistfully, 'I wish we could have a talk'.

There is no hint in these letters from her father of any estrangement, and certainly no suggestion that Maeve should return to Dublin. *Harper's Bazaar* offered her the kind of opportunities she could never have found in Ireland, and made her an irreplaceable contact for those at home. Letters written to her by Madison Avenue literary agent Mavis McIntosh show that up to the spring of 1949, Maeve was attempting to find publishers for both *The Man Who Walked like a Dancer* and her father's autobiography, which had been appearing in instalments in the *Sunday Press*.

Working at *Harper's Bazaar*, she was at the heart of fashion. Before the war, Carmel Snow had published Christian Dior's first sketches; then in 1947, when he opened his own fashion house with the revolutionary collection that became known as the New Look, hers was the magazine that launched it in America. With longer, full skirts (sometimes with padded

Una Bolger and Robert Brennan on their wedding day, 6 July 1909.

Maeve, *c.* 1926, at St Mary's National School, Belmont Avenue, Dublin.

Maeve, aged about twelve, with her mother in the back garden at Cherryfield Avenue.

The house at Coolnaboy, Co. Wexford, where Una grew up and Maeve spent summers as a child.

48 Cherryfield Avenue, Ranelagh, where Maeve lived with her family from December 1921 to September 1934.

Maeve Brennan as the Virgin Mary in a Nativity play, Immaculata Seminary, Washington, DC, 1935 or 1936.

Maeve in Washington, about 1938.

Maeve, shortly before she left Washington for New York, 1941.
In her right lapel she wears the *fáinne* that proclaims her a speaker of Irish.

Maeve about 1948, photographed by Karl Bissinger in the New York apartment of the theatre critic Thomas Quinn Curtiss.

Maeve with Bluebell, the black Labrador, East Hampton, New York, 1962.

Maeve with an unidentified companion, on board the Holland–America Line liner *Noordam*, early January 1963.

Maeve with William Shawn, *New Yorker* offices, January 1968.

Maeve with Bluebell and two other dogs, early 1970s.

hips), tight waists and a soft, feminine shoulder line, the New Look was a dramatic contrast to the prevailing European fashions, which were still cut and made with economy in mind. Wartime shortages had curtailed fashion development there, and little had changed from the late thirties, so that typical daywear still looked like uniforms, with strong padded shoulders and short skirts. Free of these austerities, the US had already produced youthful, sporty fashions, typified by the designs of Claire McCardell, but the New Look triumphed in America as it did elsewhere.[45]

The New Look marked a revolution not only in the way women looked, but in the way they acted, as all across America they moved out of factories, offices and shops and into kitchens, to leave jobs open for returning soldiers. By wearing clothes that used extravagant amounts of fabric, women expressed confidence in the economy, and in men as breadwinners; they were learning to shop as never before, to support the recovery of industry. 'Feminine' fashions did not mean more respect for women, however. Powerful anti-feminist polemic had been appearing in print for some time. In 1942, Philip Wylie's misogynistic *Generation of Vipers* instituted 'Momism', blaming all the ills of America on mothers' suffocating and enfeebling seduction of their sons; his book's title became familiar enough for Sylvia Plath to use it in a poem.[46] In 1947, Ferdinand Lundberg and Marynia Farnham's *Modern Woman: The Lost Sex* purported to show that higher education prevented women from achieving sexual fulfilment. Advertisers began to put pressure on women's magazines to focus on women exclusively as consumers: what a later generation would call 'dumbing down'.[47]

The era of washing whites whiter was about to begin. For the moment, though, with confidence still high before the Korean War, life for fashionable young single women in New York had never been better. Carmel Snow's office at *Harper's Bazaar* was always filled with flowers; her door and windows stood open, and each issue of the magazine was spread out on the floor so that the editors could walk around and through it, before it was put together. Even the street outside was exhilarating. Madison was Maeve's favourite avenue, 'good at any hour of the day or night, and at any season': 'Whenever I walk along Madison Avenue,' she wrote in 1961, 'I think of fine clothes and gaiety and the possibility of having both at once,' [*LWL* 125]. Maeve dressed with immense care by the late 1940s, always with a fresh flower, usually a rose, in her left lapel. Her hair shone, and she wore it drawn tightly back from her face. Her waist was tiny, her clothes expertly tailored, and though some noticed that her legs were not her best feature, her shoes always had high heels.[48]

In 1948, Maeve asked Karl Bissinger to take photographs of her. They met in the apartment of the wealthy Irish-American theatre critic Thomas

Quinn Curtiss, where Bissinger had already photographed Denis Johnston. Maeve, in a black dress, her hair tied up in a thick ponytail, sat and stood with a cigarette, in front of a fire of logs, for several shots. One of them, appearing on the cover of her second posthumous short-story collection *The Rose Garden* (2000), and in many newspapers and magazines since, has become well known. Maeve sits without smiling, looking over her left shoulder. She looks exquisite, but wary.[49]

In Dublin, Bob's old friend from both the *Irish Bulletin* and *Irish Press*, Anna Kelly, still known as 'Fitz', had become involved in a new project. By the end of 1948, plans for a new, glossy, Irish 'society' monthly were well advanced. Priced at one shilling, it would publish text, photographs and cartoons, reporting on the activities of both the Anglo-Irish gentry and the rising Catholic middle class, with numerous doctors' weddings pictured along-side horse shows and hunt balls. As wartime austerities relaxed, it aimed to bring its readers up to date with new trends in fashion, film, theatre and books. Each issue was destined for a long life in dentists' waiting rooms. Anna Kelly wrote to Maeve, asking her to contribute a column from New York. Maeve obliged, and in March 1949 the first issue of *Social and Personal* carried 'News from New York', with her byline. With all the skill she had learned at *Harper's Bazaar*, Maeve supplied a deft, condensed, sometimes sardonic, overview of Manhattan's latest trends, especially in theatre, with details of the kind she would later develop in her 'Long-Winded Lady' essays for *The New Yorker*:

> Greta Garbo lives in New York now. Someone is always seeing her walking along Madison Avenue, or walking along Eighth Street, or sitting in some restaurant somewhere. She seems to leave echoes wherever she goes. I myself saw her one day, marching, or rather shambling along Madison Avenue in a slouch hat, and looking just as romantic and beautiful as ever she looked in the movies.

Irish writers, she reported, were visiting New York, and finding readers. Devin Garrity, of publishers Devin-Adair, had started an Irish book club:

> [H]is choice of books is excellent, and a big surprise to those accustomed to the usual bog-and-thunder variety of stuff that has been foisted abroad in the name of Ireland. So far he has offered books by Mary Colum, Mary Lavin, Lennox Robinson, Michael McLaverty, Sean O'Faolain, Helen Landreth and Benedict Kiely . . .

Still in the same piece, Maeve mentions work by Bryan McMahon, Anne Crone, Donagh MacDonagh and Sean O'Casey. Denis Johnston, 'Michael'

Mac Liammóir and Vivian Mercier, she tells her readers, have all spoken recently at the Irish Arts and Literary Society:

> Vivian Mercier is living down in the village and teaching at Columbia University. Sometimes, on Friday night, he turns up at Tim Costello's Third Avenue bar for an hour or so. Oliver St John Gogarty also visits this place once in a while, usually, they tell me, in the afternoon.

On 8 March, Fitz wrote to her from the *Irish Press*, that 'they' were very pleased with her first 'letter', adding, 'Do us Spring in New York, and be as gay and lighthearted as you like'.[50] Maeve's 'News from New York' appeared again in the April issue. Pyramid schemes had been all the rage, she wrote, and she knew one or two people who had made money: 'Everyone is tired now, though, and you don't hear so much about it.' Arthur Miller's *Death of a Salesman* was the season's big theatre hit, but Maeve gave more space to her former colleagues at the Catholic University of America, where Leo Brady, of the Drama Department, had just sold the film rights to his first novel, *Edge of Doom*, to MGM for a reported $150,000.[51] Hemlines in New York were rising, 'but the majority of women seem content enough to stick to about thirteen or fourteen inches from the floor. The New Look costs too much to be so easily discarded.' Spring had come to New York and the parks were crowded. Television broadcasting, begun just before the war, was expanding rapidly and Maeve reported that 'the television people' were now showing old films: ' . . . and that is the best thing I've yet heard about television. Actually I prefer to chase the old movies myself – there are at least twenty houses in the city devoted exclusively to foreign and old movies and I'd just as soon see them on a full-sized screen.'

For the May issue, Anna Kelly visited New York herself, and sent an account of an evening at 'The Swankiest Restaurant in the World': the Colony, on 61st Street. She described how the Ladies' Room attendant took care of patrons' dogs, and how her escort presented her with 'a beautiful corsage composed of a frozen rose', while gallantly swallowing his dismay at her age: 'My warm gratitude immediately thawed that rose. At home nobody ever did this. At home the only thing I might expect to find in my hand on a night out would be a glass of stout, for which I'd have to pay myself.'

In June, 'News from New York' was unsigned, although Maeve's name appeared in the Contents and the style was unmistakably hers. *South Pacific* was on Broadway, with Mary Martin singing 'I'm Gonna Wash that Man Right out of My Hair'. Maeve, for whom hair-washing was a major operation, expressed wonder that Martin washed her hair on stage nightly, adding that the show was 'so good that people's voices rise to a squeak describing it'.

The Lafayette Hotel, on the corner of 9th Street and University, had closed for ever:

> It was a favourite place for artists and writers, and for other nice, quiet people who just liked to sit around and pretend to remember Paris, because it was a very French sort of place . . . Apparently the only people who didn't mind seeing the old place go were the waiters, who are reported to have cackled nastily and returned in a body to France.

No further contributions from Maeve appeared in *Social and Personal*, but she joined *The New Yorker* in 1949, and its editor Harold Ross did not approve of staff writers contributing to other publications.

NINE

The View from the Kitchen

Magazines were prospering in New York at the end of the 1940s. As rapid postwar innovation in products and services brought more and more advertising, their glossy obsolescence suited the city's pace, and its ability to shed and remake itself while retaining a familiar personality. Almost twenty-five years old, with some quarter of a million subscribers, *The New Yorker* was flourishing more than most. Unlike *Harper's Bazaar*, its subscribers and editors were mostly men, although women read it and wrote for it. Week by week it wrote the city, and the idea of the city, into being.[1] While still at *Harper's Bazaar*, Maeve had a couple of short pieces published in *The New Yorker*; then in 1949, managing editor William Shawn invited her to join the staff.

E. B. White, who had written for the magazine since 1925, exemplified its high standard of graceful, clear, grammatical writing. Generations of children remember him for *Charlotte's Web* and *Stuart Little*, students and professional writers for *The Elements of Style*, based on the precepts of William Strunk, Jr, one of his professors at Cornell. White's essay 'Here is New York' appeared not in *The New Yorker*, however, but in the monthly *Holiday*. Written while he was staying at the Algonquin Hotel, as a visitor to the city from Maine during the hot summer of 1948, it carried all the authority of his patiently crafted *New Yorker* prose. 'Here is New York' surveyed the city in the aftermath of a war fought from the air. More than fifty years later, the attack on the World Trade Center would show its closing paragraphs to have been distressingly prophetic. Its opening was equally insightful, and at the time of its publication, aptly described Maeve's situation:

> On any person who desires such queer prizes, New York will bestow the gift of loneliness and the gift of privacy. It is this largess that accounts for the presence within the city's walls of a considerable

section of the population; for the residents of Manhattan are to a large extent strangers who have pulled up stakes somewhere and come to town, seeking sanctuary or fulfillment or some lesser grail.[2]

By the time she joined *The New Yorker*, Maeve had pulled up almost all her stakes, or had had them pulled up for her. She had loyal friends like Brendan Gill and Tim Costello, and there were many others, men and women, who found her fascinating, but she lived alone, and a little mysteriously, an expert in both loneliness and privacy. Then in 1950, another link was severed. Derry had returned to live in Washington after the war, so Maeve saw her and the children less frequently, but now Gilbert Jerrold returned from one of his trips to Algeria, took ill and died.

Maeve's 1953 *New Yorker* story 'The Clever One' tells of a springtime visit to her younger sister in Washington. It calls Derry by her full name, Deirdre, mentions her four children, and even names Garfield Street, where the Jerrolds lived in a large colonial house at number 3510. By the time the story was published, however, Derry had long left Washington. In the summer of 1950, just months after her husband's death, she had closed up their house and returned with her children to live near her parents in Dublin. Maeve helped her to pack.[3]

'The Clever One' shows Maeve's realisation that she and Derry have exchanged roles without her noticing. All through their childhood, Maeve had been the elder, the taller, the cleverer, the more grown-up. Now, however, as a mother and householder, Derry has become an adult, according to the customs of their tribe, while Maeve has somehow not. They sit in Derry's 'large, pleasant living room', while Derry's children are in the garden, 'giving themselves wholeheartedly to some raucous game', and the vagueness of that description contrasts with Maeve's detailed memory of the way she and Derry had played and talked in their Ranelagh garden some twenty-five years earlier. Hemming a dress for her daughter, or running outside to investigate when her children begin to fight, Derry is only marginally interested in their shared past, but its content and dynamic are still urgently present for Maeve. She is the little girl who has been so busy learning about the world, and talking or making jokes about it, that she has forgotten to grow up. Her own lack of children – and indeed of a 'large, pleasant living room', in which she might entertain guests as grown-ups do – expresses that reality.

Sometime in the late 1940s, she had left the apartment on 10th Street and moved to 22nd Street, near Ninth Avenue. That was one of the few places where she had a real kitchen, but when the landlord infuriated her by removing 'the one thing that might have held me to the place', a magnificent gilt mirror that hung between two windows, Maeve moved again, to 15 East 9th Street, to two high rooms with a fireplace, where she had all the walls painted white. There was no proper kitchen, but at least she had a cat. The perfect city pet, good at independence and privacy, the cat was a link with her Dublin childhood. It lay on the terrace outside her windows, or went climbing in search of adventure, while she walked about the city, or sat and wrote.[4]

What grail Maeve sought in New York City is not known, unless it was to become a writer. At *The New Yorker*, though, she found sanctuary, and at least some fulfilment. She had many friends there already – word was that Brendan Gill had urged Shawn to hire her – but her arrival caused a stir nonetheless. '[T]o be around her was to see style being invented,' William Maxwell wrote, years later.[5] Barely five feet tall, she almost always dressed in black, and the high heels of her Papagallo shoes sounded along the corridors with the same brisk 'little short step' that Mairéad Parker remembered at Coolnaboy. Her ponytail made her look younger than she was, but she was never without dark lipstick and thick mascara, and a red rose, or a carnation, in her lapel.[6] Like her mentor Carmel Snow, Maeve drew a fine line between art and artifice: witness her exasperation that 'if you buy a rose, the florist can't wait to break it off at the neck and garrote it with wire and sticky green paper, and strip all the leaves and thorns'.[7]

It was not surprising that Maeve should be more elegant than most in her new place of work – *The New Yorker* was a haven for rumpled writers – but Maxwell was probably not just referring to her appearance, for her speech and writing were admirably succinct, and she more than held her own among the magazine's famous humorists. As he continued: 'If you heard laughter at the water cooler, the chances were that a remark of hers had given rise to it.' Whatever private hurts she carried, Maeve's sense of the ridiculous remained intact, as did her wit; like her predecessor Dorothy Parker, she could be merciless. The people she didn't like found her watchful, silent, and even dangerous; otherwise, though, she was funny, charming, and sometimes absurdly generous.

From the time of her arrival, Maeve moved in the 'higher circles' of Brendan Gill, Joseph Mitchell and Charles Addams, stars of the magazine, all of whom, at one time or another, were smitten by her. Gardner Botsford, who had joined *The New Yorker* in 1941 as a 'Talk of the Town' reporter, was not often part of those circles, but he too found her irresistible: 'warm-hearted, generous, and smart as a whip'. He would become a protective friend to her in later years, and would write of her in detail in his 2003 memoir, *A Life of Privilege, Mostly*.[8] For those who knew her only slightly, though, Maeve's warm heart came as a surprise. When Philip Hamburger's mother died in 1952, he returned home from the hospital to find Maeve pacing in circles outside his building. She gripped his hands and told him that she had come to sympathise. Married, with two small sons, he had never met her outside office circles before, but Maeve often came in at night to work and he had got into the habit of leaving a packet of Camels on his desk for her. She never said thank you, and he never asked, but every morning, the cigarettes were gone.[9]

R. Hawley Truax was the administrative legal brain behind *The New Yorker*, responsible for the issuing of cheques and the allocation of space. His niece Mary Rudd, always known as Mary D., had recently joined the staff as secretary to William Shawn. Several years younger than Maeve, and many inches taller, she admired Maeve, and was surprised one day to hear Truax remark that he would have to find her an office somewhere else.

'Why, Uncle Hawley?' she asked.

'She's like a fairy princess; she'll be too distracting,' was the reply.[10]

Faith McNulty had thought Maeve was 'like a pixie'; to Philip Hamburger, she was 'a changeling'. She was tiny, engaging, and Irish, but her Irishness had nothing to do with Irish America; instead, probably because she took care that it should, it reminded people of Yeats, and that whole Pre-Raphaelite complex of images and ideas they thought of as 'Celtic'. In the early 1950s, however, her impeccable grooming provided a degree of paradox that made those educated Americans unable to take their eyes off her. And the uninhibited language they heard her use made them listen in fascination, and sometimes horror. Editors at *The New Yorker* weighed all words carefully, but reserved a special queasy caution for profanity. Harold Ross had once written to a colleague, 'I am an old-fashioned double-standard boy who is shocked at nothing, absolutely nothing, in a stag gathering, but who is embarrassed poignantly at any word or reference which used to be called off-color, in mixed company.'[11] One commentator said that Maeve had 'a longshoreman's mouth', another, 'a tongue that could clip a hedge'. Perhaps her experience as an honorary man at McSorley's and elsewhere made her adopt what was then a male register of speech. Or it may be that she felt herself so far from home, and in surroundings so unreal, that it amused her to use language that would have appalled her family. In any case, after her arrival, the receptionists who guarded the lobby near the elevator (and anyone who happened to pass by), grew accustomed to hearing Maeve exclaim 'Oh fuck!' And at a party hosted by E. B. and Katharine White in Turtle Bay, all the guests heard her voice ring out, 'Fuck you, Brendan Gill, you goddamn Roman Catholic!'[12]

Maeve's office was on the twentieth floor of 25 West 43rd Street, on the long corridor that Philip Hamburger had nicknamed 'Sleepy Hollow', where Gill, Joseph Mitchell and Hamburger himself also worked, as did William

Maxwell. All *New Yorker* staff writers had tiny private spaces carved out by Truax, where they could – and did – sit in silence until they began furiously to type. Maxwell remembered the effect of Maeve's presence:

> Brendan Gill's office was next to Maeve's and there was so much slipping of notes under his door, and hers, and mine, and so many explosions of laughter as a result of our reading them that – we learned through the grapevine – Mr Shawn decided it wasn't good for the office morale, and Maeve was moved down the hall to the other side of the building.[13]

Glass panels in the metal doors dribbled light into the corridor of Sleepy Hollow, but Maeve worked with her door open, and instead of the dingy cells the men tolerated, her little office became a bright and fragrant space, where she would sit behind her typewriter, wearing enormous reading glasses. She smoked constantly, but so did everybody else, and Maeve wore Russian Leather perfume that wafted along the corridors and gathered in her room. She brought in potted plants, and had the walls painted white, the ceiling Wedgwood blue, telling Mary D. about Carmel Snow's flower-filled office at *Harper's Bazaar*, and Snow's custom, every time she bought a coat, of having a green ribbon sewn into the lining, five inches above the hem. For a woman who travelled as much as Snow did, and had as many clothes, it was a practical way of identifying her own garments to the assistants who might have to fetch them, but Maeve, who admired Snow immensely, would no doubt also have heard in it an echo of her Parnellite past, and the ballad line, 'All around my hat I will wear a green ribbon . . .' It was the sort of detail Maeve liked, and the kind of advice she often passed on, half in mockery, about how to live. Perhaps she was thinking of Diana Vreeland's famous 'Why Don't You?' pieces in *Harper's Bazaar* in the 1930s ('Why don't you wash your blond child's hair in dead champagne to keep it gold? . . . put all your dogs in bright yellow collars and leads like all the dogs in Paris?'). 'If you go on a diet,' Maeve told Mary D., 'just have two cups of good soup: that'll get you through lunch.'

Sometimes Maeve and Mary D. ate an impromptu lunch together, or went out for a drink, but Mary D. quickly learned that Maeve could not be pinned down. She had a horror of being trapped – by a person or an engagement – and preferred not to commit herself to arrangements in advance. Already what her friends came to know as Maeve's 'demons' were in evidence: people sometimes set up social engagements for her, to which she didn't turn up, or invited her to big parties, where she became so uneasy that she drank to dramatic excess. Nevertheless, the two women became friends: Mary D. too had been educated by nuns – though her American Sacred Heart convent had been more benign than Cross and Passion – and she shared with Maeve a combination of independent, humorous intelligence and pleasure in their femininity. To bait an inquisitive colleague, Maeve would write mischievous notes to Mary D. and leave them on her desk. 'I loved Maeve,' Mary D. said, fifty years later. 'We enjoyed each other: we laughed; we gossiped.' Maeve instructed her on the importance of having nice underwear – she herself would buy bras at Saks for $50 each – but she also encouraged her to write. Mary D. recalled her own first *New Yorker* 'casual', about an apartment burglary; 'She got me writing,' she said.[14]

Not many friendships like this between heterosexual women flourished at *The New Yorker*, even after the revival of the women's movement in the 1960s. British writer Kennedy Fraser didn't join the magazine until 1968, but in the 1990s she recalled that another young woman had come there at the same time as she did. '[S]omehow the world we had each entered and whose myths we took on as protective camouflage made it strangely difficult for two young women to ally themselves in simple friendship,' she reflected.[15] *Harper's Bazaar* had been run by women who felt no need to prove themselves to men, and if the younger women who worked there could meet Carmel Snow's exacting standards, its culture allowed them to be themselves. The *Bazaar*'s offices on Madison Avenue were fragrant and colourful, but *The New Yorker* felt more like a university: a place where women adapted to male norms. When Frances Kiernan arrived there in September 1966, having just graduated from Barnard College, she observed her surroundings:

> [T]here was gray everywhere I looked: on the floors, on the reception room walls, on the walls of the long dingy corridor I was told to follow, on the doors of the narrow shoe-box offices that lined that corridor. The *New Yorker* offices looked exactly like the Barnard English department.[16]

The New Yorker had hired and published women from the beginning, of course, and some – notably Katharine Angell, who married E. B. White in 1929 – had risen high within it, but its culture remained firmly, if subtly, male. The magazine had an identifiable idiom, to which hundreds, if not thousands, of writers pitched their work, the best of them carving out an individual style within or around it. But because that idiom was coded masculine, a woman who wrote unmistakably in her own voice, as Maeve did, ran the risk of being considered only as a 'minor' writer. It was the same double bind that Hans Christian Andersen had articulated in 'The Little Mermaid', one of Maeve's favourite stories. Seen in this context, her insistence on the codes of femininity in clothes, make-up and office decoration – and even her alliance with Mary D. – were powerful, provocative, statements.

At first, Maeve wrote only the unsigned fashion notes for which she had been hired, and short, unsigned, 'Briefly Noted' book reviews. Then, in December 1950, *Harper's Bazaar* published her first short story. Set in the Ladies' Room of a hotel, 'The Holy Terror' is a mischievous exploration of the politics of such places in the mid-twentieth century – the sort Anna Kelly had noted in her May 1949 piece on New York for *Social and Personal*. This hotel is in Dublin, however, and Maeve's story is also a dark study in malevolence, expressed unerringly in an Irish idiom. Like *The Visitor*, it avoids all the national politics about which she knew so much, and makes no use of the riverbanks and gardens her father's letters so carefully describe. Instead, it concentrates on people, their capacity for spite or triumphant grudge, and their convoluted strategies for getting the better of each other. Its descriptions are precise, and deadly. To sophisticated, travelled, American readers, it showed a grim, dark underside of what they would routinely encounter in Ireland, but might perceive as picturesque, or imagine they understood.

Mary Ramsay is the Ladies' Room attendant at the Royal Hotel.[17] She has been described by an American journalist as 'a real Dublin character, possessed of dry Irish wit', but the story mercilessly details her storing up of negative capital as she saves not only the tips she receives daily, and never spends, but the nuggets of shameful information collected over thirty years that she relies upon to keep her safe. Her sense of revenge is like that of Mrs King in *The Visitor*, but instead of Mrs King's dry gentility, she has a Rabelaisian bulk and lack of inhibition. (Bob and Una in Dublin had a large-bodied daily help whom Maeve found intrusive and coarse, and may have used as a model.) Ungainly and grotesque, Mary Ramsay is 'rough-voiced, rough-handed, rough-mannered in every way'. Without humour, the story gives her a comic presence that leaves no room for a victim and so avoids the dreadful emotional nakedness of Anastasia King, while the same strategy conceals its author's vulnerability behind a satiric disdain. 'The Holy Terror' has no attractive characters, and makes no demands on sentiment. Relentlessly negative about the Dubliners it describes, it nevertheless reserves most of its angry derision for the Americans – like the hotel visitors who tip Mary Ramsay – who were the publishers and readers of *Harper's Bazaar*, and were travelling in increasing numbers to Ireland. 'You are so gullible,' it seems to say; 'you see so little of what is really going on.'

Maeve's trip to Ireland in 1947 or 1948 – almost certainly her first since 1934 – had allowed her to juxtapose her adolescent memories with the realities available to the wealthy foreign visitor. She looked like a glamorous American, but her ear for Irish speech — and thus her ability to crack its codes — was pitch-perfect. Much of what she wrote in the years that followed would exploit that ability to 'pass'. 'You couldn't take your eyes off her,' people said, but that very visiblity allowed her to observe in depth, without her observation being observed.

Early in Maeve's *New Yorker* career, two strands emerge in her writing. Bypassing adolescence and making straight for childhood, a long thread of memory brings her back again and again to Ireland, to Coolnaboy and Wexford town, and to Cherryfield Avenue, where repeatedly and insistently she takes apart the family and home in which she was born and grew up, examining them to see how they were put together. Meanwhile, a thread of acceptance binds her into New York and treats her as an adult, offering something that is neither a family nor a home, but will do in their place, at least for now. Her studies of relationships between rich New Yorkers and their Irish servants, between waiters and patrons in a restaurant, or between the fictional characters in books she reviewed, lack the urgency of Maeve's Irish stories, but she brings to them the ironic insights of the undetected outsider, and hides coded messages within them.

Harold Ross, the *New Yorker's* legendary founding editor, died in December 1951. William Shawn, already holding everything together at the magazine, was tipped to take his place. On 5 January he published Maeve's first signed book review. *Seven Novels by Colette*, introduced by Glenway Wescott, merited one full page (with space for a cartoon), and three single columns set among advertising on the following pages. Entitled 'The Need for Love', Maeve's review began:

> Colette, that inhumanly gifted Frenchwoman, writes about lovers, but not as pairs. She gives her attention to those most in love, the more needy ones, and traces in her stories the concessions they have to make, and keep on making, in order to be loved. She writes of the destructiveness of love, of the gradual erosion of the spirit through need, and of the simple truth that in the world of sexual love ordinary strengths count for almost nothing and the thought of equality, or even of fairness, is ridiculous . . . Her world contains only two people, one of them struggling to be allowed to stay; this is the only struggle that counts.

Maeve writes with critical authority about Colette's whole output: she revered Colette, and treasured a framed photograph of her by Louise Dahl-Wolfe. Her review shows none of the self-protecting malice of 'The Holy

Terror', but reaches behind Colette's own brittle surface to deal tenderly with the human frailties she depicts. In Maeve's review, when the Chéri of one short novel's title goes away from the older woman who used to love him, he is 'no longer an elegant, self-centered young man but a human being so chilled by rejection that he will never be able to get warm again'. It is as though she is writing about Anastasia King in *The Visitor*, or about herself.

Five weeks later, on 9 February, Maeve had another signed review in the magazine, this time of the Italian writer Elsa Morante's recently translated first novel, *House of Liars*. The length is the same, and Maeve's engagement with the book equally revealing, for it is a novel written in the form of a young woman's memoir about her parents, 'people driven awry by their own flamboyant daydreams, which they are unable to realize and equally unable to outgrow'. Quoting a passage about the tawdry luxuries Francesco bought for Anna in their early marriage, she writes:

> These things, so futile to dwell on and so impossible to forget, attach themselves to every incident of this story – fragments of the most unreasonable, most intractable, and most inconsolable part of the nature of these unhappy people, with their splendid dreams and feeble lives . . . Miss Morante's people might seem operatic in their transports of fury and despair if it were not for the dreadful, trivial details that their daughter drags up out of her mind to commemorate their bewilderment and the punishment they brought upon themselves.

Anticipating the theme of her Derdon story, 'Family Walls' (1973), on which she worked for many years, Maeve distinguishes between the feelings that lie inside and outside the 'house of liars': 'Disillusionment and wisdom alike lie outside the walls of their house. Inside is only protest, and the echoes of protest, going back to the time of their childhood, when they heard their parents' voices raised in the same complaint they make now.' Her closing lines, about Morante's narrator, read like Maeve's verdict on the society the famous 'fight for Irish freedom' has produced and the legacy it has left: 'Perhaps she fears that a dream realized or a cause redeemed begins to diminish or even to get corrupt, and that is why, even in her awake mind, the problem of these lives, and of her life, cannot be solved.'

The characters with whom Maeve seems most at home have long memories, and are fated to speak the lines that have been assigned to them by the generations that went before, or perhaps that they themselves have chosen in their unthinking youth. If they realise this, and fret over it, she feels sympathy; if their repetitions are mindless or complacent, however, she hates them. Like a small child, she is absolute in her antipathies and radiant in approval, and this feature of her own fiction is at the same time one of her most effective tools as a critic. In the 1950s, according to Gardner Botsford, who edited them, she wrote almost all the seven-to-twelve-line 'Briefly Noted' reviews of fiction in *The New Yorker*. With deadpan elegance, 'she explained what a book was about, and said if it was good or not'. Here, for instance, was how she disposed of Daphne du Maurier's *My Cousin Rachel*:

> Miss du Maurier's magic touch is unhappily not in evidence in this witless tale of a nineteenth-century lady who may or may not have been a poisoner. Her name was Rachel, she was married twice, she dabbled in herb recipes and remedies, and she had, we are told, a mysterious spell over men.[18]

But when Doubleday published her old friend Dorothy Macardle's novel *Dark Enchantment* in 1953, she was kinder:

> A comfortable, romantic, and gently frightening tale of a young English girl, Juliet, on a working vacation in a charming inn in southern France, and of the beautiful and mysterious witch who from time to time comes down from her lair in the woods above the inn to terrorize the young couple who are Juliet's employers as well as her friends.[19]

Meanwhile, *Harper's Bazaar* had accepted another of Maeve's own stories. 'The Poor Men and Women', about Rose and Hubert Derdon, appeared in the April 1952 issue; a typescript copy among Maeve's papers gives her address as 15 East 9th Street.[20] The title echoes words used in *The Visitor* (where Katharine told Anastasia King, 'Don't ever say beggar'), and the story's layout makes it clear that here Maeve is embarking on a large project. People and places have histories and memories enough for a novel. Rose and Hubert Derdon stand firmly located in place and time, and the odd contradictions of their personalities establish them as real. Rose gives freely to the poor men and women who call to her door; she is forty-seven, a lover of flowers and plants, and of the changing daytime sky. Still, the story tells us, 'a wearisome discontent . . . had begun in her spirit very young' [*SA* 128]. She and Hubert have been married for twenty-seven years, as Bob and Una Brennan were in 1936 (when Una was forty-seven). They are not Bob and Una, however, but fully realised fictional characters, entirely under the control of their creator. It is clear that they live in 48 Cherryfield Avenue, Ranelagh. The sky that Rose watches all through one twilight, as she sits by her window, recovering from flu, may have come from Maeve's 10th

Street apartment, but there is no mistaking the laburnum tree, or the garage and tennis club beyond the garden wall, or the table of ferns in the bow window at the front.

The Derdons have one son, who is a priest; indeed the story's opening words describe Rose as the 'priest's mother'. He is an unsatisfactory character, however, more easily discernible in the negative space where Rose broods over his absence than when he appears, and speaks. Maeve will write more stories about the Derdons, and John will feature in several of them, but this is the only one he enters as a character directly, rather than through his parents' musings and memories. Even here, where we see his fair skin and limp fair hair, his black clothes, and eyes that are 'light blue, troubled, even aghast', the few words he speaks lack direction and we know nothing of his inner thinking. Why Maeve should have created such a two-dimensional character to set alongside her rich imaginings of Rose and Hubert is not immediately clear, but it may be that he represents the ultimate sterility of their lives. Rose has some of Una's characteristics, which may have included a certain cowed behaviour around her husband, but Una was a strong-minded woman of confident, quiet refinement, who had dodged bullets and visited prisons and then become an accomplished diplomatic wife, and it is hard to imagine her with Rose's craven snobberies. It seems rather that Maeve wanted to portray something that struck or troubled her about the emotional landscape of Ireland, much as she did in *The Visitor*. John has 'vanished forever into the commonest crevasse in Irish family life – the priest-hood'. Like the ring that Anastasia King threw into the waters of the old quarry, he represents the abnegation of sexual life in a country where the ironic, intrepid, optimistic culture Maeve remembered had come to be dominated and censored by an elderly, celibate clergy.

None of Maeve's further stories of the Derdons appeared in print for another ten years. Perhaps she showed them to William Maxwell, but the first story of hers that *The New Yorker* bought was of a completely different type. 'The Joker' had an upper-class American setting and most of its characters were American. More importantly, perhaps, it was set at Christmas. Part of *The New Yorker*'s success was its calendar quality: in parallel with honouring the local alongside the global, week by week, it noted the seasons of the year with covers, cartoons and fiction, even as its non-fiction articles ranged over decades.[21] The issue of 27 December 1952 marked the hung-over aftermath of Christmas (60 pages, as against 104 the previous week). In one cartoon, a father in pyjamas registers surprise as a child in pyjamas blows a hole in the house wall with the 'Martian Disintegrator' he has found under the Christmas tree. The caption of another, by Charles Addams, reads, 'The little dears! They still believe in Santa Claus', while the full-page

Gothic artwork shows adults whispering at the door of a room as children load logs on to the fire, blowing the flames high with bellows.

'The Joker' shared space in that issue with 'Interval in a Lifeboat' by Saul Bellow. Its setting is different from that of *The Visitor* and 'The Poor Men and Women', but once again, a poor man comes to the door and offers to sing in return for a handout of money. The preoccupation is the same as in the earlier stories: poverty, and charity, and how some people 'to all appearances the same as everybody else' come to be deprived of the entitlement to sit with others at a table in a house and eat. Isobel Bailey calls her Christmas Day guests 'waifs' (Maeve considered this as a title), and takes a complacent pleasure in her own kindness to them, unaware that they see the contempt in which it is rooted. 'When do people get that fatal separate look?' the story asks. 'Are waifs born?' Early on, it offers an answer: 'that waifs were simply people who had been squeezed off the train because there was no room for them. They had lost their tickets. Some of them never owned a ticket. Perhaps their parents had failed to equip them with a ticket' [RG 53]. As the story progresses, however, that explanation falters, giving way to angry satire.

Isobel Bailey is mistress of a large and comfortable redbrick house, with firelight and fine linen. Although at thirty-one she is still young, she is never childish. Her maids have strict orders to shut the door to beggars, for she believes only in organised charity. This year for Christmas dinner, she and Edwin, her successful lawyer husband, have invited an awkward, arty dressmaker called Amy Ellis, Jonathan Quin, a young reporter, new in town, and Vincent Lace, an Irish poet. Maeve has buried a private joke in Jonathan Quin's biography, for he is gauche and speechless, and has come to New York, where he knows no one, from 'a little town in North Carolina'. Her close friend and mentor Joseph Mitchell had been in New York for twenty-three years in 1952, and knew everyone, but he had come there at twenty-one from Fairmont, North Carolina, a small farming town, and before joining *The New Yorker* had worked for eight years as a newspaper reporter. The poet Vincent Lace is a ruined shambles of a man, given to flowery, nostalgic speeches. Deluded by praise in his youth, he has lived prodigally and come to nothing, but the few lines he speaks in retaliation after Isobel has mocked his 'reputation for standing treat and giving' are enough to punch a large hole in the Christmas feast. Their effect anticipates what happens later, when a poor man brought into the kitchen leaves his own contemptuous mark on the meal. Only Delia, the 'bony Irish maid', fully appreciates what is going on: 'Her thin hair was pressed into stiff waves under her white cap, and she appeared to hear nothing, but she already had given Alice, the cook, who was her aunt, a description of Vincent Lace that had her doubled up in evil mirth beside her hot stove' [RG 61].

The poet and the maids are all from Ireland, whose culture specialises in cutting people down to size. Delia and Alice relish the exquisite absurdities of Vincent Lace's rhetoric. Later in the story, when Lace has redeemed himself somewhat and the other waifs have supported him with genuine kindness, it is Delia who makes 'rough noises of merriment and outrage' as she tells of the ungrateful tramp who has decamped from the kitchen, leaving the butt of his Christmas cigar half buried in the hard sauce intended for the plum pudding.

'The Joker' was one of several titles Maeve considered for this story. It seems to sum up a world of disillusion about the real status accorded to people who have always done what they believed was expected of them, but who have been misinformed: 'left to travel without a ticket'. Maeve can 'pass' in upper-class American company, but, like her father, she is essentially a colonial subject. Much of Bob's and her own considerable intelligence has been devoted to seeing the funny side of things, and being entertaining; but although the jester may achieve much of importance in situations of political imbalance, neither she nor her father has ever had, or will have, real power. Ten years earlier, when the Irish Minister visited Boston, a newspaper columnist who was not one of Bob's regular contacts had spotted this and had seized with relief on racial stereotype to account for it. Writing in the *Boston Evening American* on 6 May 1943, Austen Lake described 'An Hour with Eire Minister' with some bemusement:

> I found . . . that some of what Robert Brennan said was swayed by a habitual idealism that amounts to distorted perspective . . . through his conversation ran a curious blend of muffled pugnacity, whimsical humor and amiable philosophy that puzzles one until you realize that it is a national trait.
>
> None can be more generous with their favors or more devastating in their disapproval. None delve more deeply into the past for arguments relating to the present. None can make conversation so charming an art. There were all these native elements in Robert Brennan.[22]

At the beginning of the twentieth century, Erskine Childers could characterise his own heroic patriotism (both British and Irish) as 'the gay pursuit of a perilous quest'. Fifty years later, Bob's autobiography, *Allegiance*, told the story of the 'fight for Irish freedom' with an abundance of hilarious anecdotes and comic exchanges, but failed to find an American publisher. It was published in Dublin in 1950, and in June 1952 Padraic Colum wrote from New York to congratulate him:

Dear Bob,

I want to tell you how much I enjoyed ALLEGIANCE. After all the
solemn books that have been written on 'Revolutionary Ireland and
its Settlement' it is delightful to read a book which gives the gay atmosphere of so many of the happenings. We know that without the good
spirits the boys coud'nt [*sic*] have carried on . . .[23]

By the mid-twentieth century, though, humour about serious things was
out of fashion; it survived chiefly among the dispossessed and in former
colonies, and provoked only puzzlement at the centres of power.

Maeve prided herself on being different, and on coming from a special
place that was Ireland. 'She wasn't one of us,' *The New Yorker*'s Roger
Angell said, 'she was one of her!'[24] That position conferred extra glamour,
but it also inevitably exposed her to patronising stereotype and isolation.
The release of John Ford's film *The Quiet Man* in 1952 coincided with (and
actively fostered), the marketing of Ireland to American tourists, but it also
constructed a new stereotype for Irish women, and one that fitted Maeve
better than any until now.[25] Maureen O'Hara (born in Dublin in 1920 and
brought up in Beechwood Avenue, Ranelagh, as Maureen Fitzsimons), was
the feisty, fiery, Irish-speaking Mary Kate Danaher. She was the only significant woman in a male community, and her red hair, shawls, handknits and
red flannel skirts, shown in glorious Technicolor, made her a fashion icon
too. The clothes she wore in *The Quiet Man* echoed images in Paul Henry's
(by now well-known) paintings of the west of Ireland, and soon they featured
in the work of Irish dress designers.

Ever since Lady Aberdeen and Peter White had set up the Irish Village
for the Chicago World's Fair in 1892–1893, and Douglas Hyde had made
the wearing of homespuns a policy of Irish Ireland, tweed had been central
to Ireland's sense of its place in a globalising economy. In 1951, an American
consultant advised the government of the need to understand seasons and
sizes, and recommended that the coarse wool produced on the wet mountains of the west of Ireland should be supplemented by finer imports. 'It
would be unwise to retard the future of an industry where ingenuity and
manpower play so great a part and the future is so lucrative,' he wrote,
'because of the use of an unsuitable basic commodity.'[26] His advice was
accepted: Ireland was about to join the world of international fashion.

Dublin designers Irene Gilbert and Raymond Kenna pioneered the use
of the new, finer tweeds woven in Ireland, but it was Sybil Connolly's name
that became famous. Connolly found an early supporter in Lady Dunsany,
and was highly effective in reaching an international market.[27] In July 1953,
the new Irish Export Board, Córas Tráchtála, sponsored a visit to Ireland

by American fashion writers and buyers on their way to see the Paris collections, and Carmel Snow recruited a group of colleagues to visit her native land.[28] They stayed at the Shelbourne Hotel and travelled to Dunsany Castle in County Meath to view and photograph Sybil Connolly's autumn collection in an appropriately romantic setting. Caroline Mitchell wrote in the *Irish Times* on 18 July that 'the Irish designer has got in first with a collection that should bring the dollars pouring into this country,' continuing that 'While the collection was worth looking at on its own account, there was just as much fashion interest among the audience. Seldom can so many fabulously-dressed women have gathered together in any Irish setting.' Two days later, a new production of J. M. Synge's *The Playboy of the Western World* opened at the Gaiety Theatre, starring Siobhán McKenna as Pegeen Mike and Cyril Cusack, recently returned from Hollywood, as Christy Mahon. Siobhán McKenna too would do her part in promoting the red flannel skirt as a high-fashion item. The visit of the fashion writers was a resounding success for Sybil Connolly, who herself travelled to New York that September.[29]

Maeve was in Dublin that summer of 1953, probably as a member of the Córas Tráchtála party. It was her first opportunity for nineteen years to spend an extended period in Ireland. The country was poor and chilly, for Ireland had experienced no postwar boom. 'Rural electrification' was promised, but had not yet been achieved, and thousands were emigrating with every sailing from Cobh. Nineteen fifty had been a Holy Year. Large Catholic churches were being built and consecrated, especially in the new Dublin suburbs, and bishops and priests walked regularly in procession in the streets, dressed in linen and lace, while women in dark overcoats and headscarves looked on. Sexual morality was rigidly enforced, backed up by a number of religious-run 'Magdalen laundries': a nineteenth-century institution long abolished in Britain, but in twentieth-century Ireland dedicated to hiding unmarried mothers and 'wayward' girls from public awareness, while exploiting their labour. In July, a list of seventy books banned by the censor included *The Wildes of Merrion Square: The Family of Oscar Wilde*, by Patrick Byrne, and *For Esmé – with Love and Squalor and Other Stories* by the celebrated *New Yorker* writer J. D. Salinger.

The previous 13 December, *The New Yorker* had published an essay by Betty Wahl Powers, recently arrived to live in Ireland with her husband, the writer J. F. Powers, and their young children. She described walking down Grafton Street on a rainy November day:

And the rain rolled off tweed coats, oily with age, and off dirty gabardine coats and stiff rubberized cloth and crackling plastic capes, or

soaked slowly into the dull-plaid blankets that the poorer women made
do for both cloak and hood, some of them carrying a baby rolled into
a fold in front, perhaps for begging purposes . . .

Soon after arriving in 1953, Maeve wrote to William Maxwell: 'It is
wonderful to be in Dublin, but no-one seems to know I'm here if you know
what I mean. It was the same the last time. The city looks great but it feels
forlorn and stoical.'[30] She had been to Dickson's seed shop in search of a
rose catalogue for Maxwell: he grew roses at his summer house in Yorktown
Heights, New York. She had also visited Derry and her four children, who
all appeared to be thriving; the eldest boy, Jan, was twelve, Yvonne, nine;
Alan was six and Suzanne almost three. Maeve visited them regularly in
the years that followed, always arriving with exotic gifts, animated conversation and wonderful anecdotes about New York. She made no attempt to
behave as Irish people might think an aunt ought to; instead, as she lit
another cigarette or poured a drink, she would tell the children, 'I'm the
horrible example' – of what not to do.[31]

From Dublin, Maeve went to Galway, her first visit since that one-day
trip for her father's play in 1932. She loved it even more than before, and
thought about renting 'an ancient enormous house on the River Corrib on
the edge of the city', though she does not seem to have done so. With Una,
she travelled to Wexford, where she wrote to Maxwell again. She had been
sending the *Saturday Evening Post* to Bessie regularly, and Nan Brennan
had a print of one of Karl Bissinger's photographs. Her Wexford relatives
knew about her published writing too ('The Morning after the Big Fire'
and 'The Clever One' had appeared in *The New Yorker* earlier that year),
but Maeve had not seen any of them since her last visit as a schoolgirl nineteen years before. Travel was not easy, but she hired a car and driver, and
took Una to visit her old home.

Wat and Katie at Coolnaboy now had eight children, none of whom
Maeve had met before, and they welcomed her warmly. Her uncle John
Bolger had moved back to live with them in Coolnaboy, or was about to
do so. Like Cooldearg in Maeve's 'Stories of Africa', the house he had
inherited from his uncle at Pouldearg was almost a ruin; he had not paid
his rates for years, and now the farm had to be sold to defray debt. Maeve
was finding her mother's company a strain: 'I nearly got a headache listening
to her chatter,' she wrote, with the intolerance of one who does not spend
much time being bored. She was thirty-six years old, but, as an unmarried woman, the Irish society she had come home to would have had
difficulty in granting her adult status. Her dramatic hair and make-up,
the long cigarette-holder she used constantly, and the seams in her nylon

stockings fascinated the children, but they must have left her adult relatives bemused. Women were expected to be reticent and self-effacing, but Maeve was exuberant and even dominant.

St Clair McKelway may have accompanied Maeve on that trip. Certainly somebody sent her a telegram from Paris to her parents' house on 1 September, saying 'rooms reserved'.[32] Twelve years older than Maeve, of Scottish Presbyterian ancestry but born in North Carolina, McKelway was a handsome and highly talented non-fiction writer who had joined *The New Yorker* in 1933, after a six-year stint in Asia that included three years as editor of the *Bangkok Daily News*. He had also spent some time on the *Herald Tribune*. Before the war, he had been *The New Yorker*'s managing editor for three years, on the then considerable salary of $15,000, but had been a full-time writer since, with a drawing account from the magazine. This meant that all his pay came in the form of advances on earnings from future writing, and since he was not only charming and sociable, but manic-depressive and alcoholic as well, he was constantly – and deeply – in the magazine's debt.[33] He and Maeve were alike in their flamboyant generosity and complete inability to manage money. Harold Ross once remarked that Mac spent so recklessly, he seemed to think 'all the money was going to be called in at midnight': he regularly left bills unpaid. He was also a compulsive pursuer of women, and had professed himself delighted when the publication of the Kinsey Report on male sexuality in 1948 'relieved him of such terrible guilt'.[34] Some of his friends called him 'Marry the girl Mac', and William Maxwell wrote that '[h]e courted women ardently until the vows were said and then his interest in them faded'.[35] By 1953, he had been married and divorced three times, and he was courting Maeve.

Maeve was due back in New York by 19 October. Visiting Coolnaboy again, and meeting all those children, must have been disturbing for her, as must the realisation of how little she now had in common with her family. Christmas was the most difficult time for her, as well as the season on which she pinned the most hope. Some call the twelve days of Christmas 'Never-Never-Land': a time out of time, and Maeve may have had that in mind when she used the title in her work. 'The Joker' calls Christmas itself 'the most complete day of the year, when everything stopped swirling and the pattern became plain'. It is a description of memory, rather than of a lived present, and recalls the precious long-ago Christmases Maeve remembered in Dublin. In her Irish childhood there had been no Thanksgiving to rival them, and no minority population big enough to challenge their significance. A folder among her papers contains drafts of stories about Christmas – 120 leaves in all – including several versions of 'The Joker'.[36] With them is a single handwritten page: above a tiny drawing of a rudimentary house (gable with door, and path; no windows), are the following notes:

Christmas   Disappointment   – general

     Outsiders   – isolated

Christmas, the day when the pecking o[rder] is completely revealed. The insiders bolster themselves against their own disappointment by inviting outsiders.

Another story, never published, opens: 'Every year, around the middle of November, Harry Webster would feel the dread of Christmas beginning to creep up on him. At first he would be able to ignore the signs of the jolly season . . .'

Brendan Gill, Joseph Mitchell, Charles Addams and most of the other men Maeve spent time with were married, with children, and would disappear into domesticity at Christmas. St Clair McKelway, though, was as much an outsider as she was. (He once dealt with the gloom he felt in the holiday season by taking a train to Albany on Christmas Day, enjoying the deference of dining-car staff who assumed he was travelling on important business. He boarded the next train back, however, only to discover the same staff in the dining car.)[37] Early in 1954, as the building of New York's skyscrapers proceeded, Maeve's white-painted apartment on 9th Street was 'torn out from under [her] by the wreckers' [*LWL* 218], and she married McKelway.

Maxwell again: 'It may not have been the worst of all possible marriages, but it was not something you could be hopeful about.'[38] Maeve was thirty-seven, McKelway forty-nine. They held a 'very fancy' reception with canapés and drinks at Nicholson's on 57th Street, between Lexington and Third Avenue, and Bob Brennan came from Ireland, perhaps by air. BOAC Stratocruisers flew the thirteen-hour journey between New York and London daily now, featuring 'Spacious upstairs cabin and smart downstairs cocktail lounge. All fully reclining seats . . . full-length sleeper berths at slight added cost' – and the planes stopped at Shannon.

New Yorker writers who met Maeve's father that day for the first and only time understood that he was an important person. Tim Costello left his saloon on Third Avenue to attend and meet him once again, but Una was not present. Her health probably did not allow her to travel. McKelway and his new father-in-law, both newspapermen at heart, had a certain amount in common. Affable as Bob may have seemed to his daughter's wedding guests, however, neither he nor Una, devout Catholics both, can have been pleased about Maeve's marrying a thrice-divorced man. Ireland was ever more isolationist and anti-liberal as de Valera held on to power at seventy-two and Archbishop John Charles McQuaid consolidated the devotional effects of the 1950 Holy Year with thunderous fundamentalist pronouncements on marriage, and on sex in literature and drama. His proclamation of 1954 as the Marian Year led to statues being erected all around Ireland as an antidote to the corruption represented by images of women in films and magazines.[39] They showed Mary as the Immaculate Conception, after the dogma proclaimed by Pope Pius IX exactly a hundred years earlier, and given a distinctive visual identity by the famous apparitions at Lourdes in 1858. The Madonna with infant became confined to Christmas cards, as the slim white standing figure with blue sash made Mary's virginity her most important attribute. To many of the Brennans' friends in Dublin, prohibited by their archbishop from attending religious services in any but Catholic churches and schooled to look on divorce as the ultimate evil, Maeve's 'mixed' and secular marriage would have seemed both tragic and disgraceful. In New York, even the people who liked and admired both Maeve and Mac were uneasy. Faith McNulty had seen McKelway in action when he spotted an attractive woman: 'his eyes started out, and his nostrils flared,' she said, and she thought it 'weird' that Maeve should marry him; William Shawn's assistant Edith Oliver seemed shocked.

From Nicholson's, the newly-weds moved with a considerable part of the crowd to their new apartment near the United Nations headquarters, on East 44th Street. At that second gathering, the invariably discreet Shawn caught Philip Hamburger's eye and shook his head slightly: this marriage was not a good idea. Roger Angell, who would become famous as a writer about baseball, was not yet a member of the *New Yorker* staff, but he was the son of one of its mainstays and the stepson of another, and remembers that Mac and Maeve seemed 'like two children out on a dangerous walk: both so dangerous and so charming'.[40] He had reason to know, for as an enlisted man in the Pacific during the Second World War he had witnessed Mac, then chief PRO for the Twentieth Air Force, go spectacularly crazy and lock himself in a Quonset hut in Guam, from where he sent a series of cables to Washington, accusing everyone from Admiral Nimitz down of sabotaging the B29 programme. Mac was recalled without delay, and hospitalised, and spent the rest of the war in Washington, but characteristically, years later, he would turn the episode into a lengthy and elegant article for *The New Yorker*. Angell had a house at Snedens Landing, an unusual community of artists, writers and theatre people in Rockland County, on the steep, wooded east bank of the Hudson, an hour's drive north of New York City.

Mac had been living in Snedens too; Maeve had spent weekends there and, after their marriage, she would have the opportunity to study it in detail.

Between 14 November 1953 and 21 April 1956, *The New Yorker* published six stories by Maeve about a community called Herbert's Retreat, and drafts of still more remain among her papers, with evidence that she was attempting to stitch them together as a novel. When her stories appeared in book form, 'The Joker' was placed among them, with its original 'Bronxville' changed to 'Herbert's Retreat'. All seven stories share a satiric preoccupation with the ways of the privileged, but the six original 'Herbert's Retreat' stories have a setting that gives them a larger stage. Herbert's Retreat is a 'tightly locked, closely guarded' community of thirty-nine white-painted houses on the Hudson, and a private road winds through the woods from one to another. It is clearly modelled on Snedens Landing. As the stories take shape, their major characters emerge. Leona Harkey is rich, ambitious, clumsy and biddable, and Charles Runyon is the bitchy, ageing theatre critic from New York who exploits her hospitality and directs her life according to his own whims and interests. George Harkey is Leona's most recent husband, whom she has married so as to be able to demolish his cottage, which spoiled her view of the river. He is a credit manager at a department store, a hapless fellow, but like Vincent Lace, when he realises that he has nothing to lose, he will tell the truth. Edward Tarnac is another such outsider: a former golden boy and member of this exclusive community, he has squandered his substance and drunk to excess, and is now an embarrassment, living in a run-down Washington Square hotel, but he too will confront the complacencies of the privileged and propertied.

The mixing and drinking of martinis punctuates all activities in these stories. Everybody drinks too much, except the maids, all of whom are from Ireland and, as in 'The Joker', it is their derisive eyes that see everything, their unmodulated, irreverent voices that tell everything. Maeve's 'Herbert's Retreat' stories are rich with coded messages about what the maids see and how they understand it. Had she been describing African-American domestics; had she herself come to *The New Yorker* from Antigua, say, as Jamaica Kincaid did some years later, rather than from Ireland, readers might have had a different understanding of the relationships she portrayed between the homeowners of Herbert's Retreat and their maids.[41] As it is, most critics seem to have read these stories as shallow and inconsequential, with the maids as merely comic characters.[42] Maeve's fluency in the language of America's most privileged people would have led her readers unconsciously to locate the stories' point of view among the homeowners she wrote about, much as Jonathan Swift's English readers at first saw nothing unreasonable in his 1729 pamphlet *A Modest Proposal*, which suggested that a solution to Ireland's ills would be the fattening of Irish children for use as food. Another of the writers Maeve most admired, Oliver Goldsmith, was similarly misunderstood in eighteenth-century England, by people who did not realise that, as an Irishman, he had a different perspective from theirs.[43]

Unlike many of her colleagues on *The New Yorker*, Maeve did not come from a wealthy family, although the status she enjoyed as the daughter of an ambassador must have led some of them to assume that she did. The Ireland she and her family came from was fraught with class distinctions and class awareness, but the differences were small, and the separating membranes relatively porous. Maeve's own relatives, or her classmates at Cross and Passion or Scoil Bhríghde, would never have ended up as servants, but some of the children she sat beside at national school in Oylegate and Donnybrook undoubtedly did. The prevailing culture in Ireland was one of homogeneity, moreover, so that relatively well-off children used the same schoolbooks and attended the same churches as poor, while social networks were so firmly rooted in the local that a few well-placed questions could elicit information about almost anybody. Wealthy American society would have been equally exotic to Irish Catholic women of all classes, and even someone as privileged as Maeve did not escape an element of stereotyping, as listeners exclaimed at her accent or her turn of phrase. She must constantly have heard references of the kind she attributes to her character Charles Runyon in these stories, who likes to refer to Bridie as 'that splendid Irishwoman of Leona's'.

Bridie emerges from the same part of Maeve's imagination or memory as do Rose Derdon's mother Mary Lambert, and the Ladies' Room attendant Mary Ramsay. She is 'Leona's massive Irish maid', 'big Bridie, the bully', whose 'big behind' sprawls across the back seat of the private bus that takes all thirty-nine maids from Herbert's Retreat to Mass on Sundays. Her 'beady Irish eyes' and scornful stare watch through the window of Leona Harkey's kitchen, contemptuously registering everything that goes on. When she enters a room, noise and violence come with her. Her characteristic expression is a 'glare of pure hatred', and the other maids fear her, yet these stories show her truculence arising from rage, and her rage from dispossession and hurt. Another story, 'The Bride', published in August 1953, showed the same hurt, but without the satire.

Bridie and the other maids have some of the poignancy of Joseph Mitchell's 1940 *New Yorker* interview with 'Lady Olga', the bearded lady Jane Barnell, who told him 'No matter how nice a name was put on me, I would still have a beard', or of the images fashion photographer Diane Arbus began to make in 1958 of 'freaks' in New York City.[44] Grotesque and often repellent, Maeve's portraits clearly show the women's suffering humanity, not least in the way they persist in referring to themselves as 'girls'. Their only power lies in their ability to tell stories, and it is this that Maeve celebrates, and participates in, when she writes about Herbert's Retreat.[45] Her training as a fashion writer gives her a devastating way of revealing people through the clothes they wear, but her ear for conversation, and especially for spoken narrative, comes from her life in Ireland.[46]

In 'The Divine Fireplace', Stasia (yet another Anastasia) is forty-seven, with a pointed white face and very large ears, and on Sunday she wears a beige gabardine suit with green nylon gloves, green plastic handbag, and green sandals whose straps wind twice around her ankles:

> Somebody had once complimented her on her merry Irish eyes, and she had endeavored to live up to the remark ever since, rolling her eyes enthusiastically until it became a habit, and showing that she, at any rate, knew what was going on in the room and behind the scenes, even when there was nothing going on at all. Stasia's merry, knowing looks frightened some of her employers and irritated others. Stasia didn't care. 'Some people have no sense of humor,' she would say when she lost a job . . . Stasia was famous for her sense of humor, which she brandished like a tomahawk. And she was a great storyteller. All the maids were agreed on that. And the funny faces she made. Stasia was a scream. [*RG* 96]

All the action in 'The Divine Fireplace' is seen through Stasia's eyes, and most of it is told in her voice, inflected sometimes to convey the way she hears her employers speak. It is a story of greed, excess and moral bankruptcy, told through images like the thick, juicy steak left bleeding all night on the living-room carpet, after Stasia's employers have destroyed their own kitchen, then attempted to cook dinner over the fire, and through language that contrasts the careless pretensions of the rich with the maids' frugal Irish Catholicism. For these maids and the culture they come from, fireplaces are not fashion accessories, but dirty and troublesome necessities, and only God is divine, so that a barking laugh is already audible behind the story's title. The maids are on their way to Mass as the story is told, throwing the language of religion into relief. Debbie Tillbright adores her house, adores fireplaces; Norma Lamb is divorced and finds her new freedom 'divine, simply heaven'. Tearing out the stove to reveal the bricked-up fireplace, these people leave 'a hole as big as a coffin' in the wall. In other stories, Bridie refers to Charles Runyon as 'Mr God', and describes him mixing drinks: 'He stands up in front of the bar in there like a priest saying Mass, God forgive me, and mixes a martini for himself, and one for her, and maybe an odd one for the husband.'

In the Latin Mass of the 1950s, the priest turned his back to the congregation to mix water and wine from cruets and consecrate them. The silence, precision and suspense of that ceremony provided a blasphemously perfect analogy that threw the employers' culture into grotesque contrast with that of their hard-working, God-fearing maids.

That description of Charles Runyon mixing drinks probably owes something to the only lasting friendships Maeve made in Snedens Landing. Gerald Murphy was sixty-six in 1954, and his wife Sara was seventy-one. Although now president of his family's Mark Cross company, which sold luxury leather goods on Fifth Avenue and advertised regularly in *The New Yorker*, Gerald had also been a distinguished painter, and he and Sara were friends and patrons of artists. Legendary hosts, who embodied *savoir-vivre*, in the 1920s on the Côte d'Azur they had been at the centre of a circle that included Pablo Picasso, F. Scott Fitzgerald, Cole Porter and Ernest Hemingway, and most literary critics see them as the models for Dick and Nicole Diver in the first part of Fitzgerald's 1934 novel, *Tender is the Night*. They had suffered tragedies and betrayals since then, but five years earlier they had bought Cheer Hall, a beautiful stone house in Snedens Landing, renovating it imaginatively and moving in in 1950. They entertained there, less lavishly than in the past, but still with style, and Gerald specialised in mixing complicated cocktails. He liked to recall the comment their friend, the playwright Philip Barry, made, at their Villa America in Antibes, that when Gerald mixed cocktails he was like a priest saying Mass.[47]

Gerald was cultured, cosmopolitan and highly aware of his Irish antecedents, although he had long rejected the Church. Both he and Sara lavished on all their friends the kind of steadfast kindness Maeve had not known since she stayed with Wat and Bessie at Coolnaboy as a child. The Murphys embraced her wholeheartedly – Brendan Gill said they were 'enraptured' by her – and she loved them in return, and got a special pleasure from their house.[48]

Precise, detailed descriptions of clothes in Maeve's 'Herbert's Retreat' stories mock the snobbish materialism of *The New Yorker*'s advertising even as they draw a series of characters who lack, precisely, character. They offer an *écriture féminine* that would have been instantly intelligible to most of the magazine's women readers, but they may also have been part of a running joke with Gerald Murphy, whose own clothes sense was legendary. 'The Stone Hot-Water Bottle', published in November 1954, is filled with playful references to Ireland and to clothes. It centres on the competing snobberies of Charles and Leona during a visit to Leona's house by her deceased husband's aunt, a titled Englishwoman called Lady Ailesbury-Rhode. Ailesbury Road, Dublin, running from Donnybrook Church to Merrion, is one of the city's most expensive residential streets, not far from where the Brennans used to visit the Poor Clares' monastery. Charles tells Leona that she should stop wearing velvet: 'Tweed, yes, but only in its thinnest, most gossamer interpretations. That thing you're wearing looks like tree-trunk bark. Thin, soft tweed in divine colors: mauve, of course; periwinkle, of course; olive, apricot, cerise, maybe' [RG 74]. Only a month or so earlier, Anne Scott-James of the London *Sunday Express* had written of dress designer Sybil Connolly that:

> In less than two years she has transformed the traditional clothes of the Irish peasant into high fashion. She has got the world's most elegant women into black shawls and red flannel and homespun bainin [undyed white] tweed and hand crochet . . . [H]er new tweeds are wonderfully light and soft, and the colours: ink-blue, charcoal, and a warm red. They are handwoven in the same cottages, but from new, finer yarns.[49]

In more than one of these stories, Leona Harkey wears a 'fireside skirt' that recalls Maureen O'Hara's red flannel skirts in *The Quiet Man*. In 'The Stone Hot-Water Bottle', Charles prescribes a new one for her: 'A tremendous fireside skirt with a hem that measures at least a mile around . . . made of awning canvas, striped in mauve and the very clearest yellow, and quilted, and lined with thin black cotton' [RG 75]. It echoes the description of Sybil Connolly's 1954 'Kitchen Fugue': a dress whose full skirt was made of striped linen tea towels.[50]

Stone hot-water bottles, open fires and pots of tea made with tea-leaves, not tea-bags, were the daily necessities of life in Ireland in the 1950s, as they had been in the 1920s and '30s. In the centrally heated Petit Trianon life of the postwar Americans Maeve satirised, however, they were luxuries and status symbols, achieved through the exploitation of Irish women, as Maeve documents. She may have been describing herself when she wrote of Charles Runyon that he 'edited himself carefully, because the truth of his background was too crowded and hearty to suit the slender, witty, cynical being he had become'. If that is so, then the 'Herbert's Retreat' stories speak of guilt and self-disgust. In any case, as Christopher Carduff has noted, a 'ravenous nostalgia' runs through all Maeve's work, paralleling the 'ravenous grudge' she described in 'The Holy Terror'.[51] Throughout her adult life, to the point of eccentricity, Maeve drank tea and sought out open fires. In 'The Anachronism', social climber Liza Frye will not allow her mother to have either tea or a fire, but Mrs Conroy makes a plaintively convincing case for both, and finally outwits her daughter. Her surname, of course, reveals that she is Irish.

Maeve was a woman without a kitchen: an Irish immigrant in America who had ended up paradoxically not just outside the drudgery of kitchens, but excluded from all their warmth and comfort. The stories she wrote about Herbert's Retreat honour the work and perception of less privileged Irish women, but they also lament and rail against her own exclusion.

TEN

The Long-Winded Lady Observes

Around the end of 1953, when Maeve was about to marry St Clair McKelway, Faith McNulty used to see her carrying a small black-and-white handbag made of skunk fur. McNulty had recently joined the staff of *The New Yorker*. She wrote about natural history and Maeve had praised one of her first pieces, criticising the use of fur in fashion, so she found the bag surprising. Before long, however, the bag was no more:

> Now the end has come. I had that little black-and-white skunk bag that I was inhumanly fond of and I had the idea of having a collar made to match it, so I took it to a *very good* little shop downtown and asked the girls there if they'd get me the collar. They said yes and called their man, and he said sure he could make the collar but he would have to have the bag to match the color of the skin. He said he would have to have the bag. So after some protest, I left the bag and carted my belongings away in a paper bag, and today they called up in *agony* to say that the little man had turned up with the collar, but when they said 'Where's the bag?' he said 'Well, I didn't think she'd want the frame, so I threw it away.' He *said* he only wanted the bag to match the skin, and then he *chopped* up this madly expensive bag and made a measly little collar out of it.
>
> Well, there you are, in case you've paid any attention.

That account appeared as the second half of an item in *The New Yorker*'s 'Talk of the Town' on 23 January 1954. Under the title 'Skunked', it followed a mock-pompous preamble that was typical of the column: 'A rather long-winded lady has just given us an example of the death of the faculty of attention, which she believes is rampant. Let her present it in her own heart-rending words . . .'

The piece marked a breakthrough for Maeve. Inclusion in 'Talk' was what almost every *New Yorker* writer aspired to: here appeared the writing that caught the heartbeat of the time and made the magazine indispensable to hundreds of thousands of readers every week. *The New Yorker* had published seven of Maeve's short stories in the previous two years, and another would appear in the next issue: she had truly arrived. 'Talk of the Town' was the first item of text in each week's magazine, and William Shawn himself hovered anxiously over its content. The style of Maeve's piece (unsigned, like all 'Talk' pieces then), could scarcely have been further from the column's usual, impersonal, senior-common-room register. She writes in a feminine code, a parody of 'girl talk', the breathless italics making a vivid piece of aural and visual description seem like a fuss about nothing, or a joke. But highly subversive messages can be passed in safety if the words appear sufficiently frivolous, and amusing as it is, this first 'Long-Winded Lady' piece is a pointed commentary on the way men and women respectively pay attention to what women say.[1]

Brought up on spy stories and whodunits, on crosswords, puns and secret passwords, and speaking Irish as well as English, Maeve, like her fictional Lily Bagot, always loved codes. A code is useless, however, unless there are are others like oneself who will read and understand it. The popularity of Maeve's contributions to 'Talk of the Town' made it clear that there were indeed those among the magazine's readers who heard what the Long-Winded Lady was saying, even if they were not typically the male householders whose names appeared on its subscription list.

By 1954, 55 per cent of *New Yorker* readers were women (up from 47 per cent in 1949), and most of them were college-educated, although many had dropped out to marry before graduating.[2] Women of all classes were retreating – or being herded – out of the workforce and back into 'the home'. Connie Field's 1980 documentary film *Rosie the Riveter* tells the story of the skilled women workers forced to give up paid employment when the war ended, to leave jobs available for returning servicemen. In the same period, McCarthyism cut off oxygen from feminist education and activism, as 'redbaiters' viewed women's organisations with increasing suspicion.[3] In the years that followed, fashions in clothing emphasised womanly curves, while advertisements for new household appliances and new, wipe-clean materials like Formica insisted that housework could be fun.[4] Betty Friedan's *The Feminine Mystique* (1963) gave a name to the language and imagery of relations between women and men in White America in the 1950s, for after the war, middle-class women had begun to abandon education and the public domain to marry younger and younger, have more and more babies, and exercise power primarily by purchasing.

The New Yorker's success as an advertising medium for the things that married women bought, or persuaded their husbands to buy, allowed it to pay for the funniest cartoons and the most interesting fiction, and to commission articles based on lengthy, expensive research. These included Rachel Carson's 'Silent Spring', published in June 1962, having been first mooted in February 1958, and Truman Capote's 'In Cold Blood', which took him six years to write and appeared in the magazine in September and October 1965.[5] When 'new journalist' Tom Wolfe launched an attack on the magazine that same year, he poured scorn on the way it had catered for its 'suburban-bourgeois' women readers throughout the 1950s, and, with misogyny masquerading as literary criticism, described its fiction as 'the laughingstock of the New York literary community'. Ben Yagoda, author of the most comprehensive study of the magazine, seems to agree, characterising the period 1952–62 as 'The Bland Leading the Bland'. He comments on the genteel tone of the fiction, its many Irish settings, and the large proportion of stories by women. But as Frances Kiernan wrote in 1988, 'if you believe that fiction at its best can enrich or even change our lives, mustn't you constantly bear in mind that women have lives too?'[6] For women readers and their teenage daughters in the 1950s, trapped in the 'feminine mystique', the macho excitement of the worlds of test pilots or criminals was simply not available. Relegated to the suburbs, excluded from the 'real' world, and cautioned against appearing aggressive, the intellectually frustrated women who experienced Friedan's 'problem that has no name' developed a facility for gauging shades of meaning. It was not difficult for them to decode stories that told their truths quietly and with subtlety.

'Skunked' was to be the first of many communications from 'our friend, the long-winded lady'. The next appeared on 18 September, and took up most of the first column of 'Talk':

A rather long-winded lady we hear from occasionally, whose spirit is generous and who is a forthright spendthrift as far as italics go, writes as follows: 'I was in a new *small* supermarket the other evening, waiting to have my things put in a bag, when I saw a shabby tall man with red eyes, who had obviously been drinking heavily since the *cradle* . . .'

The piece ends: 'I mean to say that the impulse toward good involves *choice*, and is complicated, and the impulse toward bad is *hideously* simple and easy, and I feel sorry for that poor tall red-eyed man.'[7]

Maeve achieved what only a handful of writers on *The New Yorker* in her generation did, in establishing an identifiable persona within the 'Talk' column, but the manner of her achievement was more daring than it looked, for she was unique in making a woman's voice heard regularly in that forum.

Yagoda writes that her pieces, 'lent Talk an eloquence, a quality of observation, a connection to the city streets, a nonfacetious humor, a personality,
and an ineffable sadness it had lacked'.[8] Like the 'gossips' or 'old wives' of
earlier times, though, she paid a price in dignity for the right to be heard,
for surely a 'lady' invariably described as 'long-winded' could not have
anything of consequence to say. Yet the sobriquet could well have been
Maeve's own idea: it would have been like her to draw ironic attention to
the prevailing feeling that women talk too much.

Another piece appeared on 26 February 1955 as the lead in 'Talk':

> That long-winded lady we hear from occasionally has sent us another
> communication, this time on the subject of modern design. 'I like to
> have a cup of tea first thing in the morning,' she writes, 'and for that
> reason, whenever I have to spend a night or two away from home, I
> pack a small electric kettle and a box of Keemun [tea] . . .'

The piece proceeds to describe the niceties of making tea, and the disaster
of a modern teapot with a hollow handle that became dangerously hot.

The Long-Winded Lady was acquiring a persona, but she was not Maeve,
and Maeve would not be revealed as the author until 1969, when William
Morrow published forty-seven of her pieces under the title *The Long-Winded
Lady*. Maeve was a hard-working professional who wrestled words and ideas
on to paper with commitment and originality; she would sit at her typewriter all day, eating only a couple of hard-boiled eggs as she finished an
assignment.[9] She was also a woman from Ireland who carried her country
with her every day of her life, and a hard-drinking, straight-talking intellectual and wit who held her own among the men in Costello's on Third
Avenue. By contrast, the Long-Winded Lady of the 1950s was a two-dimensional figure such as *The New Yorker*'s advertisers imagined, supported by
a husband or a private income, and venturing forth from her home only to
shop. A lengthy advertising campaign for *Woman's Day* ran in the magazine
about this time. Addressed not to women readers, but to the men who bought
advertising space, it showed various images of a fashionably dressed woman
striding out, all of them captioned: 'She's got to GO OUT to get *Woman's
Day* . . . and *Woman's Day* isn't all she buys!' *The New Yorker*'s Long-
Winded Lady might have been the employer of an Irish maid in one of the
'Herbert's Retreat' stories, or a reader of *Woman's Day*; certainly she was
neither a working woman nor Irish.

William Maxwell was a steady presence in Maeve's life as she wrote the
Long-Winded Lady pieces and her book reviews, all the time working on
her own fiction. Nine years older than she was and happily married, he

edited her short stories, and soon became the person for whom she wrote. Famously, he edited Frank O'Connor too, and Sylvia Townsend Warner, J. D. Salinger, Eudora Welty, John Updike, and many others among *The New Yorker*'s best-known fiction writers.[10] Humane and scrupulous, he seemed not to notice the testosterone battles that raged all around him, but understood how questions left unanswered in childhood dictated the shape of many writing lives. He honoured women's writing as much as men's.

Maxwell's own 1937 novel, *They Came Like Swallows*, was strongly autobiographical, as was much of his later work. It offered Maeve a model of how to write about childhood, describing the interior of a house in intent detail as a way of invoking the child's consciousness that had lived there, but presenting it with the subtlety and compassion that come from seeing through layers of subsequent life. Like Maeve, Maxwell in childhood had felt the shadow of things that had happened before his birth and had suffered agonising disruption and dislocation. For him, the accident that led to his brother's leg being amputated, and the Spanish influenza that carried off his mother when he was ten, would be the edges of the broken tooth at which his tongue probed constantly. He read what Maeve had written about her Dublin childhood, and encouraged her to write more. From February 1953 to January 1955, alternating with the brittle, cynical, 'Herbert's Retreat' stories, *The New Yorker* published seven pieces about the Brennans' life in Cherryfield Avenue. They are, as Maxwell says in his Introduction to *The Springs of Affection*, slight; it is also true, however, as he continues, that 'they are definitely stories, written with great care and radiant with the safety and comfort of home'. What is most striking about them, given all we know about Maeve's life, her other writing and her self-presentation in those years, is the stories' trusting simplicity: the lack of artifice that allowed the woman who ate all her meals in restaurants and never went out without make-up to reveal the child she had been. The stories speak of wonder at how much had been contained within a world that was so small.

The theme music of the Cherryfield Avenue stories was domesticity: the wallpapers and floor-coverings of the house; the cement, grass and flowers in the gardens back and front; callers at the door; the family at tea, and the washing-up afterwards. It was the antithesis of the life Maeve was leading with Mac. Since their marriage, they had lived in various apartments and residential hotels in Manhattan, always upping sticks and moving on, drinking, partying, writing and running up debts (which *The New Yorker* paid). They did not buy a house, and Maeve did not become pregnant. One night in 1955, staying in two rooms on the eighth floor of one of Washington Square's old hotels, she watched a woman feeding pigeons on the street below, and amused herself by building a house out of a pack of playing cards that had been specially slit so as to fit together. The piece she wrote, about the buildings she had lived in that had been torn down, or were about to be, appeared as a *New Yorker* feature piece, with her byline, on 16 July, entitled 'The Last Days of New York City'. 'All my life, I suppose, I'll be running out of buildings just ahead of the wreckers,' she wrote [*LWL* 219]. It was as though she were volunteering for a necessary task, for she would spend much of her writing life thereafter on elegies for lost buildings.

In Dublin at the end of 1954, Maeve's brother married Emer Coghlan, daughter of the Brennans' old neighbours on Belgrave Road. Seumas Coghlan had become a successful businessman, and his daughter and Robert Patrick made an elegant couple. Robert Patrick (or 'Mans', as his father called him), was now a qualified engineer, and couldn't wait to get back to the United States. Derry paid the young couple's fare; Maeve sponsored them for immigration, and they arrived in New York in 1955, staying at her and McKelway's apartment until they found their feet. Siobhán McKenna was in New York throughout the winter of 1955–1956 too, playing Miss Madrigal in Enid Bagnold's *The Chalk Garden*. She was much in demand in the Irish saloons on Third Avenue.[11] Maeve and Mac sometimes took Robert Patrick and Emer to Costello's, and Mac invariably stopped at a flower stall on the way to dinner and presented each of the women with a rose. Emer found him 'a most delightful man'.[12]

Brendan Gill's 1975 autobiography, *Here at* The New Yorker, tells a story about a woman at Costello's who may have been Maeve before her marriage:

> I think of one of the most gifted of our writers, a pretty girl always immaculately groomed, and of how she would sit beside her lover, smoking cigarette after cigarette and drinking drink after drink, never speaking a word, until in the early morning the moment had come for her to punish him by passing out, and her exquisite head would pitch forward upon the bar, as if guillotined.[13]

Maeve's Irish relatives remember her as voluble – talking about everything and anything, and always smiling – but New Yorkers more often saw her as a loner, silent and watchful. She did not seem to care whom she offended. Once, when nobody came to take her order at Costello's as she sat in a booth, she lifted a heavy, full sugar bowl and dropped it on the floor.

Robert Patrick and Emer moved to Brooklyn Heights, and Emer gave birth to a son – another Robert Brennan – in October 1955. He stayed overnight just once at Snedens Landing as a small child, but the visit was not a success. He remembers someone dragging him through a field of very tall grass, and that there was a huge black dog there.[14] Afterwards, he told his mother tearfully, 'She shaked me.' Most of Maeve's domestic affection was lavished on her animals. She observed children respectfully, but could be diffident in their presence, and the chain-smoking Snedens Landing life, with its martinis and hangovers, was not child-friendly. In 1958, the Caterpillar Tractor Company offered Robert Patrick Brennan a new job in Peoria, Illinois, and he, Emer and little Robert left New York. Their second son, Peter, was born in Peoria in 1960.

The 'huge black dog' was a Labrador bitch called Bluebell — perhaps named after the 'darky bluebells' of the Dublin children's rhyme – who would be Maeve's faithful companion for many years to come. Bluebell became 'Niobe' in several *New Yorker* stories, but recovered her real name when the stories about her were collected in *In and Out of Never-Never Land* in 1969.

Between December 1952 and November 1954, twelve of Maeve's short stories had appeared in *The New Yorker*. Three more followed in 1955, along with 'The Last Days of New York City', but after 'The Divine Fireplace' in April 1956, none of her fiction appeared in the magazine for three years, and no Long-Winded Lady pieces for almost two. Given that *The New Yorker* kept stories in its 'bank' for years, publishing them only when it identified a perfect fit between time and topic, this must mean that she had written little since her marriage that pleased her, or her editors. Maeve had always been a solitary writer, and often worked at night, but Mac's ebullient personality and the social life of Snedens Landing probably left her in much less control of her time than she was used to. For one so urgently committed to her work, it must have been disheartening indeed.

One signed book review did appear over her name. In the issue for 11 May 1957 Maeve reviewed *The Wapshot Chronicle*, by John Cheever, another Maxwell protégé. Entitled 'Mortal Men and Mermaids', the review echoes with Maeve's memories of reading Hans Christian Andersen and conveys both the spirit and the structure of the book. She admires Cheever's celebration of 'mortal love, different for all of us as our celebrations of it are different', but after three years of marriage to McKelway, her critique of the way he represents women is trenchant. 'Mr Cheever', she writes, 'brings his genius to his study of men, but who can say what blew through the caverns of his brain when he turned to deal with the women?' Each of the Wapshot men pursues his vision of ideal woman:

> For her, they will jump into the sea they fear and adore, braving Scylla and Charybdis, night storms, whales, whirlpools, and the floating hair of drowned men.
>
> Well, here they are, the Wapshot mermaids. Melissa, Betsey, and

Leander's only love, his first wife, Clarissa, are passive, gentle, lovely, childlike, innocent, beguiling creatures, helpless in their sex and in their various misfortunes, all of them half asleep, and all of them, I might add, reluctant to wake up. We do not learn a great deal about any of them – we do not need to learn it; they are what they are – and we see poor Clarissa only through the yearning eye of Leander's memory, but the quality that is remarkable and common to Melissa and Betsey is their obtuseness.

When Maeve wrote that, her neighbours in Snedens Landing included thirty-six-year-old Betty Friedan, her husband Carl and their three small children. Betty Friedan was beginning the research that would become *The Feminine Mystique*.[15]

By the time her review of *The Wapshot Chronicle* appeared in print, Maeve was on her way to Ireland for an extended visit. She spent time in Dublin with her parents, and with her sister Derry, and Derry's children: 'the best humoured children I ever saw, and the best looking, almost', and travelled to Wexford and beyond. For William Maxwell and his family she bought handwoven woollen rugs from Avoca Weavers in County Wicklow, and sent them off by mail. In New Ross she visited Sheila Hickey, a friend from early childhood, recently widowed. Sheila was the older sister of Robert Patrick's wife Emer and, like Maeve, had been three years old on the night of that Black and Tan raid in Belgrave Road, when Bob had hidden in the Coghlans' house: she remembered meeting him on the stairs the following morning. Sheila's husband had been a dispensary doctor, and his death meant that she and her children had to find another place to live immediately. When Maeve turned up at their rented house that sorrowful summer, she brought gaiety and encouragement, urging sixteen-year-old Garret to think seriously about writing, and captivating his eleven-year-old sister Cliona.[16]

Maeve went to Galway in 1957 too, and this time travelled to the Aran Islands, where Robert Flaherty had made his famous film. The driver who took her on his horse-drawn sidecar from the boat to the house where she stayed was 'terribly handsome . . . with [an] air of guilty and gleeful complicity', she wrote to Maxwell later. 'And he gave the impression of being much too big for the life he was living.' Maeve was angry because the driver handled her typewriter carelessly, 'and he was very much inter-ested in me and I sent him away'.[17] Much more than people in the rest of rural Ireland, Aran Islanders were used to exotic and glamorous visitors, but Maeve did not like the way they treated animals. She was distressed at the condition of the many donkeys she saw. Her husband joined her on that trip, and he may have been waiting for her on her return from the islands, for an undated note on the letterhead of the Great Southern Hotel, Galway, reads 'Maeve, Call me when you get in? Mac.'[18]

Back in her parents' house in Dublin, Maeve wrote a long, lively letter to Maxwell, typing fast on a page whose top left-hand corner already bore the words 'The late Mrs Enright'. She crossed them out by hand, and scribbled 'Dodder Road, Dublin' above a page of single-spaced text. Most of Maxwell's friends called him Bill, but to her he was always 'William':[19]

Dear Wm,

I know you dislike the word gingerly and you may also dislike and deny the word preposterous but I must say that I think nothing could be much more preposterous than for me to start writing a letter to you on a page that I had decided to start writing a story on and had started writing it on as you can see. But the stone deaf Daily Help who is the horror of this house as far as I am concerned decided at the same time to come in here and start vaccuuming [sic] in spite of all my gestures, pushes, and shrieks, and not being able to plug in in the only free plug she inserted her great bulk in behind my chair, displacing me and the chair, unplugged my lamp and plugged in there, but did not plug, and cannot hear, so proceeded to <u>do</u> the room from top to bottom to the sound of her own heavy breathing only, for the vaccuum [sic] had not connected. I <u>let</u> her, and when she left, having unplugged, she cast a despairing glance back at the rug, which was clean enough in the first place, and remarked that it was awful hard to keep a place clean in this weather. Desprit, she said. Smashin' fuyerr, she said, casting another glance but at my little turf fire, which I am burning mostly for appearances. Then she squeezed out and I locked the door.

Your review of the Colette book was lovely lovely lovely and if I said nothing about it earlier it is partly because I have been saying nothing and partly because you had promised me a proof and I waited around and waited around exactly as my mother would do if someone offered to take her to tea and then forgot, with my good clothes on, not daring to sit down because of the dog hairs, and said nothing and got nothing. It is the second example I have had of a growing thoughtlessness in you that delights me. The first example was so outrageous that I will not tell you about it until next year, and I am treasuring it intact until then, although I did tell McKelway about it and he laughed out loud, barked, and I took that to be a triumph for me, even though it was your responsibility really. Your responsibility is my triumph. I may never use the word triumph again and I may begin to use the word love again – now I am referring to fashions not meanings.

My father is enfeebled by the illness that struck him early this year, and my mother, who has always used her last ounce of strength every day, has revealed a thorny little personality, little but very thorny, so that instead of the pale patient and suffering cipher that used to confront people McKelway has seen only a bad little woman who hisses like a cat, laughs like a fiend, and chatters from morning till night telling interminable stories ('then he crossed the road, that road isn't there any more, it belonged to the Bewley estate, not the branch that owns the restaurants on Grafton Street, the other Bewleys who') none of the stories containing, as McKelway said, a good word about anyone. She introduces me proudly as Mrs McKelway. My father says, this is my daughter Maeve. About McKelway he says This is Mr McKelway. Her garden is unimaginably beautiful, and I am glad she stole your roses. McKelway swears she talks to the flowers, and Derry says every single bit in the garden matters separately to her, and I can see that Derry is right.

I saw my sister Emer in Washington before I left. I won't go on about that, only to say that all these echoes, the four faces of a personality – Emer, me and Derry and my mother – are startling to observe . . .

The letter continues for half of a second page: McKelway is ill, and in a nursing home:

He has been in bed and with doctors almost since arriving in Dublin, and they have finally x-rayed and discovered a Live Ulcer, so it has happened at last. They have him on the Sippy diet, named for Doctor Sippy, and he should be out in a week, and will then go to Scotland. But no finnan haddie, I'm afraid. Pain but no danger, if he does what he is told. My mother's doctor – the one he has – is a Protestant, I am glad to say, no nuns in this nursing home.

best love, and to Emmy, Maeve

Maeve seems amused by her mother's calling her 'Mrs McKelway', but clearly her parents have made her husband welcome. Bob introduces her proprietorially as 'my daughter Maeve', however. She had always been the child who most resembled him, who shared his pleasure in walking and words, and got his jokes. He was enormously proud of her, and had always encouraged her writing, but he may have begun to be jealous, as several people who knew both father and daughter suggest he was.

At the end of her last visit, in October 1953, the *Irish Digest*, a small-format, one shilling monthly, had reprinted Maeve's story 'The Clever One' from *The New Yorker*. The following December, the editor wrote to Bob, requesting a short biographical note about Maeve, for use as a panel with one of the short stories and 'Irish sketches' he was planning to publish. Two more stories appeared, 'The Lie' in January 1954, and 'The Day We Got Our Own Back', in April, but no biographical note accompanied them. Bob did write one, however, and his handwritten draft letter suggests that the *Irish Digest* may have been in breach of copyright:

> I am sending you herewith the biographical material you asked me for about my daughter Maeve.
> Before you use it however I wd ask you to write to Maeve. When I saw her in NY a couple of weeks ago she told me she was very uneasy about the Irish Digest. She said that the New Yorker never allowed anyone to reprint their material and as well as I can remember she said she had got a special concession for you in one case.
> I gathered that the N Yorker people were incensed because they had had no acknowledgement [*sic*] from you & no copy of the publication.
> Maybe a letter from you to Maeve & to the editor of the New Yorker wd put all this right. I hope so.

The carbon of the biography survives too:

> MAEVE BRENNAN is the daughter of Robert Brennan former Irish Minister at Washington. She was born in Dublin in 1917 and educated at Scoil Bhride, Stephen's Green. She took a degree in Arts at the American University, Washington and another in Library Science at the Catholic University of America. She served as Assistant-Editor of *Harper's Bazaar* before joining the staff of the *New Yorker* in 1947.[20]

Written according to the conventions of the time, it is nevertheless a surprisingly egotistical and diminishing account of Maeve. Bob's own work was appearing regularly in the *Irish Press*, the *Sunday Press* and other Irish periodicals. Since his retirement, he had published his autobiography, *Allegiance* (1950), and the thriller, *The Man Who Walked Like a Dancer* (1951), but no American publishing contract or film offer had appeared, and his earnings from writing were small. By the time of Maeve's 1957 visit, when she was forty and he was seventy-six, he may well have been both envious of her success and disapproving of the person she had become. Whatever impression Maeve got about his attitude to her, or conveyed to her friends in New York, however, later correspondence shows his affection for her undiminished. And however she may have viewed the relationship between her parents, Bob's dedication in *Allegiance* was 'To Una, a quiet, brave and very patient lady'.

Those 1950s visits must have been difficult for everyone concerned. It is not easy to go back as an adult to the places where one is still somehow a child, or for elderly people to tolerate long visits from eccentric and opinionated younger adults. Ireland in the 1950s was a reticent, frugal, chilly place, where, notwithstanding much kindness and humour in the private sphere, an increasing repression hid a culture of great cruelty in orphanages and institutions. Maeve's enthusiasms and antipathies, her uninhibited language, generosity with gifts and proffering of solutions to what she perceived as other people's problems, could be overwhelming. Her letter from Dodder Road ends with a handwritten seven-line postscript and a smiley face the size of a fingertip.

Mac did not make it to Scotland on that trip, but he did go to London. Maeve wrote from Dublin to Maxwell's wife Emily that he had 'been there for quite a long time and I think he is having what we in literary circles refer to as the Time of his Life'.[21] She joined him, and they spent some time there together before sailing back to New York in October. This was later than planned, for Maeve refused at the last minute to fly. Things had been happening to her and Mac, though it is not clear precisely what. Mac was subject to psychotic episodes when away from New York for extended periods, and he had been ill in Dublin.[22] Perhaps he – or both of them – had been drinking too much, but at the very least, their way of running up bills and leaving them unpaid had caught up with them, so that they had had to appeal to William Shawn for help. Maeve wrote to Maxwell before they left London, in the shorthand, stream-of-consciousness style of people in constant touch:

Dear William,
I will be in the office on October 15, but not until then. I suppose I should be sorry about the letter I sent you, but I don't feel very contrite. The Hamlet at the Old Vic is perfectly dreaadful [sic], no matter what you read. I can't understand why the Whites didn't like London. I refused to get on the plane, which is why we are taking this late boat. I am thinking about being hung for a sheep instead of a lamb, and I think the boat might give me a chance to think. Now there I go sounding worried and burdened and it is not like that at all – I am in fine shape, I had some of my hair dyed gold, streacked [sic] with gold – it is something else. I think if I could be alone for a month I could

write a much better book than War and Peace. I really am not worried about the income tax – it just seemed the only mentionable thing. Ever since the Wolfenden report [published 3 September 1957], the homo-sexual population of London has been walking around looking as though they were different from the rest of us, not worse or better, just different and important and fated, like problem children at school. I know the look, I used to wear it myself in Kilcullen when the nuns had explained to me in public that I was damned damned damned. I never felt so holy since. London is a dangerous city. I went walking alone one Sunday afternoon and a man chased after me in his big car. I would turn down a street to get away from him and soon he would zoom down on me from another direction. Finally – he was so awful looking – I shouted at him OH Go AWAY, I am meeting my <u>husband</u> – and I went into the Park Lane hotel and looked in the showcase there. The other night I was walking through Shepherd's Market on my way to meet McKelway in a bar, and two men approached me separately, both jingling what sounded like sixpences, at the most. I thought the least they could have done was produce a five or ten pound rustle. So many strange things have happened since I left New York that I feel extremely queer – I think the Lord must have got bored with me, this obtuse mortal, and HE decided to throw the BOOK at me. I used to be always surprised at everything I saw, but now I am dazzled all day long. But blood tells – I was looking for a nice map of London but was outraged when they offered me one with LONDON Bastion of Liberty on it – it is the one they have framed all over the place.

Despite the sudden reappearance of the republican nationalism she grew up with, Maeve is enjoying what may have been her first extended visit to London. Whatever their difficulties, she and Mac seem to be on good terms. The letter continues (after a breathless paragraph break):

It is quite early in the morning and I am having tea and the Italian lady who runs the place just came up with your letters. McKelway is asleep in all his innocence, so I read his as well as my own. What a pleasure to read these two letters, and to know that you think we should stay here as long as possible. I wonder what Shawn is thinking – I wrote to him for the money to get back. I was divided between mirth and horror, I couldn't believe things had gone so far. If he is angry with me, do you think his rage might close the gap that has always existed between us. Anyway he sent the money and we rushed over to Cook's and paid for the tickets. The man at Cook's was convulsed with joy when he saw us at the counter with all the money. I could hardly bear to see it being paid over. I think I feel as Goldsmith must have done, that any money I get is spending money, and the grownups ought to pay the big ugly bills. But we have the tickets. William, I think that for a while instead of saying it's only money we should say it's only lack of money. I saw the Chaplin picture [*A King in New York*, 1957] and I larfed and larfed. He washes a little boy's hair in a plate of soup, and then he sits in a cream cake, which turns out to have his good fur hat inside of it. Little Michael Chaplin is preulsive. (repulsive)[23]

Oliver Goldsmith, born in County Longford in 1728, was a notorious spendthrift and wanderer, but he was endlessly entertaining, and Maeve admired him hugely. William Maxwell quoted that passage about the 'big ugly bills' in his Introduction to *The Springs of Affection*; it bears out what Roger Angell said, that Maeve and McKelway together were like 'two children out on a dangerous walk'. Most of Maeve's final paragraph seems to answer news in Maxwell's own letter, or letters, about other *New Yorker* writers. As always, she leaves out question marks:

Jean Stafford talks so exactly like Ann Honeycutt (they are very close friends) that McKelway is very nervous. That is an exaggeration [*sic*]. I don't see why I should be glad to hear that Brendan is about to strike it rich but I am very glad. I am also glad the Cheevers have that Italian cook – with so many in family, do you think they would like the big mansion at Sneden's Landing. Do you think I should go to Yaddo after Cheever leaves. Has Brendan made any headway with Miss E. He was happy laying siege when I left, and you can make what you like of that. Siege. I have become quite coarse. I wish the English wouldn't say Moddom. The lady who does my gilded hair turned out to be a vegetarian and brought me a bunch of grapes from her garden in Kent. They were limp. She likes to and does dance competitively in the evenings. She is proud of being a member of the lower classes and boasted to me that her uncle was a gardener in the viceregal lodge in Dublin.

Love, Maeve

An anecdote that went the rounds at *The New Yorker* conveys some of the comic gallantry and disorder of Maeve's life with Mac. On her return from one trip to Ireland, he came to meet her at the ship, drunk.

'But I thought you were on the wagon!' she said.

'I was,' he replied, 'but I got up to give my seat to a lady.'

Back in New York, they seem to have attempted to live more carefully.

They stayed full-time at Snedens Landing instead of renting an apartment in the city, and Maeve travelled in and out of Manhattan by bus. Soon, after a three-year gap, the Long-Winded Lady appeared again, with two short essays about the A-train, the subway that carried Maeve to the bus in the evening. Neither piece hinted that the Lady was working for a living. The first, on 15 February 1958, began: 'That long-winded lady we hear from occasionally has got herself involved with subterranean transportation this winter, on which she reports as follows:

> I come in to town for a round of the shops once in a while, and last Wednesday evening, after an unexpectedly agreeable day with the new chemise dresses, I was on the A train, riding up to 168th Street, where I catch the bus that takes me out to my present home, in Palisades. There were no seats to be had, but I had a good grip on the pole at one end of the seats and I was reading the beauty column of the *Journal-American*, which the man in front of me was holding up in front of him. [Cf. *LWL* 14–16]

'I must have left my wits at Lord and Taylor,' she says, when a man offers her a seat that she hastily declines. The twittering references to shopping (removed editorially in the published collection), introduce a detailed, circumstantial account of a small contretemps of etiquette on the train, beautifully observed and described with tongue in cheek.

The second piece, on 8 March, placed the Lady on the A-train again, 'riding up to the bus terminal at 168th Street after an exhausting day at the linen sales' [cf. *LWL* 33–7]. It commented mockingly on a *Life* magazine article, read on the train, about a thirty-three-year-old woman ('a pretty girl with dark hair who has a luxurious apartment and a French maid and a very big office'), who had recently become president of the Henri Bendel department store on Fifth Avenue. *Life* quoted her as saying, 'Once you've found the right people and set them free, you can't lose', and the Long-Winded Lady, hanging on to a pole on the crowded subway, worried the sentence, shaking out possible interpretations. How to recognise a right person, she couldn't begin to guess, but as for setting them free:

> Does she take them up on the roof at Henri Bendel? Or out into Central Park? Does she set them free all at once, in a flock, or one by one? At dawn, or when? If by some mischance a wrong one starts out of a coop, how is he or she got back in again? A hand on each shoulder? Both hands together on top of the head? Net? What if a wrong one gets clear away? [*LWL* 35]

These surreal ruminations typify the humour that Maeve's friends loved in her. With hindsight, though, the underlying references to New York's high-flying, street-scavenging pigeons read poignantly, for Maeve would eventually find herself living down among them. She was forty-one by now, still remarkably glamorous, and still living an enviable life, but debt was mounting and weariness had crept in. Walter Kerr was drama critic for the *New York Herald Tribune*, and in 1957 his wife Jean had published a bestselling book about life in their big old house with him and their four sons. *Please Don't Eat the Daisies* was a madcap-housewife story in which disasters happened constantly, but the reassuring love of family members for each other kept everything safe. It became a film in 1960, starring Doris Day and David Niven, and then a television series. No such benign spin on her situation was available to Maeve, however. In 'The Divine Fireplace', published two years earlier, she had written, 'The most important fact, not vague at all, about Herbert's Retreat is that only the right people live there.'

On 4 August 1958, Una Brennan died suddenly at her home in Dodder Road, Dublin. It was the beginning of Horse Show Week, and she was almost seventy. Maeve was able to fly direct from New York to Shannon and on to Dublin for her mother's funeral, for since the end of April, Aer Lingus's sister company, Aer Línte, had offered the transatlantic service originally planned for ten years earlier. Maeve's story 'The Drowned Man' tells of Hubert Derdon's bewilderment after Rose's death. A summer story (Rose's garden is 'well worth looking at'), it did not appear until July 1963, but it clearly expresses Maeve's own distress at the death of her mother, about whom her feelings had become so ambivalent. As in 'A Young Girl Can Spoil Her Chances', Hubert feels both tenderness and profound irritation when he thinks of Rose. Here, though, blundering around their home in the days after her death, he gasps for air, unable to name his emotion in a stream of consciousness that continues through a series of immensely long paragraphs. When at last he breaks down and cries,

> The tears hurt him. They hurt his chest and his eyes and they seemed to be tracing sticky wooden lines all over his face and neck and they hurt his brain and made it ache. The tears did not run down his face and away. They poured all over him and stayed on him and encased him, and when he tried to stop crying, because he was afraid he might smother in them, imprisoned in them, they poured out all the more and there seemed to be no end to them. The tears had him in a strait-jacket, and he could not speak. Now that he could not speak, he wished

he could speak, because he longed now to tell his sister the truth and have the matter cleared up once and for all. [*SA* 210]

That last phrase is the same one that ends the Long-Winded Lady's second 'A-train' piece. It is clearly part of Maeve's own idiom, and may have belonged to her family. She uses it with irony, as if to illustrate the folly of imagining that the mess of human relationships ever can be cleared up once and for all. Hubert Derdon has some of Bob's characteristics, as Rose has Una's, but here, where emotion is registered in and on the body (those 'sticky wooden lines' of tears on the face), his consciousness can only be Maeve's own. Her letters in later years to William Maxwell make many references to her mother: to a quest for her in many places, and an attempt to know and understand who she had been. On what would have been Una's eighty-fifth birthday, 11 September 1973, during a prolonged visit to Dublin, she wrote to him about her death:

> I thought that if I could see in my mind one tree, or one house, or one hill or river, if I could see even the wall of a cottage – a remnant, a door, even, I would cry my eyes out. But the landscape that had been mysterious & familiar as it was, was quite gone. There was nothing, and nothing to cry over. She gave me an 'asylum for my affections' & I learned not to care that my affections so far exceeded her ability to understand me that she came near to drowning. But she is defined in her struggling – I remember her very well.[24]

In 'The Drowned Man', as in that letter, the idea of vacancy, of emptiness, recurs. Hubert is ashamed and angry because he believes that what he feels is not grief. He experiences too what was clearly another preoccupation of Maeve's: the sense, already expressed in 'The Joker', that some people are sent into life unprepared. In 'The Joker', they are waifs, for whom nobody has remembered to buy a train ticket, so that they remain stranded on the platform, and must eat their Christmas dinner at someone else's table. Here, Hubert wonders again and again what the secret is that everybody but him seems to know [*SA* 278].

Maeve's relatives in Ireland remember her grief at Una's funeral. Days later, in Kilmuckridge, County Wexford, her Aunt Bessie's husband Mike Parker died too, and Maeve travelled from Dublin for his funeral. She was not expected. Wat and Katie had driven from Coolnaboy to Kilmuckridge in a horse-drawn trap that morning, with several of their children, but two of their sons, Matt and Liam, had cycled.[25] Arriving late at the small church, they were astonished to see walking towards them a glamorous-looking woman with hair wound all around her head. As teenage boys, they were only vaguely aware of their grown-up cousins in America, so were even more surprised when Maeve recognised them, asking 'Are you the Bolgers?' Irish funerals are quite unlike American ones: Jessica Mitford's *The American Way of Death* (1963) drew attention to American customs that seemed to European eyes bizarre, including embalming the dead. Mike Parker's funeral was an important occasion, for he had played on the Wexford hurling team that won the All-Ireland Final in 1910, but Maeve had not lived in Ireland for many years. At Irish funerals, the whole culture regresses from its own modernity. We are at once comforted and appalled by our resemblance to our relatives, and our differences from them, as families and neighbours gather in great numbers, deferring to the oldest people present; eyes are lowered; voices murmur old-fashioned, formulaic phrases; the food is that of years ago, and everyone talks about the past. Women wore dark clothes in Ireland in the 1950s, especially at funerals. The Bolger brothers were astonished to see Maeve's brightly coloured coat that day in Kilmuckridge, and her red lipstick.

'America at home' was a phrase often used to describe household innovations and acquisitions in those years, for America was much in people's minds. A few months earlier, the *Irish Press* had marked the new transatlantic air service with articles about flight, airports, Irish-American connections and American life. On 28 April, the day of the first 'fly-out', the other major item on the front page was headed 'U.S. Cardinal to Have Arm Amputation': it concerned Cardinal Stritch of Chicago, son of a former Fenian from Ballyheigue, County Kerry, who had visited there the previous year. Tweed featured on the fashion pages, for Magee of Donegal had supplied the cloth for the flight attendants' uniforms, and the duty-free shops at Shannon Airport were full of Irish tweed, linen, lace and Waterford glass, but nylon was clearly the fabric of the future, appearing everywhere in photographs and articles. Inside, most of page 9 was devoted to the first part of a new series by Bob Brennan.

'My Wartime Mission in Washington' continued in daily instalments until 19 May, each one illustrated with photographs of Brennan with American statesmen, churchmen, writers and entertainers, including 'Wrong Way' Corrigan, Mayor Fiorello LaGuardia of New York, and the humorous writer Damon Runyon, from whom Maeve seems to have borrowed Charles's surname in the 'Herbert's Retreat' stories.[26] A quarter-page advertisement on 28 April offered round-trip flights from Dublin and Shannon ('the air crossways of the world'), to New York:

The Aerlinte Eireann Pay Later Plan means you can fly to New York and back for £15 deposit and pay the balance over 21 months.

Repayments for the return fare from Shannon are £5.15s. monthly and from Dublin £6.3s. monthly. By special arrangement the Emigrant fare can also be paid in monthly instalments.

The total cost of this round-trip ticket from Shannon was £134 14sh. At approximately $3 to the pound, it worked out at just over $400; cheaper 'emigrant' fares were offered to lure one-way passengers away from travel by sea. Air travel made America easier to imagine and brought emigrants home more often, sometimes with discomfiting results. In New York, a truck driver got $155 for a forty-hour week; an accounting-machine operator could earn $70 a week, as against £6 10sh. in Dublin for longer hours. The *Irish Times* compared prices and wages, calculating that: 'A dollar to Miss New York is half an hour's work; its equivalent to Miss Dublin is two hours' work. This explains why so many Americans can go to Europe and spend holidays there, and why there is so little holiday traffic in the opposite direction.'[27] Most of those travelling from Ireland, especially on 'emigrant' fares, were the Bridies and Agneses who would work for low wages that seemed high to their families at home – huge numbers emigrated in the 1950s – but travellers coming from New York were altogether more prosperous.

Any American, or any Irish person who had lived in America, was a 'Yank', to be envied, admired, derided, exploited, and even pitied. Maeve's fiction about the 'ravenous grudge' of Irish women less fortunate than herself would have been informed by her own experience of being on its receiving end. The nostalgia of Yanks was notorious. Without the Irish person's tight-lipped wariness, they seemed gullible and childish, in odd and unsettling contrast to the nervousness they inspired. Yanks would sit in thin clothing, complaining of the cold, or arrive wearing rough tweeds and sweaters to meet relatives who had dressed up and lit fires in their honour. They would expect hot running water, and ice in their drinks, and would cause mortal offence by commenting on the accents of people who knew that the way *they* spoke was normal. Yanks could be recognised without difficulty by their voices, and by the bright colours and synthetic fabrics they wore. Long after they had left, parcels would arrive that might be magical with nylon party dresses, books and toys, or might smell of mothballs and yield only uncomfortable, embarrassing garments and plastic ornaments. There were many little hats with veils. Aunts wrote letters to mothers with sentences like 'At least I know he's faithful, which is more than you can say about some', and Irish children gaped that an adult in the real world and not in a book could express herself so frankly. Some Yanks even came intending to stay, but it seemed inconceivable that such beings could settle down and live among Irish people. When Frank O'Connor moved back to Dublin from Brooklyn

Heights in 1959 with his young American wife and baby daughter, the letters they wrote to William and Emily Maxwell reverberated with the culture shock they experienced. A few years later, another *New Yorker* writer, Brian Friel, would turn from short stories to drama to express the dislocations Irish people were experiencing when they travelled.[28]

After the funerals, Maeve set about organising her father's life. Over his protests that he would manage well enough with a daily help, she asked her Aunt Nan, Bob's younger sister, to come and live with him. Possibly she feared that if their father remained alone, Derry would be burdened with his care, but she cannot have had so much scruple about her aunt, although she may have felt that Nan would be better off in Dublin than in Wexford. Nan Brennan was seventy-four, a small, intrepid woman who always wore brown and now lived alone in her flat in Main Street. She had looked after her sister Tess's husband John Griffin while Tess was in St Senan's Hospital, and had continued to do so after Tess's death, until he too died, and she had provided a home for Chrissie's husband after Chrissie went blind and could no longer run her own house. Such selflessness was taken for granted in unmarried women who stayed in Ireland. Like Min Bagot in 'The Springs of Affection', Nan left her own flat in Wexford to look after her widowed brother, moving into the house on Dodder Road to live with him, while Maeve returned to New York. Nan did not like Dublin. She missed her friends in Wexford and her involvement in the town's cultural life: she had been a staunch supporter of the International Opera Festival since its foundation in 1951.

Bob continued to retire into his room every day to write, but at the end of the 1950s Ireland was changing, at last becoming more interested in the future than in the past. A new American embassy was planned for Ballsbridge in Dublin: a circular building in reinforced concrete, which would engage with the surrounding redbrick houses 'more in quality and in spirit than in imitation'. In December, T. K. Whitaker, Secretary of the Department of Finance, published his groundbreaking White Paper, *Economic Development*. It marked a first step towards curbing emigration and attracting foreign investment.[29]

The New Yorker had not published fiction by Maeve since 1956. Some time in the early spring of 1959, a reader called John R. Boyce wrote to the magazine from East Northport, New York, asking if any more 'Herbert's Retreat' stories were on the way. The reply was dated 17 March, and read:

Dear Mr Boyce:
Thank you for your letter. We don't know whether there will be more stories about Herbert's Retreat, but we do hope to have something by

Maeve Brennan in a forthcoming issue. We'll see that your comments reach her.

Very truly yours, The New Yorker

This letter soon began to be passed around the office, for when Maeve received a copy in due course, she added her own reply to Mr Boyce, signing it with William Maxwell's name before passing it on:

Dear Mr Boyce

I am terribly sorry to have to be the first to tell you that our poor Miss Brennan died. We have her head here in the office, at the top of the stairs, where she was always to be found, smiling right and left and drinking water out of her own little paper cup. She shot herself in the back with the aid of a small handmirror at the foot of the main altar in St Patrick's Cathedral one Shrove Tuesday. Frank O'Connor was where he usually is in the afternoons, sitting in a confession box pretending to be a priest and giving a penance to some old woman and he heard the shot and he ran out and saw our poor late author stretched out flat and he picked her up and slipped her in the poor box. She was very small. He said she went in easy. Imagine the feelings of the young curate who unlocked the box that same evening and found the deceased curled up in what appeared to be and later turned out truly to be her final slumber. It took six strong parish priests to get her out of the box and then they called us and we all went and got her and carried her back her[e] on the door of her office . . . We will never know why she did what she did (shooting herself) but we think it was because she was drunk and heartsick. She was a very fine person, a very real person, two feet, hands, everything. But it is too late to do much about that now.

I have a lot of live authors, Mr Boyce, if you would like to as[k] about any of them, if there is anything you'd like to know about any of them, I'll be happy to oblige. Most of them have studio portraits, ready for framing, some life size, some even en famille, as we say around here in our amiable but decidedly spirited, even brisk, New Yorker Magazine way. And thank you for your kind interest in the unfortunate Miss Brennan. I am glad to know that *someone* remembers her. As for her, I am afraid she would only spit in your eye. She was ever ungrateful. One might say of her that nothing in her life became her.

sincerely, William (Bill) Maxwell

Maxwell included the text of this wonderful letter in the Introduction he wrote for *The Springs of Affection: Stories of Dublin*, published four years after Maeve's death. Juxtaposed with the quietly lit, remembered settings of her fiction, it echoes like a cackle of infectious laughter in a church, bringing into consciousness all that has been left outside. Perhaps the St Patrick's Day date on the original reply to Mr Boyce struck Maeve as ironic, or she may simply have been heartsick, as she writes, and weary, when she amused herself by imagining the magazine's Yale-educated writers as an agricultural-heroic band of Irish ditch-diggers, who down tools to carry an injured comrade home on a door that has been lifted off its hinges.

Maeve was certainly heartsick at this time. With her mother dead, her marriage to St Clair McKelway sinking ever deeper into debt, and her own writing in difficulty, she was clearly feeling diminished: 'She was very small,' the letter said; she had a 'little' paper cup and a 'small' handmirror; 'our poor author' was found curled up in the poor-box. *The New Yorker* has retained her smiling head, but, it appears, has discarded the rest: 'two feet, hands, everything'. The woman who appeared to others so intimidatingly self-possessed and groomed presents her own body as though dismembered, or reflected in a distorting mirror at a fairground. It was ten years since she had joined the magazine. She had entertained her nieces and nephews in Dublin with stories about people in New York who felt the need to see their psychiatrists every day (McKelway may have been one of them), but her own memories were her richest source of fiction, and it is hard to imagine her having recourse to a psychiatrist herself. Instead, she made jokes. It was a long-standing Irish tradition, and one she had learned as a child: sometimes, all you can do is laugh.

Maeve and Mac were effectively borrowing from their employer week by week as they lived lavishly on their *New Yorker* drawing accounts, lacking the private income many other staffers had. Maeve was beginning to realise why Mac's family had welcomed her so warmly as his fourth bride: they were grateful to anybody who seemed willing to take him off their hands.[30] On 14 June 1958, *The New Yorker* had carried St Clair McKelway's account of the delusions he had suffered in the Pacific at the height of the Second World War, when he accused Admiral Nimitz and many others of treason. For two years, however, Maeve herself had published almost nothing. Moreover, in the constant knocking-down and rebuilding of partitions between offices at the magazine, she had lost most of her work space.

Elizabeth Cullinan, a young Irish-American from the Bronx, joined *The New Yorker* in 1955, when she was twenty-two, and became William Maxwell's assistant a year later. Maeve encouraged her in her writing, and sometimes brought her unexpected gifts from Stern Brothers', across the street from the office.[31] Once it was a housecoat; another time a cashmere sweater. 'I thought it would suit you,' she said. Cullinan appreciated the gifts, though she thought the old-fashioned department store 'horrible'. Maeve was always drawn to the funky, however. She loved Stern's and mourned it when it closed [*LWL* 3].

Cullinan had never been to Ireland. The Catholic, second-generation-immigrant culture in which she had grown up was what 'Irish' meant to her, and it was a world away from the *New Yorker* offices, where Maeve embodied the magazine's urbanity and style. She could not fathom what it meant that this dainty, elegant woman in black, with the piled-up hair and dramatic make-up, a fresh flower always in her lapel, was 'Irish'. Once, hearing Maeve described as 'Irish-American', she almost fell off her chair.

Almost from the time she arrived at the magazine, Cullinan witnessed battles between Maeve and Maxwell over Maeve's story 'The Rose Garden'. Maxwell wanted to cut out a long passage, but Maeve made 'the most tremendous fuss' and refused to allow it, so the story remained unpublished. Then in 1959, when she needed money badly, Maeve capitulated, and the cut version of 'The Rose Garden' appeared on 28 March; this was the 'something by Maeve Brennan' that the magazine's letter to Mr Boyce had mentioned as appearing 'in a forthcoming issue'. Although Maeve must have felt this as a defeat, judging by a surviving typescript copy, which includes the deleted passage, it is hard not to agree with Maxwell that the story was the better for his cut.[32] The deleted passage is almost five typed pages – nearly one-fifth of the total – and describes the lame Mary Lambert's memory of a walk with her father to a lake, where the water's expanse and depth and weight terrified her, invading her imagination for ever after:

What she wanted to tell Dom, but could not tell him, and could not tell anybody, was the place that walk had led to, that she could not forget, no matter how hard she tried. She was thirteen at the time. Her father said they'd walk out as far as the lake that lay beyond the town, but he had not given her any notion of the size of the lake, or of how it looked. Perhaps it did not appear the same to him, as it did to her, but she got a great fright when she saw it, because she thought they had come to the Dead Sea. They had been walking a long time, and she was growing tired, when they came upon the lake very suddenly, over the rim of a high bank. She was scrambling along behind her father, who had boarded the bank in three long powerful strides, when the great grey floor [of] water rose up at her feet, or at her mouth, without warning. The water was much too close to her, and it made no noise. She was terrified by the stillness that came up out of it. The size of it was too much for her, and she looked quickly down past her feet, at the part nearest to touching her, to persuade herself that it was only water, and nothing to be upset about, but that downward glance undid her, because the bank did not slope gradually into the lake, but dropped straight down, and she found herself staring through the glassy surface to the farthest depths, where great mountains of water, long sunken, long dead, huddled haunch to haunch, ringed with silver shadows that increased and grew darker until they vanished in the spectral blackness of the lake bed. Mary believed that the blackness down there was not the bed of the lake at all, but that it was only the beginning of a much more calamitous fall. There would be no chance of anyone dragging her back, if she were to fall past that blackness. She could feel the water pulling at her, and she looked in terror to her father, but he was standing a few steps away, gazing impassively across to the horizon.

Mary Lambert is another of Maeve's 'freaks', like Bridie the maid, or Mary Ramsay in 'The Holy Terror', but her vulnerable subjectivity shows through in tender detail as theirs does not. Tiny, charming and fastidious herself, Maeve wrote much about women who were large, ungainly and unsmiling. Partly it is the same physical revulsion she registered at seventeen, when Gilda in a performance of *Rigoletto* turned out to be mannish and middle-aged, instead of young and fair, but she also deliberately enters the mind of these characters who are her opposites in every way. They are deprived where she is privileged; mean and grasping where she is generous; ugly where she is beautiful. Towards the end of 'The Rose Garden', a deleted sentence reads, 'Words and their meanings, and the differences between meanings, did not concern her': whereas Maeve lives through words, these women are inarticulate. They are all Irish, though, and most of them have great masses of hair; Maeve does not spare them, but she shows us their humanity. Their physical freakishness makes manifest what her own appearance concealed: the fact that they do not belong.

Mary Lambert has a short leg that makes her 'walk crookedly, leaning forward and sideways'. Her character is twisted and determined, like the staircase in her house, for she lives in the same awkward two-corner-houses-knocked-into-one, with a little shop downstairs, as Maeve's grandmother did in Wexford town. Despising those who smile, to ingratiate themselves, as she believes, she stares indifferently, making people uneasy, and the laced boots she wears are 'very solid and hard-looking, as though the feet inside them were made of wood'. With stolid emphasis, the story repeats that phrase in contradiction: 'The feet inside were not made of wood. She had great feeling in them, and in all parts of her body.'

Mary Lambert always wears a large, wide skirt that marks her territory on the bench in the rose garden, leaving her knees free to move. The parts of her body whose feeling Maeve explores so passionately are all below the waist, for the story is an astonishing assertion of female sexuality, located at a maximum remove from the feminine mystique that reserved the pleasures of the flesh for childlike, passive women. The women in 'The Rose Garden' are neither elegant urbanites like Maeve, nor the happy housewife heroines of the American media; instead, they are a working-class woman so unattractive that she almost never leaves her home, and Irish nuns in black wool shawls, infantilised by their vocation. Yet these are sexual beings. The nuns fear that the devil may yet enter them through the 'treacherous parting' in their flesh that is 'red and dark' like the roses in their garden, but Mary Lambert says 'I want the rose garden. I want it', and her urgent desire is unapologetically sensuous: 'I want to see it, I want to touch it, I want it for my own.'

The nuns in 'The Rose Garden' take a gentle, virginal delight in the blooming of their starry yellow forsythia at Christmas.[33] Then every June, that timid wintry pleasure gives way to the full-blown red explosion that Mary Lambert lives for. Maeve's experience of describing fashion colours makes up for her lack of gardening expertise:

> But with the coming of June the roses arrived in their hundreds and thousands, some so rich and red that they were called black, and some so pale that they might have been white, and all the depths between – carmine, crimson, blush, rose, scarlet, wine, purple, pink and blood – and they opened themselves and spread themselves out, arching and dancing their long strong stems, and lay with lips loose and curling under the sun's heat, so that the perfume steamed up out of them, and the air thickened with it, and stopped moving under the weight of it.

The garden dates from the time of the illustrious family who owned the ground before the convent came there – when political power in Ireland lay with families, and not with a celibate clergy and the thin-lipped politicians who did their bidding – and when the roses show clearest it looks 'as though a great heart had begun to beat under the earth, and was sending living blood up to darken the red roses, and make the pink roses purer'.

'The Rose Garden' insists that partnership and procreation depend not on beauty or grooming, but on being able to cope with life. Like Hubert Derdon in 'The Drowned Man', Mary Lambert suspects that 'the rest of the people in the world were better off, or that they had some fortunate secret, or were engaged in a conspiracy in which she was not included' [*RG* 196]. She allows Dom, a faint-hearted draper's assistant, into her bed 'because she ha[s] as much ordinary courage as any other human being'. They marry, and have two children, Rose and Jimmy, but Mary is still shut out from love. In later stories, Rose will marry Hubert Derdon and become the priest's pallid mother. Rose Derdon was almost ten when her father died, however; here, Rose is seven when Dom dies, and Jimmy two.

Maeve's attachment to the passage that William Maxwell deleted may have been aesthetic: it does provide a counterweight of imagery – cold, grey and masculine – to balance the burning female redness of the rose garden. Without it, the story's preoccupation with sex is less overt. When a child in her shop tells Mary excitedly that the lake has frozen over, she contemplates going out to look at it:

> The thought of the ice stiffening over the lake aroused great excitement in Mary also. She wanted to feel the ice, to stroke it until it burned her, and then, maybe, to secretly poke a hole in it, and lay her face down alongside the hole, and spy down into the cold and dark at the smothering there below. The thought of the powerful water, swelling and straining, bursting inside its tight binding sheet, maddened her, and she wanted to speak about it, but there was no one to speak to. She thought of the children scampering out over the tightening ice, mocking their own death with every touch of their boots, and then she was afraid, because although she had never seen any amount of ice, she knew that there might very well be soft places in it, sore parts, where the rising water pursed and pulsed and tasted its own air again.

The writing is wonderful, adding texture and depth to Mary Lambert's character, but the whole long passage about the lake fits the story awkwardly, suggesting that the memory of water is Maeve's own, along with the nightmare conviction that it spreads everywhere beneath the land. There is no lake of any size near Wexford town, but in any case, the body of water the story describes, with steep banks that conceal it from view, is less like a lake than a reservoir. Mary Lambert's father would have been seventy-three when she was thirteen, but here he has 'boarded the bank in three long powerful strides' by the time she catches up with him. Bob Brennan sometimes took Maeve walking in the Dublin mountains. A favourite destination was the reservoir built for the township of Rathmines in the late nineteenth century, on the Dodder, in the valley above Bohernabreena, where high, steep grassy banks surround the water. In 'The Rose Garden', when Mary Lambert was twenty, and a commercial traveller lodger climbed wordlessly into bed with her, she knew by the fabric of his shirt that it was not her father. 'Anyway,' she says devastatingly, 'my father hadn't that much interest in me.' The same shadow of incest lies over the description of the lake. Maeve's own father was always interested in her, and proud of her – an attitude far from the exploitations of father-daughter incest – but again she chooses to explore experiences that are the obverse of her own, visiting the dark side of herself and her relationships. Letters to William Maxwell in the years that follow refer to an abiding guilt Maeve feels about her family – chiefly, it seems, about betraying them somehow, by pursuing her writing talent. That guilt probably had its origin in her decision to leave Washington and pursue a career instead of staying at home to help and support her mother. After Una's death, the ambivalence Maeve has expressed about her mother switches its focus to Bob.

In the summer that followed the publication of 'The Rose Garden', Maeve visited her father in Ireland again. In June, his hero Éamon de Valera, aged seventy-five and almost blind, finally stepped down as Taoiseach and was immediately elected as the third President of Ireland. His successor was the pragmatic, energetic and very patient Seán Lemass, who embraced the economic policies put forward by T. K. Whitaker and at last began the process of running Ireland as a business, rather than a patriarchal household. Exports of woollen and worsted cloth had more than doubled since 1952; sales of handknitted sweaters were rising steadily, and soon new industries would join them.[34] Tourism was still a priority, as air travel began to close the gap of understanding between Ireland and America. The Brennans' old friend Jimmy O'Dea, now sixty, starred with Scottish actor Sean Connery in *Darby O'Gill and the Little People* in 1959, delivering a version of Irish folklore to American cinema audiences, and four young men called the Clancy Brothers and Tommy Makem, who were playing Irish ballads in clubs around Greenwich Village as the folk revival began, issued their first album, *The Rising of the Moon*.

St Clair McKelway came to Dublin too in the summer of 1959, but he did not spend all his time in his father-in-law's house. His writing mentions the Dolphin Hotel on East Essex Street near the Liffey, and he may have stayed there, rather than at Dodder Road. It was a fashionable haunt of hunting and shooting types, where Siobhán McKenna's husband Denis O'Dea and his friends would sometimes play poker 'through Saturday night and Sunday morning until it was time for Father "Flash" Kavanagh's 1.00 p.m. mass at St Audeon's'.[35] Mac's plan was to go at last to Scotland, where his ancestors had come from, so after a week he flew from Dublin to Glasgow, intending to move on to Edinburgh and write some 'Reporter at Large' pieces for *The New Yorker*.

The adventure that followed became known as 'The Edinburgh Caper', a paranoid picaresque with copious amounts of alcohol, all of which McKelway rendered in courtly, bewildered, meticulous detail in *The New Yorker* of 13 October 1962, and shortly afterwards expanded into a book.[36] Much as he had in the Pacific during the war, McKelway believed he had detected a complex plot, in which he had a vital part to play. Queen Elizabeth and the Duke of Edinburgh were in Canada in the summer of 1959, and Eisenhower and Khrushchev were considering a summit meeting. McKelway became convinced that the Russians were plotting to kidnap one or more of the western heads of state in Edinburgh, and that the chance remarks of people he met in bars, and even the registration numbers of the cars he saw, were coded messages from his friends in the CIA about a counter-plot. He rented limousines and drove back and forth across Scotland to report his suspicions to US intelligence officers and the consul, and even spent a night in jail, with his typewriter, after being arrested for drunk and disorderly behaviour. In his published account, the woman who flies from Dublin to join him towards the end of his time in Scotland is a 'friend' called 'Susie', said to be the daughter of a French diplomat. Her girlhood had been full of escapes and intrigue, for 'her father had always been on the run, with a price set on his head by Nazis'. 'Susie', of course, was Maeve Brennan. The book is dedicated 'To Maeve'.

Those who knew Maeve in New York and saw what happened to her in subsequent years thought that perhaps the 'Edinburgh Caper' had been a kind of apprenticeship in craziness for her. Mental illness was not unusual at *The New Yorker*, of course: many of its writers were alcoholics and depressives. Some prolific writers simply stopped, as Sally Benson did in the mid-1950s. McKelway himself took to writing meaningless words on the walls on the eighteenth floor, and several others committed suicide. Maeve's personal demons were no secret, and to Brendan Gill at least, it seemed as if she actively encouraged them.[37] McKelway's escapade in Scotland may have suggested one way of dealing with life when everything around her became too much. For the moment, however, what could not be sustained was their marriage. Maeve and Mac agreed to divorce and, late in 1959, Maeve left Snedens Landing and moved back to Manhattan, alone.

ELEVEN

The Traveller in Residence

By the spring of 1960 Maeve had left Snedens Landing for good, and with Minnie, a 'waif cat' that had just had kittens, was installed in rooms she had lived in before, on the eighth floor of the Hotel Earle in Greenwich Village. Her other cats, and Bluebell, the black Labrador, were at a kennel, where they would have to stay until Maeve could find an apartment to house them all. Gerald Murphy wrote on a postcard at the end of March to thank her for her most recent gifts – a child's mug for him; a yellow shawl for Sara – addressing the card to 'Mrs St Clair McKelway'.[1] Brendan Gill has noted that 'like the Murphys, [Maeve] could bestow distinction upon the humblest objects – a painted biscuit-tin, a table woven of straw – by the emphasis she gave them or by the unexpected uses to which she put them'.[2] Her gifts were always imaginative and thoughtful, but while many could see the hungry diffidence that lay behind them, the Murphys were among the few who reached out to nurture and embrace the giver. It seemed to Gill that they sheltered her, especially after her marriage ended, and tried to protect her against her demons. She kept the postcard.

On 18 June, the Long-Winded Lady appeared in *The New Yorker* again. Some 2,000 words describe the first evening of her return to the city that she will later call '[h]alf-capsized . . . with the inhabitants hanging on, most of them still able to laugh as they cling to the island that is their life's predicament' [*LWL* 1]. The Lady notes the small colourful pleasures of living in Manhattan, but she seems dispirited. In a good-humoured, self-deprecating way that becomes tragic when we reflect on the many brilliant women who became casualties of 1950s cultural politics, she is struggling to stay afloat. It was no small thing for a woman over forty to leave even the most eccentric marriage, especially with no prospect of alimony, and Maeve has done it in a way that was typical of her, without any but the most basic and costly preparations:

I left the packing until it was too late to be properly organized about it, and by the time the movers had left to take my things to storage, where they will stay until I find the right apartment, I was too disgusted with my own possessions to watch the van crawl down the driveway and too weary to be very pleased about anything at all. [*LWL* 37]

Soon, though, she is out on the street, buying a carnation to wear in her lapel, looking at window displays, browsing among remaindered books. One that she buys gives a clue to her identity: it is Benedict Kiely's *Poor Scholar*, about the nineteenth-century Irish writer William Carleton. A little later, eating a solitary dinner at her favourite table in the window of the University Restaurant on 8th Street, she sees a flurry of uneasy commotion in the street and hears a waiter say that a woman has dropped dead outside. Hoping it is not true, she concentrates on reading, but in the street she learns that yes, a woman of about thirty has had a heart attack and died:

I walked along to the hotel and went up to my rooms. Minnie was with her kittens, but she lifted her head when I came in and I could see her whole small face, her eyes radiant with the steady, resolute anxiety of the devoted mother. Poor waif, she had traveled a long journey with her infants that day. She purred when I touched her, but mechanically, it seemed. She remained on guard and I went to bed. I hoped the woman who died on the street had had a nice day. I don't know what I didn't hope for her. I hoped she had no one belonging to her who loved her enough to grieve for years, to cry all their lives over the thought of her lying there like that.

The passage anticipates Maeve's stories about the Bagots (who also have a cat called Minnie), in which she will reflect on family love as 'the instinctive kind of attentiveness that animals give to their young' [*SA* 307]. It echoes too with her continuing bewildered grief for her own mother. Minnie has had to travel uncertainly with her infants, just as Una did with Maeve and Derry so many times. Twice, the piece describes the little cat as a waif, as Isobel Bailey's guests were in Maeve's first published *New Yorker* story, and as she has undoubtedly begun to feel herself to be. Still, hotel rooms like this one are where she feels safest. The last words of the piece are, 'So ended the first evening following my return from where I was to where I am now – home' [*LWL* 42–3].

Home is a refuge, hastily improvised, a place where one can settle down unchallenged, yet be free to leave at will. The Long-Winded Lady describes herself, famously, as a 'traveler in residence', and Manhattan as the great, unwieldy, half-capsized ship in which she travels.[3] She wishes she could turn herself into a transatlantic traveller for a few days, or even a week, 'and masquerade with luggage and a striped steamer rug in some distant hotel lobby, and allow everybody to believe that I had a very good and important reason for being there, and that when I left I would have an urgent reason for leaving . . .' [*LWL* 119]. For her, life is a journey whose destination remains unknown, and perhaps the most satisfactory home is a boat, or a train: waifs, after all, are those who have no ticket. It is a way of explaining, even excusing, a failure to develop a rooted grown-up life. Maeve is a passenger, not a driver, and all her indefatigable walking through New York's streets in her high-heeled shoes is like the turns she might take about the deck of a liner in mid-ocean. Endlessly amazed and diverted by what she sees, she knows that none of it is really her concern. It is only when the ship begins to falter and shudder on its course – when familiar landmarks are torn down, good books by hard-working authors are sold off at bargain prices, or people drop dead or go crazy in the street – that the passenger feels an uneasy responsibility and longs for a remembered home. 'Home is a place in the mind,' Maeve had written in *The Visitor*. 'When it is empty, it frets' [*V* 8].

Four more Long-Winded Lady pieces appeared in 'The Talk of the Town' in 1960. Gradually the Lady's personality takes shape. She moves from one hotel to another about the city – even stays for a while on the moneyed Upper East Side – leaving her animals at various kennels and her possessions in storage as she searches for the place where she would really like to settle down. She suffers reversals that threaten her stability, some-times literally, as when the heel of her shoe snaps in two, but the city comes to her rescue, offering taxis to ride in, and new things to think about. Senator John Fitzgerald Kennedy is running for President; sitting barefoot in a shoe shop, she is happy to overhear two ladies condemn him as 'much too young' while they look at evening sandals, for she is forty-three, as he is. (She does not mention that, like her, he is a Catholic, whose ancestors came from County Wexford.) Back in the street, from behind her own impeccable grooming, the Long-Winded Lady pays attention to both men and women. If they are poor and ask her for money, she gives it to them.

That summer of 1960, Bluebell stayed with William and Emily Maxwell and their daughters, five-year-old Kate, and Brookie, three, at their house on Baptist Church Road in Yorktown Heights, New York. In August, Maeve was still looking at apartments in Manhattan. In September, the Maxwells came back to the city, but Bluebell, brought up in Sneden's landing, was a country dog, and whined all night in their apartment.[4] By the time Kennedy was elected President in November, however, Maeve had moved out of the city.

Gerald and Sara Murphy lived part of each year in East Hampton, close to the eastern tip of Long Island, where Sara's family was long established in a huge house above the sand dunes, beside the Maidstone golf club, and Gerald had his rose garden.[5] Many of the artists and writers who summered nearby were their friends, some of them Europeans who had followed them from Antibes after the war. Concerned for Maeve, and eager to keep her near them now that she was separated from Mac and would no longer be at Snedens Landing, the Murphys had arranged a winter rental for her at Amagansett, the next station after theirs on the Long Island Rail Road.

A big storm hit the Hamptons soon after Maeve arrived. On 10 December, Gerald sent her a postcard; he and Sara had worried about her, but were too sensitive to risk intruding:

We have been thinking of you down the little lane that leads to the sea. We wanted to call when the blizzard started but feared being upbraided for worrying about you without permission.[6]

Maeve was not put off by bad weather, however. On 4 January 1961, William Maxwell wrote to Frank O'Connor, 'We are about to surrender Bluebell permanently to Maeve Brennan, and there is talk of acquiring Bluebell's niece'. On 17 January, he reported, 'Yesterday . . . Maeve took Bluebell for good'.[7]

So began a series of rentals, when Maeve would spend the winters alone in other people's houses in the Hamptons, with Bluebell and five or more cats, making only short forays to the city. The long Atlantic beach that runs from the Hamptons to Montauk was deserted in winter, and Maeve liked to walk while Bluebell ran headlong after seagulls or a plastic ball. She wrote in her notebooks about the wind and the sea's ferocity, and the pearly fog that made everything mysterious. She would return home to light a fire, read, make tea or a martini, and write: book reviews, fiction, 'long-windeds' (as she called them), and many letters. Her own writing entered a new phase of productivity as she found a rhythm that suited her. Gardner Botsford and William Maxwell kept the dozens of letters she sent them.[8] Some of them run to many pages, others are only a few lines long; some are typed; others handwritten; almost all are undated, their pages unnumbered. Maeve describes her reading and writing – she was reading as many as eighteen or twenty new novels a week for *The New Yorker*, and submitting her 'Briefly Noted' reviews to Botsford – and after years of eating in restaurants, her attempts at cooking for herself. She wickedly recounts the doings of other *New Yorker* writers who live nearby, or who turn up out of the blue, amusing or enraging her. She writes with humble, overflowing love about Bluebell, and the cats ('small heaps of warm dreaming fur all over the furniture and the floor'), and about the kindness of the Murphys.

Sara and Gerald were almost always nearby. Maeve admired both immensely, and had long, thoughtful conversations with them, in one house or another. Along with their imaginative generosity, they shared her love of France and the French language, and Gerald, like Maeve, had grown up a Catholic. They exchanged gifts and lent each other books, and sometimes stopped by each other's houses to visit for just a minute. Maeve's letters show how much she appreciated simply knowing that the Murphys were nearby, that their affection was sincere, and that they would stay in touch while respecting her solitude. 'As we grow older,' Gerald told her, 'we must guard against a feeling of lowered consequence.'[9] For a divorced woman without property or a private income, a sense of lowered consequence was probably inevitable, but like William Maxwell, Sara and Gerald offered Maeve the inestimable gift of taking her and her work seriously. Over the next five years, she spent several winters in a little house on their property, whose storybook quality suited her. She described it once as 'a fat, romantic cottage . . . [that] might have been baked from a bit of dough left over after the giant's place on the dunes was built' [*RG* 279]. With an enormous fireplace, door and windows that left almost no room for walls, it seemed less like a house than a set for an operetta. For Maeve, whose first passion had been the theatre, and whose domestic arrangements always had a temporary, 'fit-up' quality, it was perfect.

On 4 February 1961 'The Beginning of a Long Story' appeared in *The New Yorker*. It had been almost two years since 'The Rose Garden'. Maeve kept the proofs, with William Shawn's queries and William Maxwell's pencilled responses.[10] This first story about children with fictional names begins her relentless, meditative mapping of her family's hidden currents where they remain imprinted, in the house on Cherryfield Avenue in Dublin. Early in her writing life she had created Rose and Hubert Derdon and placed them in that house, but now she introduces the child's perspective, which will find fuller expression in her stories about Lily and Margaret Bagot. Since Una's death, Maeve's writing had been bound up with trying to find her and understand her: 'I must know what she was,' she wrote to Maxwell. Her affection for his daughters Kate and Brookie may also have been part of what sent her back into the language and preoccupations of young children; certainly fatherhood made him a valuable sounding board. Shawn's notes on 'The Beginning of a Long Story' made courteous suggestions about punctuation and queried whether Johanna, who could not be more than seven, would be capable of thinking and saying the things attributed to her. 'Well, Kate's not 6 yet, and she's quite capable of saying something very like it,' was Maxwell's pencilled reply. In other notes he re-assured Maeve that they could discuss any of Shawn's commas that she didn't like, and that if she didn't want 'whiches', she didn't have to have them.

New Yorkers came and went, by train or car, between Manhattan and the Hamptons. There were a lot of parties, which Maeve did not much enjoy. Various men tried their luck with her, but her letters register only irri-tation, shading into outrage, at their advances, for her vivacious sociability could burn down as swiftly as it ignited. Gay men were easier. Her long-time friend Howard Moss, poetry editor of *The New Yorker*, was as committed to his own writing as Maeve was to hers. He shared her affec-tion for the Murphys and rented houses nearby from time to time with his companion, a hairdresser called Mark, who liked to cook elaborate meals. (He once sent Maeve a Louisiana cookbook, with recipes for owl, among other delicacies. 'I wish he had kept it for himself,' she wrote to Maxwell.) Both men were devoted to Bluebell, and Howard allowed Maeve to use his apartment at 27 West 10th Street in Greenwich Village whenever he was away. Maeve enjoyed being involved in their daily dramas, although irri-tation could set in swiftly. One Christmas the two men stayed with her in East Hampton, straining her fastidious, fragile patience to its limit. Her domesticity did not include much cooking, but she did sometimes indulge in bouts of house-cleaning. Gardner Botsford kept the long letter she wrote him, in which she described Mark's peeling potatoes directly on to the floor she had just scrubbed, and balancing a cupful of olive oil on the part of a window that someone was about to open. He left messes of toast crumbs and wet tea-bags all over the kitchen, until she reacted: 'I threw that toaster with all my might, what a crash, and what a thundering of hooves when I ran after it to start throwing it again'.[11]

Edward Albee, Moss's young neighbour in the Village, was another dog-lover and a good friend, whose play, *Zoo Story*, had been a success off Broadway in 1960. By the time his *Who's Afraid of Virginia Woolf?* was shocking and delighting Broadway audiences in October 1962, he had bought a house on the edge of a cliff overlooking the sea at Montauk. An undated letter Maeve wrote to William Maxwell tells of a chance meeting with him, and perfectly conveys the sudden animation and engagement that so many people remember about her, contrasting with her solitude and occasional aloofness. She had gone to Le Batt's in East Hampton to eat Thanksgiving dinner alone, and didn't at first recognise Albee when he looked at her and smiled:

> I said 'You look so different. You look so different.' He said 'Well I
> am older.' I saw them [perhaps Albee and his friend Bill, who lived

with him], on Saturday last. I said But you look as you must have looked when you were 20, like a snapshot of yourself when you were 20. And so he did. Another time I will tell you why I know Albee is nice, and why he hates the people who took it upon themselves to 'be nice to him'.

    Best love Maeve[12]

This letter's ending, where the storyteller promises more treats in future, is typical. With Maxwell, Maeve adopts a fairy-godmother role that is full of self-mockery, for to him she also confides her terrors and uncertainties. She sends gifts to him and Emily, and to Kate and Brookie; she looks out for houses nearby that they might rent for the summer, and scolds him for being accident prone and put-upon. She has grey hair in front now, she tells him, but will have it coloured, with 'the 30-day rinse'; she promises to buy him a better teacup the next time she comes to the office, since her efforts to scrub the stains off the one he has have failed. Above all, she writes to him about writing.

Maxwell had worked for more than ten years on his own novel, *The Château*, despairing of ever finishing it until he began to discuss it with Frank O'Connor in 1958; it became a major critical success on its publication in 1961. Maeve's letters praise his fiction lavishly, and exhort him to write more.[13] Most important, she insists, in narrative or exposition, is *voice*, and Maxwell has it. More than once, her letters refer with emphasis to '*the voice you can say anything in*'. As her 'Long-Winded Lady' essays so subtly, yet eloquently, insist, a woman writer should not abdicate her own experience in favour of a supposedly neutral male perspective, yet voice must be set free of gender in order to speak truthfully and with authority. Perhaps she was thinking of Maxwell's earlier work, where male characters, notably Lymie Peters in *The Folded Leaf* (1945), are allowed a range of emotion more usually restricted to women in twentieth-century fiction:

> I can only recall a conversation we had on the day 2 or 3 years ago when I discovered that men and women employ the same words.
>
>   The perspective is inhuman
>   The proportion is human
>   The voice is mortal.
>
> If we stand still long enough our perspective will arrange itself – if we watch steadily we will get and hold the proportion, & then if we what? Tell the truth? From the heart? We will begin to reach the PITCH of voice that is neither male nor female – simply communication – discipline, obedience & to forget the camera was ever invented. Well

look at Goldsmith, he lived the life of a woman in some ways, do you see what I mean. What I really mean is his voice, which comes across to me most clearly in his History of Animated Nature . . .'[4]

Maeve owned a treasured copy, bought cheaply in Dublin, of Oliver Goldsmith's *History of the Earth and Animated Nature*, originally published in eight volumes in London in 1774. 'He talks about babies, all animals, birds, the ocean, everything, with all pity & not a trace anywhere of that hateful Christian compassion,' her letter to Maxwell continues.

Apart from his capacity for pity, Goldsmith's lack of status or authority in his own lifetime may have been what prompted Maeve to write that he 'lived the life of a woman in some ways'. Maxwell says she was so fond of Goldsmith 'that it was almost as if she had known him' [*SA* 2], and it is easy to see how she might have taken him, half ruefully, as a role model. Maeve was beautiful, whereas Goldsmith was chinless and physically unprepossessing, but he was also small, witty, volatile and Irish, and he was a marginal character. Like Maeve, he earned good money by writing for commercial publications, but his generosity and improvidence left him constantly in debt, and he seemed constitutionally averse to settling down. Goldsmith's friends despaired of him, yet his best writings, full of humour and wisdom, continue to be read and performed.

Maeve's dismissal of Christian compassion as 'hateful' is like what she wrote about 'the people who took it upon themselves to "be nice to" Edward Albee'. Both reflect her horror of being patronised or pitied, and echo passages from drafts of her 'Herbert's Retreat' stories. In one version of 'The Joker', Vincent Lace says, 'Isabel, your understanding is an impertinence. Do you understand that? Nobody wants it', while another, unpublished, story has the following exchange between two of the Irish maids:

'She has the name of being very tolerant,' Bridie said cautiously, being careful not to interrupt this promising flow.

'Tolerant,' screeched Min, 'she'll tolerate me right off the face of the earth before she's done. Who asked her to tolerate anybody?'[5]

An undated, unpublished fragment (once again, without question marks), about Santa Claus figures who collect on the streets for charity, touches on the same idea:

Where did those good people who run charities ever get the idea that Santa Claus is interested in charity, or, for that matter, that he is interested in deserving causes. Santa Claus is not interested in charity, and he doesn't give to people who deserve, or because they deserve. He gives to everybody, whether they deserve or not. That is the whole point about Santa Claus.[16]

Maeve is constantly alert to economic inequality and to the power relations negotiated through giving: she herself always gave freely, and gaily, without condescension. Fury at being perceived as needy comes across in everything she wrote about poor men and women. For her, perfect pity requires being at one with those who are afflicted, and there is some sense – perhaps a Christian inheritance – that only among outsiders and the afflicted can the truth finally appear. Oliver Goldsmith and Hans Christian Andersen are her heroes, along with Colette, James Joyce, Leo Tolstoy, Albert Camus and the eighteenth-century essayists Richard Steele and Joseph Addison, founders of the *Spectator*. William Hazlitt, credited with revitalising English prose writing in the nineteenth century, and the English religious writer Francis Thompson (1859–1907), who wrote 'The Hound of Heaven', were special favourites.[17] Apart from Maxwell, she praises few of her contemporaries.

Hazlitt, with his benign clarity of observation, may have become a model for the Long-Winded Lady. Consider this passage from his *Table Talk: or, Original Essays* (1821):

What I mean by living to one's-self is living in the world, as in it, not of it: it is as if no one knew there was such a person, and you wished no one to know it: it is to be a silent spectator of the mighty scene of things, not an object of attention or curiosity in it; to take a thoughtful, anxious interest in what is passing in the world, but not to feel the slightest inclination to make or meddle with it. It is such a life as a pure spirit might be supposed to lead, and such an interest as it might take in the affairs of men, calm, contemplative, passive, distant, touched with pity for their sorrows, smiling at their follies without bitterness, sharing their affections, but not troubled by their passions, not seeking their notice, nor once dreamt of by them. He who lives wisely to himself and to his own heart, looks at the busy world through the loop-holes of retreat, and does not want to mingle in the fray. 'He hears the tumult, and is still.' He is not able to mend it, nor willing to mar it.[18]

Reclusive though she had become in East Hampton, Maeve's generosity was undiminished. In 1962, when Mary D. at *The New Yorker* was getting married, Maeve wrote to William Maxwell about her plan for a splendid wedding present. Over forty years later, Mary Kierstead treasures the French linen sheets Maeve bought her from D. Porthault in New York, with their characteristic floral pattern and scalloped edges trimmed with hand-sewn braid. Otherwise, aside from the elderly and increasingly forgetful Sara Murphy on the one hand, and Emily Maxwell, to whom she wrote as affectionately as she did to Maxwell himself on the other, Maeve's letters scarcely mention women friends.

Many of the women she knew at this time seem to have struck her as either disgusting or pathetic. Jean Stafford, the celebrated novelist, was one *bête noire*. Maeve admired her writing, but could not abide her behaviour, and catalogued her offences in letters to Maxwell and Botsford. Stafford, who suffered from depression, was drinking heavily in the early 1960s. She had married the *New Yorker* writer A. J. Liebling at about the same time as Maeve was parting from McKelway, and when he died in 1963 and was buried in Green River Cemetery, East Hampton, Stafford came to live in the house he had owned nearby. She made much of Howard Moss, but apparently considered Maeve unworthy of notice. She was not above imposing on her for Christmas dinner when Howard and Mark were there, however, with disastrous results, which Maeve recounted in ghastly, hilarious detail in the letter to Botsford already quoted.[19] Breaches of ordinary good manners offended Maeve immensely, and she would write at length about them to her friends. It was the same with fiction: she detested lazy, dishonest writing, and the kind she characterised as 'vulgar'. She worried about various young women, however, at the magazine and in the Hamptons, who she felt were being exploited in one way or another: 'All girls should have a little money of their own and they should all be married at 17 to splendid fellow[s] of thirty. There is no getting around these old facts,' she wrote to Maxwell.[20] It is as though a voice in her head is saying again that 'a young girl can spoil her chances'. Her heavy irony signals the double bind in which she had seen young women find themselves since her time at *Harper's Bazaar*.

Each summer, when crowds descended on East Hampton, owners arrived to claim some of the houses, and the rents on others went up, Maeve returned to the city, or went to Ireland. At least once, Howard Moss and Mark spent the summer in 'her' little house. They took care of Bluebell while she was away and Mark made a bird-feeder to which pheasants picked their way across the snow the following winter. Another year, Bluebell spent six weeks with Edward Albee in Montauk. Returning to East Hampton, reunited with Bluebell, Maeve became immediately more light-hearted. Here, writing to Maxwell in 1961 or '62, she is able to be cheerfully dismissive about a grumpy housekeeper:

Dear William,

All is well. Bluebell beautiful and really much thinner. Autumn over the Atlantic. Pine cones. Waves banging away against the land, I suppose the sand is still land. The Lady Who Helps Me stiffly resentful, I don't know why, except that of course I know why and I wish she would go into opera where she belongs. Gerald Murphy's roses are literally beyond belief – they are Irish roses, huge, all midsummer. He talks about you and talks about you. I hope everybody is being nice to you and that you are getting your tea.

    Best love

      Maeve[21]

Maeve wrote and wrote. Four more Long-Winded Lady pieces appeared in 1961, and six in 1962. In fiction, she was trying out various themes, rejecting some and keeping others for further work. Rose and Hubert Derdon appeared in two stories in 1962. Another one, 'The Bohemians', published on 9 June, was about a Dublin family called Briscoe, who lived in much the same house as theirs on Cherryfield Avenue, but nothing more was heard of them. Then a series of stories featured a 'rather fat' black Labrador retriever called Niobe (her name became Bluebell when the stories were republished in book form), and five cats, who lived in an eccentric little house on the beach in East Hampton.

According to William Maxwell, it was after she began to live alone following her separation from St Clair McKelway that Maeve began to write 'what are clearly her finest stories', about Rose and Hubert Derdon.[22] In fact, the Derdons had been with her for many years when 'An Attack of Hunger' appeared in print in 1962, on Maeve's forty-fifth birthday. Rose and Hubert had featured in one *Harper's Bazaar* story ten years earlier, and 'The Rose Garden' was about Rose's mother; this was the couple's first appearance in *The New Yorker*, however.

'An Attack of Hunger' arises from the barren desert of the Derdons' marriage. Their house in Cherryfield Avenue has become shabby, and sensuality is so entirely absent that a simple appetite for food seems shameful. Six months after her son John has vanished into the priesthood, Rose Derdon mourns him: 'All the things she had collected together and arranged about the house could blow away, or fall into a pitiful heap, if it were not that the walls of the house were attached on both sides to the walls of the neighboring houses' [*SA* 157]. Alone, she fantasises thinly about widowhood, and about becoming John's housekeeper. When Hubert comes home and clumsily destroys the fire she has carefully set, her anger explodes in a tantrum of tears and recrimination. In her 'delirium of loss', she walks along Sandford

Road and Eglinton Road – the same route Maeve has described in 'The Barrel of Rumors', with the same big trees and benches along Eglinton Road – making for Donnybrook church. The story contains one of Maeve's very rare slips of memory, for when Rose Derdon turns to the right at the bottom of her own street and walks along Sandford Road before crossing to the other side, the traffic that passes her is driving on the right, as it does in America, instead of on the left.

'A Young Girl Can Spoil Her Chances', with its calculations of ages, dates and anniversaries, is the story Maeve seems to have begun shortly after arriving in New York, but the version that appeared in *The New Yorker* in September 1962 is long, complex, and structurally much more ambitious than anything she had done before. Rose's memories and Hubert's proceed in counterpoint, while the implacable, disappointed enmity between them – a given in the earlier story – begins to unfold and peel apart.

Una Brennan was dead, and Bob Brennan old and frail, but still receiving the magazine in Dublin every week, when their daughter prepared this story for publication. In it, straight streets contrast with the winding paths of a city park in ways that may represent the differences between fact and fiction, or memory and imagination, as Maeve insists on truths that cannot be reached through facts alone. During his lunch break from the men's outfitters where he works in Grafton Street, Hubert Derdon takes an unaccustomed walk in the streets around St Stephen's Green. The Green, in the heart of Dublin city, is square, and bounded by high iron railings. Inside the railing, hidden by the trees that press against it, is a Victorian park with green lawns and fountains, bright flowerbeds, a large duck pond, and paths that curve and cross each other. This was where Hubert and Rose used to walk, early in their marriage; it is the place where their happiness is lodged, but Hubert has not entered it for thirty-three years, and will not go in today either, although he thinks he will. As he walks the straight streets outside, his mind meanders through the park, among images of Rose. His memories all morning have been bitter and angry; full of reproach about the way Rose has reared their only son and excluded him from his child's life. In those early days, though, in her navy-blue wedding 'costume' and white blouse, she used to seem to him like Helen of Troy, when 'her slender hips appeared commanding and alien, and she was his'.

Death frames this story, and so does needlework. It is the forty-third aniversary of Rose's father's death, and a prominent grocer called Kinsella is being buried. Hubert remembers that when he first saw Rose, she was sitting behind the counter in her mother's shop, working on a scrap of crochet. The colour is not mentioned, but she wraps her work in a big handkerchief or a piece of a pillowcase, so perhaps it is white cotton lace, which must be kept clean: it suggests lingerie, or bedlinen, or an infant's clothing. At the end of the story, when Hubert arrives home after a day of private agony and anger, he finds Rose sitting by the fire, working on a piece of 'gray wool crochet' that is to be part of an afghan. The elderly and drab has replaced frivolity in their lives, but it is Hubert's obdurate inability to depart from the straight lines of his own custom that has condemned him to remain estranged from Rose, just as his insistence on the sort of logic found in print has left him excluded from the warmth and softness that marriage to her seemed to promise. As the story ends, he emerges from behind his newspaper to snub Rose one more time:

> Rose left Hubert to read the full account of Mr Kinsella's life and circumstances, which he had read earlier with less attention, because it had been in yesterday morning's news, and she herself looked idly through the back pages of the old Sunday paper, and found several items that she had missed on her first reading. When she remarked on this to Hubert, he observed that she had never learned to read properly, that she was a careless reader who skipped too often and did not concentrate on what she was reading, and it was a pity, because it was hard to form a good habit when you were older, and just as hard to break a bad habit once it had taken hold of you. [*SA* 98]

Maeve's mastery of point of view makes that last sentence echo ironically in the mind long after the story has given way to the blank space that follows it on the page.

On 9 December 1962, Bob wrote to her from Dublin: 'Lessons & more Lessons etc. is a little masterpiece . . . I would rate it very high, as high indeed as Frank O'Connor's "The Majesty of the Law"'. He ends, 'Happy Christmas from Nan and me.'[23] O'Connor's 'The Majesty of the Law' was first published in 1935. Maeve's 'Lessons and Lessons and Then More Lessons', published on 10 November 1962, was a short piece about two nuns seen years before in the University Restaurant on 8th Street, who had set off memories of her time at boarding-school [*LWL* 220–4]. Maeve kept her father's letter, but there is no record of his reaction to her two Derdon stories, which had also appeared that year. Bob was old by now, however, and not in good health – he dated his letter '1926' instead of '1962' – and he may not have fully read or understood his daughter's longer stories.

Maeve sailed for Europe within days of receiving her father's letter, but not to spend Christmas with him. On 7 December, Hawley Truax had written to her from *The New Yorker*, enclosing a cheque for $1,600. It was her fee for the coveted 'first reading' agreement with the magazine, whereby it would have first refusal on everything she wrote the following year, and would pay at higher rates than before for everything it published. Maeve's writing had been going well, but McKelway had left her with serious debt, and recent years had been more than difficult. No doubt she still had 'big ugly bills', but here was spending money aplenty – coming at the time of year she dreaded most. Maeve booked a ticket on the Holland America line's *Westerdam*, and sailed for Amsterdam on the day before Christmas Eve.

A Long-Winded Lady essay mentions 'Amsterdam, Marseille and Algiers' as places the Lady has never been, but thinks of visiting. Though not published until the following July, it was presumably written before her December voyage:

> My suitcase would translate me to everybody's satisfaction and espe-
> cially to my own satisfaction. And I would go to a city where the people
> spoke a language I did not understand, so that I could listen as much
> as I liked and still not eavesdrop. It is so nice to be able to listen to
> voices without being delayed by what is being said. I would go to
> Amsterdam. [*LWL* 119]

Maeve made her first Atlantic crossing at seventeen, in undreamt-of luxury, on the aptly named *Manhattan*. For most of her life thereafter, balancing Irish and American identities as a 'traveller in residence', she found equilibrium in the non-place of a long sea voyage. Terry Coleman describes the 'sense of a sea-going abstraction from ordinary things' that the captains of Atlantic liners shared with their first-class passengers, calling it 'an exac-erbated sensibility, of feeling everything more intensely'. He notes how the shipping lines' advertising exploited this sense of theatrical make-believe:

> In the mind of the passenger, nothing existed except himself and one
> or two of his fellow passengers to whom he was drawn by like-feeling
> and with whom he shared this intensity of isolation. The ship on which
> they sailed was for the moment their only piece of land.[24]

Maeve undoubtedly felt that too, but her midwinter trip was typically quixotic: it took eleven days to get to Holland, and nine to get back, this time on the *Westerdam*'s sister ship, the *Noordam*. In between, she had just two days in Amsterdam. Photographs taken on board the *Noordam* show her sitting with a drink beside an unidentified but attentive-looking man of about her own age. She wears a dark, sleeveless dress; her hair is piled in shining waves on top of her head; she looks relaxed and beautiful.[25]

Maeve spent her two days at 'the swanky Amstel Hotel', as she called it in a letter to Mary D., now living in London with her new husband, Wilson Kierstead. Half a mile from the centre of Amsterdam, the hotel stands five storeys high on the bank of the river from which it takes its name, on the corner of the broad and airy Sarphatistraat.[26] Beneath its windows, bicycles and barges go by all day. It was (and is) one of Europe's leading luxury hotels, and Maeve loved it. Long afterwards, her letters to William Maxwell make reference to Amsterdam, to the view from her hotel window there, and her wistful desire to go back, and stay for ever. Immediately on her return to New York, however, she had to travel again. A 'frantic' letter from her sister Derry informed her that Bob was dangerously ill, and she flew to Dublin for four days. There, as she wrote to Mary D., she found a 'very old hospital and a very old sad disappointed in his middle daughter man'.

Bob cannot have been happy about his middle daughter's circumstances. Her financial situation must have seemed precarious, despite the first-reading agreement and accompanying cheque, and he was in no position to help her. He had never accumulated wealth; his diplomatic pension gave him a comfortable income, but it was tiny in American terms and would die with him in any case. More importantly, however little he approved of her marriage to McKelway, as a pillar of de Valera's Ireland he must have found the fact of his daughter's divorce repugnant. With John F. Kennedy in the White House, Irish people were identifying in a new way with America, but the economic innovations of Lemass and Whitaker were still in their infancy. Instead of reinforcing faith in free-market capitalism as an antidote to communism, therefore, Cold War politics and anxiety about the Cuban missile crisis brought a renewed reliance on Catholicism. Divorce, illegal and foreign, was a symbol of all the corruption in a frighteningly godless world. Bob may have wished to keep his daughter's situation secret; or perhaps he was simply old, tired and out of touch; she herself may have preferred to remain unknown in Ireland; certainly, nobody welcomed Maeve to Dublin as an important writer returning home. After the Amstel Hotel, in the dark and damp of an Irish winter her father's modest house by the Dodder must have seemed a cold and cheerless place.

East Hampton offered a safe haven from the grimness of these memories of Ireland; Maeve's Bluebell stories reflect her life there. In two of them, the animals' owner is Mary Ann Whitty. Her name, borrowed from the redoubtable bedridden great-aunt in Coolnaboy, Mary Kate, could easily belong to one of the maids in Herbert's Retreat, but this Mary Ann is clearly Maeve in her beach-side existence: an independent woman, a solitary survivor, entertained by life. 'In and Out of Never-Never Land', a Fourth of July adventure and the longer of the two stories, appeared in *The New Yorker* on 6 July 1963. Evidently written soon after Maeve took up residence in the little house at the foot of the Murphys' lawn, it combines with her letters of that time to illustrate the consolation the place offered her:

> [Mary Ann Whitty] was sitting in her living room, which was remarkable to her because it was hers alone, and because it contained her furniture, her books, her dog, and her cats. The furniture was shabby, the books were worn and showed the signs of long storage, the cats wore mixed furs, and Bluebell, the black Labrador retriever, was not as serene as a dog of her age and nature ought to be. Bluebell had spent too much time in too many different kennels.
>
> Mary Ann did not care that her household was a trifle bedraggled. What mattered to her was that all her possessions were collected in one place. [*RG* 283]

Words like 'tranquil', 'placid' and 'complacent' underline the contentment Maeve felt in the little fairytale cottage. Mary Ann is used to eating in restaurants, but has managed to become expert in preparing 'very small plain dinners'. Every night, she chops and peels and arranges saucepans on top of the stove, while Bluebell and the cats look on attentively.[27]

'In and Out of Never-Never Land' is the only one of Maeve's stories in which a character who resembles her takes on, however tentatively, a nurturing adult role. Seven children feature in the story, whose climax is the connection Mary Ann achieves with the youngest girl, a resourceful, headstrong six-year-old called Linnet, who may have been modelled on one of Maxwell's daughters. Linnet has walked across the lawn in her nightdress to Mary Ann's house in the early hours of the morning, following a dramatic fire. Mary Ann gives the child a shawl and a glass of milk, then sends her home:

> 'May I come back to see you?' Linnet asked.
>
> Mary Ann looked at her. Linnet was small and friendly, and Mary Ann, who feared trustfulness, had often rebuffed her, but now she put her hands out and tightened the shawl around the little shoulders. 'Yes,' she said, 'but right now, this minute, you must run home. Your mother will be frightened if she finds you not in your bed. Then come back later and tell me everything about the fire. I'll have questions ready. All right?'

Maeve may have been mistaken during her trip to Ireland about her father's attitude to her, but back in New York, her friends formed a lasting impression of him as envious and domineering. Gradually, after her mother's death, she had been rehabilitating her memory of Una, replacing irritation and dismissal with 'ravenous nostalgia'.[28] Now, in the stories she told about her family, Bob became the villain. He had even changed his wife's name from Anastasia to Una, Maeve told Elizabeth Cullinan – inaccurately, as it happened, for as we have seen in Chapter 1, her mother had been signing herself 'Una' since 1907. A long, rambling, handwritten letter from Maeve to Maxwell shows her grappling with problems of creativity while floundering in memory as she searches for her mother. It appears to have been written from Howard Moss's apartment in New York in the summer of 1963, while Moss was in London and Maxwell was on holiday with his family in Fire Island, not far from East Hampton. Maxwell, who had begun learning to play the piano in 1962, when he was fifty-four, had a passion for Mozart. Maeve continues what must have been a dialogue with him, about 'the voice you can say anything in'.[29]

Dear William,
I hope you are well & cheerful & that everything is Happyville.

Mary Ann Whitty was a figure of confusion – the product of a confused imagination – she is dead. Poor Mary Ann, we will hear no more of her.

I recognised the voice that speaks in the second part (passage) [i.e. 'movement'?] of Mozart's Symphony No. 29 in A Major instantly, & knew I knew it, and also that I had never heard it before. I wish I could remember what impulse led me to go downstairs and ask for a Mozart symphony & also for an opera. I took the symphony off the shelf myself – they gave me Don Giovanni. After listening to the symphony many times, over & over, I realised that the voice is my mother's voice as she would have sounded if she had been happy – her <u>other</u> voice. It is instructive – it is the <u>voice you can say anything in</u>. I remember we were talking about that voice once. There is a mosquito bothering me. Ouida never numbered her pages & I am not going to any more. About the voice – it is the <u>voice you can say anything in</u>, I can't think of that enough. A week ago last Wednesday, I began to understand that when I first saw the view from the Van Cortland [hotel in New York] I was seeing the second manifestation of my mother – it is to see what is infinite, always changing, endlessly responsive, and capable of <u>containing</u> anything, & everything . . . I was never able to protect her . . .

Later in the letter, Maeve returns to the subject of her mother, allowing us to observe something of the process by means of which Maxwell's patient listening to her memories allowed material for her stories to float to the surface. Maxwell had never been in Ireland, but in the early 1960s he was immersed in things Irish through his work with Frank O'Connor, and their letters show him probing his friend's memory for texture, colour and nuances of feeling, as he must have done with Maeve. Here she offers him moments of childhood memory captured in the building where Howard Moss lived:[30]

. . . I was trying to describe the walk up these stairs of Howard's carrying my ~~typewriter~~ suitcase. It was one of those awful days & the door was open on the second floor & workmen were in there (Albee's new duplex) – they looked up when I appeared going by & they <u>paused</u> & went back to work. As I tried to describe that pause I was pulled away from them and straight to her, & I described them, their pause, & then her pauses – different if you walked in on her when she was cooking, in the kitchen, sewing at the machine, reading, or at her plants – if you came in when [she] was at her plants she looked at you <u>suspiciously</u>. I was always her <u>witness</u>. Then, I was describing the elevator in the Van Cortland – the same day or so, & I found myself instead describing the first ride I ever had in an elevator – she took me & Derry up to an office my father had once – we were very small. You see it all now. I have told you everything I know, except that at last I am able to ~~express~~ offer the gratitude to you that I was never able even to admit until today.

> Your loving & grateful friend
> Maeve
P.S. She gave me everything, and now she has given me the <u>city</u>.

Elizabeth Cullinan met Bob at a party in Ireland in those years after Una's death, and was struck by his close physical resemblance to Maeve. On the younger woman's return, however, Maeve rejected that comparison out of hand. She looked like her mother, she told Cullinan, not like her father. Other undated letters to William Maxwell also touch on difficulties with her family. This note, scrawled with a thick pen on a sheet of typing paper turned crossways, probably also in 1963, is typical:

Wm,
. . . [W]ould you tell me at once how to <u>transfer</u> the <u>disgusting guilt</u> I feel about my <u>family</u> to my poor work – I can <u>do</u> something about that can't I? Now you see it is quite a neuroses [sic] – to be ashamed to have anything – even ashamed to enjoy a most cheerful & independant [sic] talent. Kindly solve in one line.

> Yrs M.

A letter from the end of 1963 touches on the same theme:

> The pain radiated by the Envious One is terrible to endure. The pain
> that envious people feel, it is frightful, it must be. And this shame I
> feel all my life – I was as ashamed of having a little talent as another
> would be of being born without a nose . . .

Nineteen sixty-three had begun with Bob's illness and Maeve's flying
visit to Ireland. It continued with events and innovations that brought the
United States and the island of Ireland close together in ways that had not
before been dreamt of. It seems also to have drawn the two parts of Maeve's
life into painful juxtaposition, and made it brutally clear that Ireland was
not her home.

US President John F. Kennedy visited the land of his ancestors in June.
The places he travelled through had seen much emigration and decline, but
like John Wayne eleven years earlier in *The Quiet Man*, Kennedy invested
the landscape with new heroism and virility. Telefís Éireann, only eighteen
months in operation, rose to the challenge of sustained outside television
broadcasting. Framed colour photographs of the President joined the Sacred
Heart on the walls of homes all over Ireland. Everywhere Kennedy went,
thousands turned out to cheer him, then bought television sets to follow
his continued progress. Suddenly, even in the remotest corners of the
country, people could watch American films in their own homes. On 12 July,
Time magazine ran a special issue on Ireland, calculated to encourage
American investment. On the cover, behind a photograph of Taoiseach Seán
Lemass, a leprechaun held back a shamrock-printed curtain to reveal a
modern power station; inside, a map showed seventy-eight new industrial
plants opened since 1960.[31] The Clancy Brothers and Tommy Makem made
a triumphant visit home, and played to a capacity audience in Dublin's
Olympia theatre. In two years they had progressed from Greenwich Village
folk clubs to the *Ed Sullivan Show* and Carnegie Hall, and their trademark
white Aran sweaters were soon selling by the thousand, earning money for
home knitters along Ireland's western seaboard.[32]

Years later, in a second-hand bookshop in Dennisport, Cape Cod, a Boston
College professor of Irish Studies came across a book Maeve had bought
in Dublin in 1963; her name was pencilled on the flyleaf, with the date and
place.[33] *The Gael* by Edward Lysaght, is a novel about the Irish-Ireland
movement, which had been so much part of Bob and Una Brennan's lives.
Inside it were two business cards printed 'C. Maizel, La Boutique, Main
Floor, Saks Fifth Avenue'. One of them had handwritten notes about shops
in Grafton Street, Dublin: 'Brown Thomas: Mr O'Donnell; Weir [the

jewellers]: Mr O'Sullivan'. With them, slightly larger than the cards, was a tie-on label from a sweater, printed red on white: 'Genuine Hand Knit: "Homes of Donegal", MacGinty's sweaters'. The price and size were in pencil: £6.6.0 (six guineas), Size 36. The strand of wool used to attach the label shows that it was a white Aran sweater. Not Maeve's sort of garment, it was probably intended as a gift. The accumulation of cards and label, on the other hand, was typical: Maeve always carried a large handbag, with all manner of things inside, and frequently left some of them behind when she departed.

Telefís Éireann's flagship programme from 1962 was *The Late Late Show*, which has been called the 'mid-wife to contemporary Irish liberalism'.[34] It is tempting to imagine the impact Maeve might have made in its open-ended live interview format, and the effect such an appearance might have had on her reception as a writer in Ireland, but she never appeared as one of Gay Byrne's guests.

Bob was seriously ill throughout 1963; Maeve's feelings about him were ambivalent, and during the summer, St Clair McKelway had another mental breakdown. Writing to Maxwell years later, she referred to 'the terrible summer of 1963 when he went mad and you were away'.[35] Although no longer living together, she and Mac remained on good terms and she felt a measure of responsibility for him. When Gerald Murphy, reading a manuscript Mac had written, asked Maeve what he should do with it, she told him to give it to her, that she would keep it safely. Gerald too had health problems. He and Sara finally sold Cheer Hall, their house in Snedens Landing, and in August Gerald had what he had suggested would be a minor investigative operation. The surgery turned out to be invasive and debilitating, however, for he was terminally ill with cancer. When A. J. Liebling died that same year, aged fifty-nine, Maeve's mounting antipathy to Jean Stafford in the role of widow exacerbated her grief about Gerald's condition. Then in November, John F. Kennedy was assassinated. Christmas 1963 was probably the one Jean Stafford, Howard Moss and Mark spent with Maeve in East Hampton. As the year ended, she wrote in red ballpoint pen on pink paper to Sara Murphy – a letter she seems not to have sent – 'I will be glad to see 1964. This has been an appalling year, every step of the way.'[36]

Maeve may have been living rent-free in the Murphys' little house, but air fares to Ireland were expensive, and she may also have been spending money on Mac's behalf. On 21 January, Saks, Fifth Avenue, sent her a telegram at *The New Yorker* editor's office. 'FURTHER STALLING IMPOSSIBLE UNLESS BALANCE $1,840.70 RECEIVED BY JAN 27, 1964 TO ATTORNEYS TO PROCEED AS THEY SEE FIT'. It was signed J. Jonas, Collection Manager. This was probably far from the first such document Maeve had seen – that Leona

Harkey's husband in the 'Herbert's Retreat' stories was a department-store credit manager is surely not an accident – but the fact that William Maxwell kept it hints at its effect.[37] Milton Greenstein, who took over from Hawley Truax in 1966 as legal counsel and vice-president of *The New Yorker*, inherited the task of mopping up messes like this one, and Maeve's letters in later years reflect an increasingly difficult relationship with him. For the moment, though, as her work continued to appear in *The New Yorker*, she was a staff member in good standing. William Shawn took care of his writers, among whom epic debt was not unusual, and the magazine would step in to bail her out.

Early in 1964 Maeve was writing to Maxwell about summer plans. Elaborate suggestions for his family vacation flowed into musings about tragedy in life and literature and her own state of mind as she continued to mourn her mother:[38]

Dear William,
Consider this house. I honestly want to be in the city for a part of the summer, and preferably August. I am one minute from the beach, and the interior of the house is pretty. There is a dining room and the kitchen is more than adequate as we real estate people say. You could get a temporary membership in the Maidstone [golf] club which is one minute away and they have a children's place there. Mrs P. would baby sit and tidy up and cook enough pot roast for 3 day's eating. You could see the Murphys, two minutes away. I could stay at McKelway's, because it is not like a hotel room. Many men are capable of tragedy, maybe all men, but very few women. Mary D. is. I am not. Emmy is not. Anna K[arenina], no. Emma Bovary, no. You are, and so is Gardner. Wm., your voice changed when I was talking to you. Do not imagine that I am forlorn You do not know my nature but I know it now from this long and almost unconscious watch I have kept on my mother in the determination I have always had to isolate her from everything because I must know what she was. Only I did not know what was going on. I wanted, I told you, a smoke screen, only I did not understand that it was to stand between me and myself. Last week I spoke in my melodramatic way of danger coming from a different direction, but where it was coming from is where it has always come from – ME. You must be sick of what appears to be doubletalk. Please forgive me. You have no idea of how SERENE I Am. You can hear the sea day and night here, and Emmy would adore my bedroom. It is perfecto. The guest room is really a guest wing with bath and private entrance. Anyway, bear it in mind. There is no rush. Life is easy if you let it

have its way. I must have read that somewhere. I am working hard and
hope you are working hard too. Don't forget to write to Gerald.
Maeve

By the end of 1964, eight more Long-Winded Lady pieces had appeared
in 'Talk of the Town', as well as two more Derdon stories. The latest, 'A
Free Choice', treats of Rose's girlhood in Wexford in the summer when she
first met Hubert Derdon, when each of them thought they could be safe
with the other. It is a beautiful story, which tenderly examines the small
unbearable hidden pains of people's lives, yet finishes in hope. Critics praise
William Maxwell's writing for the way it opens out the agonies of adolescence with clarity and restraint; Maeve is about the same business, but
manages to convey not only the separate loneliness of several characters,
but the humble courage and goodwill that make them try to overcome it.
The scene is a party, where Rose's train of thought recalls the discomfort
Maeve's friends say she often experienced at large gatherings. The host is
the wealthy Mrs Ramsay, whose name Maeve may have borrowed from the
central character of Virginia Woolf's *To the Lighthouse*, one of Maxwell's
favourite books.[39] The small white handkerchief her mother has given her
stands for a young girl's sense of herself. It is Irish linen, edged with hand-
made lace in a pattern of 'shells and roses and daisies and shamrocks and
ivy leaves'. Kept safely in its box, it is a small, hidden thing, but precious,
'the best handkerchief money could buy'. Rose has taken it out into the
world tonight though, and lost it at this party, and she thinks of it 'down
there on the floor under someone's feet. It would be a rag by this time.
Even if it was a rag, she would be glad to have it back.'

Rose knew that 'when a thing is gone it is gone', but when she meets
Hubert Derdon at the bottom of the stairs, he has the handkerchief, and it
is still perfect. He gives it to her, 'as though he was giving up his passport,
or his ticket of passage, or, as it was, his one and only hope of refuge in her
country'. By making the choice to place her trust in Hubert, Rose acquires
what seems to be a ticket that will carry her through life, and escapes from
another fate that might have awaited her, for her school friend Mary is a
maid in Mrs Ramsay's house.

The letters she wrote to Maxwell suggest that in 1964 much of Maeve's
attention was on Gerald Murphy's failing health. He was in severe pain,
and Sara was increasingly confused. Maeve visited Gerald, bringing little
gifts and sending messages with others when it was their turn to visit him.
She talked to him on the phone, and they discussed his plan to give some
of his more interesting clothes to Howard Moss and Mark. All his life Gerald
had loved clothes, and his wardrobe had been famous. He was anxious not

to offend, but Maeve assured him that Howard and Mark and others, herself included, would be delighted to have clothes that he had worn. Gerald died on 17 October. He had been a father-figure and a friend to Maeve, and with his death, another piece of ground broke off beneath her feet.

A few weeks later, on 12 November, Bob Brennan died in Dublin, aged eighty-three. Modest appreciations of his life and work appeared in newspapers the following day, alongside a photograph of Frank O'Connor attending a PEN club dinner at the Shelbourne Hotel, and reports that in Dublin 40,000 people had visited a three-day exhibition brought on loan from the John F. Kennedy Memorial Library. Éamon de Valera, President of Ireland, attended Bob's funeral mass at Mount Argus, as did several members of the government. He was buried beside Una at nearby Mount Jerome. Maeve flew to Dublin for the funeral. Newspaper reports give her name as 'Mrs Maeve McKelway, New York', but make no mention of her writing, or of her position with *The New Yorker*.

After the funeral, Maeve stayed on long enough to give away various items of furniture from the house in Dodder Road and sign a document relinquishing any claim to what remained. She gathered up most of her father's papers and returned to New York with them, leaving her Aunt Nan to sort out what was left in the house. Nan invited Bob's grandchildren to take mementoes and tried to persuade Derry to take the remaining furniture. Derry did not want it, however, so Nan took some of it back with her to Wexford. She and other members of the family were distressed several years later to read Maeve's story 'The Springs of Affection', in which Min Bagot sits with vengeful satisfaction in Wexford among the furniture of her dead brother and his wife.

Back in East Hampton in December, Maeve wrote a long letter to William Maxwell, most of it about Gerald and Sara Murphy. 'But what would I have done without them the last five wretched (sorry) years. Not very well, I can tell you,' she writes, recalling Gerald's gift that she called *ambiance*. She uses the French term to convey his ability to create a whole environment. She had *ambiance* too, she told Maxwell, and so did he, and so did M. Verdoux (in the 1947 Charlie Chaplin film about a man who supports his crippled wife by marrying a series of rich women and setting up a fully furnished life with each of them before murdering them). 'My father died a month ago,' she adds: 'I see him, bones, white hair, faded eyes, courage, wonder, naked envy, malice, longing, & high dreams, dedication, bewilderment, all gone, but no longer a dream, reality at last.'

On the first day of the new year she wrote to Maxwell again. After her signature she drew a smiley face, and for once added the date: 'January 1, 1965 6 pm'. Back in her routine, she is observing her natural environment to learn the spiritual lessons it has to teach:

[T]he frozen puddles in the 'driveway' shone with moonlight, although there was no moon. It was a lesson in brilliance, & what the sky said was 'Everything that happened happened a long time ago'. Very calm, calmest of all, not the remembrance of death but the remembrance of life. I suppose that is the edge we have over the dead, that we can remember. I am perfectly serious.[40]

After her father's death, and Gerald Murphy's, although Maeve continued to write, and to spend the winters in East Hampton, much had been lost. Derry's daughter Yvonne arrived in New York with her husband in August 1965, soon after their marriage. Maeve met them at the boat and escorted them around the sweltering city, with dinner at the Algonquin, and an evening at the Metropole jazz café on Seventh Avenue, to see 'the almost naked girls dancing on the shelf behind the bar' [*LWL* 80], because, she said, 'Everyone should see them once.' Maeve was charming and generous as ever, but was having trouble with her teeth: she ordered huge steaks all round, but took one bite of her own, then put the rest in a doggy bag for Bluebell and the cats.

Only one Long-Winded Lady piece appeared that year, a difficult one for *The New Yorker* in any case. 'New' journalist Tom Wolfe attacked the magazine in the *New York Herald Tribune*. His two articles on 11 and 18 April wickedly satirised the *New Yorker*'s long, thoughtful sentences as 'whichy thickets', and poured scorn on its seventy-two-year-old editor. The scrupulous William Shawn, notoriously shy of personal publicity, was devastated.[41] Although his magazine still bulged with advertising, it had grown predictable. Writers and cartoonists who had been in their unbeatable prime in the years after the Second World War were middle-aged or older, and had probably known each other too long. Down on the street, young people were wearing long hair and pale lipstick, short skirts and bell-bottomed trousers. The United States government had entered a new war, and while the magazine would soon publish some of the most effective polemic against American action in Vietnam, it seemed for the moment to have lost touch with the spirit of the times.

The Maxwells did go to East Hampton that year at last,[42] renting Maeve's little house for a month from 7 August and taking care of the animals, but her own connection to the place was wearing thin, especially as Sara Murphy grew more absent-minded. She began to spend more time in New York, knuckling down to write regularly for 'Talk of the Town' again. 'I write the long-windeds for money,' she wrote to William Maxwell, distinguishing them from her fiction, in which she still struggled to express exactly what she fleetingly saw, especially in the past. The Long-Winded Lady was her concession to the present. Walking about New York, or sitting in restaurants, she observed the miniature choreographies of comic hesitation as people misunderstood each other, advanced, retired and advanced again, and, as Carmel Snow had trained her to do, she noticed their clothes.

At *Harper's Bazaar* and *Junior Bazaar*, Maeve had learned to describe clothes with detail and precision. Notwithstanding her familiarity with her Aunt Nan's workroom, it was a skill she would never have acquired in Ireland. Carmel Snow's autobiography remarks that: '[James] Joyce remembered the "jingle jingle jaunted jingling" of a Viceregal procession, but he didn't describe, as Proust would have done, the clothes worn by the Viceroy's lady'.[43] Maeve took that lesson to heart: 'If you're writing about people in the street,' she told an interviewer from *Time* in 1974, 'you have to describe their clothes, all of them. Clothes tell a lot.' Writing to Elizabeth Cullinan around the same time, carefully explaining the difference between the colours beige and bone, she added, 'You insist on forgetting that I worked as a fashion copywriter on Harper's Bazaar for 7 years.' The same training lay behind her descriptions of different-coloured roses in 'The Rose Garden', and of velvet curtain fabrics in 'A Free Choice'.

Clothes, and ways of walking, tell almost everything about the dozens of people Maeve described in her Long-Winded Lady pieces in the 1960s. She had once written to William Maxwell about wanting to write 'as though the camera had never been invented', and here she does it. The man who walked into the Adano Restaurant, on West 48th Street, on a hot Sunday afternoon in July 1966 and hesitated just inside the door, was 'politely dressed in a dark blue summer suit, a snowy white shirt and a neat dark tie with dots on it'. Two years later, a couple, 'both about forty', walked along Sixth Avenue one evening:

I noticed the two people because of the deliberate way they walked, close together, and because the hem of her dress was about three inches below her knees. She wore a sleeveless, buttoned-down-the-front dress of pale pink cotton printed with green foliage and cream-colored flowers, and it hung straight down from her shoulders to end in a deep flounce . . . He attempted to match her informal attire by going tieless and coatless. He wore navy blue trousers, buttoned tightly around his middle, and a plain white shirt with the sleeves folded back to his elbows, and open-toed leather sandals that showed off his striped socks.

Maeve had observed this couple closely enough to write a novel about them. A piece she called 'A Young Lady with a Lap', published on 3 September 1966, manages to convey not just how one young woman dressed and walked ('like two snakes'), or how New York City looked and felt on a Saturday night in summer, but also the poignant irony of a beautiful woman who has always been looked at, but who can be amused as well as terrified by the unmistakable arrival of her own middle age.

> As I came near the Latin Quarter, a girl appeared in the crowd, walking alone. She wore a tight white crêpe dress, much whiter than flesh, and she had a small, fluffy white mink stole around her shoulders and her bosom. She was very slim, and she walked like two snakes, while her hemline slithered about her knees. She was much too clever to wear a very short dress. She showed her knees, and left the rest to her audience, to us – to all of us. We all looked. Her dress was more than very tight. It was extremely tight. Nobody looked at her knees. Everybody looked at her lap. Her hair was gold and it glittered, and so did her slippers, which were of transparent plastic edged with gold. She carried a small handbag, also of transparent plastic edged with gold, but it contained nothing except a gold lipstick, which rolled about like dice. I thought at first she must have some money tucked away in the tops of her stockings or somewhere, but as far as I could make out she had nothing at all on under her dress. [*LWL* 79–80]

New fibres and fabrics allowed girls to discard the complicated foundation garments that had come to symbolise the many constraints of their mothers' lives; the Lady's last remark is directed against herself as much as anyone.

Maeve turned fifty in 1967. The following autumn she moved to Wellfleet, Massachusetts, near the tip of Cape Cod.[44] With its long Atlantic beaches and its hospitality to artists and writers, it was another East Hampton. Accessible by rail for painters influenced by the French fashion for painting *en plein air*, nearby Provincetown had been an artists' colony in the early twentieth century. Instead of an easy trip on the Long Island Rail Road from Penn Station, though, getting to Wellfleet entailed a long and complicated journey, and Maeve was soon back in New York.

She was restless again, moving from hotel to hotel, sometimes renting an apartment but not living in it, or renting two at a time when she found a place she liked better than where she had already signed a lease. When Howard Moss went to London, she stayed in his apartment on 10th Street for a few days. A cocktail party was going on in the next apartment, and it was raining. This is how her description ended:

> Once in a while, over the low roar of conversation, there is a loud laugh, and once in a while a little shriek. Outside, all the noise in the

world is being hammered into the earth by the rain, and, inside, all the noise there is is effervescing at the cocktail party. Only in this room there is stillness, and the stillness has gone tense. The room is waiting for something to happen. I could light the fire, but my friend forgot to leave me any logs. I could turn on a lamp, but there is no animal feeling in electricity. I stand up again and walk over to the phonograph and switch it on without changing the record that I played this morning. The music strengthens and moves about, catching the pictures, the books, and the discolored white marble mantelpiece as firelight might have done. Now the place is no longer a cave but a room with walls that listen in peace. I hear the music and I watch the voice. I can see it. It is a voice to follow with your mind's eye. '*La brave, c'est elle.*' There is no other. Billie Holiday is singing.

Once, as William Maxwell recalled, Maeve decided to have parquet flooring installed in her (rented) apartment in a Greenwich Village brownstone and simply moved into the Algonquin Hotel for months.[45] Her cousin Joe Bolger, seven years younger than she, worked at the Irish embassy in Washington. The two shared a birthday, as well as a robust irreverence for the pieties among which they had been raised, and Joe, a bachelor, visited Maeve in New York from time to time, despite severe arthritis, which made stairs increasingly difficult. Maeve's solution to the problem was totally in character: she moved to a ground-floor apartment. Once, while Joe was staying with her, Maeve went to bed, leaving the same record playing over and over on the phonograph. Unable to walk across the room to turn the machine off, Joe finally threw his walking-stick at it, stopping the music once and for all. Asked how Maeve might have reacted next morning to this destruction of her property, Joe's sister Ita Doyle was amused. 'She would just have laughed,' she answered.[46] Maeve's lack of possessiveness was legendary. She left her belongings behind in hotel rooms and apartments, and gave away clothing and accessories to almost anyone who admired them. Brendan Gill and Joseph Mitchell found themselves retracing her footsteps, negotiating for the return of deposits she had paid, trying to save her from drowning in debt.

Or perhaps nostalgia was what threatened to overwhelm her. 'The Door on West Tenth Street', written when Bluebell the black Labrador had become old and fat, her muzzle grey, appeared in *The New Yorker* in October 1967. It is the most extended of Maeve's animal meditations, but for years she had been entering the consciousness of dogs and cats, interpreting their logic, deferring to their patient wisdom, envying their lack of reasoned human memory, and writing about them in her notebooks. Dogs and cats do remember, of course, and Bluebell grown old still knows that behind a certain door on West 10th Street is Edward Albee, who is her friend.[47] Bluebell doesn't care that he is a famous and controversial playwright, or that Elizabeth Taylor has just won an Oscar for playing one of his characters; it is enough for her that behind his door are the cliffs of Montauk and the Atlantic Ocean, where she has been for six weeks and longs to be again.

Maeve's memories too are waiting intact behind closed doors in the most surprising places, and their force is so strong that it is impossible to imagine her developing a life that would make the daily walk more real than *they* are. She is like the elderly bishop in her 'Stories of Africa', which she prepared for publication about this time, who during his decades of exile 'looked on that lane from Oylegate to Poulbwee as the only path he knew through a maze that had no center and no form and no secret – worst of all, no secret' [*SA* 294–5]. It is bad enough to feel excluded from a secret that everyone else knows, as so many of Maeve's characters do; it is far worse to feel full of guilt, and yet to realise, like the bishop, that '[t]here was nothing secret and hidden that he could ferret out and destroy and punish himself for and do penance for. There was nothing. There was only the maze.' This is the knowledge that Maeve cannot bear to face. Instead, she tries to do as the dog does, continuing through New York's mysterious streets with good humour, as though she hopes that one day the special door will suddenly appear.

TWELVE

The Tightrope that Wasn't There

'I think she was a genius,' Philip Hamburger said, talking about Maeve in his Upper East Side apartment in Manhattan, in December 2001.[1] It was a preface to his memories of the years when Maeve began to fall apart, when her eccentricities became more disturbing than entertaining. Her friends and colleagues understood the intensity of her investment in writing, and could see the dividends it was beginning to pay, for she was not only richly productive in the late 1960s, she was also writing consistently close to the bone. William Maxwell even remarked privately to his secretary, Frances Kiernan, that he thought Maeve was the best living Irish writer.[2] Her prose described interiors and people as though a film crew was at her disposal, complete with sound and lighting equipment. In the stories she wrote now, a gesture was enough to convey a lifetime's history. 'When Rose appeared in the doorway, Hubert felt such dislike that he smiled' is the devastating sentence that sums up the Derdons' marriage in 'Family Walls', a story Maeve appears to have worked on throughout the 1960s.[3] In 'Talk of the Town', the Long-Winded Lady's communications became irresistible epiphanies of New York life.

'A Snowy Night on West Forty-ninth Street', published in January 1967, offers portraits of women young and old in the Étoile de France, a restaurant near where Maeve lived [*RG* 224–55]. It seems to have grown from a Long-Winded Lady piece into a full-blown story. The narrative speaks like a camera: the consciousness behind it could almost be William Hazlitt's 'pure spirit', whose interest in people is 'calm, contemplative, passive, distant, touched with pity for their sorrows, smiling at their follies without bitterness, sharing their affections, but not troubled by their passions, not seeking their notice, nor once dreamt of by them'. It has something of Charlie Chaplin's compassionate mockery too, but the eye behind this camera is feminine. The codes the story uses, describing the 'wide, stout, elderly lady' whose name is Mrs Dolan, are those that women use when talking to each other, or writing privately for other women:

[Her] elaborate makeup – eyes, complexion, and mouth – looked as though it had been applied several days ago and then repaired here and there as patches of it wore off. Her hair was dyed gold and curled in tiny rings all over her head, and her face and neck were covered with a dark beige powder. Her face had spread so that it was very big, but her nose and mouth were quite small, and she had enormous brown eyes that had no light in them. She had put on a great deal of black mascara, and blue eyeshadow. The shadow had melted down into the corners of her eyes and settled into the wrinkles. She was all covered up in a closely fitted dark blue velvet dress that was cut into a ring around her neck and had long tight sleeves that strained at her arms every time she lifted her spoon to her mouth. [*RG* 236]

Almost a quarter of 'A Snowy Night' is a single long paragraph, giving the story an unselfconscious urgency, as though its action were happening in present time, as in a film. The narrator stays in shadow, almost out of sight, gesturing discreetly to where her characters, old, young and middle-aged, experience excitement and disappointment. Most lastingly, although they struggle gamely to conceal it – especially from themselves – they suffer shame. That the narrator is a woman is remarkable, for there seems little doubt that the scene is real. The reader does not question the observer's authority, but for a woman to sit alone in public places after dark, simply looking, is to risk embarrassment if not danger. Like Colette, and Edith Piaf, and Billie Holiday, Maeve made herself vulnerable in pursuit of the insights her art expresses.

Loss was weighing heavily on Maeve by this time, and much of what she wrote was elegiac. Around Manhattan's midtown, where *The New Yorker* had its offices, and where she lived for some time in a hotel room on West 49th Street, modest, domesticated buildings were being torn down to make way for new skyscrapers. The Long-Winded Lady marked their passing, as she noted changes to the landscape of Greenwich Village. She deplored the taking away of dignity, from buildings as from people.

In April 1967, 400 high-school students carrying daffodils marched through Washington Square in protest against the war in Vietnam. The Lady was moved by their youth and politeness (a word Maeve liked). It was just days since Martin Luther King had given his 'Beyond Vietnam' address to 3,000 people in Manhattan's Riverside church, and a huge demonstration was planned for the following week. Suddenly, some students of New York University dropped large wads of wet paper from the windows of their residence on to the heads of the marching teenagers. The Long-Winded Lady's description of the fright and humiliation they caused was her oblique comment on the war and on those who promoted it [*LWL* 53–61].

Only when Russian tanks moved into Prague on the night of Tuesday, 20 August 1968, did the Lady offer anything like a sustained essay about the politics of the time. Always a night person, Maeve was staying at the Algonquin. She sat up until morning, listening to coverage of the invasion from radio station WINS. Its commentator, Jerry Landay, had recently returned from Prague, bringing with him a copy of the Prague Spring's unofficial manifesto, written by Ludvik Vaculík, from which he read at intervals throughout the night.

In her early childhood in Dublin, Maeve had heard the rumbling of Crossley tenders and armoured cars, and had not forgotten them when fire trucks rumbled outside her house by the beach in East Hampton. Her parents had belonged to an Irish generation that started out as hopefully and creatively as the one that made the Prague Spring, but she herself had become an exile from the country she wanted to love. Early in the morning following the events in Prague, Maeve took a taxi to the Jan Hus Presbyterian church at 74th Street and Second Avenue, near where New York's first Czech and Slovak citizens had settled, hoping to find an early morning service. She saw little sign, however, 'that a blow had been struck that might smash the globe and would in any case leave deep and lengthening fissures in it'. Her Long-Winded Lady essay, published on 7 September, began with a quotation from Vaculík's *Manifesto* on one of her favourite themes, truth:

> The truth is not in triumphing. It is merely what remains when everything else has been squandered away . . . This spring has just ended and will never return. Everything will be known in the winter.
> [*LWL* 197]

A letter to William Maxwell, scrawled on both sides of a sheet of Algonquin Hotel notepaper and dated simply Thursday, 12.25 a.m., seems to belong to the week of the invasion. It quotes the same words of Vaculík in a postscript, apparently from memory, for there are small variations. Bluebell and the cats are in a kennel, but Maeve's delight in small things is evident once more:

Dear William,
I only a few minutes ago discovered your lovely book of poems & inside, your note. Thank you very much.

A little while ago I had coffee sent up. Mr Michael of the Rose Room sent a happiness rose with it. Every night Mr Michael sends me a happiness rose (pinched from the Rose Room) and all day the room service waiters bring me daisies, one daisy each time they come to the room.

In a little while now I will be with my treasures and I will never leave them again.

This room is full of tiny glass <u>vases</u> each with one flower in it. I learned from watching Gerald that an arrangement of different vases is 'nicer' than all flowers in one vase. Eggs in one basket, flowers all around.

Best love to you & Emmy,
Maeve

Beneath her signature she has written the quote from Vaculík, adding:

'It is dangerous TO MOCK A FOOL'
GOD[4]

A snapshot taken the previous January shows Maeve in profile, standing in a narrow office, with William Shawn in the doorway behind her.[5] Wearing a tailored suit with a flower in the lapel, she appears to be drying a teacup; she wears earrings and her hair is shining, piled on top of her head. Maeve is slim, and elegant as ever, but young people no longer wanted to look the way she did. That same year, William Shawn hired twenty-two-year-old Kennedy Fraser, recently arrived from England, to write fashion notes and book reviews for *The New Yorker*, and she raced around the building in velvet hotpants, her long hair flying.[6] Most of the talented young women who wanted to be writers or editors were offered jobs as secretaries. Frances Kiernan, who would go on to write a distinguished biography of Mary McCarthy, was one of them. She had been an English major at Barnard College, and had just graduated when she became receptionist on the twentieth floor in 1966. It seemed that most of her contemporaries at the magazine had been selected for their looks:

[E]veryone I admired seemed to be wearing a pastel-colored wool dress that came just above the knee. Looking back at the typing pool with more than a little nostalgia, I see a cluster of pretty long-stemmed flowers: perhaps a dozen young women with perfectly straight, shoulder-length hair and the palest of pale lips, trying, with varying success, to look like Julie Christie or Catherine Deneuve.[7]

Kiernan has warm memories of Maeve Brennan. As Maeve came in and out of her office, or took breaks from her own writing, she made a point of stopping to talk to the new receptionist. She brought books she thought the younger woman might enjoy, and presented her with a fine, lace-edged handkerchief when she got married the following June.[8] Maeve was clearly a person of importance. One or other of the senior men was always whisking her off to lunch, but many of them were by now in second and third marriages, some to much younger women plucked from the typing pool.

If Maeve's position as a woman at *The New Yorker* had been ambiguous when she was young and spellbindingly attractive, it cannot have been easy in her fifties. It was not a good time to be a middle-aged woman in New York. A much talked-about bestseller there in 1966–1967 was gynaecologist Robert Wilson's *Feminine Forever*. Without mentioning the generous funding he received from the manufacturers of hormone replacement drugs, Wilson described women over fifty as 'castrates' and called menopause a 'disease' and a 'living decay'. Writing that 'Estrogen makes women adaptable, even-tempered, and generally easy to live with,' he added a new chapter to the story of the 'happy housewife heroines' of the 1950s. Although later discredited, his findings carried the authority of scientific research, and were soon enormously influential. *Feminine Forever* sold 100,000 copies in its first seven months.[9]

Maeve's legendary grooming began to be less than it had been. Her hairstyle – 'taller than she was!' according to Gardner Botsford – had become progressively more elaborate, but now people noticed that she was putting her hair up less carefully than before. Her natural hair colour was dark brown, but as more grey strands appeared, she had it dyed increasingly striking shades of red. John Updike, fifteen years Maeve's junior and a star of *The New Yorker* in the 1960s, used to see her about the office. He remembers chiefly about her 'that she was small and wiry and wore her lipstick well up over her upper lip'.[10] Maeve had always slashed lipstick carelessly across her mouth, but it no longer looked either daring or elegant.

Her writing was increasingly respected, however, and when Edward Albee wrote two new, interrelated plays, he honoured Maeve both directly and indirectly. *Box* and *Quotations from Chairman Mao Tse-Tung* had their first production in Buffalo, New York on 6 March 1968, and came to New York six months later. One of the characters in *Quotations* is called 'Long-Winded Lady', and when the plays were published the following year, the dedication read, 'For Maeve Brennan and Howard Moss'. And Maeve's story, 'The Eldest Child', published in *The New Yorker* on 29 June, was selected for inclusion among 'Best American Short Stories' published that year.[11]

William McPherson, then a young book editor, met Maeve and Howard Moss at the Algonquin on a hot day in 1968, for the sort of long, boozy lunch that publishers hosted then for writers they wanted to woo. McPherson (who went on to win a Pulitzer Prize for critical writing in 1977), described Maeve as 'a woman of legendary but fading Irish beauty, spectacular red hair, and a marvelously eccentric intelligence'. She encouraged him to become a writer, and sent him a gift the next day of an Eye-Ease National 210 notebook – the sort she used herself.[12] The following year, William Morrow published Howard Moss's *Writing Against Time: Critical Essays and Reviews*, and Maeve Brennan's *The Long-Winded Lady*, her own selection of forty-seven pieces from *The New Yorker*, with a short Author's Note by way of introduction. Critics welcomed *The Long-Winded Lady*, and noted its author's unmasking; John Updike reviewed it for the *Atlantic Monthly*, crediting Maeve with having 'helped put New York back into *The New Yorker*'.

The Long-Winded Lady is dedicated 'To W.S.'. When Kennedy Fraser saw William Shawn's 'look of tender pride . . . as he placed [it] on the arched bookshelf in the living room of his Fifth Avenue apartment', she longed to write enough to fill a book that he would value as highly.[13] It was the second book Maeve published that year. While in East Hampton, she had been sending stories to Dublin-born Diarmuid Russell, of the Russell and Volkening Literary Agency in New York, who was also agent for one of William Maxwell's best-known writers, Eudora Welty.[14] His father had been George Russell, better known as Æ, whose *Irish Homestead* had inspired Bob and Una's generation all those years ago in Ireland.

In spring 1969, Charles Scribner's Sons published twenty-two of Maeve's short stories under the wry title, *In and Out of Never-Never Land*. The jacket copy noted: 'This is Maeve Brennan's first collection of short stories. But because of the reputation her stories in *The New Yorker* have earned her, she is already a writer with a place of her own in contemporary fiction.' The book is dedicated: 'For the Bolgers of Coolnaboy, Oylegate: Anastasia, James, John, Elizabeth, Ellen, Walter'. Ellen, of course, had been dead since long before Maeve was born, but the others were her mother, aunt and uncles. The stories are grouped in four sections: 'Bluebell', '48, Cherryfield Avenue', 'Mrs Bagot' and 'Two People', the last one comprising three Derdon stories, 'A Young Girl Can Spoil Her Chances', 'The Drowned Man' and 'A Free Choice'. None of the 'Herbert's Retreat' stories is included.

The 'Mrs Bagot' section is made up of six stories, all of which had appeared in *The New Yorker* between 1964 and 1968. 'The Carpet with the Big Pink Roses on It' was the first Bagot story to appear in print. Maeve must have written it during the optimistic time in the early 1960s, before the deaths of her father and Gerald Murphy began to loom, when she was making friends with the Maxwells' daughters and the Murphys' grand-daughters, watching the sea and sky, and basking in the love of her own pets. 'The Shadow of Kindness' had followed swiftly, about Delia Bagot and her dog Bennie, and Delia's coming to terms with her resemblance to her own dead mother. Next came 'The Twelfth Wedding Anniversary', published in September 1966, then 'The Sofa', 'The Eldest Child' and 'Stories of Africa', all published in *The New Yorker* during 1968.

The Bagots live in the same house as the Derdons and the real-life Brennans did, with steps down to the red-tiled kitchen, and a laburnum tree in the back garden, but whereas in the Derdon stories the house stretches and contracts like clothing over the emotions Rose and Hubert experience so violently, there is a geometry about this new work – a careful framing of the narrative in space and time – that reads like an attempt to hold the balance, or find the note, that will make sense of everything. Like so many of Maeve's characters, Delia Bagot wishes that the world would hold still long enough for her to discover what she has done wrong:

> In an instant of sickening panic Mrs Bagot saw all the mistakes of her life rush together to congeal into the one fatal mistake that had made everything go wrong from the beginning. But the instant passed and with it her glimpse of that original mistake, the fatal one, which she could have named if it had only stayed before her eyes long enough to give her a chance to get a good look at it, so that she could see it and recognize it and call it by its name and know at last, once and for all, what it was she had done that separated her from the wisdom she knew other people possessed. [*SA* 278]

Almost every one of the stories about Delia and Martin Bagot and their children begins by setting a scene, as though a table were being laid in preparation for a meal. Space is ordered in rectangles: the door into the garden; the carpet with its pattern of pink roses; the fireplace; the big window in the back sitting-room. Maeve is walking through her childhood home again, but carefully, and although the house is the same one as the Derdons', it is summer in Delia's garden. There was much of Una in Rose Derdon (and, undoubtedly, much of Maeve, as she perceived herself), but Delia's is a gentler, more generous portrait. The woman in these stories is still ruled by fear, but her own kindness is undiminished, and the tensions between her and her husband emerge sadly, without bitterness, as being the fault of neither. Several stories mention their first child, Jimmy, who died when he was three days old. Bob and Una had lost their son Manus before Maeve was born, so that her own early life must have been shadowed by her mother's grief for the child who went before her. Her sister Derry's son Noel had died at six months, and Carmel Snow, mother of three girls, also grieved for a baby boy who died: she had given birth in 1929 to a son who lived only two weeks.[15] Delia Bagot's grief haunts her, but the children and animals in these stories are assured of the kind of love Una used to express in the letters she wrote to her daughters at boarding-school. Maeve still kept those letters carefully in a big square blue box with brass corners.[16]

In and Out of Never-Never Land was well received, but there was no paperback edition, and Maeve did not become a celebrity. Had she been known in Ireland, the book must surely have been taken seriously there, and if Frank O'Connor had still been alive, he might perhaps have promoted it. As it was, without an Irish or British publisher, it was almost unobtainable in the country where most of its stories were set, and seems to have gone almost unnoticed. The feyness of the title didn't help.

Copies did make their way to Ireland, of course. Maeve sent them to Derry and her children, and to her cousin Joe Bolger, now retired and living in Dublin too.[17] When Joe's arthritis meant that he could no longer work, or live alone, his sister Ita and her husband Rory Doyle had fitted out a chalet in the back garden of their bungalow in Kilbarrack (their son Roddy's fictional Barrytown), as a self-contained apartment for him. *In and Out of Never-Never Land* found a place beside Bob Brennan's *Allegiance* in the bookcase behind Rory's armchair. Roddy Doyle was eleven in 1969, just a year older than the character he would write about in his Booker Prize-winning *Paddy Clarke Ha Ha Ha*, but he was interested in soccer and lepers and the American west, and nothing about Maeve's book attracted him.[18]

An Irish novel that also appeared in 1969 hints at how much it might have meant to Maeve to be recognised as an Irish writer: she loved Richard Power's *The Hungry Grass*, and championed it tirelessly in New York.[19] Versed in the vernacular culture of both English and Irish languages, *The Hungry Grass* was an unsentimental critique of modern Ireland, at once a comical take on Irish priesthood that anticipated the 1990s television series *Father Ted*, and a clear-eyed, compassionate study of social inequality. Though widely acclaimed internationally, the book sadly disappeared from view after its author died, aged forty-two, the year following its publication.

By the time her own first book was published in 1969, Maeve's blurred lipstick and occasionally unkempt hair were symptoms of distress. Living in a series of apartments and hotel rooms, pursued by creditors, she was separated from her animals, and as Gardner Botsford puts it, 'the voltage began to climb':

Her enthusiasms became obsessions, unpredictable but overpowering. At one point, for instance, she discovered Billie Holiday, and bought every one of her hundreds of records, which she played over and over again, for hours at a time, even in the office, on a portable phonograph.[20]

Billie Holiday was the singer Maeve had listened to in Howard Moss's apartment while his neighbours held a noisy cocktail party and the rain poured down outside. Earlier, she had played Mozart's Symphony No. 29 with the same obsessive repetition. Perhaps she hoped the music might reveal the answers to the questions that tormented her: what is it that keeps people going, and makes men and women obedient to their roles? What makes a waif?[21]

Maeve had always invested unsparingly in her writing, but the cost was beginning to show in her own life. Around 1965, she had written to William Maxwell:

I will send you a note later about the specific difference between those writers who possess the natural confidence that is their birthright, and those fewer writers who are driven by the unnatural courage that comes from no alternative. It is something like this – some walk on a tightrope, and some continue on the tightrope, or continue to walk, even after they find out it is <u>not there</u>.[22]

Cartoon characters who keep running beyond the edge of the cliff, not falling until they chance to look down, were probably outside Maeve's consciousness as she wrote that, but her tightrope image describes the precariousness of what she was doing, and recognises the same quality in the writers she most appreciated. Another note, undated and unsigned, carries the same idea: 'Wm, Camus' words on the novel apply(?) only to writers who are Bound to the <u>Truth</u>. In other words, only to those writers who have no choice.'[23]

Whether she had many readers or only a few, Maeve would keep writing. She was working on more stories. 'Christmas Eve', eventually published in *The New Yorker* on 23 December 1972, is short, and was probably written quickly. Lily and Margaret Bagot are eight and six, and despite their parents' differences, their house is peaceful as they wait for Father Christmas to arrive. Maeve's lines explain something of why she was once again retracing the steps of her childhood:

It is the solid existence of love that gives life and strength to memory, and if, in some cases, childhood memories lack the soft and tender

colors given by demonstrativeness, the child grown old and in the dark
knows only that what is under her hand is a rock that will never give
way. [*SA* 307]

More and more, as though feeling herself to be a 'child grown old and
in the dark', Maeve focuses on the idea of an elusive 'truth', the answer to
the riddle of life. Madness is a recurring theme, although it remains at the
edges of the picture, but certain truths cannot be gainsaid. Rose Derdon in
'Family Walls' (not published until March 1973) is attempting with great
difficulty to steer a course between the sharp edges of the two things she
knows to be true: that life is precious because it is fragile, and that life is
worthless, because so easily destroyed:

> [T]he courage she showed came not from natural hope or from natural
> confidence or from any ignorant, natural source, but from her deter-
> mination to avoid touching the two madnesses as they guided her,
> pressing too close to her and narrowing her path into a very thin line.
> She always walked in straight lines. She went from where she was to
> the place where she was going, and then back again to the place where
> she had been. She kept close to the house. She might as well have
> been in a net, for all the freedom she felt. [*SA* 182]

This is a variation on a theme much treated by the *New Yorker*'s
humorists, and seen most vividly in the house-woman of James Thurber's
cartoon, 'Home'.[24] Because women control domestic space, men must rattle
around outside, or risk being engulfed and suffocated; but in Maeve's story
we see how that paradigm could look to a woman. To learn to cook and
sew, to marry and have children, is to risk being left without a ticket for
the wider world, where the answers to life's painful puzzles may possibly
be found; it is to risk spending one's whole life entangled in a net. Not to
do so, however, means being without a home. When Maeve was younger,
of course, her intelligence and curiosity were what made her choose going
out over staying in, but we remember the many references in her work to
Hans Christian Andersen's 'Little Mermaid', and the painful choice it sets
out for the young girl: between staying where she is loved and safe, and
losing everything, including her voice, in order to see and know a larger
world.

Moving from one run-down hotel to another, divorced, childless, her
parents dead and her siblings far away (Emer was caring for an invalid
daughter), the nearest thing Maeve had to a permanent home was the *New
Yorker* building. Mary D., back from London with her husband and two

small sons since 1965, noticed that Maeve was 'getting strange'. Mary D. was reading manuscripts at home for *The New Yorker* and went only occasionally to the office. Maeve had always worked at night, smoking her way through the pack of Camels Philip Hamburger left on his desk for her, and sometimes in the morning Mary D. found her in the Ladies' Room, or in the tiny cubicle beside it (a 1960s provision), where women with period pains could go to lie on a couch. Much as she had loved Maeve and enjoyed her company, Mary D. grew to dread these encounters.

Maeve was planning another departure from the city. Divorced since 1966, Philip Hamburger married a beautiful widow called Anna Walling Matson, in October 1968. Anna maintained close contacts in Wellfleet, Massachusetts, where she had lived in the 1930s, and her brother, Hayden Walling, owned a house in the woods there that he agreed to rent. Maeve was soon making arrangements to move back to Cape Cod. Bluebell was getting old, with bad arthritis in her legs, and in Wellfleet, Maeve could have all her animals with her. She planned to live there for the winter, as she had in East Hampton.

From Wellfleet, Maeve wrote to the Maxwells about how happy she was, describing a house that reminded her of the *Arabian Nights*, and urging them to visit. 'I am getting very <u>old</u> looking and I <u>hate</u> it,' she wrote to Emily, but then ended her letter: 'I am going to buy a lot of noisy colours when I come to town & I am going to make a lot of noise and give Milton Greenstein what for'.[25]

Maeve always had at least five cats, sometimes twelve, or more. Her letters and the Mary Ann Whitty stories mention them constantly. They have names and personalities, and sleep in their own chosen places around her house.[26] She pays attention to the way they move, describing how they come to meet her and Bluebell after walks, then run home 'like rocking horses, with their tails arched' [*RG* 276]. For Maeve's friends, one of the first clear signs that all was far from well was when she suddenly disappeared from the house in Wellfleet, leaving the cats behind. Several references in letters to the Maxwells point to tension. Her landlord wanted only 'nice' people in his houses, she wrote; he had a very young girlfriend. Later, when she was no longer in the house, and had been reunited with her cats, Maeve wrote to Emily Maxwell, 'I would never have left the woods in Wellfleet, but honest to God that is a dreadful man'.[27]

In December 2001, just a year before her own death, Anna Hamburger recalled this painful time, not long after she and Philip married.[28] Her brother had admired Maeve greatly, she said, and had perhaps wanted to see more of her; Maeve, for her part, loved the house she rented from him. When Walling went there, however, he found no sign of Maeve, only the cats wandering around and the house damaged. Maeve would never have gone away without her cats had she believed she had any choice, so it appears that she felt pursued or otherwise persecuted. Through the tolerance and good manners of everyone concerned, no action was taken against her, but we can assume that, once again, *The New Yorker*, in the person of Milton Greenstein, was faced with a large bill.

Maeve's movements throughout her life are difficult to trace, but in the late 1960s the track becomes increasingly muddy. After Wellfleet, she spent time in Marshfield and by July she was in Duxbury, still in Massachusetts, still on the Atlantic coast, but farther north again.[29] She wrote light-heartedly to Maxwell, signing herself 'Maybelle', and added a postscript: 'I am a best-seller in Duxbury. The lady in the West Wind bookshop has sold 15 copies of In & Out (one to me, 4 to herself) & has ordered 5 more!!!!'[30] To Emily, she wrote, 'My hair is now imitation Titian. Imitation Titian is the only Titian there is, in case you don't know.'[31]

The MacDowell Colony, founded in 1907 as a place where creative artists could find freedom to concentrate on their work, is in Peterborough, New Hampshire. Maeve may have gone there directly from Duxbury, for in early 1970 she was in nearby Rindge, in wooded country near the base of Mount Monadnock, on the shores of Pearly Pond. When Elizabeth Cullinan's novel of Irish America, *House of Gold*, was published in February, Maeve reviewed it enthusiastically for *The New Yorker*. A letter she wrote to Cullinan shortly afterwards, and this one to William Maxwell, described an ice storm on Pearly Pond:

. . . On December 26 there was the most tremendous ice storm. I didn't know then that it was an ice storm, only that it was tremdous [*sic*], blowing up out of that enormous 'pond' which was frozen solid, with heavy snow covering it. I remembering [*sic*] standing sideways to the window that was nearly in the pond, it was so close, and not looking out at it even though [I] wanted to. There was a tremdous [*sic*] dance going on out there, regions and elements and firmaments all flying around. Everything was white, and everybody was too big for everybody else. There were no partners. The snow poured down and the ice rained down and the wind blew with fierce power in all directions at once as though it was making a cutting-star and I couldn't look at it, even though I did glimpse caves and caverns folde[d] and disappearing out there in the white, I was extremely reluctant to look at it, although I kept going to the window and standing beside it.[32]

MacDowell, where she stayed for some time, provided everything a writer might need, but the house Maeve rented in Rindge was bare and comfortless, without a phone, and out of sight of other habitation. It was surrounded by trees and wildlife, and at one stage she rescued a lame skunk and fed it on milk. Of course she had no car, so to buy groceries, or even cigarettes, she would call a taxi. Some of her neighbours lived in trailers, drank a lot and raced noisy icemobiles across the frozen Pearly Pond and through the woods; others were retired, educated people whose houses were historic monuments. Maeve observed them as she had people on the street in New York, dispassionately. In September 1970 she sent Maxwell a postcard of Mount Monadnock, with the message. 'The mountain that wraps its head in its arms, like Bluebell, instead of in the clouds, like some I could mention.' Across the top, she added 'I am learning to drive a <u>truck</u>.'[33]

Money was a recurring theme in the letters she wrote from New Hampshire. In one of them, a marginal note on the second page enjoins Maxwell to 'Read calmly'. An arrow points to a paragraph that makes clear what sort of chaos her financial and tax affairs were in by now. St Clair McKelway notoriously neglected to pay his taxes, and Maeve had clearly followed suit:[34]

If I don't get some money I can't move, and if I don't get some more for Nahum to give the tax people they will come in with a ~~levy~~ lien. If they come in with a ~~levy~~ lien all that business of the LETTER will come up again, and that is the last thing Mr Greenstein wants. Wm, there really was a letter and it is sitting in my file at the tax place. The accountant read it which is why he dropped me like a hot brick & is so afraid to come into the office that he gets everybody's tax returns in late. Mrs F. spoke to me about it. She was very <u>worried</u>. Milton was horrified because he didn't realise I'd try to get severance pay. If all this comes up again Milton will die of ulcers. And of course the tax man will be hoping for another letter like that. See what I mean. (They have already come in with a levy. A levy is when they come in and take whatever is there, last week, 2 or 3 days of my miserable paycheck, which has already been cut down all this year by the state tax people[)]. They claimed for a year I am certain was paid, but the accountant wouldn't even go and get it out of his file storage place, so I had to pay. Really, I feel very ill-used. It is a wonder I am not <u>paranoid</u>. A year ago this would all have seemed a nightmare, now it is only an infuriating nuisance, thrown in the path of one who is known to all as the unchallenged re-incarnation of Little Nelly of the

Holy God.[35] With the nuisance paycheck dwindling away to nothing
I can't even pay the milkman for my cottage cheese and orange yogurt,
and I have to walk 2 miles to make a phone call. Of course it may be
that none of this is really happening and that I have gone stark staring
mad . . .

Unfortunately, Maeve's money troubles were all too real. A postscript returns
to the subject:

In other words, if you could <u>bring</u> yourself to <u>convince</u> yourself that
you could <u>suggest</u> an advance, I have the feeling Mr G. wouldn't be
all that anxious to stop you, if the advance meant the tax people would
be prevented from coming in with a lien.

Another note thanks Maxwell for his efforts on her part:

I know what a struggle you must have had to get this money for me.
I signed the cheque straight over to the MacDowell Colony. Everybody
thanks you. All will be well. Love, Maeve.

Maeve's reference to 'severance pay' suggests that her formal connection
to *The New Yorker* had ended, or that she thought it had. The Long-Winded
Lady had almost disappeared from the magazine. After seven pieces each
in 1967 and 1968, and five in 1969, only the poignant 'On the Island'
appeared in 1970, after which there were no more until 'Cold Morning', in
January 1973 – effectively the last of those contributions.[36] Other letters she
wrote about this time refer to the unlikelihood that she will ever be in the
office again. Changes were under way at the magazine, but Maeve's pay
cheques continued, and she was still receiving parcels of books for review
two years later.

In fact Maeve was suffering from writer's block. Though a common
enough affliction, it must have been devastating for one who had abandoned
so much for the sake of her writing. Frances Kiernan had been away from
The New Yorker for two years following her marriage, but had returned to
work with William Maxwell in the Fiction Department late in 1969. Now
Maxwell suggested to Maeve that dictating her 'Briefly Noted' reviews to
Kiernan over the telephone might be easier than writing them. Kiernan
took down two or three of these short reviews, and was aware of Maeve's
sadness that her little black kitten was dying of leukaemia.[37] Once – perhaps
the book under review was translated from French – Kiernan mistakenly
typed 'gentile' instead of Maeve's 'genteel'. The mistake made its way past

all the magazine's checkers and appeared in print, but Maeve was kind about it, and funny. And she still had some of her old ability to boss other people into tackling their problems. Kiernan was typing Maxwell's memoir, *Ancestors*, in 1970 when Maeve paid a visit to New York City. Maxwell was in despair, having discovered that he had left the only corrected copy of one chapter in a taxi, but Maeve took over, briskly giving instructions about whom to phone – and the chapter was recovered. That was unusual, however; a story told in the office about Maxwell's relief when a new piece of Maeve's writing turned out to be publishable (perhaps her story 'Christmas Eve') was closer to the truth of her position.

Maeve was resident in the MacDowell Colony early in 1971, when George Kendall, the director, was planning his retirement. In December of that year, Maxwell sent her a telegram, also at MacDowell: 'SPRINGS OF AFFECTION RESCHEDULED FOR MID FEBRUARY. NO NEED TO STOP WORKING TO FIX THE GALLEYS. ANYTIME BEFORE THE END OF JANUARY WILL DO. LOVE, WILLIAM.'[38] In the event, Maeve's longest and most powerful story appeared in *The New Yorker* on the day after St Patrick's Day, 18 March 1972, when she was fifty-five.

References in letters Maeve wrote to Maxwell make clear that 'The Springs of Affection' had taken shape over a considerable period, in close consultation with him. While still in New York, searching for 'a room with Bluebell and the cats and a fireplace', she wrote to him on two sides of a small sheet of *New Yorker* notepaper: 'Dear Wm, You must be reminded again that you wrote that story. Certainly you will admit that you reminded me of the springs of affection – I had forgotten . . .'[39] Another letter, also handwritten on *New Yorker* letterhead and undated, says: 'I suppose you know that's your story, title and all. I was scrapping it – it *was* scrapped – but there you are, it was a Tuesday and you were "here". And the title – I had forgotten what she said. But it is all yours and don't forget that . . .'[40]

Widely hailed as Maeve's finest work, 'The Springs of Affection' is a *tour de force*. On its republication in 1997, Canadian *New Yorker* writer Alice Munro welcomed it as one of her favourite short stories of all time, while William Maxwell placed it with the great short stories of the twentieth century.[41] At about the same time, in a new Introduction to the Modern Library edition of his own 1937 novel, *They Came Like Swallows*, Maxwell wrote:

If you toss a small stone into a pond, it will create a ripple that expands outward, wider and wider. And if you then toss a second stone, it will again produce a widening circle inside the first one. And with the third stone there will be three expanding concentric circles before the pond recovers its stillness through the force of gravity. That is what I wanted my novel to be like. No directions came with this idea.[42]

In 'The Springs of Affection', it is as though Maeve has finally thrown the small stones she has carried in her pockets all her life, watching their ripples spread and intersect before subsiding. Unfortunately, though, the real stories of human life do not end in Aristotelian stillness. Bringing to a head the explorations that have preoccupied most of her fiction, 'The Springs of Affection' is Maeve's swan song, or her kamikaze flight, for it is both a glorious celebration of her skills as a short-story writer, and a suicidal assault on her own family. After it appeared, her Aunt Nan Brennan in Wexford wrote on the back of a ten-year-old snapshot of Maeve with Bluebell, taken in East Hampton and already captioned 'Meave' [sic]: 'Greatly changed for the worse, 1972'.[43] 'The Springs of Affection' seems certainly to have been the last piece of fiction Maeve produced. Apart from a couple of fragments, only two more appeared in print: 'Christmas Eve', in December 1972, and 'Family Walls', in March 1973, and the second of these had already been in proof, in a different version, more than ten years earlier. 'Once and for all', as one of Maeve's characters might have said, 'The Springs of Affection' tells the story of a couple's relationship and the history out of which Maeve's own imagination grew. If her collected stories about the Bagots have 'the organic unity and artistic integrity of a novel', as has been suggested, this story is its denouement.[44] But the past belongs to everyone who has lived through it, and Maeve had sacrificed other people's history to the needs of her own art.

Almost every fact in 'The Springs of Affection' is true, and yet the story is not. The relationships in two families over three generations, the appearance of houses and countryside, the people in the story, the work they do and the rooms where they do it, all are precise in their details and true to historical fact.[45] In 1959, Frank O'Connor had 'changed names to avoid giving pain' in sections of his autobiography, *An Only Child*, that were to appear in *The New Yorker*. 'It is an astonishment to me to find how the New Yorker gets round Ireland, even in the provinces,' he wrote to William Maxwell.[46] It was not enough to change names, however, especially thirteen years later, when communications had advanced so much. Anyone who knew Nan Brennan, and in Wexford at least, everybody did, must have recognised her biographical details in Min Bagot, and been appalled at the injustice done to her.

Min Bagot is a study in spite, a monster of heartlessness who is cunning and resentful in her dealings with all around her, but Nan Brennan had done nothing to deserve such a characterisation. Eighty-five years old when

Maeve's story was published, still living alone in her flat above the shop in North Main Street, Wexford, Nan enjoyed the affection and gratitude of her family and the well-earned respect of her neighbours. Always resolutely independent (she had claimed the old-age pension for the first time at eighty), Nan had helped out in many households over the years, and still went regularly to stay at Rosslare Strand, where her lifelong friend Bridget Sinnott lived in the hotel her husband had built in the 1920s. Bridget's son Jim and his wife Monica collected her by car and welcomed her as one of their family.[47] Her niece Nancy Walsh, Maeve's first cousin, visited her almost daily from her home in King Street, and Nancy's children called her 'Mimi', a honorary 'granny' name. Nan sometimes travelled by bus from Wexford to visit Maeve's sister Derry and her children in Dublin. Once, she insisted on completing her journey on foot when the bus conductor wanted to have her taken to hospital by ambulance, after she fell off the bus platform on to the road.[48] Nan was known as a founder member of the country's largest political party, Fianna Fáil, and a close ally of its rebel heroes (she had slept with guns under her bed when young). As late as 1976, the committee of the Wexford Opera Festival invited her to meet visiting American dignitaries.

Most hurtful, perhaps, in 'The Springs of Affection' was the reference to the time, thirty years after Martin married Delia, 'when Min was obliged to have [her sister] Clare locked up in the Enniscorthy Lunatic Asylum'. Nan and Bob's older sister Tess had indeed spent her last years in what is now St Senan's Hospital, the building with the redbrick towers on the road from Oylegate to Enniscorthy. She may have been suffering from an inoperable brain tumour: her condition began with severe headaches, and eventually became so distressing that she asked Nan to 'put her' somewhere. Nan arranged for her admission to St Senan's, where she died not long afterwards, and, as we have seen, herself took on the running of the family's old house on George Street, where Tess's husband now lived alone, just as she did for Bob in Dublin, at Maeve's request, when Una Brennan died in 1958. By the time 'The Springs of Affection' appeared in print, however, Maeve had herself spent time in a mental hospital.

'It is a wonder I am not paranoid,' she had written to Maxwell, but increasingly, she was. Bluebell the black Labrador died early in the 1970s, and with her passing Maeve lost her main comfort and source of affection.[49] As Gardner Botsford puts it, 'slowly, as this kaleidoscopic life went on, she became demented. Her living arrangements became ever more chaotic. Paranoia set in.' Botsford's own awakening to the seriousness of Maeve's condition came when she telephoned him from the writers' colony where she had been staying, sounding perfectly reasonable, but saying that she was coming to the city, as 'they' were coming after her, and asking him to meet her in a coffee shop on 44th Street, west of Sixth Avenue, at eleven o'clock sharp the next day.[50]

When he met her, Maeve told him 'in a perfectly controlled and reasonable voice' that 'they' had already tried to poison her by putting cyanide in her toothpaste. Howard Moss was in Greece, however, and she explained that since she had his keys, she would hide out in his apartment, where 'they' wouldn't find her.

'Who are *they*?' Botsford asked.

'You know perfectly well who they are. I'm not going to mention their names in a coffee shop,' she replied.

So began a time that Maeve's New York friends cannot remember without pain. Anna Hamburger, making occasional visits to the *New Yorker* offices, noticed that although Maeve still wore heavy make-up, it looked sloppy now, as though, like Mrs Dolan in 'A Snowy Night', she simply touched it up from time to time instead of reapplying it every day. Maeve's behaviour became part of *New Yorker* folklore, talked about among the staff, and recalled in several memoirs.[51] Instead of going 'home' to a room in one of the increasingly seedy hotels near the office, she began to spend her nights in the cubicle beside the women's room on the nineteenth floor. She lived there, Maxwell wrote in 1997, 'as if it were her only home. Nobody did anything about it, and the secretaries nervously accommodated themselves to her sometimes hallucinated behavior.'[52] She brought a sick pigeon in from the street and nursed it there, and when she got her pay cheque she would cash it at the Morgan Guaranty Trust on the corner of 44th Street and Fifth Avenue, then stand outside, across the street from the office, and hand out cash to passers-by.

In 'The Springs of Affection', Min Bagot finally loses patience when Clare gives away 'every piece but one of the blue-and-white German china their mother had treasured . . . Min never got over the loss of that china.' Min is the last of Maeve's studies in stinginess – a character whose petty economies stand for a shrivelling of soul, who places material possessions above human warmth. Maeve's own loudest cries against the demands of sanity took the same form as those she had described in her fiction. When Anastasia King in *The Visitor* failed to find a home with her self-satisfied grandmother, she enacted a symbolic destitution on the pavement outside her house; now Maeve did the same with the magazine that was like a parent to so many of its writers. Always generous, and sometimes embarrassingly so, she began to give things away with such a vengeance that she could not be ignored.

To stop her giving all her money away, Milton Greenstein began to dole it out to her in small instalments, but Maeve became convinced that he was stealing from her, and decided to sue. She had taken to wearing a tan trenchcoat, and a beret that completely covered her hair, and gradually she stopped speaking to her closest friends. She called Edward Albee an Antichrist, and one by one, Brendan Gill, Joseph Mitchell, Gardner Botsford, Howard Moss and William Maxwell found that she passed them without speaking. One after another, they urged William Shawn to do something, but Shawn's whole instinct had always been to tolerate and protect: 'She's a beautiful writer,' was the only response Ved Mehta heard him make.[53]

Maeve's cries for help grew louder. One morning, Philip Hamburger arrived at work to find the glass panel in the door of his office smashed. The door was closed, but the office had been wrecked, and precious photographs of his two sons, taken by Thérèse Mitchell, Joseph's wife, had had their glass, and even their frames, broken. Maeve had also broken the glass in Mitchell's door, and in Milton Greenstein's. All three had expressed concern for Maeve, and had tried to help her. They were reminded of the 'hesitation cuts' seen on the wrists of attempted suicides. Finally, with great difficulty, William Maxwell, Gardner Botsford and Howard Moss got Maeve into the University Hospital. Mental patients could not be hospitalised without their consent, but she finally signed herself in, and received the care she needed.[54] With medication, she became stable enough to be released.

William Shawn published Maeve's story 'Christmas Eve' in the 23 December issue of the magazine in 1972, and what turned out to be her last published fiction, 'Family Walls', the following March. In proof since 1962, 'Family Walls' had changed considerably by the time it appeared in print, with the Derdons' son John now edited out. In the earlier version, Hubert arrived home from work to see the kitchen door close on both Rose and the teenaged John. In this version, John's personality is more clearly drawn than anywhere in Maeve's published work, and it is he, not Rose, who inspires Hubert's instinctive and memorable recoil:

Then he heard the kitchen door open and John coming up the steps. John walked heavily in his heavy boots. He wore the boots always because Rose insisted that he had weak ankles and that his feet and ankles needed extra support. Hubert thought Rose imagined John's delicate chest and weak ankles to give herself an excuse to keep the boy from playing games and going on outings with the rest of his class . . .

When John appeared in the doorway Hubert felt such dislike that he smiled. He saw the confusion caused by the smile, and he saw John's hand fasten on the doorknob, as Rose's hand always fastened on something, the back of a chair, or her other hand, before she spoke. Hubert was irritated and not for the first time by the bewilderment on John's face. Hubert knew that a fourteen year old boy who looks as though he has suffered is only acting in the hope of getting pity for himself, and in the hope of being excused for whatever he has done that he should not have done.

'The tea is ready,' John said, and he tried to smile . . .[55]

Maeve never showed Maxwell work in progress, and never submitted a story to the magazine until she could stand by every word of it, but his editing, visible in the galleys of some of her other stories, is probably responsible for the tightening of this one.[56] Given the extent to which Maeve's fiction drew on her memory and on those of her parents, it is worth noting that what appears to be a change made for aesthetic reasons has the effect of rendering more implacable the situation she struggles to understand through writing about it. Here, as in 'The Springs of Affection', her protagonists treat each other more cruelly than she may at first have intended them to do. Her work had for some time been more urgently real to her than her life, but these final stories gain some of their power from the reckless despair that seems to lie behind them.

In 1973, thirty-nine years after leaving Ireland, Maeve decided to move back there. She left New York on 5 July, and although she had told her friends that her younger sister would not speak to her following the publication of 'The Springs of Affection', Derry's house in Dublin was where she went to stay. Joe Bolger was the only person in Ireland who had known her well in her own environment, but by the time she arrived in Dublin, he was in Cappagh Hospital full time. Perhaps he told Maeve when she visited him about his chalet behind the Doyles' house in Kilbarrack. After a few weeks, Maeve phoned Ita Doyle from Derry's, telling her 'I think I've stayed here long enough', and asking 'Would you have room?'

Rory and Ita have given their own account of the months Maeve spent with her typewriter in the chalet in their back garden.[57] Theirs was a busy, kindly, tolerant household, where Maeve stayed in the background and nobody disturbed her. The Doyles knew she had been ill, but saw no sign of it; her eyes were bright, her clothes stylish, and her hairstyle elaborate. 'If there was a hair out of place, it was meant to be,' Ita said.[58] She remembered meeting Maeve in Dodder Road twenty-five years earlier, and liking her immediately, but the Doyles expected Maeve to be different from them, and she was. She rarely took meals with the family, and ate little when she did. Her curtains stayed closed in the daytime, but they could hear her typing furiously, early in the morning and late at night. Parcels of books arrived for her from *The New Yorker*, and she sent off reviews by mail (probably to Gardner Botsford for 'Briefly Noted', for no signed reviews appeared over her name in this period).

On 8 August Maeve wrote six pages by hand to William Maxwell:

Dear Wm,
Many thanks for your letter of August 2, which arrived here just this minute. I have a tiny house here, one room with bath, all new, built 3 or 4 years ago for my cousin Joe Bolger, who is, I am very sad to say, obliged to live at Cappagh Hospital. I am behind the Doyles' house & I have enormous seagulls, little grey pigeons and several flocks of other different sorts of birds. At the end of the road is the Irish Sea, an inlet of it, & a broad wall that I walk along. I have not been inside Stephen's Green yet, but there are oceans of flowers out here. There are also 4 kindhearted cheerful children aged 13 to 21, all of them hard-working & good-looking. I only see them from time to time. I do not keep the same hours as the family. At first when I came it was sunny every day & quite warm, but lately there have been grey days here & there & rain, not the constant rain I was half hoping for, but real Irish rain just the same.

William, your letter was postmarked August 3, & the same postmark on two other letters from New York which arrived this morning. August 3 was last Friday, & by my calculations I should have had a paycheck mailed from the office on that day – the first paycheck after my 'vacation' – I took 4 weeks & have been here 4 weeks & a half. It will be five weeks tomorrow since I left New York. This is getting very long-winded – I thought a check was due to be mailed to me Fri. Aug. 3 but apparently it was not mailed. Could you enquire from somebody, Edith Agar maybe.

You should get this next Monday, 13th. If the check arrives in the meantime, I will send you a cable to ignore this letter. I will send the cable to Baptist Church Road – that way I will get at all of you. I mean, that way I will send greetings to all of you. I thought Barbara Lawrence[59] looked better & seemed happier than she has been for years & years. I saw her about 3 weeks before I left. There is a little dog here, a white terrier with floppy spaniel ears & big floppy spaniel feet. Did you read Faith McNulty's wonderful piece on the whales?
    Love, Maeve

THE TIGHTROPE THAT WASN'T THERE

Maeve went walking a lot from the Doyles', especially along the seafront at the end of Kilbarrack Road – once she went as far as the Marine Hotel in Sutton with nineteen-year-old Pamela, and got soaked to the skin – and every Thursday she walked to the local shopping centre to buy *Ireland's Own*. Seventy years after Bob Brennan and Jim Bolger had written for it, *Ireland's Own* was still published in Wexford and still carried no advertising for tobacco or alcohol. It was lowbrow, rural and determinedly wholesome, and Maeve loved it. She sat reading it in a café at the shopping centre every week, with a cup of coffee and a slice of apple tart. Sometimes she took the bus to the city, to shop or go to the theatre, and came home by cab. As always, she was lavishly generous, regularly bringing back gifts for the family, and taking Ita on at least one memorable shopping expedition.

Beyond noticing that she wore trousers – unusual for a woman of her age in Ireland in 1973 – and that she was never without her cigarettes, Roddy Doyle at fifteen had little to do with his cousin. He spent that summer listening to the Yes album, *Close to the Edge*, with its twenty-minute tracks of real rock music, but when his father lost patience and told him to 'Turn down that bloody noise' Roddy noticed that it was Maeve who spoke up to defend him. In conversation she was entertaining, and sometimes surprising, as she talked about her life in New York: when thirteen-year-old Shane interrupted her to ask who Mac was, she answered, 'He was my husband. I divorced him. I was his fourth wife.' As divorce would not become legal in Ireland for another twenty years, this made her seem impossibly exotic.

Maeve thought she would stay in Dublin. She spoke to the Doyles about finding a flat, and at one point a woman estate agent came regularly to collect her and drive her around, looking at places she might rent. She became involved in a scheme to rescue baby donkeys, and mourned the fact that the old Moira Hotel was about to be pulled down. On 11 September she wrote to Maxwell again, filling fourteen sides of notepaper. She was still happy, and had no plans to return to New York, but the same abstract, obsessive note is present in this letter as in earlier ones written when she was losing her grip on reality, and she may have begun to neglect her medication:

Dear William,
Only to say that things are moving along at an even keel & have been ever since I arrived here. The first time I saw the Liffey I was surprised – she looked so real. I have been to the play a few times. I saw a Russian drama, two Irish dramas, & a terrible <u>offering</u> about a psychoanalyst by

an American who is teaching at Trinity College here. The newspapers are my great diversion, but I am cutting myself down from 5 papers a day to 1 – the Irish Times. The weather has changed. It is autumn now, today is my mother's birthday. I get up at 6. The typewriter is here in the room with me – I hold on to it as the sensible sailor holds on to his compass. You would think a person would find the way through his hands & his eyes, but my way, I find, is through my ears & the soles of my feet. Walking has always been wonderful for me, & here, it is more than wonderful. I always felt better when I was walking along with my feet on the ground & here, every once in a while, I think 'this is Irish ground' and, I know 'where I am' and where I am, I am where I used to be, except that 39 years of flat and unmarked country lies between me & what used to be. We came here in September 1934. I suppose it is the wasteland I am looking at & I can tell you that it is not a bad sight at all. Certainly not distressing. But of course I am looking at my 'wasteland' from another side of the world – I have crossed the ocean since I saw you last. This 'wasteland' I speak of is not a <u>desert</u> – it is a plain, and I am very glad I did not know I would have to cross it, & very very glad I didn't know where I was when I was in the middle of it. The most I ever knew was that I 'didn't know where I was'. If you think, sadly perhaps, that I have regrets, you are <u>wrong</u>. I have no regrets at all. It is as it was when my mother died. I thought then that if I could see in my mind one tree, or one house, or one hill or river, if I could see even the wall of a cottage – a remnant, a door, even, I would cry my eyes out, but the landscape that had been mysterious & familiar as it was, was all gone. There was nothing, and nothing to cry over. She gave me an 'asylum for my affections' & I learned that my affections so far exceeded her ability to understand me that she came near to drowning. But she is defined in her struggling – I remember her very well.

But now, there is this <u>plain</u> I speak of, William, it is <u>extremely</u> flat, but if you imagine me surveying it with an eye that is heroic because of being tearless you are wrong again. There is nothing to survey. All it is, maybe all the wasteland ever is, is a separation between now & then, between the 'knower & the known'. What I am conscious of, is of having the sense of true perspective, the true sense of perspective, that is in fact only the consciousness of impending, imminent revelation. 'I can see'. But 'I can see' is not to say 'I see'. I don't believe at all in revelations – but to have, even for a minute, the sense of <u>impending</u> revelation, that is being alive. The rest is nothing but touch, & touch, for me was my cats & my Bluebell. It is nice to be able to say that I spent my years. I would hate to have to say that I misspent them. If I should be hit by a car, please comfort yourself with the knowledge that <u>I died happy</u>, although, dear me, outside the <u>church</u>. <u>THE</u> church.

I have three plans, three distinct and independent geometric forms, that have raised themselves in my mind. I hope to send you a typed photograph of the first one before the end of this month.

Love, Maeve

Ita Doyle returned from shopping in nearby Raheny one day to find Maeve in the hall, her bags packed. 'I'm going now, Ita. I think I've stayed long enough,' was all she said, and when her taxi arrived, she was gone. For Roddy, it was like the day he came home from school to discover that the kittens that had been in the garage were no longer there. The analogy is a surprising reminder of Maeve's own 1966 story 'I See You, Bianca', about a New York cat whose owner looks for it in vain [*RG* 250–9].

Maeve remained in Dublin for some time, although she made no contact with the Doyles. Then Ita had a phone call from Store Street Garda Station in the city centre. Maeve had turned up there, worrying that her niece was in danger, and asking for police protection for her. She seemed confused. Ita spoke to her briefly, and asked if she would like to come back to stay, but Maeve insisted that she was fine.

Maeve seems to have returned to the United States soon after. She sent Ita a letter of condolence when Joe Bolger died the following year, but she may have made one more visit to Ireland. David Marcus, literary editor of the *Irish Press*, had spotted her stories in *The New Yorker* and secured permission to republish one of them in his 'New Irish Writing' page. When he learned that Maeve was in Dublin, he and his wife, the novelist Ita Daly, invited her to a dinner at their house, but the evening ended in embarrassment when she and a visiting American became embroiled in a bitter argument.[60] Maeve invited her hosts to lunch at the flat where she was living in Ballsbridge, but when they arrived, they found no sign of her.

In the middle of 1974, Maeve was in New York. Scribners had brought out a new collection of thirteen of her stories, including the latest ones, and six from the 1950s about Herbert's Retreat. The title, *Christmas Eve*, hinted at the author's condition, however, for the book appeared in the spring. The dedication read 'For Deirdre and Gilbert Jerrold'. On 1 July, under the title 'Moments of Recognition', *Time* magazine ran a review by Helen Rogan alongside a short, unsigned interview, and a photograph of Maeve by Jill Krementz. The photograph shows Maeve with her hair much shorter than before, but swept up and held in place by hairspray; she wears earrings like small leaves, and looks straight at the camera with narrowed eyes. Her expression is benign, but the hand that reaches into the neck of her light-coloured coat suggests unease. She lives alone, the interviewer tells us, in a midtown hotel on West 44th Street, 'just opposite the Algonquin' and only a few steps from *The New Yorker*. The interview ends: 'She has been quietly side-stepping the literary life for years and treasuring anonymity. As she remarks, with a sidelong smile, "The fewer writers you know the better, and if you're working on anything, don't tell them".'

Reviewers loved the subtlety of Maeve's stories about the Derdons and the Bagots, but Harvard critic Robert Kiely, writing in the *New York Times Book Review* on 4 August, dismissed the 'Herbert's Retreat' stories. Maeve tucked a copy of his review into the back of her big blue box with brass corners. She was far from well, and seems to have left New York again soon after. The blue box, full of papers and photographs, ended up in Carrolls, the Movers, in Duxbury, Massachusetts, and eventually found its way to a used book store after she failed to claim it.

Maeve's 1968 story, 'The Eldest Child,' was anthologised in 1975, in a collection that also included work by Colette, Edith Wharton, Alice Munro and Mary Lavin, but 'she wouldn't take her medication,' Gardner Botsford said, 'and she went zing! right off the end again.'[61] Once again, her colleagues got her into hospital, but she decided that they were conspiring against her. Only Botsford and Elizabeth Cullinan continued to visit. Colleagues heard that Botsford had paid to have Maeve's cats kept in a kennel, so that they would not have to be destroyed. Cullinan found herself elected as Maeve's carer, visiting the hospital often, running errands and bringing her magazines.[62] She was amazed at how 'Irish' Maeve became in hospital, as though all the veneer of her New York life had fallen away. She spoke about Ireland, and her early life, and gave the younger woman small treasures, including a postcard sent to her mother as a girl in Coolnaboy. She told the story – whether true or imagined – of her romance with Walter Kerr at CUA in Washington. 'I can still feel how much I loved him,' she said. And Cullinan was the one she phoned in great distress one day about this time, saying 'Oh Elizabeth, I've sneezed out all my teeth!' All Maeve's teeth had been crowned for years, so that to see her without the crowns was dreadful, but Cullinan was able to persuade a dentist to repair the damage swiftly. Maeve turned against Cullinan too eventually though, when her fantasy of living in the vacant apartment next door to her failed to materialise. Maeve wanted someone to care for her as though she were a child, and had imagined that Cullinan could be that person.

Maxwell seems to have been the one who contacted Maeve's brother

Robert Patrick in Illinois, possibly through his employers, Caterpillar Tractor, to tell him of her condition. Robert Patrick, Emer and their two sons had spent a total of eight years in Central and South America. Although they had returned from Brazil in 1968, Robert Patrick had had little contact with his sister since her divorce. Now he flew to New York to visit her, and invited her to come and live with him and his family when she was discharged from hospital.

Robert Patrick and Emer's younger son Peter was fifteen, and looking forward to getting his driver's licence, when Maeve came to live in their house on High Point Road, Peoria, late in 1975. His brother Bob was away at university. The Brennans had a subscription to *The New Yorker*; they knew that the Long-Winded Lady in 'Talk of the Town' was Maeve, but Peter had no memory of having met his aunt before. Already over six feet tall, he found himself towering over a tiny woman with greying hair and enormous glasses who spent most of her time typing and smoking in the bedroom his older brother had vacated. Sometimes she would go out walking with the family's Dobermann pinscher, Laoch (Irish for 'hero'), and Peter would slip into her room to check that she had not left a cigarette burning where it might start a fire. The big old ashtray in Maeve's bedroom was always full, and something often smouldered there. In the kitchen, Maeve left pots to boil dry. She made no attempt to cook, but she would make tea, and strong coffee in an old percolating coffee pot that sat on the stove. Completely unused to sharing domestic space, she would reach in front of her sister-in-law to fill a kettle for tea as Emer stood washing something at the kitchen sink.

While Maeve took her medication she was sane enough, and especially enjoyed the company of Laoch, who was two or three years old and very friendly. Inevitably, though, she stopped the medication when she felt well. At least once, Peoria police discovered her in a park opposite City Hall, feeding pigeons and handing out money. She gave them her brother's telephone number, and he and Emer drove downtown to pick her up. Then one day, much as she had done with the Doyles in Dublin, Maeve suddenly announced that she was leaving. She moved to a room in a boarding-house, where the family was able to maintain contact with her for a while. One of the first places Peter Brennan drove to after he got his licence was the blue house with a porch where Maeve was living. She had no phone, however, and eventually she went back to New York without telling her brother.

In the spring of 1976, Nicholas Furlong, a journalist and historian from Wexford, was in New York to take part in a lecture series organised by the Irish American Cultural Institute. When he spoke at Fordham University in the Bronx on 'The Quakers of Ireland and the Founding of Pennsylvania', he noticed among the audience a woman with grey hair and a long skirt, who sat close to the front but appeared preoccupied with her own thoughts, occasionally rummaging in the large bag she held on her lap. 'She might even have eaten a biscuit while I was talking,' he said, remembering the incident many years later. To him she looked like 'a poor soul who might have come in just to sit down', so he was surprised to see her there again the following week, when he spoke about 'The Surviving Irish Royal Families'. Only after the woman had left the building at the end of this second lecture did one of his hosts tell him that she was Maeve Brennan, whose father had been Bob Brennan from Wexford, Irish Minister to Washington during the Second World War. Furlong, who remembered seeing Bob in Wexford during his own boyhood, and had grown up across the street from Maeve's Aunt Nan, was astonished, and dismayed to have missed the chance of speaking to Maeve. Historian Margaret MacCurtain also lectured in that series, but she noticed no such woman in her audience. Clearly, Maeve had made the journey to the Bronx to hear a speaker from Wexford; clearly too, she had ceased to be part of mainstream society.

William Maxwell had left his job as fiction editor at *The New Yorker* on 1 January 1976. A new policy of the magazine's business department had forced all staff aged over sixty-five to retire on that date, and he was sixty-seven; only William Shawn was exempt.[63] A new Plexiglas partition was erected outside the receptionist's desk on the twentieth floor, with a locked door to keep out all but authorised visitors, and staff were instructed not to let Maeve into the offices, for fear of violence. Even so, in September 1976, a new contribution from the Long-Winded Lady appeared in *The New Yorker* [*LWL* 261–5 and *RG* 'Preface']. Called 'A Daydream', it is a lyrical evocation of the 'sand and sea and roses' of East Hampton, with Bluebell and seagulls. It comes back to earth on the nubbly white counterpane of a bed in New York City, where an air conditioner combats the ninety-three-degree temperature outside. It ends, '. . . there are a number of places I am homesick for. East Hampton is only one of them.' The resigned tone, and the white counterpane, hint that it may have been written in a hospital.

For the people who cared about Maeve, her condition, so far as they were aware of it, was heartbreaking. But she was an adult, and one who had always been protective of her privacy, however profligate she might have been with gifts, anecdotes, advice and even, from time to time, for certain people, confidences. Nobody owned her, or had authority over her. Crucially, too, the time of her illness coincided with a major reduction in the status and authority of mental-health professionals:

> The combination of the antipsychiatry movement, a new breed of civil rights lawyers and the arrival of antipsychotic drugs all served to support policy-makers in their decision to lower the mental hospital population by discharging large numbers of patients and supporting more restrictive commitment laws.[64]

In the wake of the civil rights movement of the 1960s, a nineteenth-century system of involuntary confinement for the mentally ill, which had reached its peak in the mid-1950s, was swifty dismantled in favour of what became known as 'care in the community'. Now only those deemed dangerous were obliged to remain in hospital. While this had advantages for many patients, it led to a huge increase in the number of people living rough, since those dependent for their stability on medication typically stopped taking it, as Maeve did, when left to their own devices. Increasing conservatism in the 1980s led to these policies being revised, but until they were, Maeve was free simply to disappear for long stretches of time, and that was what she did. Like the lost cat Bianca in her own 1966 story, 'She was nowhere to be found. She was nowhere. There [was] no end to [her] story because nobody [knew] what happened to her' [*RG* 258].

If Maeve's former colleagues at *The New Yorker* spoke about her by the late 1970s, it was only among themselves, for their own powerlessness to help her more effectively had caused them deep distress. From time to time, though, she would suddenly reappear. Former colleagues might see her in the street, or sitting among the homeless people around the Rockefeller Center, but she gave no sign of recognition.[65] Philip Hamburger was singularly favoured the last time he saw her, however. It was in the street, somewhere in the Forties, not far from the *New Yorker* offices, and all at once Maeve was before him, saying crisply, 'Hello, Philip.' Joseph Mitchell, one of her closest friends over many years, was particularly astonished when he heard of it.

The discreet silence of Maeve's friends was probably the reason why Mary Hawthorne, recently appointed as an editor, had never heard of Maeve Brennan when she arrived for work on the twentieth floor one morning in 1981 to find a very small woman in a long, untidy black skirt, with grey, unwashed hair, sitting in silence outside the Plexiglas partition, staring at the floor. She sat there till evening, and returned the next day.[66] Hawthorne took the trouble to ask some questions, and learn more about Maeve, but she never saw her again.

In 'I See You, Bianca', Maeve had written plaintively that 'It should not be a problem, to have shelter without being shut away' [*RG* 256], and Milton Greenstein had made efforts to ensure that, in Maxwell's words, 'there was a place she could go to when she chose, and be fed and sheltered'. Even in her state of disarray, Maeve contrived to take care of herself somehow. Although they had no direct contact with her, those in control at *The New Yorker* knew that withdrawals were being made from the bank account they had opened in her name. And she was writing. On 5 January 1981, the day before her sixty-fourth birthday, *The New Yorker* published a final communication from the Long-Winded Lady.[67] Maeve had always been scrupulous about sending Christmas and New Year greetings to her friends, and this was clearly intended as a letter to one or more of them: perhaps a family letter to the Maxwells. In it she is completely herself: wry, profound, resigned and, as so many people remembered her, kind.

It is heartening to think that Maeve's intelligence and pleasure in life remained, even though this impeccably stylish woman had stopped bothering to make herself presentable. Once again, she expresses herself in terms of clothing:

I went off to make some coffee for myself, and while I waited for the water to boil I considered all the nonrandom 'observations' I had so portentously lined up for your inspection. While I looked them over, they began to vanish, and finally they had all vanished – all gone, and a good thing too. They would have made very dull reading.

They were a stilted crowd and rather disagreeable, as though they had found themselves at a party that was not quite what they'd expected and where their clothes were all wrong. They all wore elaborate taffeta ball gowns that seem to belong in the eighteenth century, and each ball gown was a different shade of green.

They vanished one by one, but their departure seemed sudden, and I think now they weren't observations at all but complaints, and, if so, they have gone into the complaints department, where I never look around at all. There are too many mirrors in there for my liking.

The piece goes on to describe a familiar shadow that leads the writer back once more to Cherryfield Avenue in Ranelagh, and to a memory of happy childhood, when she belonged to a family, and a house, in a street that was a community. As Maeve's letters so often did, it ends with loving wishes; this time, it expresses them as a prayer, of the kind she would have heard many times in her Catholic childhood:

I must tell you now that I am praying to Almighty God for blessings on your house, with extra blessings to go with you whenever you leave the house, so that wherever you are you will be safe.

Blessings on your house. Happy New Year.

Epilogue

She began to believe that she had been remembered at some time far back, at some moment when she had thought herself down and out and forgotten and derided. It had all been only in her imagination, that she had been forgotten. She had not been forgotten at all.

– Maeve Brennan, 'A Free Choice'

Maeve Brennan's work began to be rediscovered at about the same time as new mental-health legislation allowed others to intervene on her behalf and find accommodation for her in a nursing home.

When Mary Hawthorne saw Maeve for the first and only time in 1981, and realised that this mysterious and pathetic-seeming woman had sat patiently all day outside the *New Yorker* offices, she was concerned enough to make enquiries. And when her interest led her to read Maeve's work, and then to track down the former *Harper's Bazaar* photographer Karl Bissinger, she was amazed at the portrait that emerged. Bissinger's contact sheets from thirty years earlier showed an exquisitely self-possessed young woman, while the magazine's back numbers revealed a profound and subtle writing talent whose prophetic insight was evident only in retrospect.

McKelway died in 1980, Maeve's sister Emer in 1986, then in 1987, the University of Delaware Library acquired a large collection of papers that had been Maeve's, including several typescripts of her father's work, which she had brought back to the US after his funeral. Another collection came to light when Charles Justice, of Blowing Rock, North Carolina, bought her big blue box with brass corners, full of papers and photographs, in a second-hand bookshop in Massachusetts. It had come there following a fire at Carrolls, the Movers, in Duxbury, where Maeve had left it in storage some-time after 1974.

In summer 1988, William Maxwell wrote a brief essay about Maeve for the short-lived literary journal *WigWag*. He had been rereading *The Long-Winded Lady* after nearly twenty years, and comparing it to Turgenev's *A Sportsman's Notebook*. He did not mention the forty or so of her short stories that he had himself edited, or what had become of their author, but his essay was enough to send Christopher Carduff, a senior book editor at

Houghton Mifflin and a Maxwell devotee, in search of her other work. In Carduff's own words, he fell in love, and began to try to have the stories reissued, rescuing them from the sometimes unfortunate order in which they had appeared in Maeve's two published collections.[1]

Fiction writer Ellen Wilbur, of Cambridge, Massachusetts, encountered Maeve's work in 1989, when 'The Drowned Man' appeared alongside one of her own stories in an anthology called *Wives and Husbands: 20 Short Stories about Marriage*. Despite a long-time interest in Ireland, Wilbur had never heard of Maeve Brennan.[2] Much impressed, she asked the actor and playwright Mary Manning (by then living in Cambridge for many years) what she knew about this enigmatic writer. Born in 1906, Manning had played Lady Sterne in Bob's play *Bystander* in Dublin more than fifty years before. She had known Maeve as a child and was able to tell Wilbur a little about her career and devastating illness. Wilbur's interest was piqued. She searched out Maeve's other work, and then proceeded to promote it enthusiastically among friends and fellow writers.

Around 1990, Richard Rupp, a professor of English at Appalachian State University in Boone, North Carolina, acquired Maeve's blue box from his friend Charles Justice.[3] He managed to track Maeve down to the Lawrence Nursing Home in Arverne, New York, and telephoned her there late in 1992. Staff at the nursing home did not know that she had been a writer, and Maeve herself seemed to receive the news with some surprise. She told Rupp that she was 'going home now', and he took her to mean that she intended to walk to Cherryfield Avenue in Dublin. Rupp was able to provide the nursing home with an address for some of Maeve's relatives, and the following March, her niece in England received a packet containing a photograph of Maeve, taken in the nursing home, and a note from her in a faltering hand. '. . . . I write every day in the Irish Press and get paid,' Maeve has written. 'I am married to John Kyoss. That is not how it is spelled & I have a lot of children, boys and girls.' The picture shows her looking cheerful, grinning at the camera. The word 'Kyoss' could be 'Jyoss'. Perhaps at the end of her days, Maeve's fantasy husband was James Joyce.

Maeve was well cared for at the Lawrence Nursing Home, which prides itself on allowing patients to keep their pets with them. Her niece planned to visit her, but Maeve died suddenly, of heart failure, on 1 November 1993, aged seventy-six. *The New Yorker* contacted Robert Patrick, now blind and living in retirement in Florida, and between them they organised a memorial service in a Catholic church not far from the *New Yorker* offices. Maeve's nephew, Robert M. Brennan, and about twenty former colleagues attended. Her body was cremated, and her ashes sent to her family.

In 1997, in the US, Houghton Mifflin published *The Springs of Affection:*

Stories of Dublin, with a loving and thoughtful Introduction by William Maxwell. Christopher Carduff had placed the stories Maeve wrote about the house where she had grown up in a sequence that at last allowed them to be read as the major work they are. Alice Munro, Edna O'Brien and Mavis Gallant provided warm endorsements for the cover; Edward Albee was one of those who took part in a memorial celebration at the Algonquin Hotel, and the *London Review of Books* published an eloquent and thoughtful five-page essay on Maeve by Mary Hawthorne.[4] Three years later, Harper-Collins published a paperback edition in London.[5] It did not include Maxwell's Introduction, in which he had written, 'I don't know whether in Ireland she is considered an Irish writer or an American. In fact, both countries ought to be proud to claim her.' In the end, both countries have claimed her: each of the four Maeve Brennan books now in print received sheaves of enthusiastic reviews on publication. At the beginning of a new century, hers is a voice that can explain what it felt like to live then, in Ireland and in New York. More importantly, perhaps, it helps us to understand what it means to live now.

PERMISSIONS

NOTES

Author's Note and Acknowledgements

1. *Irish Times*, 2 January 1998.
2. Full information on sources appears in the Notes and the Permissions. In order to protect the privacy of people still living, I have silently edited Maeve Brennan's letters in a very few places.

Introduction

1. See e.g., Susan Engel, *Context is Everything: The Nature of Memory* (New York: W. H. Freeman, 1999), and Ciaran Benson, *The Cultural Psychology of Self* (London: Routledge, 2001), p. 47.
2. Jacques Le Goff, 'Writing Historical Biography Today', *Current Sociology/La sociologie contemporaine*, Vol. 43, No. 2/3 (1995), pp. 11–17, at pp. 13 and 14.
3. An important new study, published when work on this book had been completed, is P. J. Mathews, *Revival: The Abbey Theatre, Sinn Fein, The Gaelic League and the Co-operative Movement* (Cork: Cork University Press, and South Bend: University of Notre Dame Press, Critical Conditions: Field Day Essays and Monographs 12, 2003).

1. The Bolgers of Coolnaboy

1. *Cúil* means a corner, a tucked-away place; it is the first element in many Wexford place-names. Within a mile or so of Coolnaboy are Coolamain, Coolakip, Coolaknick and Coolaknickbeg. Thanks to Dónall Mac Giolla Easpaig of Oifig na Logainmneacha, the Irish place-names office.
2. I am deeply grateful (in the order in which I first spoke to them) to Máire Peoples, Ita Doyle, Yvonne Jerrold, Roddy Doyle, Johnny and Eileen Bolger, Lizzie Doyle, Mairéad Parker, Breda Dunne, Matt Bolger, Joan Doyle, Jim Bolger and Rory Doyle, for allowing me to interview them, and for sharing their memories of

Maeve Brennan and of the Bolger and Whitty families of Coolnaboy and Pouldearg.

3. See Alan Gailey, *Rural Houses of the North of Ireland* (Edinburgh: John McDonald Publishers, 1984), chapters 8 and 9, and Frank McDonald and Peigín Doyle, *Ireland's Earthen Houses*, with photographs by Hugh McConville (Dublin: A. and A. Farmar, 1997).

4. George Bassett, *Wexford County: Guide and Directory* (Dublin: Sealy, Bryers and Walker, 1885). Maps and road signs spell the name of the Bolgers' nearest village as 'Oilgate', but neither place-name has any connection with oil. The Oyle (in Irish, *An Aill*: 'the cliff'/ 'the raised ground') is the older name.

5. Family tradition as told by Bessie Bolger to her husband's niece, Mairéad Parker. Author's interview with Mairéad Parker, 12 July 2001. Like many Wexford families (with names like Lambert, Devereux, D'Arcy, Keating, Roche), the Whittys' origins were Anglo-Norman.

6. Family historian Matt Bolger, Enniscorthy, interview with the author, 23 March 2002.

7. Yvonne Jerrold, John Bolger's great-granddaughter, was told that he fell in the lane at Coolnaboy on the day the family was to move in: interview with the author, 3 December 2002.

8. NAI, Census of Ireland, 1901, Co. Wexford.

9. Máire Peoples, interview with the author, 25 August 2000.

10. Compare David Fitzpatrick, 'Marriage in Post-Famine Ireland' and Brendan M. Walsh, 'Marriage in Ireland in the Twentieth Century', in Art Cosgrove (ed.), *Marriage in Ireland* (Dublin: College Press, 1985), pp. 116–31, 132–50, and Joseph Lee, *The Modernisation of Irish Society 1848–1918* (Dublin: Gill and Macmillan, 1989 [1973]), pp. 1–9, for late marriage and celibacy among landowning families.

11. Family tradition records that Eliza Harper, née Whitty (1848–1925), known as 'Nannie', emigrated to the United States with her husband. They had one child, who died, following which Eliza's husband left her, and she suffered a breakdown, before returning to Ireland at her brother's invitation. She and her husband are buried together, however, in Crossabeg cemetery, near Oylegate.

12. For a study of women and housework in Ireland, see Caitriona Clear, *Women of the House: Women's Household Work in Ireland 1922–1961* (Dublin: Irish Academic Press, 2000).

13. Nancy Scheper-Hughes, *Saints, Scholars and Schizophrenics: Mental Illness in Rural Ireland* (Berkeley: University of California Press, 1979); this book caused outrage in Ireland on its publication. For the sibling bond: Maureen Murphy, 'The Fionnuala Factor: Irish Sibling Emigration at the Turn of the Century', in Anthony Bradley and Maryann Valiulis (eds), *Gender and Sexuality in Modern Ireland* (Amherst: University of Massachusetts Press / American Conference

for Irish Studies, 1997), pp. 85–101, and poet Nuala Ní Dhomhnaill in conversation with the author. Irish versions of the international ballad 'The Two Sisters' feature a treacherous mother-in-law or maid instead of the murderous sister of the English and Scottish versions, while in the poetic lament tradition, the wife and sister of a dead man typically engage in mutual insults, each asserting the primacy of her own relation with him: see Angela Bourke, 'Lamenting the Dead', in Angela Bourke, Siobhán Kilfeather, Maria Luddy, Margaret MacCurtain, Gerardine Meaney, Máirín Ní Dhonnchadha, Mary O'Dowd and Clair Wills (eds), *The Field Day Anthology of Irish Writing, vol. 4: Irish Women's Writing and Traditions* (Cork: Cork University Press, 2002), pp. 1365–98. Examples could be multiplied.

14. Lee, *The Modernisation of Irish Society*, p.18. See also Caitriona Clear, *Nuns in Nineteenth-Century Ireland* (Dublin: Gill and Macmillan; Washington, DC: The Catholic University of America Press, 1987).

15. Mary Agnes Whitty nursed the sick in the Crimean War, while her sister Ellen (Mother Vincent Whitty), was a formidable administrator and spiritual leader. Aged 42 in 1861, she was Superior-General of the Mercy order in Dublin when the new Bishop of Brisbane, James Quinn, begged her to assist him in Australia. She founded more than twenty convents, schools and hospitals in Queensland, but never forgot Pouldearg where she had grown up. On her death in March 1892, the *Australian* noted that she had loved the Slaney, and its flocks of wild duck, geese and swans, and that 'to the end of her days she recalled the bright arc of the salmon's leap'. See Sister Mary Xaverius O'Donoghue, *Mother Vincent Whitty: Woman and Educator in a Masculine Society* (Melbourne: Melbourne University Press, 1972), pp. 5–6. Mother Vincent is commemorated with a statue in Brisbane, and in the name of Whitty Street, Canberra.

16. Yvonne Jerrold (Una Brennan's granddaughter), e-mail to the author, 15 October 2000.

17. The Loreto Convent and school in Enniscorthy were opened in 1872. See Dan Walsh (compiler), *Images of Ireland: Enniscorthy* (Dublin: Gill and Macmillan, 1998), pp. 68–9.

18. Clear, *Nuns*, pp. 50, 104, 120–5. See also Margaret MacCurtain, *Godly Burden: Catholic Sisterhoods in Twentieth-Century Ireland*, in Bradley and Valiulis (eds), *Gender and Sexuality in Modern Ireland*, pp. 245–56.

19. Compare Mary Carbery, *The Farm by Lough Gur* (Cork and Dublin: Mercier, 1937), where Sissy contrasts life on the farm with that of her convent boarding-school.

20. Photographs taken in 1906 and 1909 of outings from Wexford and New Ross show several bicycles, all with solid tyres: Nicholas Furlong and John Hayes, *County Wexford in the Rare Oul' Times: County Wexford from the Earliest Photographs*

(1850–1914), Vol. 1 (Wexford: Old Distillery Press, 1985), Nos. 101, 104.

21. Membership card, Private collection, Cambridge, UK.

22. Douglas Hyde, 'On the Necessity for De-Anglicizing Ireland', in *The Revival of Irish Literature* (London, 1894). For a discussion, see Declan Kiberd, *Inventing Ireland* (London: Jonathan Cape, 1995), pp. 140–5.

23. Published together in 1905 as *The Philosophy of Irish Ireland*. See Patrick Maume, *D. P. Moran* (Dublin: Historical Association of Ireland, 1995).

24. Kevin Whelan, *The Tree of Liberty: Radicalism, Catholicism and the Construction of Irish Identity 1760–1830* (Cork: Cork University Press, in association with Field Day, 1996), pp. 169–73.

25. For women's lives in all classes in Ireland in the nineteenth century see, for example, Clear, *Nuns*, pp. 1–35, and Bourke et al. (eds), *Field Day Anthology of Irish Writing, vol 5.* (Cork: Cork University Press, 1987), *passim.*

26. See Maureen Murphy, 'The Fionnuala Factor', and Hasia Diner, *Erin's Daughters in America: Irish Immigrant Women in the Nineteenth Century* (Baltimore and London: Johns Hopkins University Press, 1983).

27. See Carol Coulter, *The Hidden Tradition: Feminism, Women and Nationalism in Ireland* (Cork: Cork University Press, 1993), pp. 19 ff.; Margaret Ward, *Unmanageable Revolutionaries: Women and Irish Nationalism* (London: Pluto Press, 1995 [1989]), pp. 4–39.

28. One reason given for the League's success was the unprecedented opportunity this afforded for social interaction between men and women.

29. See Michael J. F. McCarthy, *Five Years in Ireland: 1895–1900* (London: Simpkin, Marshall, Hamilton, Kent; Dublin: Hodges Figgis, 1901), pp. 481–8; Ward, *Unmanageable Revolutionaries*, pp. 47–50.

30. Ward, *Unmanageable Revolutionaries*, pp. 40–87.

31. A correspondent in *Bean na h-Éireann*, the organisation's monthly magazine, Vol. 1, No. 6 Aibreán [April] 1909: 'The women of Irish Ireland have the franchise . . . They stand on equal footing with the men in the Gaelic League, in Sinn Féin, and the Industrial Movement . . . The fact that they have not received the imprimatur of a hostile Government will worry no Nationalist woman.'

32. See Nell Regan, 'Helena Molony', in Mary Cullen and Maria Luddy (eds), *Female Activists, 1900–1960: Irish Women and Change* (Dublin: Woodfield Press, 2001), pp. 141–68.

33. Medb Ruane, 'Kathleen Lynn', in Cullen and Luddy, *Female Activists*, p. 69; cf. Robert Welch (ed.), *The Oxford Companion to Irish Literature* (1996), p. 259.

34. *Echo*, Gaelic League Notes, Friday, 24 January 1908.

35. Otherwise known as Ned Foley and Fred Cogley, of Wexford.

2. Bob and Una

1. Five generations of the Brennan family have named a son Robert. This work will refer throughout to Maeve's father as 'Bob' (as his family and friends did), so as to distinguish him from his father Robert and his son Robert Patrick.

2. Nicholas Furlong and John Hayes, *County Wexford in the Rare Oul' Times: County Wexford from the Earliest Photographs (1850–1914)*, Vol. 1 (Wexford: Old Distillery Press, 1985), especially Nos 219–26.

3. Ibid., Vol. 1, No. 218.

4. Ibid., Vol. 1, No. 171. In later years, the railway was extended for three more miles, and the new Rosslare Harbour eventually made Wexford port redundant.

5. NAI, Census of Ireland, 1901 Co. Wexford. The 1911 census shows Bob's three sisters as younger than that of 1901 would predict: Teresa's age is given as 28, Annie's as 24, and Christine's as 20. A family of lodgers shared the house with them. Their mother, too, seems to have been coy about her age, giving it as 40 in 1901, and 50 in 1911; on her death in 1938 she was said to be 'in her 82nd year' (*Echo*, 1 October 1938).

6. Bob Brennan's autobiography, *Allegiance* (Dublin: Browne and Nolan, 1950), p. 4, mentions five children, but only four appear to have survived to adulthood.

7. Joseph Ranson, C.C., *Songs of the Wexford Coast* (Wexford: John English, 1975 [1948]), p. 27. Thanks to Nicky Furlong for this reference. Ranson collected the song fragment from an old man in Wexford in April 1943.

8. R. Brennan, *Allegiance*, pp. 3–4; George Bassett, *Wexford County: Guide and Directory* (Dublin: Sealy, Bryers and Walker, 1885); author's interviews in Wexford, March 2002.

9. R. Brennan, *Allegiance*, p. 4. His hair and eye colour were recorded in Waterford Prison after his arrest in 1916: NAI, Prisons 1/39/23 (Waterford), No. 231.

10. NLI MSS, Robert Brennan Papers (Acc. 5584, uncatalogued), typescript essay, 'Mainly Meandering: The Best Detective Story', written for the *Irish Press* circa 1957.

11. R. Brennan, *Allegiance*, p. 246; Robert Brennan, *The Man who Walked like a Dancer* (London: Rich and Cowan, 1951), p. 72; his essay, 'The Best Detective Story', calls *The Wrong Box* 'one of the funniest mysteries written in English', adding 'I have never had enough time for reading, but I have read this book many times': NLI MSS, Robert Brennan Papers.

12. Robert Louis Stevenson and Lloyd Osbourne, *The Wrong Box* (London: Longmans, Green and Co., 1889), p. 35.

13. NLI MSS, Robert Brennan Papers.

14. R. Brennan, *Allegiance*, pp. 4, 16–17; Cf. *SA* 316, 328, 333.

15. R. Brennan, *Allegiance*, pp. 5–6. For a photograph taken on the occasion of Hyde's visit, see Furlong and Hayes, *County Wexford*, Vol. 1, No. 158.

16. Jeanne Sheehy, *The Rediscovery of Ireland's Past: The Celtic Revival, 1830–1930* (London: Thames and Hudson, 1980), p. 147; Maureen Keane, *Ishbel: Lady Aberdeen in Ireland* (Newtownards: Colourpoint, 1999), pp. 67, 234–5.

17. The Arts and Crafts Society of Ireland was founded in 1894. By the early twentieth century, it had begun to influence church decoration away from German glass and Italian marble and towards Irish products: Sheehy, *Rediscovery*, pp. 152–6.

18. The Light Railways (Ireland) Act of 1889 provided subsidies to encourage railway companies to extend their services into the so-called 'congested districts' of the west. Henry first went to Achill Island in 1910. From 1925, his work was widely used in railway posters. See S. B. Kennedy, *Paul Henry* (New Haven and London: Yale University Press, 2000).

19. S. J. Connolly (ed.), *The Oxford Companion to Irish History* (1988), p. 599.

20. *Echo* (Enniscorthy), 17 January 1908, front page.

21. NAI, Census of Ireland, 1901, 1911, Co. Wexford.

22. Patrick Bolger, *The Irish Co-operative Movement* (Dublin: Institute of Public Administration, 1977).

23. See Patrick Maume, *D. P. Moran* (Dublin: Historical Association of Ireland, 1995).

24. Margaret Ward, *Unmanageable Revolutionaries: Women and Irish Nationalism* (London: Pluto Press, 1995 [1989]), pp. 55–7; Máire Nic Shiubhlaigh, *The Splendid Years*, (Dublin: J. Duffy, 1955), p. 17; R. F. Foster, *W. B. Yeats: A Life, Vol. I: The Apprentice Mage* (Oxford: Oxford University Press, 1997), p. 261. For the play's authorship, see James Pethica, 'Our Kathleen: Yeats's Collaboration with Lady Gregory in the Writing of Cathleen ni Houlihan', *Yeats Annual*, No. 6 (1988); Antoinette Quinn, 'Staging the Irish Peasant Woman', in Nicholas Grene (ed.), *Interpreting Synge: Essays from the Synge Summer School 1991–2000* (Dublin: Lilliput, 2000), pp. 117–34.

25. W. B. Yeats, *Collected Poems* (Second edition, London: Macmillan 1985 [1950]), p. 393.

26. R. Brennan, *Allegiance*, p. 11. For a discussion of the play, the Inghinidhe and Maud Gonne, see Antoinette Quinn, 'Cathleen ni Houlihan Writes Back: Maud Gonne and Irish Nationalist Theater', in Anthony Bradley and Maryann Valiulis (eds), *Gender and Sexuality in Modern Ireland* (Amherst: University of Massachusetts Press/American Conference for Irish Studies, 1997), pp. 39–59.

27. The nativity play was also based on traditional oral poetry in Irish (which Hyde would go on to publish in his *Abhráin Diadha Chúige Connacht*, or *Religious Songs of Connacht*, in 1906); this time, however, the material came from apocryphal religious traditions that had circulated in European folklore since long before the Reformation and Counter-Reformation. One of the play's stories, about a tree that bowed down when the pregnant Virgin Mary expressed a craving for its fruit, came from the international ballad called 'The Cherry-tree

Carol'. The other story was part of a charm against abdominal pain, once current all over Europe, and still found in Irish: about a couple who offer the Holy Family only a bed of flax husks to sleep on, but are later grateful when Mary cures the man's severe pain. Priests in Kilkenny objected to the staging of the play, as possibly leading to confusion between superstition and dogma, and it had to wait until 1911 for its first performance at the Abbey. See Robert Welch (ed.), *The Oxford Companion to Irish Literature* (1996), s.v. 'Abbey Theatre', and Janet Egleson Dunleavy and Gareth W. Dunleavy, *Douglas Hyde, A Maker of Modern Ireland* (Berkeley: University of California Press, 1991), pp. 223–5.

28. See Sheehy, *Rediscovery*, pp. 152–63, and compare Tom Peete Cross and Clark Harris Slover, *Ancient Irish Tales* (New York: Barnes and Noble, 1996 [1936]), p. 155.

29. *Bean na h-Éireann*, Vol. 1, No. 6, April 1909, p. 1.

30. *Ireland's Own*, Vol. 1, No. 1, 26 November 1902.

31. See Helen Brennan, *The Story of Irish Dance* (Dingle: Brandon, 1999).

32. R. Brennan, *Allegiance*, p. 17.

33. Sometimes rendered in Irish orthography as 'haoghaire faoghaire' (by analogy with Dún Laoghaire – Dunleary – the native name of Kingstown, steamship port for Dublin).

34. R. Brennan, *Allegiance*, p. 17.

35. *Irish Homestead*, 29 May 1909; see also Nicholas Allen, *George Russell (Æ) and the New Ireland* (Dublin: Four Courts Press, 2003).

36. Nic Shiubhlaigh, *The Splendid Years*, p. 15.

37. For nostalgic pastoral, see Seamus Deane, *Strange Country: Modernity and Nationhood in Irish Writing since 1790* (Oxford: Clarendon Press, 1997), p. 90. For the 'ranch war', see David S. Jones, 'The Cleavage between Graziers and Peasants in the Land Struggle', in Samuel Clark and James S. Donnelly, Jr. (eds), *Irish Peasants: Violence and Political Unrest, 1780–1914* (Manchester: Manchester University Press, 1983), pp. 374–417.

38. See, for instance, Edward Lysaght's novel, *The Gael* (Dublin and London: Maunsel & Co., 1919), which is set in the years after 1905, pp. 83–4.

39. R. Brennan, *Allegiance*, pp. 9–10. Brennan suggests that the other woman IRB member was Maud Gonne; Ruth Taillon, however, in her *When History Was Made: The Women of 1916* (Belfast: Beyond the Pale Press, 1996), p. 19, considers Kathleen Clarke, wife of IRB leader Tom Clarke, to be a more likely candidate.

40. Published in the *Irish Times Weekend Special*, 25 November 2000, p. 2.

41. *Bean na h-Éireann*, Vol. 1, No. 10 (August 1909), p. 8.

42. R. Brennan, *Allegiance*, p. 24.

43. A pattern was at once an expression of popular religion and a commercial opportunity. Like many others, this well had been closed a century earlier, when progressive landowners found the traditional, often Rabelaisian, practices at

holy wells to be distressingly medieval: see John O'Donovan, *Ordnance Survey Letters, Wexford*, Vol. 2, p. 95 (typescript copy of 1840 original, Department of Irish Folklore, University College Dublin). See also Anna Rackard and Liam O'Callaghan, *FishStone Water: Holy Wells of Ireland*, with an Introduction by Angela Bourke (Cork: Atrium, 2001), pp. 7–12, 78–9.

44. R. Brennan, *Allegiance*, pp. 25–6.

45. Manus is a name usually associated with County Donegal, but this may have been a version of 'Munn', a traditional name in County Wexford. Munn was an early Christian saint in whose honour a holy well was reopened in Brownscastle, Co. Wexford, in 1912.

46. See especially 'The Eldest Child', *SA* 264–72.

47. Rosemary Cullen Owens, *Smashing Times: A History of the Irish Women's Suffrage Movement 1876–1922* (Dublin: Attic Press, 1996 [1984]), p. 52, calls Sears 'a keen supporter of women's rights' and notes that he sent a message of support to a mass meeting of suffrage women in Dublin, June 1912 (ref. to *Irish Citizen*, 8 June 1912).

48. R. Brennan, *Allegiance*, p. 31; Joseph Lee *The Modernisation of Irish Society 1848–1918* (Dublin: Gill and Macmillan, 1989 [1973]), p. 152.

49. R. Brennan, *Allegiance*, pp. 45–6; NLI MSS, Robert Brennan Papers, 'Printed Programme of Emmet Commemoration Concert, Enniscorthy, 1 March 1916'.

50. NAI, General Register of Prisoners, Waterford (1 October 1914–18 December 1929): 39/23 V16–32–7.

51. R. Brennan, *Allegiance*, pp. 95–6.

3. *Belgrave Road*

1. My thanks to Deirdre McMahon. The letter de Valera wrote from Mountjoy Prison on 11 May 1916, telling his wife that his death sentence had been commuted, ended 'Kiss Viv, Máirín, Éamon and Brian for me. Be of good courage. May God keep you under his special care till we meet. As ever, Dev': *Irish Times Weekend Special,* 25 November 2000, p. 2. See also Marie O'Neill, *Grace Gifford Plunkett and Irish Freedom: Tragic Bride of 1916* (Dublin and Portland, Oregon: Irish Academic Press, 2000).

2. Kevin O'Connor, *Ironing the Land: The Coming of the Railways to Ireland* (Dublin: Gill and Macmillan, 1999), p. 97. This chapter and the next are indebted to Deirdre Kelly, *Four Roads to Dublin: The History of Ranelagh, Rathmines and Leeson Street* (Dublin: O'Brien Press, 1995), and to Séamas Ó Maitiú, *Rathmines Township, 1847–1930* (Dublin: City of Dublin Vocational Education Committee, 1997).

3. Kelly, *Four Roads to Dublin*, pp. 229–30.

4. See Christopher W. Haden and Catherine O'Malley, *The Demesne of Old*

Rathmines: An Historical Survey of Upper Rathmines, Dartry and Milltown (Dublin: Campanile Press, 1988), pp. 39–41.

5. Round towers, dating from the tenth to the thirteenth century, are unique to Ireland and were a common motif of the Irish Revival. Consecrated in 1914, the Church of the Holy Name replaced a wooden chapel of ease built in 1898; it may have been modelled on a twelfth-century church in Lusk, north of Dublin, whose square tower embraces an earlier round tower.

6. Diarmuid Breathnach agus Máire Ní Mhurchú, *1882–1982 Beathaisnéis a Dó*, (Baile Átha Cliath: An Clóchomhar, 1990), pp. 38–9. Thanks to Honor Ó Brolcháin for additional information.

7. Medb Ruane, 'Kathleen Lynn' in Mary Cullen and Maria Luddy (eds), *Female Activists: Irish Women and Change 1900–1960* (Dublin: Woodfield Press, 2001), pp. 61–88. Cf. Bríd Mahon, *While Green Grass Grows: Memoirs of a Folklorist* (Cork: Mercier, 1998), pp. 148–50.

8. *Ranelagh News*, October 1983, p. 4.

9. My thanks to Celia de Fréine for this information.

10. Birth certificate, Robert Brennan and Maeve Brennan Papers, University of Delaware Library, Special Collections, Newark, Del., USA, F60. The fact that Maeve described herself as 'a 1916 baby' led to her birth date being given in some sources as January 1916.

11. NAI, Census of Ireland, 1911, Dublin, and Thom's *Directory*, 1916.

12. Robert Brennan and Maeve Brennan Papers, University of Delaware, F18, essay, p. 8.

13. Robert Brennan, *Allegiance* (Dublin: Brown and Nolan, 1950), pp. 114–15; cf. Timothy G. McMahon (ed.), *Pádraig Ó Fathaigh's War of Independence: Recollections of a Galway Gaelic Leaguer* (Cork: Cork University Press, Irish Narratives series, 2000).

14. R. Brennan, *Allegiance*, p. 118. One of them was later published as *The False Finger Tip* (Dublin and London: Maunsel and Roberts, 1921); the other may have been *The Toledo Dagger* (London: John Hamilton, 1926).

15. Frank Gallagher ('David Hogan'), *The Four Glorious Years* (Dublin: Irish Press Ltd, 1953). The book's title is taken from de Valera's speech on the occasion of the Dáil's accepting the Treaty with Britain in January 1922 (p. 375).

16. See Gallagher, *Glorious Years*, pp. 3–5.

17. Dr Kathleen Lynn Diary, 1916–1955, Royal College of Physicians, Ireland. My thanks to Margaret Ó hÓgartaigh for this and subsequent references.

18. R. Brennan, *Allegiance*, p. 161.

19. Ronan Fanning, Michael Kennedy and Eunan O'Halpin (eds), *Documents on Irish Foreign Policy, Vol. I, 1919–22* (Dublin: Royal Irish Academy and Department of Foreign Affairs, 1998), No. 102, August 1921; R. Brennan, *Allegiance*, p. 162.

20 R. Brennan, *Allegiance*, p. 164.

21. Ibid., pp. 167 ff.; Gallagher, *Glorious Years*, p. 46.

22. Kathleen McKenna, 'The Irish Bulletin', *The Capuchin Annual*, 1970, pp. 503–27, at p. 511.

23. Gallagher, *Glorious Years*, p. 47.

24. Dr Kathleen Lynn Diary.

25. Ruane, 'Kathleen Lynn', p. 76. The hospital is now the Charlemont Clinic.

26. Dr Kathleen Lynn Diary.

27. R. Brennan, *Allegiance*, p. 190.

28. Gallagher, *Glorious Years*, p. 48.

29. R. Brennan, *Allegiance*, p. 196.

30. My thanks to Honor Ó Brolcháin for this information.

31. Yvonne Jerrold, e-mail to the author.

32. Leah Levenson and Jerry H. Natterstad, *Hanna Sheehy-Skeffington, Irish Feminist* (Syracuse, NY: Syracuse University Press, 1986), p. 129.

33. Ruane, 'Kathleen Lynn', p.79; Levenson and Natterstad, *Hanna Sheehy-Skeffington*, p. 131.

34. Gallagher, *Glorious Years*, p. 252; T. Ryle-Dwyer, *Eamon de Valera* (Dublin: Gill and Macmillan, 1980), p. 145.

35. Gallagher, *Glorious Years*, pp. 83–119; R. Brennan, *Allegiance*, pp. 264 ff.; McKenna, 'Irish Bulletin'; see also Keiko Inoue, 'Propaganda of Dáil Éireann: from Truce to Treaty', *Éire-Ireland*, Vol. 32, Nos 2 & 3 (Summer/Fall 1997), pp. 154–72.

36. NLI MSS, Robert Brennan Papers (Acc. 5584, uncatalogued).

37. R. Brennan, *Allegiance*, pp. 267–8.

38. Ibid., p. 244; see also Gallagher, *Glorious Years*, pp. 120–1.

39. R. Brennan, *Allegiance*, p. 246.

40. Erskine Childers, *The Riddle of the Sands: A Record of Secret Service* (London: Penguin, 1952 [1903]), pp. 88–9.

41. All eight articles were published in pamphlet form as *Military Rule in Ireland* (Dublin: The Talbot Press, 1920); see pp. 11–12.

42. R. Brennan, *Allegiance*, pp. 249–52.

43. Roddy Doyle, *A Star Called Henry* (London: Cape, 1999), pp. 241–6, and interview with the author.

44. Gallagher, *Glorious Years*, pp. 160–98; Gallagher's diary of the hunger strike, published as *Days of Fear* (London: John Murray, 1928), was dedicated 'to the memory of Erskine Childers'.

45. Gallagher, *Glorious Years*, p. 77; Childers, *Military Rule*, pp. 44–5.

46. R. Brennan, *Allegiance*, p. 286.

47. Ibid., p. 290.

48. Ibid., pp. 298–301.

49. NAI, DE 2/526; cf. ibid., Memo 23, 18 March 1921, De Valera to RB, 1 April 1921.

50. R. Brennan, *Allegiance*, p. 322; NAI, DE 2/526, Memo 61, Under-Secretary to de Valera, 16 April 1921: cf. McKenna, 'Irish Bulletin', p. 517.

51. See, e.g., Garret FitzGerald, review of Fanning et al., *Documents on Irish Foreign Policy*, Vol. 1, *London Review of Books*, 21 January 1999, p. 20, where he comments scathingly on No. 114, a memo sent by RB, 20 October 1921, probably from Paris, on the need for diplomats to dress appropriately and the expense they incur in doing so.

52. Lizzie Doyle, interview with the author, Coolamain, Co. Wexford, 12 July 2001.

53. R. Brennan, *Allegiance*, p. 322.

4. *Cherryfield Avenue*

1. See William Maxwell, 'Introduction' to *SA* 3.

2. Copy of building lease in author's possession, and NAI, Census of Ireland, 1911, Dublin; cf. Deirdre Kelly, *Four Roads to Dublin: The History of Ranelagh, Rathmines and Leeson Street* (Dublin: O'Brien Press, 1995), pp. 112, 245. The Bewley houses later became part of Gonzaga College and the National College of Ireland. Bailey, Son and Gibson had offices at 4 St Andrew Street, Dublin in 1911: they were a leading Dublin firm of wholesale stationers throughout the twentieth century before being taken over by Smurfits. Their houses, Cherryfield and Hollybank, were demolished in 1996 to make way for a townhouse development.

3. Census returns made soon after they were built offer glimpses of the people who moved in. In 1911, the last house behind Gibson's was occupied by Maude Townshend, aged 53, and Karolina Bast, aged 33, born in Germany and described as a boarder. Both were members of the Church of Ireland, and gave their occupations as 'Suffragist'. Invited in the last column of the census form, 'If Deaf and Dumb; Dumb only; Blind; Imbecile or Idiot; or Lunatic' to write the respective infirmities opposite the names of afflicted persons, both women have written 'Unenfranchised'.

4. Maeve Brennan's description of the houses as 'built of red brick' [*SA* 15] is inaccurate; elsewhere, however, she refers to 'the gray houses across the street' (*SA* 249), and cf. *RG* 204.

5. See Gaston Bachelard, *The Poetics of Space*, trans. Maria Jolas, with a new Foreword by John R. Stilgoe (Boston: Beacon Press, 1994 [1958]); Witold Rybczynski, *Home: A Short History of an Idea* (New York: Penguin, 1987 [1986]), and Paul Oliver, 'A Lighthouse on the Mantelpiece: Symbolism in the Home', in Paul Oliver, Ian Davis and Ian Bentley, *Dunroamin: The Suburban Semi and its Enemies* (London: Pimlico, 1981), pp. 173–92.

6. Cf. Oliver et al., *Dunroamin,* pp. 176–8.

7. See Mona Hearn, 'Life for Domestic Servants in Dublin, 1880–1920', in Maria Luddy and Cliona Murphy (eds), *Women Surviving: Studies in Irish Women's History in the 19th and 20th Centuries* (Dublin: Poolbeg, 1990), pp. 148–79.

8. Joseph Lee, *The Modernisation of Irish Society, 1848–1918* (Dublin: Gill and Macmillan, 1989 [1973]), p. 13, notes that the number of commercial travellers in Ireland had risen from 500 to 4,500 in the previous 50 years.

9. C. S. Andrews, *Dublin Made Me* (Dublin: Lilliput, 2001 [1979]), p. 41: 'If we had read the *Diary of a Nobody* we would have seen ourselves and our social values reflected in every page.' George and Weedon Grossmith's comic classic of lower-middle-class London life was published in 1892.

10. For information about the Brennans' neighbours and details of their built environment, I am indebted to the late Aodhagán Brioscú, retired architect, Dublin, who died on 14 January 2003 as this work was being prepared for publication. Born Hubert Briscoe on 28 March 1920, he lived next door to the Brennans throughout their time in Ranelagh.

11. Frank Gallagher ('David Hogan'), *The Four Glorious Years* (Dublin: Irish Press, 1953), pp. 375–6.

12. Robert Brennan, *Allegiance* (Dublin: Browne and Nolan, 1950), pp. 334 ff.; NLI MSS, Robert Brennan Papers (Acc. 5584, uncatalogued).

13. Ronan Fanning, Michael Kennedy and Eunan O'Halpin (eds), *Documents on Irish Foreign Policy, Vol. 1, 1919–22* (Dublin: Royal Irish Academy and Department of Foreign Affairs, 1998), Introduction, p. xiii.

14. R. Brennan, *Allegiance,* p. 343.

15. Ibid., p. 352; Maurice Harmon, *Sean O'Faolain: A Life* (London: Constable, 1994), p. 59.

16. Andrews, *Dublin Made Me,* p. 278. See also Kelly, *Four Roads to Dublin,* pp. 240–1.

17. R. Brennan, *Allegiance,* pp. 261–2.

18. Aodhagán Brioscú, interview with the author, January 2002.

19. R. Brennan, *Allegiance,* p. 331.

20. Margaret Ward, *Hanna Sheehy Skeffington: A Life* (Cork: Attic Press, 1997), pp. 258–68.

21. Raymonde Kerney to RB (two letters, in French), private collection, Cambridge, UK.

22. Private collection, Cambridge, UK.

23. For their daughter's memoir of growing up in this house, see Roddy Doyle, *Rory and Ita* (London: Cape, 2002).

24. See Terence Brown, *Ireland: A Social and Cultural History 1922–1985* (London: Fontana, 1985 [1981]), pp. 90–1: '[According to the 1926 census], two-thirds of girls between thirteen and fifteen years of age who did not take up agricultural employment became domestic servants, helping to create a total of 87,000

such persons in the state as a whole.' For an account of the eating habits in Dublin in the 1920s and '30s, see Tony Farmar, *Ordinary Lives: The Private Worlds of Three Generations of Ireland's Professional Classes* (Dublin: A. and A. Farmar, 1995 [1991]), pp. 87–98.

25. Aodhagán Brioscú, letter to the author, February 2002.

26. 'The Old Man of the Sea' [*SA* 21–9]; 'The Poor Men and Women' [*SA* 128–47]; 'The Beginning of a Long Story' [*RG* 204–22]. For poor people calling to farms in the nineteenth century, see Mary Carbery, *The Farm by Lough Gur: The Story of Mary Fogarty (Sissy O'Brien)* (Cork: Mercier Press, 1973 [1937]), p. 58.

27. *V* 19, 54, 67.

28. Aodhagán Brioscú, interview with the author.

29. See, for example, *Washington Star*, 28 August 1938: 'Mrs Brennan is an artist at needlework'.

30. *SA* 43; see Nuala O'Connor, 'Maeve Brennan, Irish Writer in Exile', unpublished MA thesis, Anglo-Irish Literature, University College Dublin, The National University of Ireland, Dublin, 2001, pp. 22–4.

31. Gerry Clarke, tennis veteran, telephone interview with the author, Dublin, 2001.

32. See Rose Doyle, 'Vintage Garage Still Motoring On', *Irish Times*, 5 November 2003. My thanks to Frank Smith for additional information.

5. *Remembering Shadows*

1. Rupert was the name of one of Maeve's cats in the 1960s. When 'The Twelfth Wedding Anniversary' was published in *The New Yorker*, 24 September 1966, the big orange cat was called Sebastian.

2. A committee was formed with the object of starting a republican newspaper, and succeeded in collecting £25,000, or half its target amount. The *Freeman's Journal* came on the market, but a bid to buy it failed, and the campaign died. Apart from the £2,000 or so used in promoting the venture, all the money was returned to the subscribers. See Mark O'Neill, *De Valera, Fianna Fáil and the 'Irish Press'* (Dublin and Portland, Oregon: Irish Academic Press, 2001); Peter Pyne, 'The New Irish State and the Decline of the Sinn Féin Party, 1923–1926', *Éire-Ireland*, Vol. 11, No. 3 (1976), pp. 33–65, at 44, and RB, typescript essay, 'The Start of the Irish Press', Robert Brennan and Maeve Brennan Papers, University of Delaware Library, Special Collections, Newark, Del., USA, F17.

3. Aodhagán Brioscú, interview with the author, January 2002.

4. See, for example, RB, 'Mainly Meandering: Jack B. and Charades', typescript, NLI MSS, Robert Brennan Papers (Acc. 5584, uncatalogued); published in the *Irish Press*, *c.* May 1957. For the RDS, see Terence Brown, *Ireland: A Social and Cultural History 1922–1985* (London: Fontana, 1985 [1981]), p. 114.

5. Selskar Kearney, *The False Finger Tip* (Dublin and London: Maunsel and Roberts, 1921).

6. Robert Brennan and Maeve Brennan Papers, University of Delaware, F10, ff.

7. The athlete's 'foreign' name is in fact Old Irish. *Lí Ban* ('colour/beauty of/among women') occurs more than once as a woman's name, but in the twelfth-century manuscript known as the Book of Leinster, Laegaire Liban is a man. His story appears in translation in Standish Hayes O'Grady's two-volume *Silva Gadelica* (1892), exactly the sort of book read by romantic nationalist intellectuals like Robert Brennan. Laegaire was 'the handsomest youth in all Connacht', who fearlessly went to the rescue of an abducted woman and was rewarded with everlasting life in the fairy kingdom.

8. The Briscoe boys next door were not allowed to bring comics into their house: Aodhagán Brioscú, letter to the author, February 2002.

9. See Thom's *Directory*, 1925. Rosamond Jacob wrote in her diary on 4 November 1925 that she and the Brennans' friend Dorothy Macardle had gone with Dorothy's uncle in his car to look at a flat at 16 Herbert Place (which they eventually took) and a house on Cherryfield Avenue that Dorothy's father, Sir Thomas Macardle, head of the Dundalk brewing family, had offered to buy for her (NLI MS 32, 582 [49], Rosamond Jacob Diary, 4 November 1925). My thanks to Nadia Smith for this reference. Jacob and Macardle became lifelong friends after they shared a cell in Mountjoy, 1922–1923, under the Free State government: Damian Doyle, 'Rosamond Jacob (1888–1960)', in Mary Cullen and Maria Luddy (eds), *Female Activists: Irish Women and Change 1900–1960* (Dublin: The Woodfield Press, 2001), pp. 169–92, at 178–9.

10. I am grateful to Mr Mulroney for generously sharing his memories with me in 2002 and to Daragh Queenan for permission to quote from the website of St Mary's College, Rathmines: http://www.stmaryscollegecssp.ie/harcourt/contentframe.html. See also Brian Mac Aongusa, *The Harcourt Street Line: Back on Track* (Dublin: Currach Press, 2003).

11. Maeve's niece recalls that a Bishop Heffernan visited the family after many years in Africa, but he came to Derry's house in Dublin in the 1950s, not to Cherryfield Avenue in the 1920s (Yvonne Jerrold, personal communication).

6. *Cross and Passion*

1. See Frances Kiernan, 'Fiction at *The New Yorker*', *American Scholar*, September 1998: 'The third piece [of fiction], which ran in back, was usually but not always reminiscence. At *The New Yorker*, memoirs had always been handled as fiction'. Compare Ben Yagoda, *About Town:* The New Yorker *and the World it Made* (New York: Da Capo, 2000), pp. 72, 250–5.

2. *So Long, See You Tomorrow* (New York: Vintage, 1996 [1980]), p. 27. Originally

published in *The New Yorker*, it is here presented as a novel, but reads more like a memoir, which is what the author calls it, tentatively, on p. 6.

3. Compare Ciaran Benson, *The Cultural Psychology of Self* (London: Routledge, 2001), p. 47: 'As it unfolds discursively over time the tale told is the result of a rich succession of choices and selections governed and shaped by the dynamics of the many nows and "present thoughts" which make up the stream of experience which is my particular life. My "life" will always be an edited version.'

4. Peter Pyne, 'The New Irish State and the Decline of the Sinn Féin Party, 1923–1926', *Éire-Ireland*, Vol. 11, No. 3 (1976), pp. 33–65.

5. Pyne, 'The New Irish State', p. 56. A report of the meeting appeared in the republican newspaper *An Phoblacht*, 15 January 1926.

6. Pyne, 'The New Irish State', p. 60.

7. Robert Brennan and Maeve Brennan Papers, University of Delaware Library, Special Collections, Newark, Del., USA, F17. There is another copy in NLI MSS, Robert Brennan Papers (Acc. 5584, uncatalogued). See also Mark O'Neill, *De Valera, Fianna Fáil and the 'Irish Press'* (Dublin and Portland, Oregon: Irish Academic Press, 2001).

8. O'Neill, *De Valera, Fianna Fáil and the 'Irish Press'*; see also Tim Pat Coogan, *De Valera: Long Fellow, Long Shadow* (London: Arrow, 1995), pp. 414–21.

9. Private collection, Cambridge, UK.

10. Robert Brennan and Maeve Brennan Papers, University of Delaware, F32.

11. Thanks to Nuala O'Connor and Dr Dolores MacKenna for sharing their memories and those of their contemporaries.

12. Gardner Botsford, *A Life of Privilege, Mostly* (New York: St Martin's Press, 2003), p. 221.

13. For discussion of the culture of this period, see Terence Brown, *Ireland: A Social and Cultural History, 1922–1985* (London: Fontana, 1985 [1981]), pp. 13–137, and J. J. Lee, *Ireland 1912–1985: Politics and Society* (Cambridge: Cambridge University Press, 1989), p. 159.

14. See Alannah Hopkin, *The Living Legend of St Patrick* (London: Grafton, 1989), pp. 106–44.

15. My thanks to Mother Abbess, Poor Clares' Monastery, Simmonscourt Road, for replies to my queries.

16. Dated 2 October 1930, Private collection, Cambridge, UK.

17. See R.J. Schork, *Joyce and Hagiography: Saints Above!* (Gainesville, Fla.: University Press of Florida, 2000).

18. R. F. Foster, 'Protestant Magic: W. B. Yeats and the Spell of Irish History', in his *Paddy and Mr Punch: Connections in Irish and English History* (London: Allen Lane, The Penguin Press, 1993), pp. 212–32; W. J. McCormack, *Sheridan Le Fanu and Victorian Ireland* (Oxford: Clarendon Press, 1980) and 'Irish Gothic and After, 1820–1945', in Seamus Deane, Andrew Carpenter and Jonathan

Williams (eds), *The Field Day Anthology of Irish Writing*, 3 vols (Derry: Field Day, 1991), Vol. 2, pp. 831–949; see also Seamus Deane, *Strange Country: Modernity and Nationhood in Irish Writing since 1790* (Oxford: Clarendon Press, 1997), pp. 89–94: 'Landlord and Soil: *Dracula*'.

19. For a political-sexual reading of the Dracula story, see Deane, *Strange Country*, pp. 90–1, 213, n. 99.

20. James Joyce, *Dubliners* (Harmondsworth: Penguin, 1957 [1914]), p. 198.

21. Nuala O'Connor, interview with the author, December 2000. Philip O'Leary writes (e-mail to the author, 3 November 2002): 'In 1935, "An tAthair Micheál" was delighted to see so many detective novels being translated by An Gúm since "ná fuil aon úrsgéalta eile glan morálta ach iad" [they are the only clean, moral novels] (*Father Mathew Record*, October, 1935, p. 483). On the other hand, An tAthair Eric P. Mac Fhinn thought they were morally questionable (*Ar Aghaidh*, October 1934, pp. 7–8)'.

22. MB to RB, 21 February 1934: Robert Brennan and Maeve Brennan Papers, University of Delaware, F19.

23. My discussion of Micheál Mac Liammóir (born Michael Wilmore, in London) and Hilton Edwards is indebted to Christopher Fitz-Simon, *The Boys: A Double Biography* (London: Nick Hern, 1994).

24. Yvonne Jerrold, 9 August 2001, e-mail to the author.

25. MB to William Maxwell, 1957: University of Illinois Library, Rare Book and Special Collections Library, Urbana-Champaign Campus, William Maxwell Papers, 1–37/38.

26. Walking tour: Typescript, 'Jim Connolly of Boston, Soldier, Sailor, Storyteller', NLI MSS, Robert Brennan Papers. Summerville: R. Brennan, *Allegiance*, p. 26.

27. NLI MSS, Robert Brennan Plays, ms 32,545, No. 2.

28. NLI MSS, Robert Brennan Papers.

29. Letter from R. Jacob and card from H. Sheehy-Skeffington, NLI MSS, Robert Brennan Papers.

30. Thanks to Yvonne Jerrold for this information.

31. '[S]coil ina gcothófaí spiorad na náisiúntachta mar ba chóir,' 'Lúise Ghabhánach Ní Dhufaigh ag Insint a Scéil Féin', in Mairéad Ní Ghacháin, eag., *Lúise Ghabhánach Ní Dhufaigh agus Scoil Bhríde* (Baile Átha Cliath: Coiscéim, 1993), p. 5.

32. Erskine Childers, *Military Rule in Ireland* (Dublin: The Talbot Press, 1920), pp. 13–14.

33. Donn Piatt, 'Gearrchuntas ar Stair Scoil Bhríde', in Ní Ghacháin, eag., *Lúise Ghabhánach Ní Dhufaigh* pp. 34–7.

34. Robert Brennan and Maeve Brennan Papers, University of Delaware, F60.

35. Private collection, Cambridge, UK. The word 'pleasure' is unclear.

36. Robert Brennan, 'Mainly Meandering', NLI MSS, Robert Brennan Papers.

37. French was taught through Irish. Louise Gavan Duffy wrote on Maeve's report in 1932, 'Bhí súil agam le dul chun cinn níos fearr i mbliana' ('I had hoped for better progress this year'). In 1932–1933 the report was 'Go lag, ach d'oibrigh sí go maith agus chuaigh sí chun cinn' ('Weak, but she has worked hard and made progress'); by 1933–1934, 'Go h-an-mhaith. D'oibrigh sí go dícheallach' ('Very good: she has worked diligently').

38. Souvenir pamphlet, *Dublin Gate Theatre: Productions 1928–33*, in Robert Brennan and Maeve Brennan Papers, University of Delaware, F61.

39. Roddy Doyle, *Rory and Ita* (London: Cape, 2002).

40. For information about James and Bridget Sinnott, and Nan Brennan's friendship with them, I am indebted to their son Mr Jim Sinnott, Rosslare Strand, County Wexford.

41. Maeve's claim, recorded by Gardner Botsford, that her Aunt Nan 'had run away with [a] chartered accountant when she was not yet twenty, only to have him die in her arms in Genoa a week later', finds no echo in the memories of those who knew Nan Brennan, but such a story may have been told about Maeve's great-aunt from Pouldearg Eliza Harper, née Whitty, known as Nannie, mentioned above in Chapter 1: Botsford, *Privilege*, p. 221.

42. My thanks to Pat Walsh, Wexford, grandson of Chrissie Williamson, for these details.

43. NLI MSS, Robert Brennan Papers.

44. Micheál Ó hAodha, *Siobhán: A Memoir of an Actress* (Dingle, Co. Kerry: Brandon, 1994), p. 19.

45. NLI MSS, Robert Brennan Papers.

46. See Pádraig Ó Siadhail, *Stair Dhrámaíocht na Gaeilge* (Indreabhán: Cló Iar-Chonnachta, 1993).

47. See above, p. 29; Janet Egleson Dunleavy and Gareth W. Dunleavy, *Douglas Hyde: A Maker of Modern Ireland* (Berkeley: University of California Press, 1991), pp. 224–5.

48. Robert Brennan and Maeve Brennan Papers, University of Delaware, F60.

49. J. J. Lee, *Ireland 1912–1985*, p. 168.

50. Almost a year before the change of government, a 'traffic conference' at Dublin's Gresham Hotel had assembled representatives of shipping lines and railway companies to co-ordinate international travel. For a lively account of the Congress, and of Ireland in 1932, see Tony Farmar, *Ordinary Lives: The Private Lives of Three Generations of Ireland's Professional Classes* (Dublin: A. and A. Farmar, 1995 [1991]), pp. 73–145.

51. Charles McGlinchey, *The Last of the Name*, with an Introduction by Brian Friel (Belfast: Blackstaff Press, 1986), p. 20.

52. Aodhagán Brioscú, 'Eucharistic Congress in Dublin 70 Years Ago', *Knocklyon News*, June 2002, p. 22.

53. Máire Mhac an tSaoi, speaking on RTÉ Radio 1, Marian Finucane programme, 25 March 2002. See also her autobiography: Máire Cruise O'Brien, *The Same Age as the State* (Dublin: O'Brien Press, 2003), pp. 121–4. The *Father Mathew Record* published photographs of several street altars.

54. M. O'Toole, *More Kicks than Pence* (Dublin: Poolbeg, 1992), p. 132. Maeve's essay, published on Monday, 20 February 1933, with the encouragement of family friend Dorothy Macardle, the *Irish Press* theatre critic, described the first volume of the *Dublin Society's Weekly Observations*, in which were collected pamphlets issued by the Society (later the RDS) in 1736–1738. She noted remarkable similarities between its rhetoric and the Fianna Fáil Party's 'Buy Irish' campaign. I am most grateful to Dr Brian Ó Conchubhair, Boston College, for this reference.

55. NLI MSS, Frank Gallagher Papers, ms 18361 (1–8).

56. Ibid., ms 18361 (5).

57. Gallagher to de Valera, 19 July 1933: ibid., no. 18361 (6).

58. For conditions at the *Irish Press*, see O'Neill, *De Valera, Fianna Fáil and the 'Irish Press'*; J. J. Lee, *Ireland 1912–1985*, pp. 217–19, and cf. Tim Pat Coogan, *De Valera*, pp. 442–3.

59. The Legion's commander in Morocco was Francisco Franco.

7. Mr Brennan Goes to Washington

1. School reports, 1933 and 1934, Robert Brennan and Maeve Brennan Papers, University of Delaware Library, Special Collections, Newark, Del., USA, F60.

2. See Hasia Diner, *Erin's Daughters in America: Irish Immigrant Women in the Nineteenth Century* (Baltimore and London: Johns Hopkins University Press, 1983), and cf. Leslie Matson, *Méiní, The Blasket Nurse* (Cork: Mercier Press, 1996), pp. 23–44.

3. See Cormac Ó Gráda, *Ireland: A New Economic History 1780–1939* (Oxford: Clarendon Press, 1994), pp. 434–41; Conrad M. Arensberg and Solon T. Kimball, *Family and Community in Ireland*, third edition (Ennis: Clasp Press, 2001 [1940]), pp. 144–5 and cf. Richard White, *Remembering Ahanagran: Storytelling in a Family's Past* (Cork: Cork University Press, 1999 [1998]).

4. Private collection, Cambridge, UK.

5. Donal McCartney, *UCD: A National Idea. The History of University College Dublin* (Dublin: Gill and Macmillan, 1999), pp. 63, 69, 82.

6. The first envoy was Professor Timothy Smiddy. See D. W. Harkness, *Restless Dominion* (New York: New York University Press, 1970), quoted in Tim Pat Coogan, *De Valera: Long Fellow, Long Shadow* (London: Arrow, 1995), p. 422. See further Ronan Fanning, 'The Anglo-American Alliance and the Irish Question in the Twentieth Century', in Judith Devlin and Howard B. Clarke

(eds), *European Encounters: Essays in Memory of Albert Lovett* (Dublin: University College Dublin Press, 2003), pp. 185–220.

7. 'Desolation' etc.: M. J. MacManus to Frank Gallagher, 1935, quoted in J. J. Lee, *Ireland 1912–1985: Politics and Society* (Cambridge: Cambridge University Press, 1989), p. 219.

8. This and the other letters written to RB from Cherryfield Avenue and quoted below: Robert Brennan and Maeve Brennan Papers, University of Delaware, F19.

9. It had opened on 30 January 1934.

10. Pádraig Ó Siadhail, *Stair Dhrámaíocht na Gaeilge 1900–1970* (Indreabhán: Cló Iar-Chonnachta, 1993), p. 175.

11. *Peig. i. A Scéal Féin do Scríobh Peig Sayers*, eag., Máire Ní Chinnéide (Dublin: Talbot Press, 1936); transl. Bryan MacMahon, *Peig* (London: Oxford University Press, 1973); see also Diarmuid Breathnach agus Máire Ní Mhurchú, *1882–1992: Beathaisnéis a Dó* (Dublin: An Clóchomhar, 1990), pp. 79–81.

12. Neal Garnham, in S. J. Connolly (ed.), *The Oxford Companion to Irish History* (1998), p. 493.

13. *Irish Times*, 10 and 12 February 1934. My thanks to Mike Cronin for information on this point.

14. Brian Lynch, 'RTÉ Radio – the Voice of the Nation', *The World of Hibernia*, Autumn 2001, p. 92.

15. *Irish Times*, 12 December 1933, reports that New York has 22.2 telephones to every hundred of the population: 'Dublin, of course, comes nowhere; for the whole Free State – not to mention Dublin alone – contains nothing like 100,000 instruments.' Cf. *Oxford Companion to Irish History*, s.v. radio.

16. C. S. Andrews, *Dublin Made Me* (Dublin: Lilliput, 2001 [1979]) p. 298.

17. A reference to the Pioneer Total Abstinence Association, founded in Dublin on 28 December 1898.

18. A Hollywood blockbuster tear-jerker, set in England and based on Noël Coward's 1931 play of the same name; it won three Academy awards in 1933.

19. Also called *Pioneer Builders, The Conquerors*, directed by William A. Wellman, was released in 1932.

20. The initials suggest Geraldine (or perhaps Greta) O'Brien, or O'Byrne, but I have not succeeded in identifying her.

21. In March 1947, 'Roddy the Rover' (Aodh de Blacam) attributed the joke to Bob Brennan in the *Irish Press*, noting his return to Ireland as Director of Broadcasting. Thanks to Brian Lynch, print archive, RTÉ.

22. Quoted in Luke Gibbons and Kevin Rockett, *Cinema and Ireland* (London: Croom Helm, 1988). See also Joe McMahon, 'The Making of the Man of Aran', in John Waddell, J. W. O'Connell and Anne Korff (eds), *The Book of Aran* (Kinvara: Tír Eolas, 1994), pp. 289–98.

23. Private collection, Cambridge, UK.

24. I am grateful to the current owner of 48 Cherryfield Avenue for allowing me to consult the house deeds.

25. Aodhagán Brioscú, interview with the author. The books were *Grádh agus Crádh* [Love and Heartbreak], a short novel by Úna Ní Fhaircheallaigh, published in 1901 at one penny, and *Blátha Bealtaine* [Flowers of May], by Máire de Buitléar, published in 1902, and priced twopence. The Briscoes too moved on in 1934, buying a larger, redbrick, house in Westfield Road, Harold's Cross.

26. Elizabeth Cullinan, interview with the author, New York, 16 December 2001.

27. I thank Mrs Deirdre Jerrold for recalling details of the family's journey. The *Manhattan* was also the ship on which Douglas 'Wrong Way' Corrigan returned from Ireland to New York in 1938 (see pp. 132–33).

28. Private collection, Cambridge, UK.

29. See, e.g., George Bornstein, 'Afro-Celtic Connections: From Frederick Douglass to *The Commitments*', in Tracy Mishkin (ed.), *Literary Influence and African-American Writers* (New York: Garland, 1996).

30. Private collection, Cambridge, UK.

31. Carmel Snow, with Mary-Louise Aswell, *The World of Carmel Snow* (New York: McGraw-Hill, 1962), p. 101.

32. My thanks to Pat Walsh, Wexford, for permission to reproduce this photograph.

33. Máire Ní Fhaoláin, 50 Ranelagh Road, Dublin, to MB, 16 October 1936. Private collection, Cambridge, UK.

34. My thanks to George D. Arnold, University Archivist and Head of Special Collections, American University.

35. Cregan's husband, Dr Jim Ryan from County Wexford, was now Minister for Agriculture. *Old John*, about a faithful dog, was published in English in 1936 and in Irish translation in 1938, as *Sean-Eoin*.

36. Mairin Cregan, *Rathina* (London: George Allen and Unwin, 1944 [1942]), p. 185. Máirín Cregan also wrote plays for adults. See Bourke, et al. (eds), *The Field Day Anthology of Irish Writing, vol. 5, Irish Women's Writing and Traditions* (Cork: Cork University Press, 2002), pp. 1011–19 and 1044.

37. *Washington, DC Pocket Guide* (Princeton and London: Berlitz, 2001), p. 17.

38. For discussion, with key texts, see Margaret O'Callaghan, 'Women and Politics in Independent Ireland, 1921–1968', in Bourke, et al. (eds), *Field Day Anthology of Irish Writing, vol. 5*, pp. 120–76; see also Margaret Ward, *Hanna Sheehy Skeffington: A Life* (Cork: Attic Press, 1997), Chapter 13, 'Feminism, Republicanism, Communism: 1932–1937' (pp. 303–29), and Mary E. Daly, '"Oh, Kathleen Ni Houlihan, Your Way's a Thorny Way!": the Condition of Women in Twentieth-Century Ireland', in Anthony Bradley and Maryann Valiulis (eds), *Gender and Sexuality in Modern Ireland* (Amherst: University of Massachusetts Press / American Conference for Irish Studies, 1997), pp. 102–26.

39. Ward, *Hanna Sheehy Skeffington*, pp. 318–21.
40. For a discussion of these issues, see Carol Coulter, *The Hidden Tradition: Women, Feminism and Nationalism in Ireland* (Cork: Cork University Press, Undercurrents series, 1993).
41. Roddy Doyle, *Rory and Ita* (London: Cape, 2002), p. 133. Dates from correspondence in private collection, Cambridge, UK.
42. Lillian Eichler, *The New Book of Etiquette* (New York: Garden City, 1937), private collection.
43. NLI MSS, Robert Brennan Papers (Acc. 5584, uncatalogued). The venues for most of the earlier performances are unknown.
44. Robert Brennan and Maeve Brennan Papers, University of Delaware, F19. Marian Johnson was a fellow member of the *AUCOLA* staff.
45. Private collection, Cambridge, UK.
46. On Wednesday, 6 April 1938, the Social Calendar page of Washington's *Evening Star* carried a portrait of Una, Emer, Maeve and Derry in evening dress. They sit without smiling, perhaps in their own living-room, all looking to their right. The accompanying text reads: 'Mrs Robert Brennan, wife of the Irish Chargé d'Affaires, and their three daughters, Miss Emer Brennan, Miss Maeve Brennan and Miss Deidre [*sic*] Brennan. Mr Brennan, who has been secretary of the Legation for some years, has been spoken of as Minister from his government to succeed Mr Michael Mac White, now Minister to Italy. The Chargé d'Affaires formerly was editor of a paper in Ireland and with his family has made many friends here.'
47. Cutting in NLI MSS, Robert Brennan Papers.
48. *Irish Press*, 30 April 1958, p. 6, and Yvonne Jerrold, personal communication.
49. Private collection, Cambridge, UK, and Yvonne Jerrold, correspondence and interview with the author, 4 December 2002.
50. For information about CUA records, and for the notes that follow, I am indebted to Dr Timothy Meagher, University Archivist, and Heather Morgan, The American Catholic History Research Center and University Archives, Catholic University of America.
51. John J. Mahoney, BA. 1949, 'Home of my Heart', *CUA Magazine*, Summer 1999.
52. NLI MSS, Robert Brennan Papers. Derry used to make dresses for her mother and sisters.
53. Ibid.
54. Typescript with corrections by RB: ibid.
55. Private collection, Wexford.
56. Mary D. Kierstead, interview with the author, 18 December 2001; Gardner Botsford had also heard that Walter Kerr was 'smitten' by Maeve: telephone interview with the author, 17 December 2001. Jean Collins, born in Scranton, Pennsylvania, in 1923, collaborated with Walter Kerr in adapting Franz Werfel's

novel *The Song of Bernadette* for the stage at CUA, and married him in 1943, when she was 20, and still a student (her Master's degree in Fine Arts was conferred in 1945).

8. *Away from Home*

1. In preparing Maeve Brennan's stories for publication in *The Springs of Affection* and *The Rose Garden*, editor Christopher Carduff made several small changes, with William Maxwell's approval, to bring the stories into line with one another, including making regular the age differences between the Bagot children.

2. Robert Brennan, *Ireland Standing Firm and Eamon de Valera: A Memoir*, ed. Richard H. Rupp (Dublin: University College Dublin Press, 2002), p. 9.

3. Carmel Snow with Mary Louise Aswell, *The World of Carmel Snow* (New York: McGraw-Hill, 1962).

4. Snow and Aswell, *The World of Carmel Snow*, pp. 7–27; cf. Lord and Lady Aberdeen, *We Twa: Reminiscences of Lord and Lady Aberdeen* (London: W. Collins and Sons, 1927 [1925]), pp. 324–35. My thanks to Philip Harvey.

5. Snow and Aswell, *The World of Carmel Snow*, pp. 8–10, 118. Cf. John Cooney, *John Charles McQuaid, Ruler of Catholic Ireland* (Dublin: O'Brien, 1999), pp. 21–4.

6. Snow and Aswell, *The World of Carmel Snow*, pp. 26–7.

7. NLI MSS, Robert Brennan Papers, Máirín Bean Uí Riain to RB.

8. Snow and Aswell, *The World of Carmel Snow*, pp. 95–6.

9. Ibid., pp. 153–5.

10. University of Illinois Library, Rare Book and Special Collections Library, Urbana-Champaign Campus, William Maxwell Papers, 1–37/38.

11. MB to William Maxwell, 1957: University of Illinois Library, Maxwell Papers, 1–37/38.

12. Robert Brennan, *Ireland Standing Firm*, pp. 64 ff.

13. His date of death is given as 8 September 1898.

14. Robert Brennan and Maeve Brennan Papers, University of Delaware Library, Special Collections, Newark, Del., USA, F40.

15. See Mary E. Daly, '"Oh, Kathleen Ni Houlihan, Your Way's a Thorny Way!": the Condition of Women in Twentieth-Century Ireland', in Anthony Bradley and Maryann Valiulis (eds), *Gender and Sexuality in Modern Ireland* (Amherst: University of Massachusetts Press/American Conference for Irish Studies, 1997), pp. 102–26.

16. Terence Brown, *Ireland: A Social and Cultural History, 1922–1985* (London: Fontana, 1985 [1981]), p. 147 and *passim*.

17. Mary E. Daly, 'Oh, Kathleen Ni Houlihan', quoting Brendan Walsh, *Some Irish Population Problems Reconsidered* (Dublin: Economic and Social Research Institute, 1968).

18. Karl Bissinger, telephone interview with the author, 16 December 2001.

19. Karl Bissinger, *The Luminous Years: Portraits at Mid-Century*, ed. Catherine Johnson, with an Introduction by Gore Vidal (New York: Harry N. Abrams, 2003).

20. Photograph and V-mail in private collection, Cambridge, UK.

21. Francis W. Lovett, letter to the author, 26 November 2002, based on his contemporary notes.

22. Brendan Gill, *Here at* The New Yorker (New York: Da Capo, 1997 [1975]), pp. 75–6, 222–8, 253.

23. Ibid., pp. 140–3.

24. See Seán Rothery, *Ireland and the New Architecture, 1900–1940* (Dublin: Lilliput, 1991).

25. Private collection, Cambridge, UK.

26. Gill, *Here at* The New Yorker, pp. 31–2, 129.

27. Philip Hamburger, interview with the author, 15 December 2001.

28. My thanks to Yvonne Jerrold for this suggestion.

29. Christopher Carduff, 'Editor's Note' in *V* 86.

30. Ibid., p. 85.

31. See above, p. 128.

32. Roddy Doyle, *Rory and Ita* (London: Cape, 2002), p. 132.

33. See, for example, Gill, *Here at* The New Yorker, pp. 303–9.

34. Information from Mr Stephen J. McNeill, Tullamore, by courtesy of Dr Timothy O'Neill.

35. Faith McNulty, 'Foreword', in John McNulty, *This Place on Third Avenue: The New York Stories of John McNulty* (Washington, DC: Counterpoint, 2001), p. xii. For an Irish 'rambling house', compare Eric Cross, *The Tailor and Ansty* (Cork: Mercier, 1942).

36. Philip Hamburger, interview with the author, 15 December 2001, and MB, 'Author's Note' in *LWL* 2.

37. Faith McNulty, telephone interview with the author, December 2001.

38. R. Brennan, *Ireland Standing Firm*, pp. 88–93.

39. Government of Ireland, *Dáil Debates*, 1 May 1947, p. 1,907. For a discussion see Maurice Gorham, *Forty Years of Irish Broadcasting* (Dublin: Talbot Press for Radio Telefís Éireann, 1967), pp. 156 ff.

40. *Irish Times*, 10 March 1947. My thanks to Brian Lynch, RTÉ Archive, for this reference.

41. Private collection, Cambridge, UK.

42. Gorham, *Forty Years*, p. 159. See also *Irish Press*, 28 April 1958, p. 3.

43. Robert Brennan and Maeve Brennan Papers, University of Delaware, F5.

44. Des MacHale, *The Complete Guide to 'The Quiet Man'* (Belfast: Appletree Press, 2000), pp. 29–36; Luke Gibbons, *The Quiet Man* (Cork: Cork University Press,

Ireland into Film series, 2002), and Patrick F. Sheeran, *The Informer* (Cork: Cork University Press, Ireland into Film series, 2002), pp. 18–21.

45. My thanks to Dr Elizabeth McCrum for her expert help with fashion history.

46. Philip Wylie, *Generation of Vipers* (New York: Rinehart, 1946 [1942]). Plath wrote 'The Babysitters' in October 1961: see Jacqueline Rose, *The Haunting of Sylvia Plath* (Cambridge, Mass.: Harvard University Press, 1991), pp. 165–204.

47. Ferdinand Lundberg and Marynia Farnham, *Modern Woman: The Lost Sex* (New York: Harper and Brothers, 1947).

48. Faith McNulty and others, telephone interviews with the author, December 2001.

49. See also the cover of this book. Another image from the same session appears in Gardner Botsford, *A Life of Privilege, Mostly* (New York: St Martin's Press, 2003).

50. Private collection, Cambridge, UK.

51. Charles Vidor, Mark Robson, 1950.

9. *The View from the Kitchen*

1. Mary F. Corey, *The World through a Monocle:* The New Yorker *at Midcentury* (Cambridge, Mass. and London: Harvard University Press, 1999), pp. ix–x. Compare the subtitle of Ben Yagoda's study: *About Town:* The New Yorker *and the World it Made* (New York: Da Capo, 2000).

2. E. B. White, *Here is New York*, with a New Introduction by Roger Angell (New York: The Little Bookroom, 1999 [1949]), p. 19.

3. MB to Yvonne Jerrold, 1965, Private collection, Cambridge, UK.

4. *LWL* 114, 218 and *The New Yorker*, 23 January 1954.

5. *The New Yorker*, 15 November 1993, p. 10.

6. Author's interviews with Faith McNulty, Mary Kierstead and Elizabeth Cullinan, December 2001.

7. 'Skunked', in 'Talk of the Town', *The New Yorker*, 23 January 1954.

8. Gardner Botsford, telephone interview with the author, 17 December 2001, and *Privilege*, pp. 212–22.

9. Philip Hamburger, interview with the author, 15 December 2001.

10. Mary Kierstead, interview with the author, 18 December 2001.

11. Harold Ross to Frank Crowninshield, 20 April 1933, in Thomas Kunkel (ed.), *Letters from the Editor:* The New Yorker's *Harold Ross* (New York: The Modern Library, 2000), p. 77.

12. Some versions of this story name Charles Addams, rather than Brendan Gill.

13. William Maxwell, 'Introduction', in *SA* 5.

14. Mary Kierstead, interview with the author, 18 December 2001.

15. Kennedy Fraser, *Ornament and Silence: Essays on Women's Lives* (New York: Knopf, 1996), pp. 234–5.

16. Frances Kiernan, 'Fiction at *The New Yorker*', *American Scholar*, September 1998.

17. 'Mary Lambert' in the original *Harper's Bazaar* version.

18. *The New Yorker*, 9 February 1952, p. 109.

19. Ibid., 12 December 1953.

20. Private collection, Cambridge, UK.

21. See Kiernan, 'Fiction at *The New Yorker*'.

22. NLI MSS, Robert Brennan Papers.

23. Ibid.

24. Roger Angell, telephone interview with the author, 18 December 2001.

25. See Luke Gibbons, *The Quiet Man* (Cork: Cork University Press, 'Ireland into Film' series, 2002).

26. Edward J. Cohen, 'My Advice on Irish Tweeds', condensed in *Irish Digest*, June 1953, from *Dollar Exporters' Newsletter*. The Minister for Lands had invited Edward J. Cohen, of the Malcolm Kenneth Company, men's outfitters in Boston, to visit the Gaeltarra Éireann woollen mill in Kilcar, County Donegal, and advise on strategies for gaining a larger share of the American market.

27. Robert O'Byrne, *After a Fashion: A History of the Irish Fashion Industry* (Dublin: Town House, 2000).

28. Carmel Snow, with Mary Louise Aswell, *The World of Carmel Snow* (New York: McGraw-Hill, 1962), p. 184.

29. *Irish Times*, 18 July 1953; *Irish Press*, 24 July 1953. See also O'Byrne, *After a Fashion*, pp. 21–33.

30. University of Illinois Library, Rare Book and Special Collections Library, Urbana-Champaign campus, William Maxwell Papers, 1–37/38.

31. Yvonne Jerrold, interview with the author, April 2003.

32. Private collection, Cambridge, UK.

33. Yagoda, *About Town*, pp. 325–6 gives details: in 1954, for example, McKelway owed the magazine $7,138.76. Cf. Brendan Gill, *Here at* The New Yorker (New York: Da Capo, 1997 [1975]), pp. 146 ff., who remarks that Joseph Mitchell was the only writer to avoid the drawing-account trap by insisting on a salary. Additional material about Maeve Brennan's marriage to St Clair McKelway is from my interviews with *New Yorker* writers.

34. Faith McNulty, telephone interview with the author, December 2001.

35. Faith McNulty and Philip Hamburger, interviews with the author, December 2001; Maxwell, 'Introduction' in *SA* 4–5.

36. Robert Brennan and Maeve Brennan Papers, University of Delaware Library, Special Collections, Newark, Del., USA, F30.

37. Ved Mehta, *Remembering Mr Shawn's* New Yorker: *The Invisible Art of Editing* (Woodstock and New York: Overlook, 1998), pp. 293–4.

38. Maxwell, 'Introduction' in *SA* 4.

39. See John Cooney, *John Charles McQuaid, Ruler of Catholic Ireland* (Dublin: O'Brien, 1999), pp. 288–309.

40. Roger Angell, telephone interview with the author, 18 December 2001.

41. Compare Mary F. Corey, *The World through a Monocle:* The New Yorker *at Midcentury* (Cambridge, Mass. and London: Harvard University Press, 1999), Chapter 7, 'Managing with Servants', pp. 124–48.

42. Robert Kiely, in the *New York Times Book Review*, 4 August 1974, found the 'Herbert's Retreat' stories 'shallow, obvious, ill-composed and all but devoid of fresh observation, intellectual subtlety, and emotional depth'; William Maxwell called them 'heavy-handed and lack[ing] the breath of life', *SA* 5.

43. See Robert Welch (ed.), *The Oxford Companion to Irish Literature* (1996), p. 220.

44. Joseph Mitchell, *Up in the Old Hotel and Other Stories* (New York: Pantheon, 1992), p. 105; the piece ends as Barnell says, 'If the truth was known, we're all freaks together.'

45. See Joan N. Radner (ed.), *Feminist Messages: Coding in Women's Folk Culture* (Chicago: University of Illinois Press, 1993).

46. John McNulty, who wrote about Costello's saloon, had the same facility, although the Irish community he grew up in was in Massachusetts. Like Maeve's grandmother Bridget, McNulty's widowed mother, born in Ballyhaunis, County Mayo, had kept a small shop and entertained her family nightly with stories and mimickry. See Faith McNulty, 'John as He Was', in John McNulty, *This Place on Third Avenue: The New York Stories of John McNulty* (Washington, DC: Counterpoint, 2001), pp. xiii–xiv.

47. For the Murphys, see Amanda Vaill, *Everybody Was So Young: Gerald and Sara Murphy, a Lost Generation Love Story* (New York: Broadway Books, 1998), and Calvin Tomkins, *Living Well is the Best Revenge* (New York: Viking, 1971). For the quote from Philip Barry, see Vaill, pp. 163 and 334.

48. See Brendan Gill, *A New York Life: Of Friends and Others* (New York and London: Poseidon, 1990), p. 319, and University of Illinois, Maxwell Papers 1–37/38.

49. Condensed in *Irish Digest*, October 1954, pp. 21–3.

50. O'Byrne, *After a Fashion*, p. 28.

51. Christopher Carduff, 'Editor's Note' in *V* 83, 85.

10. *The Long-Winded Lady Observes*

1. See Joan N. Radner and Susan S. Lanser, 'Strategies of Coding in Women's Cultures', in Joan N. Radner (ed.), *Feminist Messages: Coding in Women's Folk Culture* (Chicago: University of Illinois Press, 1993), pp. 1–24.

2. Ben Yagoda, *About Town:* The New Yorker *and the World it Made* (New York: Da Capo, 2000), p. 311.

3. See, for example, Daniel Horowitz, *Betty Friedan and the Making of the Feminine Mystique* (Amherst: University of Massachusetts Press, 1998), pp. 149–52.

4. See Jeffrey L. Meikle, *American Plastic: A Cultural History* (New Brunswick and London: Rutgers University Press, 1997), pp. 153–82.

5. Yagoda, *About Town*, pp. 313–15, 346–8.

6. Frances Kiernan, 'Fiction at *The New Yorker*', *American Scholar*, September 1988.

7. *LWL* 156–7. The collected 'Long-Winded Lady' pieces are published without most of their original italics.

8. Yagoda, *About Town*, p. 306.

9. Gardner Botsford has observed that 'She was a writer through and through: she simply could not *not* write, filling endless notebooks with observed incidents, trial phrases and sentences, and overheard conversations': *A Life of Privilege, Mostly* (New York: St Martin's Press, 2003), p. 213.

10. See, for example, Michael Steinman, *The Happiness of Getting it Down Right: Letters of Frank O'Connor and William Maxwell* (New York: Alfred A. Knopf, 1996).

11. Micheál Ó hAodha, *Siobhán: A Memoir of an Actress* (Dingle, Co. Kerry: Brandon, 1994), pp. 60–1.

12. Emer Coghlan Brennan, telephone interview (ii) with the author, 24 January 2002.

13. Brendan Gill, *Here at* The New Yorker (New York: Da Capo, 1997 [1975]), pp. 312–13. This book never mentions Maeve Brennan by name; she was seriously mentally ill when it appeared.

14. Robert M. Brennan, telephone interview with the author, 26 January 2002.

15. Horowitz, *Betty Friedan and the Making of the Feminine Mystique*, pp. 165–6.

16. Cliona Hickey and Garret Hickey: telephone interviews with the author, 2002 and June 2003.

17. University of Illinois Library, Rare Book and Special Collections Library, Urbana-Champaign Campus, William Maxwell Papers, 1–37/38.

18. Private collection, Cambridge, UK.

19. University of Illinois Library, Maxwell Papers, 1–37/38.

20. Letter and biographical note: NLI MSS, Robert Brennan Papers; in fact Maeve joined *The New Yorker* in 1949.

21. University of Illinois Library, Maxwell Papers, 1–37/38.

22. At some point in the 1950s, McKelway travelled to Europe to recover the body of his only son, who had been killed in the war. He was devastated to be given only a child's coffin, which contained all that was left of the young man (Yvonne Jerrold, personal communication).

23. The correction is Maeve's. University of Illinois Library, Maxwell Papers, 1–37/38.

24. University of Illinois Library, Maxwell Papers, 1–37/38.

25. Matt Bolger, Enniscorthy, interview with the author, 23 March 2002.

26. Edited by Richard Rupp, from a typescript found by Yvonne Jerrold among RB's papers in Dublin. Published in book form, with a memoir of de Valera, as Robert Brennan, *Ireland Standing Firm and Eamon de Valera: A Memoir*, ed. and intro. Richard H. Rupp (Dublin: University College Dublin Press, 2002).

27. F. W. Peard, 'What it Costs to Live in New York', *Irish Times*, 5 August 1958.

28. Steinman, *Happiness*; Angela Bourke, 'Brian Friel: Storyteller of Home and Away', in *It's Us They're Talking About: Proceedings of the McGlinchey Summer School, 2001* (Clonmany, Co. Donegal: McGlinchey Summer School, 2002), pp. 79–85.

29. 'Design for New U.S. Embassy in Dublin', *Irish Times*, 9 August 1958; J. J. Lee, *Ireland 1912–1985: Politics and Society* (Cambridge: Cambridge University Press, 1989), pp. 342–8, and R. F. Foster, *Modern Ireland, 1600–1972* (London: Penguin, 1989 [1988]), pp. 578–9.

30. Rory and Ita Doyle, interview with the author, February 2003.

31. Elizabeth Cullinan, interview with the author, 16 December 2001.

32. Private collection, Cambridge, UK. Previously unpublished extracts below are from this typescript.

33. Maeve probably means winter jasmine, another yellow-flowered shrub that is not laburnum, for forsythia blooms in spring; compare *V* 67.

34. See, for example, Deirdre McQuillan, *The Aran Sweater* (Belfast: Appletree Press, 1993).

35. Ó hAodha, *Siobhán*, p. 62.

36. St Clair McKelway, *The Edinburgh Caper* (New York: Holt, Rinehart and Winston, 1962).

37. See Brendan Gill, *A New York Life: Of Friends and Others* (New York: Poseidon, 1990), p. 320, and cf. Yagoda, *About Town*, p. 283; Kennedy Fraser, *Ornament and Silence: Essays on Women's Lives* (New York: Knopf, 1996), p. 239; Gardner Botsford, *Privilege*, p. 222, and Ved Mehta, *Remembering Mr Shawn's* New Yorker: *The Invisible Art of Editing* (Woodstock and New York: Overlook, 1998), p. 294.

11. *The Traveller in Residence*

1. Private collection, Cambridge, UK.

2. Brendan Gill, *A New York Life: Of Friends and Others* (New York: Poseidon, 1990), p. 319.

3. *LWL* 2 (Author's note, 1969). Cf. Mary Hawthorne, 'A Traveller in Residence', *London Review of Books*, 13 November 1997, pp. 1–5. Gardner Botsford's memoir recalls that when Maeve made a month-long trip to Ireland by freighter,

she was happy to be the only passenger: *A Life of Privilege, Mostly* (New York: St Martin's Press, 2003), p. 212.

4. William Maxwell to Frank O'Connor, 26 September 1960, in Michael Steinman (ed.), *The Happiness of Getting it Down Right: Letters of Frank O'Connor and William Maxwell* (New York: Alfred A. Knopf, 1996), p. 139.

5. For Gerald and Sara Murphy, see Amanda Vaill, *Everybody Was So Young: A Lost Generation Love Story* (New York: Broadway Books, 1998).

6. Private collection, Cambridge, UK.

7. Postcard, Gerald Murphy to Maeve Brennan, 10 December 1960: Private collection, Cambridge, UK; Maxwell to O'Connor, Steinman, *Happiness* pp. 142, 144.

8. See Botsford, *Privilege*, pp. 212–22. Letters addressed to Maxwell and his family are preserved in the Rare Book Room of the University of Illinois Library at Urbana-Champaign, and form the basis of much of what follows in this chapter: University of Illinois Library, Rare Book and Special Collections Library, Urbana-Champaign Campus, William Maxwell Papers, 1–37/38: approximately 260 pieces.

9. William Maxwell, 'Introduction', in *SA*, p. 10.

10. University of Delaware Library, Special Collections, Robert Brennan and Maeve Brennan Papers, F36.

11. Botsford, *Privilege*, p. 216.

12. University of Illinois Library, Maxwell Papers, 1–37/38.

13. Steinman, *Happiness* pp. 72–3 and *passim*.

14. University of Illinois Library, Maxwell Papers, 1–37/38.

15. Robert Brennan and Maeve Brennan Papers, University of Delaware, F30, F21.

16. Private collection, Cambridge, UK.

17. University of Illinois Library, Maxwell Papers, 1–37/38.

18. William Hazlitt, 'On Living to One's Self', *The Complete Works of William Hazlitt in Twenty-One Volumes*, (Centenary Edition, ed. P. P. Howe, Vol. 8 (London and Toronto: J. M. Dent, 1931), p. 91.

19. Botsford, *Privilege*, pp. 215–20.

20. University of Illinois Library, Maxwell Papers, 1–37/38.

21. University of Illinois Library, Maxwell Papers, 1–37/38.

22. William Maxwell, 'Introduction', in *SA* 6.

23. Private collection, Cambridge, UK.

24. Terry Coleman, *The Liners* (Harmondsworth: Penguin, 1977 [1976]), pp. 15–16.

25. Private collection, Cambridge, UK.

26. Letter, Hawley Truax to MB: Robert Brennan and Maeve Brennan Papers, University of Delaware, F19. Photographs: private collection, Cambridge, UK. Letter, MB to Mary Kierstead: private collection.

27. Compare letter, MB to William Maxwell, apparently 1964: 'I slept from April 2 until 2 weeks ago, but now I am awake nearly all the time. I make omelets

every day. The noise from the pan is not omeletey, but the result is fine – I use up about a half a pot of jam on each omelet. There is always a certain amount of smoke as well as the cooking noises & a great deal of commotion on the floor where Bluebell & Basil are, & on the window ledge & on top of the refrigerator & in the sink & on the laundry basket, where Rupert, Daisy, Tommy, Pansy & Juno are, all very anxious. And it's true you do have to break eggs.' University of Illinois Library, Maxwell Papers 1–37/38.

28. 'Editor's Note' in *V* 85.

29. University of Illinois Library, Maxwell Papers, 1–37/38. For the whereabouts of Maeve Brennan, Howard Moss and William Maxwell in summer 1963, see Robert Brennan and Maeve Brennan Papers, University of Delaware, F19: aerogramme letter dated [Jul?]y 1963, from Howard Moss to Maeve Brennan, 27 West 10 St, New York City 11, NY, USA c/o Moss, and Steinman, *Happiness*, pp. 205–9. For Maxwell, the piano and Mozart, see Steinman, *Happiness*, pp. 198 and *passim*.

30. Since 1958 O'Connor had been working on the autobiographical writings that became *An Only Child* and *My Father's Son*, which Maxwell edited for *The New Yorker*: see Steinman, *Happiness*, pp. 72 and *passim*.

31. My thanks to Mary E. Daly for this reference. Lemass and his wife made a tour of US cities the following October to solicit investment in Ireland.

32. See Deirdre McQuillan, *The Aran Sweater* (Belfast: Appletree Press, 1993).

33. My thanks to Philip O'Leary, who bought the book and shared its history with me. Its author later changed his name to McLysaght.

34. Lance Pettit, *Screening Ireland: Film and Television Representation* (Manchester and New York: Manchester University Press, 2000), pp. 166–70.

35. University of Illinois Library, Maxwell Papers, 1–37/38.

36. Private collection, Cambridge, UK.

37. University of Illinois Library, Maxwell Papers, 1–37/38.

38. Ibid.

39. A proof copy gives the character's name as 'Mrs Haddon': however, Hadden is the name of a prominent Wexford family: Robert Brennan and Maeve Brennan Papers, University of Delaware, F42. Maxwell wrote enthusiastically to Frank O'Connor about Woolf's manuscript notes for *To the Lighthouse*, preserved behind glass in Room 318 on the top floor of the New York Public Library: Steinman, *Happiness*, pp. 234–5; cf. Maxwell's novel, *The Château*, where Harold Rhodes names this book as his favourite.

40. University of Illinois Library, Maxwell Papers, 1–37/38.

41. See Ved Mehta, *Remembering Mr Shawn's New Yorker: The Invisible Art of Editing* (Woodstock and New York: Overlook, 1998), p. 221 ff.; Ben Yagoda, *About Town: The New Yorker and the World it Made* (New York: Da Capo, 2000), p. 334 ff.; Mary T. Corey, *The World through a Monocle: The New Yorker at*

Midcentury (Cambridge, Mass. and London: Harvard University Press, 1999), p. 139; Botsford, *Privilege*, pp. 228–32.

42. Steinman, *Happiness*, p. 243.

43. Carmel Snow, with Mary Louise Aswell, *The World of Carmel Snow* (New York: McGraw-Hill, 1962), p. 7.

44. Postcard, 'David' to MB, postmarked 7 October 1967, redirected from the *New Yorker* offices to General Delivery, Wellfleet, Mass.: private collection, Cambridge, UK.

45. William Maxwell, interview with Jacki Lyden, National Public Radio, Washington, DC, 'Weekend Sunday', 14 December 1997; cf. 'Introduction', *SA* 10–11.

46. Ita Doyle, interview with the author, April 2003.

47. At a memorial reading of Maeve Brennan's writings at the Algonquin Hotel, a publicity event tied into the publication of *The Springs of Affection* in 1997, Albee read this story and explained his relationship to it: Christopher Carduff, memo to the author, 13 November 2001.

12. *The Tightrope that Wasn't There*

1. Philip Hamburger, interview with the author, 15 December 2001.

2. This was in 1969 or soon after; Frances Kiernan, e-mail to the author, 11 April 2003. Maxwell mourned the loss of his friend Frank O'Connor, dead since March 1966: see his 'Frank O'Connor and *The New Yorker*', in Michael Steinman, *The Happiness of Getting it Down Right: Letters of Frank O'Connor and William Maxwell* (New York: Alfred A. Knopf, 1996), pp. 263–70.

3. *The New Yorker*, 10 March 1973. This was MB's last published story, but a substantially different proof copy is dated 3 December 1962: Robert Brennan and Maeve Brennan Papers, University of Delaware, Special Collections, Newark, Del., USA, F47.

4. University of Illinois Library, Rare Book and Special Collections Library, Urbana-Champaign campus, William Maxwell Papers, 1–37/38.

5. Private collection, Cambridge, UK.

6. Kennedy Fraser, *Ornament and Silence: Essays on Women's Lives* (New York: Alfred A. Knopf, 1996), pp. 231–3.

7. Frances Kiernan (author of *Seeing Mary Plain: A Life of Mary McCarthy* [New York: W. W. Norton, 2000]), 'Fiction at *The New Yorker*', *American Scholar*, September 1998.

8. Frances Kiernan, e-mail to the author, 11 April 2003, and telephone interview, 29 June 2003. For the white handkerchief, cf. the discussion of 'A Free Choice' on p. 237.

9. Robert Wilson, *Feminine Forever* (New York: M. Evans & Co., 1966). The

circumstances of its writing were widely discussed in the media following publication in July 2002 of new findings by the US federally funded Women's Health Initiative that the oestrogen/progestin pill produced by Wyeth-Ayerst posed a serious danger to women's health.

10. John Updike, letter to the author, 11 December 2001; Gardner Botsford and Elizabeth Cullinan, interviews with the author, December 2001.

11. Edward Albee, *Box and Quotations from Chairman Mao Tse-Tung: Two Interrelated Plays* (New York: Atheneum, 1969); my thanks to Philip O'Leary. Martha Foley and David Burnett (eds), *The Best American Short Stories 1969* (New York: Houghton Mifflin, 1969).

12. William McPherson, 'To Capture the Fugitive Day', *Washington Post*, 4 December 1984.

13. Fraser, *Ornament and Silence*, p. 241.

14. See Michael Kreyling, *Author and Agent: Eudora Welty and Diarmuid Russell* (New York: Farrar, Straus and Giroux, 1991). A letter from Maeve to William Maxwell, written in East Hampton, mentions that she has 'sent six stories to D Russell and said that for various reasons it might be as well to avoid "doing" anything till the other two were in. I don't really care, but I thought I would say it anyway.' (University of Illinois Library, Maxwell Papers, 1–37/38.) The six stories may be those about Mrs Bagot; a further two appeared in *The New Yorker* after *In and Out of Never-Never Land* was published.

15. Carmel Snow, with Mary Louise Aswell, *The World of Carmel Snow* (New York: McGraw-Hill, 1962), p. 69; Yvonne Jerrold, e-mail to the author.

16. Private collection, Cambridge, UK.

17. See Roddy Doyle, *Rory and Ita* (London: Cape, 2002) pp. 266–70.

18. Roddy Doyle, *Paddy Clarke Ha Ha Ha* (London: Secker & Warburg, 1993) and interview with the author, Dublin, 26 March 2001. See also his *Rory and Ita*, pp. 265–70.

19. Published in London in 1969 by The Bodley Head. Elizabeth Cullinan, interview with the author, December 2001.

20. Gardner Botsford, *A Life of Privilege, Mostly* (New York: St Martin's Press, 2003), p. 220.

21. Compare *SA* 202–3 and *RG* 53.

22. University of Illinois Library, Maxwell Papers, 1–37/38.

23. Ibid.

24. James Thurber, *Vintage Thurber*, vol. 1 (Harmondsworth: Penguin, 1983 [1963]), p. 417.

25. University of Illinois Library, Maxwell Papers, 1–37/38.

26. When the Maxwells rented her house in East Hampton in the summer of 1965, Maeve wrote notes to the children about two of the cats: 'Dear Brookie, When Rupert was born his front paws were not connected with his arms except by

his skin. He used to try to crawl along on his shoulders. Remind me to tell you how I mended his tiny legs. He was V. Brave'. And to Kate: 'Please have a private word with Juno now & then. She is a very confidential cat': University of Illinois Library, Maxwell Papers, 1–37/38.

27. Ibid.

28. Interview with the author, New York, 15 December 2001.

29. A postcard signed 'Susan' and postmarked July 1969 is addressed to Maeve at Box 235A, Duxbury, MA: private collection, Cambridge, UK.

30. University of Illinois Library, Maxwell Papers, 1–37/38.

31. Ibid.

32. Ibid.

33. Ibid.

34. Ibid.

35. A popular devotion in Ireland in the early twentieth century. Ellen Organ, born in Waterford in 1903 and known as Little Nellie of Holy God because of her reported piety, died before her fifth birthday at the Convent of the Good Shepherd, Sunday's Well, Cork.

36. Her two final pieces were 'A Daydream' (20 September 1976) and 'A Blessing' (5 January 1981). See *LWL* 262–8.

37. Frances Kiernan, telephone interview with the author, 29 June 2003.

38. University of Illinois Library, Maxwell Papers, 1–37/38.

39. Ibid.

40. Ibid.

41. *SA,* blurb and Introduction.

42. William Maxwell, *They Came Like Swallows* (New York: Modern Library, 1997 [1937]).

43. Private collection, Wexford.

44. Christopher Carduff, quoted in *Publishers Weekly*, Vol. 244, No. 45 (3 November 1997), p. 20.

45. As in 'An Attack of Hunger' (*SA* 165), however, Maeve seems to forget that Ireland drives on the left.

46. Steinman, *Happiness*, p. 125.

47. Author's interviews with Pat Walsh and Jim Sinnott. About 1958, when the wife of Bridget's other son, Dick, was in hospital, Nan Brennan moved into their house to look after the children, and political scientist Richard Sinnott remembers that she sewed nametapes on to all his clothes before he went as a boarder to the Irish College at Ring, County Waterford. A nationalist and a seamstress, Nan wrote his name in Irish and stitched the labels securely, but she had no husband or son, and hadn't used Irish in years, so his name appeared as though it were a girl's: Risteárd Ní Shionóid.

48. Yvonne Jerrold, interview with the author, 4 December 2002.

49. In 1970, Bluebell was having cortisone injections for bad arthritis; by the time of 'A Daydream' (1976), she has been 'dead for years'.

50. Botsford, *Privilege*, p. 221, and telephone interview with the author, 17 December 2001. Botsford names Yaddo, in Saratoga Springs, NY, rather than MacDowell, as the colony Maeve had come from when he first realised the seriousness of her condition, but the Yaddo website does not list Maeve among the writers resident there since 1926.

51. Maxwell, 'Introduction', in *SA* 11–12; Ved Mehta, *Remembering Mr Shawn's New Yorker: The Invisible Art of Editing* (Woodstock and New York: Overlook 1998), pp. 294–6; Mary Hawthorne, 'A Traveller in Residence', *London Review of Books*, 13 November 1997; author's interviews with *New Yorker* writers.

52. Maxwell, 'Introduction', *SA* 11.

53. Mehta, *Remembering Mr Shawn's* New Yorker, p. 295.

54. Gardner Botsford, Elizabeth Cullinan, Philip Hamburger, Mary Kierstead, interviews with the author, December 2001.

55. Robert Brennan and Maeve Brennan Papers, University of Delaware, F47.

56. Christopher Carduff, 'Editor's Note' in *V* 86–7.

57. Roddy Doyle, *Rory and Ita*, pp. 270–6.

58. Rory and Ita Doyle, interview with the author, February 2003.

59. A Wellfleet neighbour who had once worked at *The New Yorker*. My thanks to Kate Maxwell and Alec Wilkinson.

60. Thanks to David Marcus and Ita Daly for this information.

61. Susan Nennzig Cahill (ed.), *Women and Fiction: Short Stories by and about Women* (New York: New American Library, 1975). Gardner Botsford, telephone interview with the author, 17 December 2001.

62. Elizabeth Cullinan, interview with the author, December 2001.

63. Ben Yagoda, *About Town: The New Yorker and the World it Made* (New York: Da Capo, 2000), p. 389.

64. See Pauline M. Prior, *Gender and Mental Health* (London: Macmillan, 1999), pp. 149–52, at p. 150. Prior cites A. Scull, *Decarceration: Community Treatment and the Deviant: A Radical View* (New Jersey: Polity Press, 1984).

65. William Maxwell, 'Introduction', *SA* 11, and author's interviews with *New Yorker* writers.

66. Hawthorne, 'A Traveller in Residence'.

67. 'A Blessing', *LWL* 266–8.

Epilogue

1. Joan Iaconetti, 'At Houghton Mifflin, Reprints and Rediscoveries', *Publishers Weekly*, Vol. 244, No. 45 (3 November 1997), p. 20, and Christopher Carduff, conversations with the author.

2. Michael Nagler and William Swanson (eds and introd.), *Wives and Husbands: 20 Short Stories about Marriage* (New York: New American Library, 1989). Ellen Wilbur, interview with the author, September 2000.

3. Richard Rupp, e-mail to the author, 25 September 2000. The box contained a typescript of Robert Brennan's *Allegiance*, which Rupp edited. He returned the box and the remainder of its contents to Maeve's family in Dublin.

4. Hawthorne, 'A Traveller in Residence'.

5. Maeve Brennan, *The Springs of Affection* (London: Flamingo, 2000).

INDEX